Alastair Sawday's

SPECIAL
PLACES TO STAY
IN
BRITAIN

Typesetting, Conversion & Repro:	Avonset, Bath
Maps:	Maps in Minutes, Devon
Printing:	Jarrold Book Printing, Norwich
Design:	Springboard Design, Bristol
UK Distribution:	Portfolio, London
US Distribution:	St Martin's Press, New York

First published in 1998 by Alastair Sawday Publishing Co. Ltd
44 Ambra Vale East, Bristol BS8 4RE, UK.

Alastair Sawday's

SPECIAL PLACES TO STAY
IN
BRITAIN

"Home is not where you live but where they understand you."
CHRISTIAN MORGENSTERN

ASP

Alastair Sawday Publishing

ACKNOWLEDGEMENTS

At last! We now have a full-time editor and project co-ordinator, Jackie King. She took the office home with her and has succeeded brilliantly with this, her first, book.

Without Julia Richardson, our Publishing Manager, however, Jackie would have been lost in the jungle of it all. Julia has guided and helped her in the kindest and most generous of ways. They have been ably helped by Lisa (Pea) Saunders, who - rapidly and good-naturedly - tackled any task Jackie and Julia set her.

Thanks, too, are due to the devoted team of inspectors: Tom Bell (editor of our Hotels & Inns book) and Simon Greenwood (editor of our Irish book), who criss-crossed the country with enormous good humour; and Tony Mudd, who came on board later, with our gratitude. A small army of part-time inspectors flew off at a moment's notice and I am grateful to them all.

Behind the scenes there are supportive spouses and partners who also deserve our gratitude; from Jackie, a huge 'thank you' to David and Marina. We are indebted to our readers and supporters who have sent in recommendations and comments, all of which we take very seriously.

Thanks go to Nicola for streamlining our systems and to the team of Alastair Sawday's Tours, a constant source of encouragement, fun, ideas and support. They are a critical part of this publishing machine. So, too, is our accounts department; Hercules had an easier time in the Augean stables.

Series Editor:	Alastair Sawday
Editor:	Jackie King
Production:	Julia Richardson
Additional writers:	James Belsey, Jenny Walters
Administration:	Amy Clifton, Nicola Crosse, Lisa (Pea) Saunders
Inspections:	Julie Albeson, Wendy Arnold, Annie Coates, Nicola Crosse, Trish Dugmore, Juliet Harkness, Penny Houghton-Brown, Lorna James, Marina King, Hannah Klewin, Auriol Marson, Mike Millbourn, John Rees, Peter Sorrell, Bridget Sudworth, Will Ward-Lewis, Rachel Wilkinson, Betka Zamoyski
Accounts:	Sheila Clifton, Movita Clutterbuck, Maureen Humphries
Cover illustration:	David Sorrell
Cover design:	Caroline King
Photographs:	Andrew & Miriam Dow, Sara Hay, Ray Smith, Bridget Sudworth

INTRODUCTION

The Sunday Times recently wrote that our books are 'full of attitude'. They certainly are!

I am going to make a bold, and perhaps reckless, comparison: this book does, or attempts to do, for B&Bs, Hotels and Inns what the CAMRA guide does for ale, what Radio 4's Food Programme does for food, what the Soil Association does for agriculture and food. We celebrate variety, individuality, good taste and high standards.

You have seen how corporations buy up private hotels and 'brand' them; so that wherever you are you can be sure of the same 'standards'. Good buildings are torn down to make way for ugly ones. More insiduously, the hand of Big Brother is to be seen everywhere, standardising and destroying the stamp of individuality.

But help is at hand. Turn the pages of this book and you will see over 600 different types of B&B, hotel and inn, over 600 unpredictably individualistic sets of people willing to look after you. Each has something special, be it facilities, welcome, comfort, service, etc... some have it all. We have chosen each place because we like it, for one reason or another... and they all reflect the differing tastes of their owners; that, after all, is half the fun.

BUT, and this is important, you must read the descriptions carefully; they tell you what to expect. Read between the lines; we tend to focus on the aspects that we like most. Some houses are chosen largely because the buildings are dazzling; others because the people are captivating. Some are engagingly chaotic; others are professional in every way. Usually the whole 'package' is irresistible.

There is scarcely a note of ugliness, meanness, bad taste, 'froideur', discomfort anywhere in the book. And the corporate culture doesn't get a look in.

WHO IS THIS BOOK FOR?

For dreamers, romantics, individuals. It is definitely not for seekers after status, designer-chic, conformity and perfect predictability.

INTRODUCTION

IS THIS BOOK DIFFERENT?

A resounding yes. The maps are brilliant, the colour photos are a great help and the directions are a godsend. Please know that it is we who write this book, not the owners. More than one has dropped out because we would not use 'accommodation guide' banalities or agree to gloss over weak points.

Above all, the writing is fresh, honest, vivid and original - that is not easy with just 100-odd words, 620 times. We have struggled to eliminate any hint of estate agents' English and such words as *offers*, *boasts*, *affords*, *situated*, *located*, *comprises*, etc.

HOW DO WE CHOOSE?

The introductory paragraph says it all! We think we have found many of the best hotels, inns and houses in the UK. They pay to feature, but nobody can buy their way into this book. Our reputation depends on providing a brilliant selection so we dare not include the wrong places. We do de-select people and places which have proved unpopular, and for every house that is in the book there are many others that were considered inappropriate.

We try to re-inspect every other year, and we take criticisms very seriously; we dropped a house from the guide at the last minute because of severe comment from readers. We hate to do so, because often there is nothing inherently wrong with the house or people; it may just be that they are not doing quite what is needed to please guests.

RATINGS

We have none; most ratings are meaningless if you are looking for character, aesthetic appeal, lovely people. Some of the most horrible hotels and B&Bs I have been to have been highly rated by others. A rating system that would be of any use to us would be hopelessly subjective, so we try to use good descriptive language instead.

MEALS

If you think British food is still awful do, please, try the meals in these places. Many of the owners are cooks of real imagination and flair; British food is now often delicious. Note, too, how many of these places use locally-produced or their own home-grown ingredients.

It will be rarely, if at all, that you will come across packaged butter and jams, mini-cereal packets, little UHT milk containers, processed food and fast food. Please let us know if you do!

HOW TO USE B&Bs

They are all different, but if you treat them with the kindness and humanity that you reserve for your own friends you cannot go wrong. Some will draw you into the bosom of the family; some will leave you to do your own thing. In some you can bury yourself in the library or in front of the log fire; in others there is no sitting room but perhaps a large garden to enjoy.

The key piece of advice I have to offer is: remember that these are not hotels. There is no room service, no staff to carry luggage, no chamber-maid to pick up your washing or make up your bed. These things may happen, but you should not expect them.

Above all, **please** don't book a room and then cancel at the last minute or not turn up.

PRACTICAL MATTERS

Deposits: Some places ask for them; others don't.

Cash, cheque or credit card: most B&Bs don't take credit cards, while hotels do. If you are paying ahead from overseas you could try using Eurocheques.

Children: the symbol tells you if children are welcome, but do ring ahead to discuss.

Smoking: the symbol tells you if there is no smoking at all but ask before lighting up, some may allow it in certain rooms only.

Tipping: most hotels expect it while B&Bs certainly do not. Our own view is that tipping is embarrassing and anachronistic. It is acceptable to make your own decision.

Dogs: a tricky one. There are few places where I can take my own dog because many owners, although happy to have dogs in public rooms insist that they sleep in the car. So check ahead, and even if your host is happy, be prepared to compromise if other guests don't fall in love with your adorable little rottweiler.

INTRODUCTION

BOOKINGS AND CANCELLATIONS

We haven't got this right yet. There have been hair-raising tales of guests booking a whole house and not turning up, of hostesses cooking exquisite dinners and waiting up late for people who then ring to say 'sorry, we're not coming until midnight'.

Conversely, some guests have been unfairly stung for cancelled bookings. You would be wise to check on each owner's cancellation policy; they are all different.

Our own advice, before we become irreversibly involved, is that a contract exists as soon as you make a booking, whether by phone or by letter. It is fair that you should lose your deposit, unless perhaps it was for a huge group or family deposit to a place that then re-lets the space.

Please treat your future hosts with sensitivity over this; they are trying to make a (usually very modest) living and it is simply not fair to muck them about.

PRICES

They should be clear in the text, with details of single supplements given. If breakfast is not included, the price is given separately.

CYCLISTS

Cycling and walking are the most 'sustainable' ways of travelling in the countryside. But traffic creates traffic - people are frightened to take to busy roads on two wheels. The National Cycle Network is a flagship project designed to create routes which are suitable for everyone. A typical route comprises both minor roads and special traffic-free sections. By the millennium some 3,000 miles of cycle network should be in place. There's a National Cycle Network map at the back of the book. For more information call Sustrans on 0117 929 0888.

Many owners will pick you up from a rail station or cycle path for a small, or no, charge. Railways are marked with a thin black line on the maps.

THE HOTELS AND INNS

We are delighted to include some hotels and inns in the book, for there are many that are as individual or as special, in one way or

INTRODUCTION

another, as any of the B&Bs. I only wish there were more. Let us know of your own favourites, for we will soon be publishing a separate book about hotels and inns.

THE INTERNET

We are definitely going to be ON LINE in 1999.

WHEN IN ROME...

The majority of our owners are hugely accommodating and we would ask you in return to be sensitive to the very different lives that you will, briefly, be part of.

One owner pulled out this year because, for her, the final straw was a 'Sawday' guest coming down to breakfast in bare feet - something she felt was bad manners.

Conversely, one of our new owners said he takes it as a compliment if guests pad around without shoes - it means that they're feeling at home.

To do as your host does all the time would be exhausting, but a little sensitivity will go a long way.

A LAST DIATRIBE AGAINST STANDARDISATION

Note the following items of intelligence from the Scottish Tourist Board's Star System material:

'The inspector makes an assessment in each of a potential 51 areas... Grading Officers will take into account 'quality and condition'. 'Taste or fashion' will not influence...' (!)

You can get marked down for sounds of family coming from the kitchen, puddles on your drive and coarse grass.
You get top marks for providing a full information pack about the local area but nothing is said about talking **to** guests.
Even your hair gets marked - a touch out of control and you lose some points, and many points if it is entirely out of control.

And lastly, a standard quote from an AA report: *'The bedrooms provide pleasant comforts... The public rooms provided good comforts together with the facility to carry out functions'.*

We hope *our* write-ups whet your appetite.

INTRODUCTION

ENVIRONMENTAL POLICY

We are keen to reduce our negative impact on the environment and, to that end, have asked a special unit at Edinburgh University to assess our current 'performance' and recommend action, such as tree-planting on a scale to compensate for the company's overall impact on the environment.

We hope to become the 'world's first carbon-neutral' publishing company!

FINALLY

Above all this guide shows you the way to enjoy Britain at its very best. We still have some glorious countryside, matchless villages and houses, and - better - a profoundly civilised interest in other people. So, set forth with an open mind - we know that you'll have a good time.

Alastair Sawday

A WORD FROM *Country Living*

Country Living - one of Britain's top-selling lifestyle magazines - has long celebrated the richness and diversity of our countryside and the small rural businesses which are so important to the people who live there. so it is with great pleasure that once again *Country Living* supports *Special Places to Stay in Britain* which lists 625 bed and breakfasts, hotels, pubs and inns. Many are family-run enterprises and bring valuable income to country communities. In addition they give urban dwellers the opportunity to visit and explore the rich pastures, woodlands, moors and valleys that combine with beautiful villages and thriving market towns to make up our unique rural landscape.

Alastair Sawday's philosophy of what makes a special place to stay is very similar to that of *Country Living*'s. We have always awarded marks for stunning views not full length mirrors, for modest posies of fresh flowers not colour televisions, for breakfasts featuring home-made local or organic produce not for whether you can order it from your bedroom. So in buying this book and, I hope, also becoming a regular reader of *Country Living* magazine, you are giving yourself a clear advantage over other travellers. Finding your way through the maze of holiday accommodation on offer in this country isn't easy, but armed with *Special Places to Stay in Britain*, plus *Country Living*'s regularly published 'Escapes' guides, you can't go wrong. Whether you plan to go away for a week or a weekend, I am sure the British countryside will inspire and refresh you.

Susy Smith
Editor
Country Living magazine

SYMBOLS

Explanations of symbols - treat each one as a guide rather than as a statement of fact.

Working farm.

Children are welcomed but cots, high chairs etc are not necessarily available. The text gives restrictions where relevant.

Pets welcome - possibly to sleep in the house as long as they are properly trained. There may be a supplement to pay. Please discuss with owners beforehand.

Vegetarians catered for with advance warning.

Owners use organically-grown ingredients, whether 'certified' or chemical-free from their own garden.

Full facilities for disabled people.

Accessible for people of limited mobility.

No smoking anywhere in the house.

This house has pets of its own: dog, cat, duck, parrot...

Credit cards are accepted.

Premises are licensed.

DISCLAIMER

We make no claims to pure objectivity in judging our special places to stay. They are here because we like them. Our opinions and tastes are ours alone and this book is a statement of them; we cross our fingers and hope that you will share them.

We have done our utmost to get our facts right but apologise unreservedly for any mistakes that may have crept in. Sometimes, too, prices shift, usually upward, and 'things' change. We would be grateful to be told of any errors or changes, however small.

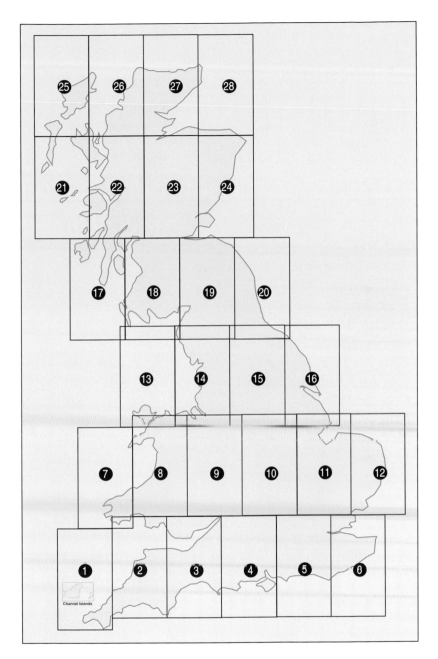

General Map

CONTENTS

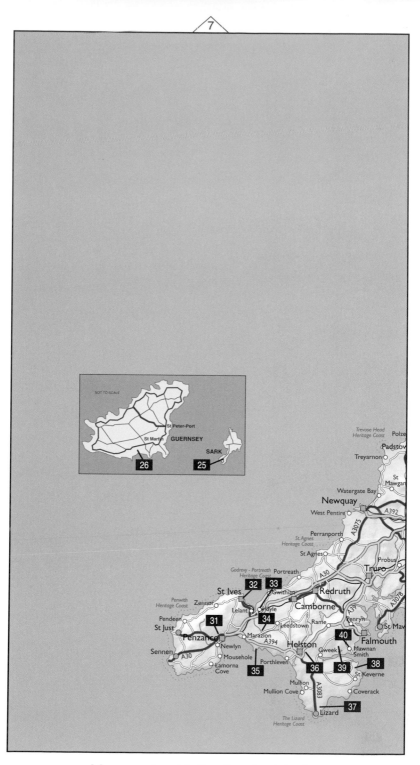

Map scale: 14.3 miles to 1 inch

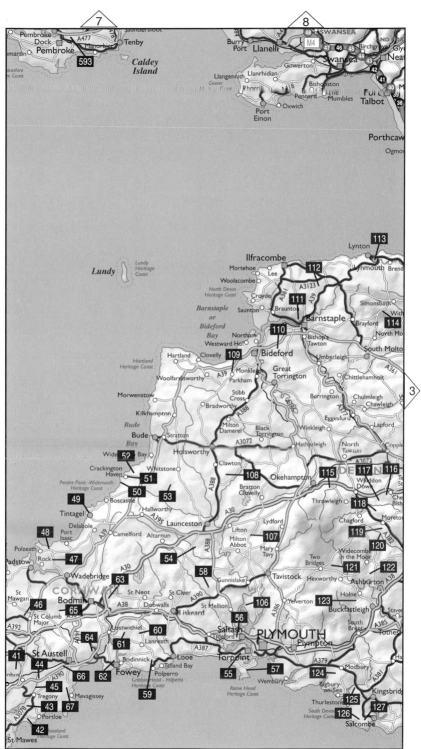

©RH Publications 1997

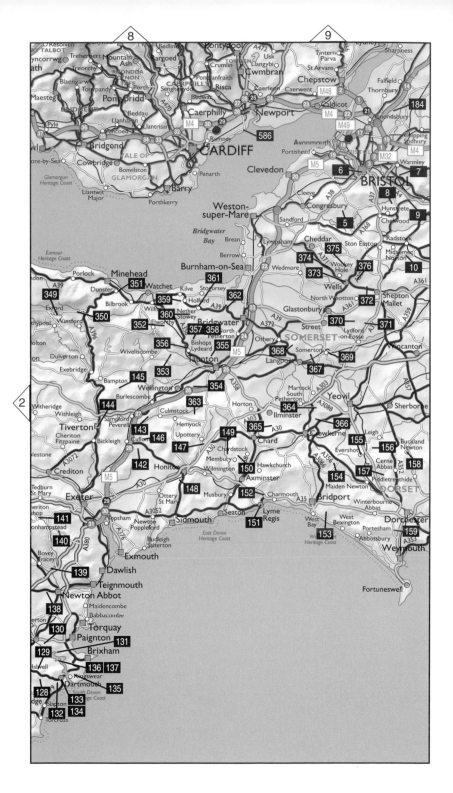

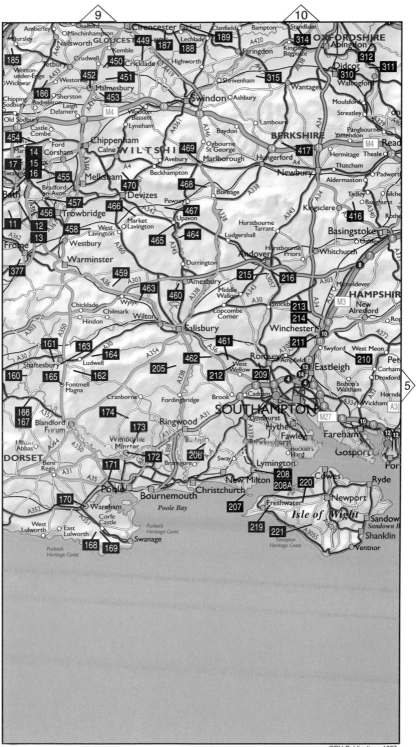

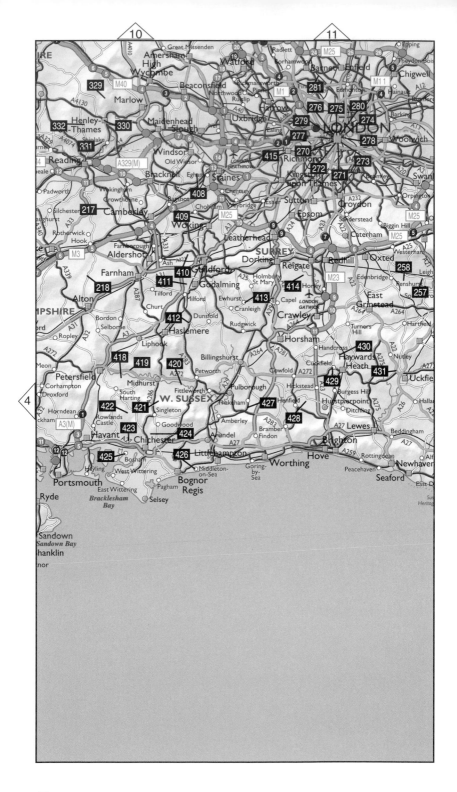

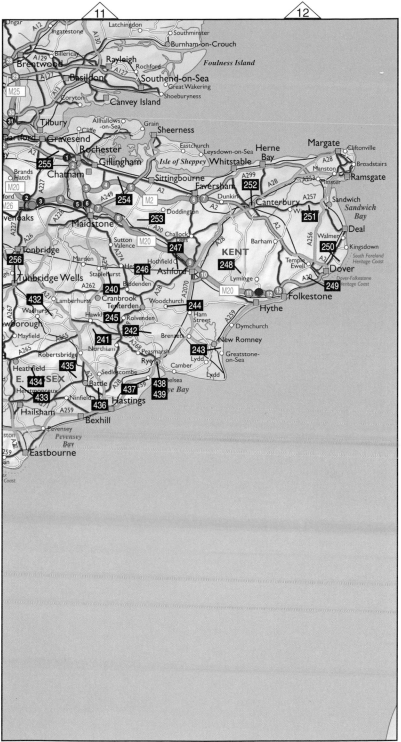

Ongar
Ingatestone
A12
A1/29
Billericay
A130
Latchingdon
Southminster
Burnham-on-Crouch
Brentwood
Rayleigh
Rochford
A127
A12
Foulness Island
28
A127
Basildon
Southend-on-Sea
A13
Great Wakering
M25
Corytón
Shoeburyness
29
Canvey Island
30
Tilbury
Allhallows-on-Sea
Grain
31
Cliffe
Sheerness
Dartford
Gravesend
Eastchurch
Leysdown-on-Sea
Herne Bay
Margate
Cliftonville
A2
Rochester
Isle of Sheppey
Whitstable
A28
Broadstairs
Brands Hatch
255
Gillingham
Sittingbourne
A299
252
A28
Manston
Ramsgate
Chatham
Faversham
A2
Minster
251
Sandwich
M20
A227
254
M2
Dunkirk
A2
Canterbury
Sandwich Bay
M26
253
Doddington
A257
Sevenoaks
Maidstone
A249
A20
Challock Lees
Barham
250
Walmer
Deal
Kingsdown
Tonbridge
Sutton Valence
M20
247
KENT
A256
A2
South Foreland Heritage Coast
256
Marden
Hothfield
248
Temple Ewell
Dover
Tunbridge Wells
A262
Staplehurst
246
Ashford
9
Dover-Folkestone Heritage Coast
432
A26
240
Biddenden
A20
10
M20
249
Lamberhurst
Cranbrook
Woodchurch
11
12
Folkestone
Wadhurst
Tenterden
244
Hythe
245
Ham Street
Mayfield
242
Rolvenden
Dymchurch
Crowborough
A265
241
Northiam
Brenzett
New Romney
Robertsbridge
Peasmarsh
243
Greatstone-on-Sea
435
Rye
Lydd
Heathfield
Sedlescombe
Camber
Lydd
E. SUSSEX
434
Battle
437
438
Winchelsea
Hastings
Herstmonceux
433
Ninfield
439
Rye Bay
Hailsham
436
A259
Bexhill
Pevensey
Eastbourne
Pevensey Bay
A259

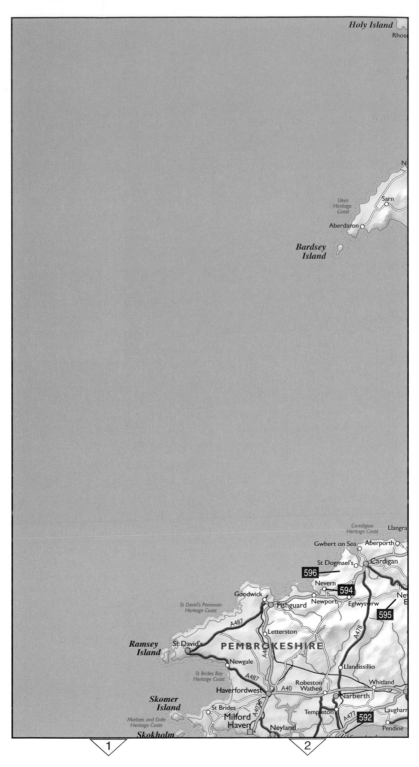

Holy Island
Rhos

N

Lleyn
Heritage
Coast

Sarn

Aberdaron

Bardsey
Island

Ceredigion
Heritage Coast

Llangra

Gwbert on Sea   Aberporth

St Dogmael's   Cardigan

596

Nevern

594   Ne
E

Goodwick   Newport
St David's Peninsula
Heritage Coast   Fishguard   Eglwyswrw

595
Letterston
A487

A478

Ramsey   St David's   PEMBROKESHIRE
Island

Newgale   Llandissillio
St Brides Bay
Heritage Coast   A487
Robeston   Whitland
Haverfordwest   A40   Wathen
Skomer
Island   St Brides   Narberth
Marloes and Dale   Templeton   Laugharn
Heritage Coast   Milford   A477   592
Skokholm   Haven   Neyland   Pendine

1   2

7

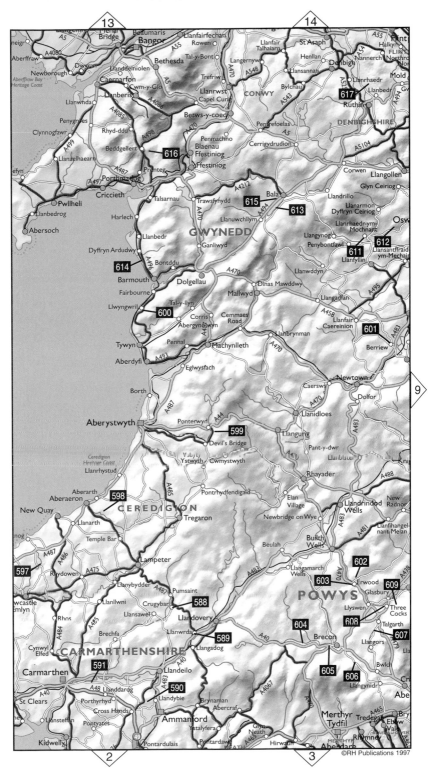

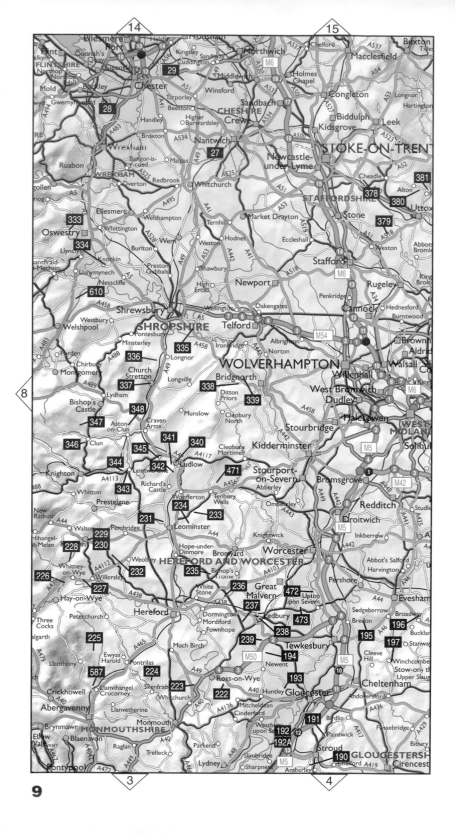

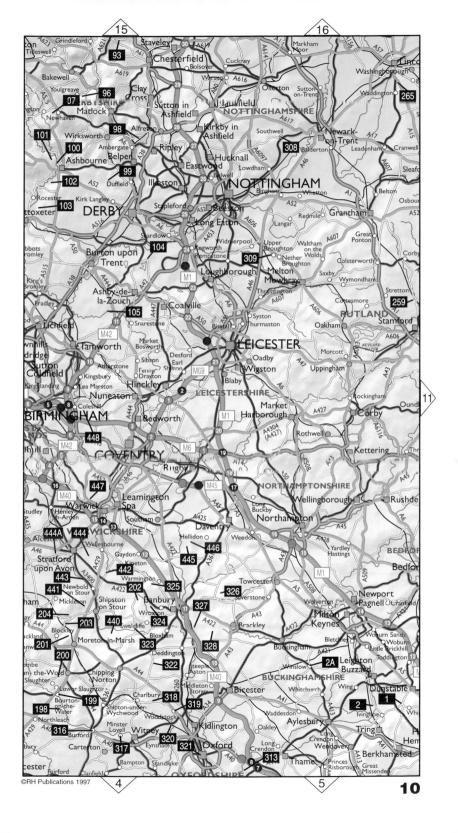

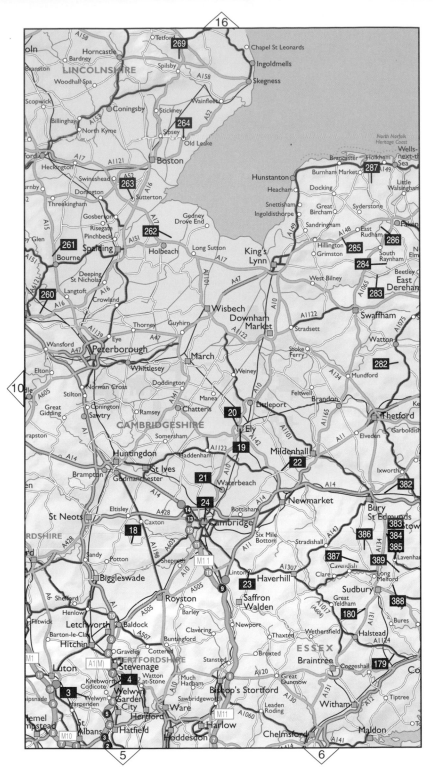

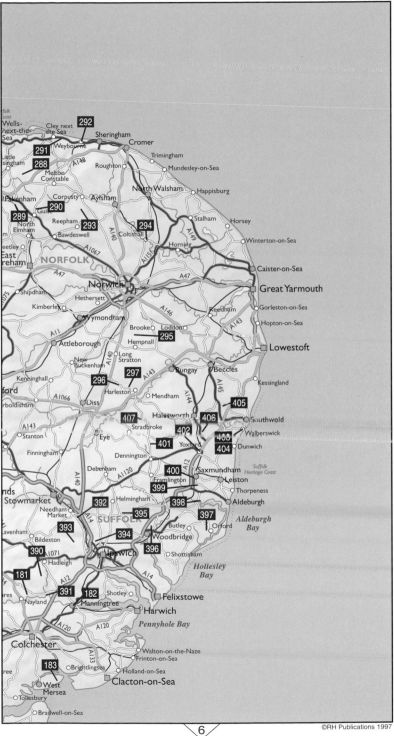

St Bees
Heritage

North Anglesey
Heritage Coast

Cemaes
Bay   Amlwch

A5025

Llanerchymedd

Anglesey

Benllech Bay

Great Orme
Heritage Coast

Holyhead   A5025

Llangoed

Llandudno

Holyhead Mountain
Heritage Coast

Valley ISLE OF ANGLESEY

Deganwy

Colwy

Treardur Bay

Holy Island

Llangefni

Menai
Bridge

Beaumaris

Conwy

Aber

Penmaenmawr

Rhosneigr

A5

Llanfairfechan

Rowen

Aberffraw

A4080

Bangor

A55

Llan
Talha

Newborough

Dwyran

Llanddeiniolen

Bethesda

Tal-y-Bont

Langernyw

Aberffraw Bay
Heritage Coast

Caernarfon

Cwm-y-Glo

A5

Trefriw

A548

Llanwnda

Llanberis

A4086

Llanrwst
Capel Curig

A470

CONW

A4085

Betws-y-coed

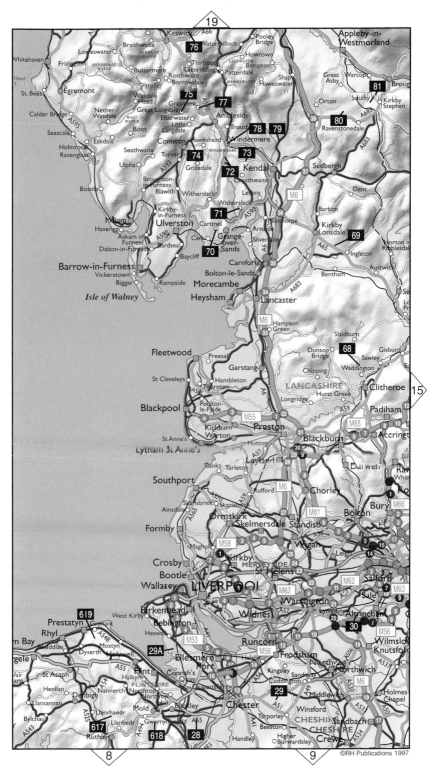

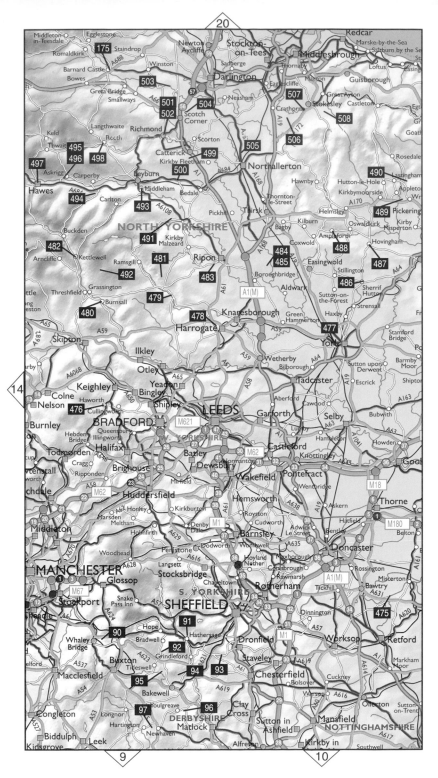

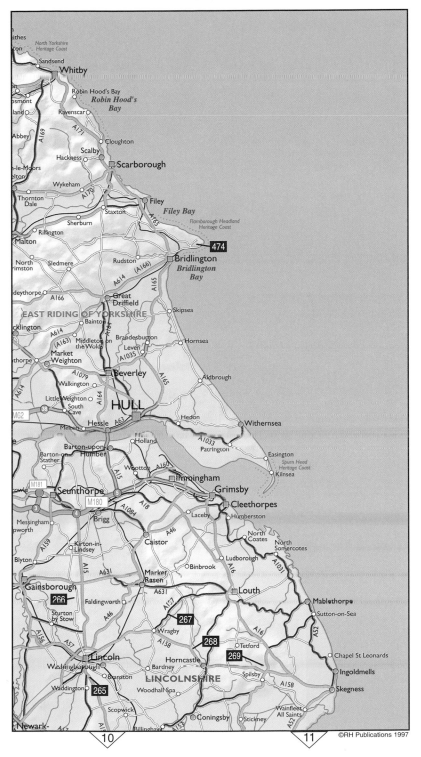

©RH Publications 1997

16

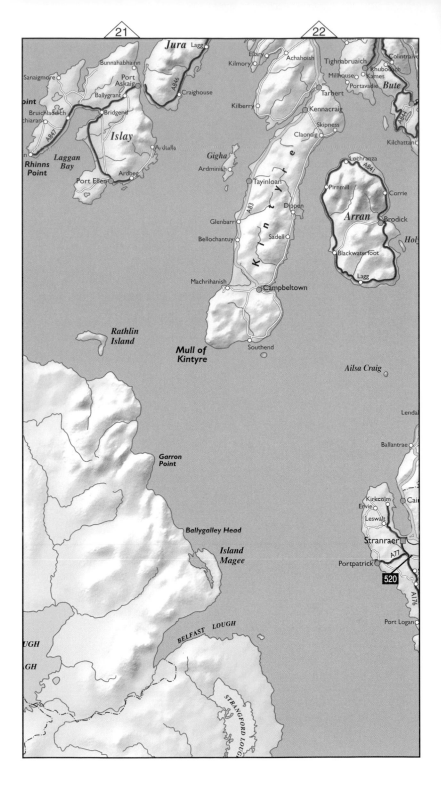

Jura Lagg
Bunnahabhainn
Sanaigmore
Port Askaig
Ballygrant
Bridgend
Bruichladdich
chiaran
Islay
Ardtalla
Rhinns Point
Laggan Bay
Port Ellen
Ardbeg
Craighouse

Elary
Kilmory
Achahoish
Tighnabruaich
Millhouse
Kames
Portavadie
Bute
Colintraive
Rhubodach
Kilberry
Tarbert
Kennacraig
Skipness
Claonaig
Kilchattan

Gigha
Ardminish
Tayinloan
Kintyre
Dippen
Glenbarr
Bellochantuy
Sadell
Machrihanish
Campbeltown
Mull of Kintyre
Southend

Lochranza
Pirnmill
Corrie
Arran
Brodick
Blackwaterfoot
Holy
Lagg

Rathlin Island

Ailsa Craig

Garron Point

Lendal
Ballantrae

Kirkcolm
Cai
Ervie
Leswalt
Stranraer

Ballygalley Head
Island Magee

Portpatrick
520
Port Logan

BELFAST LOUGH
UGH
GH
STRANGFORD LOUGH

17

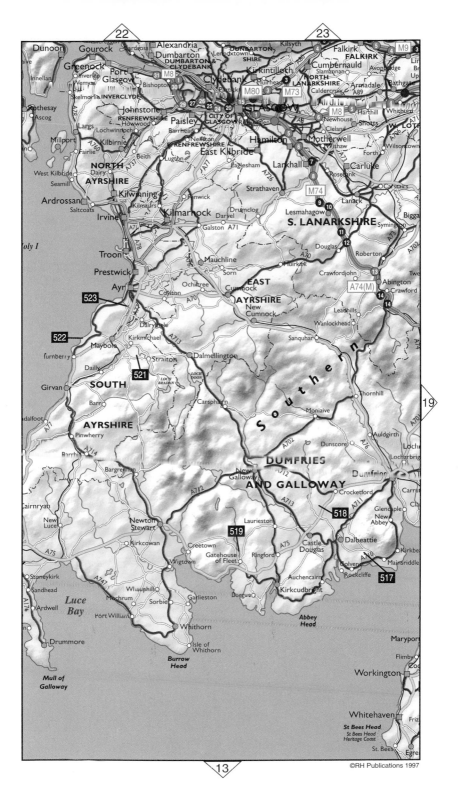

©RH Publications 1997

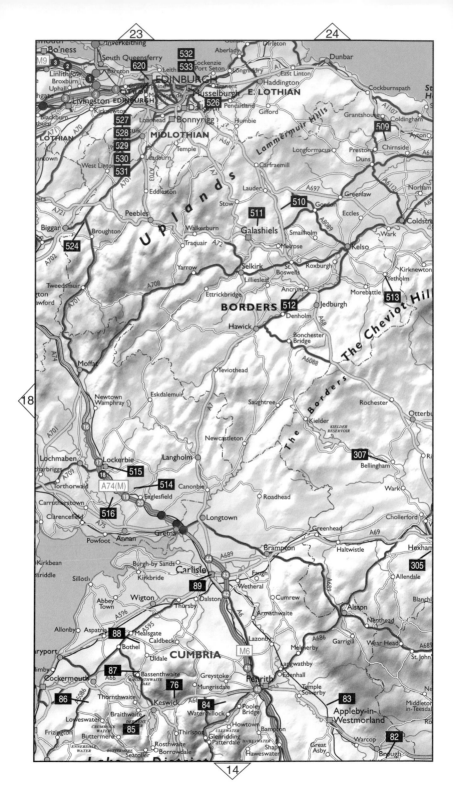

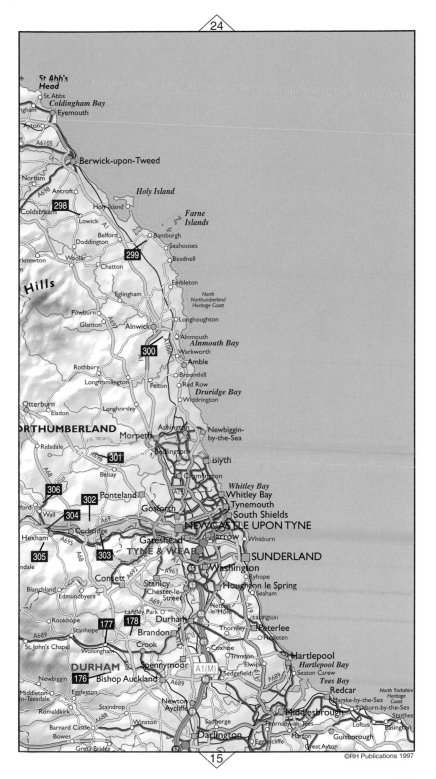

St Abb's
Head
St. Abbs
Coldingham Bay
ngham
Eyemouth
Ayton
A6105

Norham
Berwick-upon-Tweed
A698 Ancroft
Holy Island
Coldstream 298 Holy Island
Lowick A1
Belford *Farne*
Doddington Bamburgh *Islands*
rknewton Wooler 299 Seahouses
Chatton Beadnell

Hills Eglingham Embleton
North
Northumberland
Heritage Coast
Powburn Longhoughton
Glanton Alnwick
Alnmouth
Alnmouth Bay
300 Warkworth
Rothbury Amble
Longframlington Broomhill
Felton Red Row
Druridge Bay
Otterburn Widdrington
Elsdon Longhorsley
ORTHUMBERLAND Ashington Newbiggin-
Morpeth by-the-Sea
Ridsdale Bedlington
301 Blyth
Belsay Cramlington
306 *Whitley Bay*
302 Ponteland Whitley Bay
ford Gosforth Tynemouth
Wall 304 South Shields
Corbridge NEWCASTLE UPON TYNE
Hexham A695 Jarrow Whitburn
Gateshead
305 TYNE & WEAR SUNDERLAND
303 Washington
Blanchland Consett A963 65 Ryhope
ndale Stanley Houghton le Spring
Edmundbyers Chester-le- Seaham
Street A691
Rookhope Langley Park Hetton- Easington
177 178 le-Hole
Stanhope Durham Thornley Peterlee
St. John's Chapel Brandon Hesleden
Woolsingham Crook Coxhoe
Newbiggin Trimdon Hartlepool
DURHAM Spennymoor Sedgefield *Hartlepool Bay*
176 Bishop Auckland A1(M) Elwick Seaton Carew
Middleton- A689 60 A689 *Tees Bay*
in-Teesdale Eggleston Newton Redcar *North Yorkshire*
Romaldkirk Aycliffe 59 *Heritage*
Staindrop Marske-by-the-Sea *Coast*
Barnard Castle Winston Sadberge Saltburn-by-the-Sea
Bowes Thornaby-on-Tees Middlesbrough Staithes
Greta Bridge Darlington Loftus
67 Eggescliffe Marton Guisborough Easington
Great Ayton

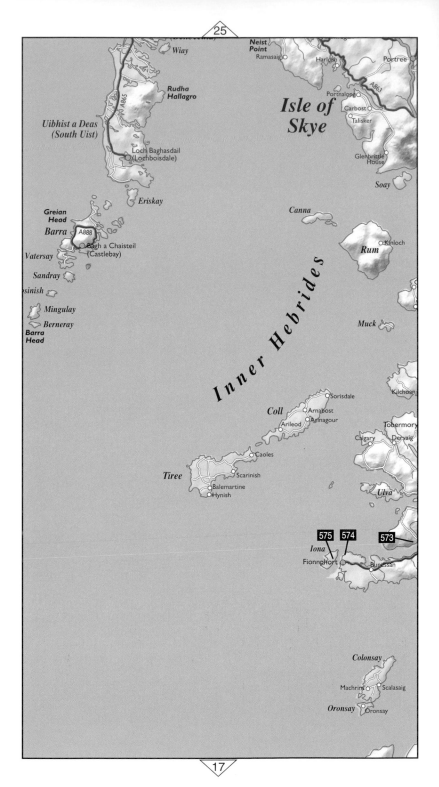

Wiay

Ramasaig○

Harloch○

Portree○

Rudha
Hallagro

A863

Portnalong○

Uibhist a Deas
(South Uist)

A865

Carbost○

Talisker○

Isle of
Skye

Loch Baghasdail
○(Lochboisdale)

Glenbrittle
House

Soay

Eriskay

Canna

Greian
Head

Kinloch○

Barra

A888

Rum

Bàgh a Chaisteil
○(Castlebay)

Vatersay○

Sandray

○sinish

Mingulay

Muck

Berneray

Barra
Head

Inner Hebrides

Sorisdale○

Coll

Arnabost○

Kilchoan○

Arileod○

Arinagour○

Tobermory

Calgary○

Dervaig○

Caoles○

Tiree

Scarinish○

Balemartine○

Ulva

○Hynish

575 **574** **573**

Iona

Fionnphort○

Bunessan○

Colonsay

Machrins○

Scalasaig○

Oronsay ○Oronsay

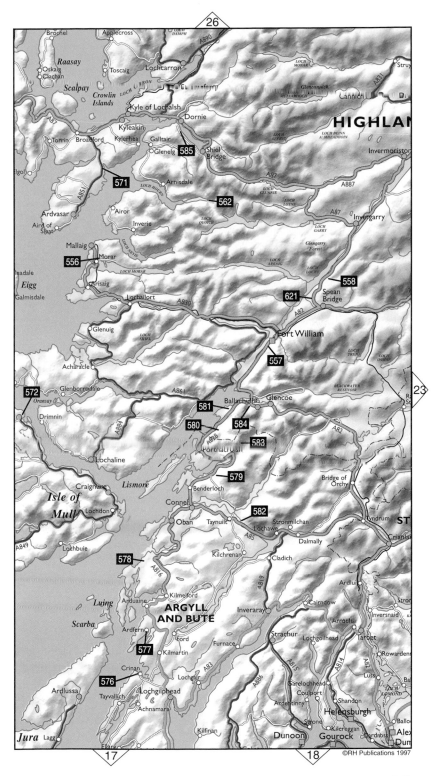

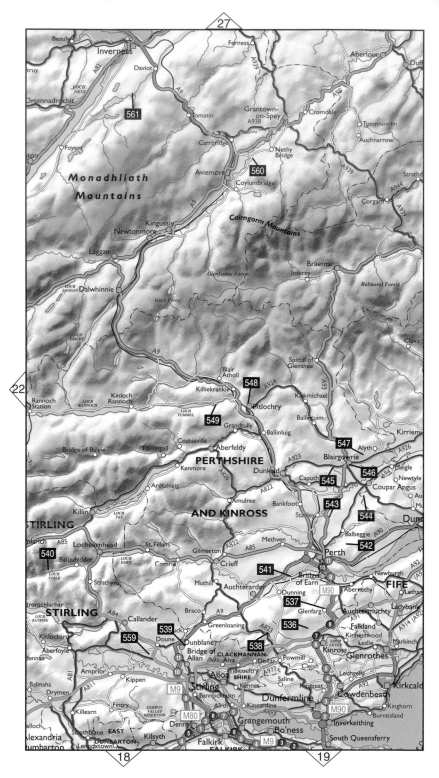

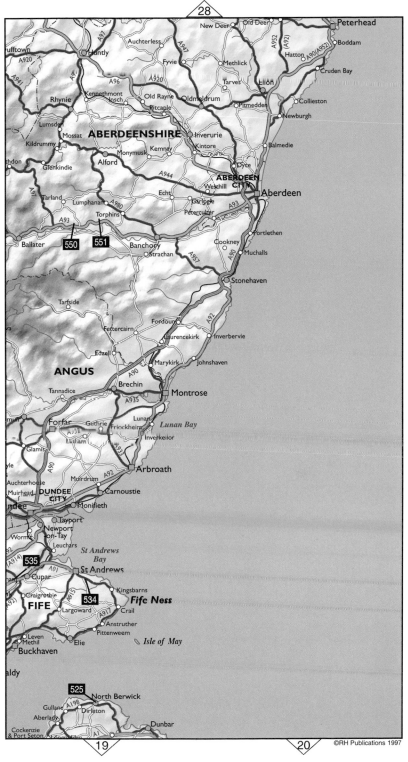

Peterhead

New Deer   Old Deer   Boddam

Auchterless   Hatton   Cruden Bay

ufftown

A920   Huntly   Fyvie   Methlick   Tarves   Ellon

A96   Rhynie   Kennethmont   Old Rayne   Oldmeldrum   Pitmedden   Collieston

Insch   Ritcaple   Newburgh

Lumsden

Kildrummy   Mossat   **ABERDEENSHIRE**   Inverurie   Balmedie

Monymusk   Kemnay   Kintore

thdon   Glenkindie   Alford   Dyce

ABERDEEN CITY

Tarland   Lumphanan   A944   Westhill   Aberdeen

Echt   Garlogie

Torphins   Peterculter

Ballater   **550**   **551**   Banchory   Cookney   Portlethen

Strachan   Muchalls

Tarfside   Stonehaven

va   Fettercairn   Fordoun

ANGUS   Laurencekirk   Inverbervie

Edzell   Marykirk   Johnshaven

Tannadice   Brechin   A935   Montrose

Forfar   Guthrie   Lunan   *Lunan Bay*

Letham   Friockheim   Inverkeilor

Glamis

yle   Auchterhouse   Muirdrum   Arbroath

Muirhead   **DUNDEE CITY**   Carnoustie

ndee   Monifieth

Wormit   Tayport

Newport-on-Tay

Leuchars   *St Andrews Bay*

535   St Andrews

ham   Cupar

Craigrothie   Kingsbarns

FIFE   **534**   *Fife Ness*

Largoward   Crail

Anstruther

Leven   Pittenweem   *Isle of May*

Methil   Elie

Buckhaven

aldy

525   North Berwick

Gullane   Dirleton

Aberlady   Dunbar

Cockenzie & Port Seton

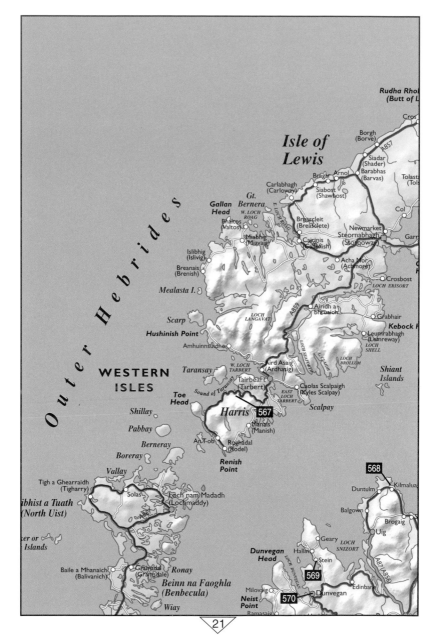

Rudha Rho
(Butt of L

Cros

Borgh
(Borve)

Isle of
Lewis

Siadar
(Shader)
Barabhas
(Barvas)

Bragar Arnol
Carlabhagh   Siabost
(Carloway)   (Shawbost)

Tolast
(Tol

Gt.
Bernera
W. LOCH
ROAG

Gallan
Head

Breascleit
(Breasclete)

Newmarket
Steornabhagh
(Stornoway)

Col

Bhaltos
(Valtos)

Cairinis
(Carlabhish)

Miabhig
(Miavaig)

Garr

Islibhig
(Islivig)

Acha Mor
(Achmore)

Breanais
(Brenish)

Crosbost

LOCH ERISORT

Mealasta I.

Airidh a
bhruaich

Grabhair

Scarp

LOCH
LANGAVAT

A859

Kebock

Hushinish Point

Leumrabhagh
(Lemreway)

LOCH
SHELL

Amhuinnsuidhe

LOCH SEAFORTH

LOCH
BROLLUM

W. LOCH
TARBERT

Aird Asaig
(Ardhasig)

Shiant
Islands

Taransay

Tairbeart
(Tarbert)

Caolas Scalpaigh
(Kyles Scalpay)

EAST
LOCH
TARBERT

Toe
Head

Sound of Taransay

WESTERN
ISLES

Scalpay

Shillay

Harris   567

Manais
(Manish)

Pabbay

An T-ob   Roghadal
(Rodel)

Berneray

Boreray

Renish
Point

Vallay

568

Tigh a Ghearraidh
(Tigharry)

Duntulm   Kilmalua

Solas   Loch nam Madadh
(Lochmaddy)

Balgown

ibhist a Tuath
(North Uist)

Brogaig

Uig

er or
Islands

Geary   LOCH
SNIZORT

Dunvegan
Head

Hallin

A87

Stein

Baile a Mhanaich
(Balivanich)

Gramsdal
(Gramsdale)

Ronay

Milovaig

569

Beinn na Faoghla
(Benbecula)

570

Dunvegan

Edinba

Wiay

Neist
Point

Ramasaig

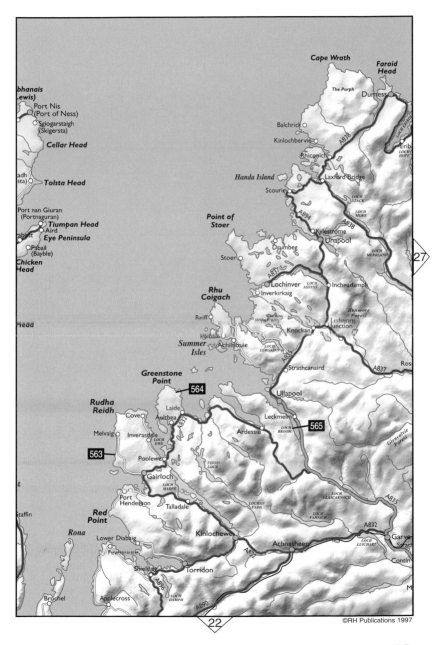

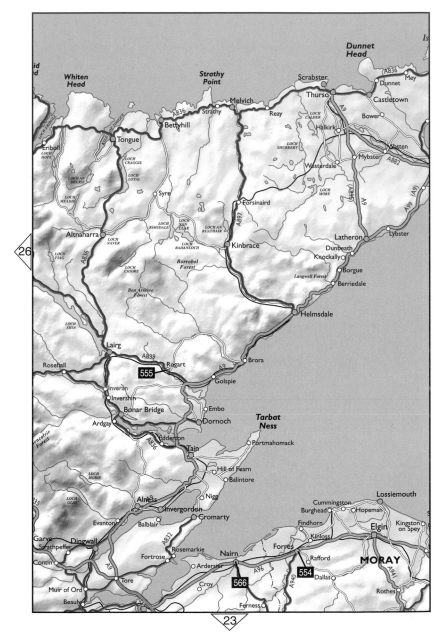

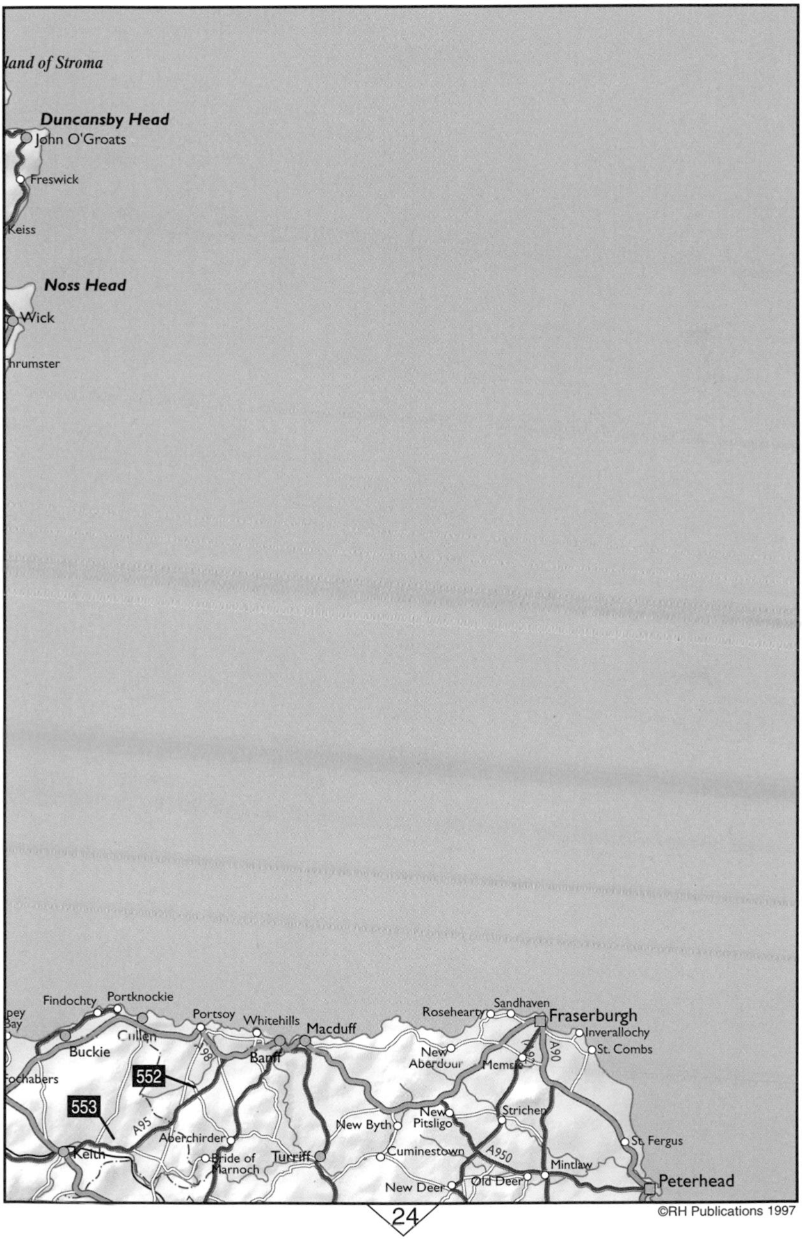

land of Stroma
Duncansby Head
John O'Groats
Freswick
Keiss
Noss Head
Wick
hrumster
Findochty
Portknockie
pey Bay
Buckie
Cullen
Fochabers
552
553
Portsoy
Whitehills
Macduff
Banff
Keith
A95
A98
Aberchirder
Bride of Marnoch
Turriff
Rosehearty
Sandhaven
Fraserburgh
Inverallochy
St. Combs
A90
New Aberdour
Memsie
A92
Strichen
New Pitsligo
New Byth
Cuminestown
A950
St. Fergus
Mintlaw
New Deer
Old Deer
Peterhead
24

©RH Publications 1997

Tucked beneath the Chilterns in 20 acres of grounds (and lakes) this 16th-century water-mill, a mile from the village, has a very pretty room in the 'Hay-loft'. Most of the chintz-and-antique bedrooms are in a converted stable-block - hotel privacy in a B&B - and you may stay all day, gazing at the lake from the conservatory and victualling yourself from the little kitchen. Rachael is an easy no-rules hostess and can lend you a bike... or offer fly-fishing, tennis, pool and 'ping-pong'.

Rooms: 2 twins and 5 doubles, all en suite.

Price: £30 p.p. Children £7.50. Single supp. £5-£15.

Breakfast: 7-9 am (week); 8.30-10 am (weekend).

Meals: Occasionally dinner, by arrangement, £15 p.p.

Closed: Never!

Bedfordshire, Buckinghamshire & Hertfordshire

From Dunstable, SW on B489. Right at roundabout by Plough pub. Bellows Mill in 3rd road on left.

Map Ref No: 10

Rachael Hodge
Bellows Mill
Eaton Bray
Dunstable
Bedfordshire LU6 1QZ
Tel: 01525 220548
Fax: 01525 222536

1

Come to the Old Vicarage and be welcomed into the heart of this charming family. With a church across the way and gracious, comfortable rooms, it is a lovely house, built by the Rothschilds in 1865 when they bought the village of Mentmore. Guests can use the large drawing room and savour Susie's delicious recipes in the dining room or *al fresco* in the lovingly-tended gardens with spectacular views over unspoilt countryside. Bedrooms are peaceful and airy (one overlooks the swimming pool). Waddeson Manor is nearby; London is less than an hour away.

Rooms: 1 twin, en suite (bath) and 1 double, en suite (shower).

Price: £25 p.p. Children under 12, £10 when sharing.

Breakfast: 7.30-9am.

Meals: Dinner £15 p.p. Available on request.

Closed: Occasionally.

Sarah's conversion, architectural rather than religious, has turned a fascinating church into a fascinating home, complete with tower and spiral staircase, original stained glass and stone-mullioned windows. Yet, with stealth and a sure touch, the comforts have crept in. Any austerity has been exorcised. Each of the bedrooms has its own church window; one has a Winnie the Pooh mural; and a bathroom has painted fish swimming round the walls. Sarah is ease personified and cooks a delicious breakfast in the magnificent kitchen/schoolroom. This is a one-off.

Rooms: 1 twin, 1 double and 1 single, sharing 1 bathroom and 1 shower room.

Price: Twin/double £20 p.p. Single, £25.

Breakfast: Flexible.

Meals: Excellent restaurants & pubs nearby.

Closed: Never!

At Cheddington roundabout left signposted Mentmore. Follow, past gates to Mentmore Towers. Old Vicarage is on right opposite church.

Map Ref No: 10

From Aylesbury, A413 towards Buckingham. On reaching Winslow centre, turn left into Horn St between The Bell Hotel and The George, church on left.

Map Ref No: 10

Charles & Susie Kirchner
The Old Vicarage
Mentmore
Buckinghamshire LU7 0QG
Tel: 01296 661227
Fax: 01296 661227

Sarah Hood
The Congregational Church
15 Horn Street
Winslow
Buckinghamshire MK18 3AP
Tel: 01296 715717
Fax: 01296 715717

A mere thirty minutes by train from central London, this is an oasis. Surrounded by cornfields, woods and lovely views, the house is large and old yet wonderfully cosy. The kitchen is bright and informal and we can imagine Claire cooking brilliantly and competently for dinner served in the pretty dining room. There are antiques, Limoges porcelain, lovely soft furnishings and informal bedrooms with comfortable beds. Claire, friendly and chatty, is very easy going and sweeps visitors of all ages into her welcome. There's a large, quiet garden.

Rooms: 2 twins, (1 en suite bath and 1 with private bathroom).

Price: £26.50 p.p. Single supp. £8.50.

Breakfast: Flexible.

Meals: Dinner, £20 p.p. by arrangement.

Closed: 20 December-3 January.

Lutyens built this wonderful house in 1901 for his mother-in-law, the Dowager Lady Lytton. Set down a long drive in six acres of beautiful gardens and fields, each elevation of the house is different. Architectural peculiarities - such as internal, octagonal windows - abound and Samantha Pollock-Hill has applied her considerable artistic skills to the interior. Unusual colour schemes offset magnificent antiques, tapestries and chinoiserie. The family is happy to share its lovely home with guests and can converse in a clutch of languages.

Rooms: 1 double, en suite (shower), 1 family suite with bathroom and 1 double with private shower sometimes available.

Price: Double £30 p.p. Single occ. £40. Family suite £75 for the room.

Breakfast: Flexible.

Meals: Dinner £20 p.p. Wine £5 p.p.

Closed: 20 December-3 January.

From A1 junc 4, follow signs to Wheathampstead (B653). After Brocket Hall, follow signs to Kimpton. After 2nd r'bout, go 2.2 miles and turn left to Porters End. Paddock Lodge is 1st house on left after 0.5 miles.

Map Ref No: 11

Claire van Straubenzee
Paddock Lodge
Porters End
Kimpton
Hertfordshire SG4 8ER
Tel: 01438 832423

Into Knebworth on B197, turn into Station Rd which becomes Park Lane. 300m after crossing M'way bridge, left into Public Footpath into Homewood drive. Bear left through lodge gates where drive forks.

Map Ref No: 11

Samantha Pollock-Hill
Homewood
Knebworth
Hertfordshire SG3 6PP
Tel: 01438 812105

Bristol postcode, but another world, a delightful, accessible, rustic world of honeysuckle and scented roses, wrapped around by a bountiful walled garden and bee-buzzing wildflower meadow... an idyllic farmhouse picture. It's all here: flagstones, terracotta tiles, old pine, Aga, dresser - and crisp white linen. Rooms are cosy, pretty and stylish, subtly colourful, the whole house alive and informal. Breakfast by the open fire in winter; on hazy days, laze in the garden and hear the flutter of butterflies' wings, then watch the sunset.

Rooms: 2 doubles: 1 en suite (bath) and 1 with private bathroom.

Price: £20-£25 p.p.

Breakfast: 7.30-9am.

Meals: Available nearby.

Closed: Christmas.

Bristol, Bath & North East Somerset

From Bristol take A38 for Airport. 5 miles out, turn left on B3130 towards Winford. On leaving village bear right up Regil Lane, for 1.5 miles. After Regil Stone, Farm is 5th on right.

Map Ref No: 3

Judy & Roger Gallannaugh
Spring Farm
Regil
Nr. Winford
Bristol BS40 8BB
Tel: 01275 472735

Unabashedly 1920s mock-Tudor with an oak-panelled hall and a great engraved fireplace, this is a generous house on the edge of the Bristol Downs, perfectly placed for country quiet in the evening after city bustle in the daytime. Light from the garden floods in and Philippa, with long experience of five-star hotels, revels in doing a proper job. The breakfast menu is mouth-watering and the morning papers come with it. The guestrooms are 'fully equipped', pastel-decorated and eminently comfortable; your hosts are affable and intelligent in their (semi-) retirement.

Rooms: 1 twin, en suite (bath) and 2 doubles (1 en suite shower and sitting room and 1 with shower and private w.c.).

Price: £27 p.p. Single occ. £33-£40.

Breakfast: Flexible.

Meals: Available locally.

Closed: Christmas & New Year.

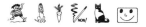

From M5 take exit 17 onto A4018. At 4th r'bout take 3rd exit into Parry's Lane. Left into Saville Rd. 3rd right into Hollybush Lane. Turn 1st left immediately after 2nd road hump into Downs Edge. Drive to end.

Map Ref No: 3

Alan & Philippa Tasker
Downs Edge
Saville Road
Stoke Bishop
Bristol BS9 1JD
Tel: 0117 968 3264
Fax: 0117 968 3264

The house is full of books, paintings and character - a place that, rather than provide a kettle and telly in each room, provides the whole house for you to be at home in. Valerie is artistic and musical (there is a piano to play) and interested in people. John Wood the Younger lived here; it has an unusual entrance, a secret garden... and is right beside the (clockless) Saxon/Norman church. The atmosphere is cosy: Liberty curtains and a log fire, leaded windows, winding stairs, semi-circular bathroom windows, open fireplaces and a walled garden. Booking essential. *Children over 8 welcome.*

Rooms: 1 double with basin and 1 twin sharing bathroom and separate shower.

Price: From £16 p.p. No single supp.

Breakfast: Until 9.30am.

Meals: Dinner, 4 courses, £11 p.p. with notice (not Thurs). B.Y.O. wine. Good pub food locally. Packed lunch possible.

Closed: December, January & February.

From A420, A431 into Bitton, turn right beside White Hart. Church on left, 25 yards of garden wall then 3 entrances on left. Granchen is middle one. Mrs Atkins would like to talk you through these instructions on booking.

Map Ref No: 3

Valerie Atkins
Granchen
Church Road
Bitton
Bristol BS30 6LJ
Tel: 0117 932 2423

An exceptional house in a quiet, secluded hamlet, yet minutes from Bath and Bristol. Julia exudes warmth and enthusiasm and is utterly natural. Both she and Patrick love their garden - immaculate lawns, deep herbaceous borders, croquet lawn, masses of roses and clematis, burgeoning fruit and vegetable garden and views to the Mendips. "I could hardly tear myself away" wrote our inspector. On warm days breakfast is served on the terrace and guests have exclusive use of the drawing room. Julia has deep local knowledge. *Children over 12 welcome.*

Rooms: 1 twin/double, with extra single bed, en suite (bath and shower).

Price: £28 p.p. No single supp.

Breakfast: Flexible.

Meals: Dinner, £15-£20 p.p. by prior arrangement. Good food available locally, too.

Closed: Mid-December-mid-January.

Come at the right time and the beautiful crops of sulphur-yellow rapeseed and vibrant blue linseed blanket the Addicotts' acres. The flax from linseed is used to heat the sturdy listed house - it has stone mullion windows, open fires and big bedrooms. Your hosts manage the mix of B&B-ing and farming with an easy-going humour. There are dressers with old china, Chinese rugs on wooden floors and swathes of Bath stone. The owners are involved in women's issues and agriculture in Uganda so there is a smattering of Africana. They are also passionate supporters of Bath Rugby Club.

Rooms: 1 double, with en suite (bath); 1 twin and 2 doubles with shared bathroom/shower.

Price: From £24 p.p. Single occ. £30.

Breakfast: Flexible.

Meals: Dinner available locally.

Closed: Christmas & New Year.

From Bath, A4 west. At r'bout by Globe Inn, left onto A39 towards Wells. Through Corston (ignore Burnett sign), after 0.5 miles take B3116, SHARP right. After 1 mile left signed Burnett and next right. House 100 yds on left.

Map Ref No: 3

Patrick & Julia Stevens
Brooklands
Burnett
Keynsham
Bristol BS31 2TF
Tel: 0117 986 8794

From A4 W of Bath take A39 through Corston. 1 mile on, just before Wheatsheaf Pub (on right), turn right. Signposted 200m along lane on right.

Map Ref No: 3

Gerald & Rosaline Addicott
Corston Fields Farm
Corston
Bath
Bath & N.E. Somerset BA2 9EZ
Tel: 01225 873305
Fax: 01225 873305
e-mail: corston.fields@3wa.co.uk

A large old Mendip-style 'long cottage' with mullioned windows, beams made of ships' timbers and... a vineyard! The flavour is Somerset and old stone barns and you are temptingly close to the treasures of Bath and Wells, the gardens and concerts at Stourhead and Gregorian chant in Downside Abbey. Bedrooms are light and pretty, with fresh flowers and good towels. No sitting room but tea in the beautiful walled garden is a rich compensation. Interesting, child-friendly hosts. Excellent value.

Rooms: 1 twin/family and 1 small double/single, sharing bathroom.

Price: £15-£17.50 p.p

Breakfast: Flexible.

Meals: Available locally at excellent pubs.

Closed: Never!

This house grew over three centuries (14th to 17th). The dovecote is 14th-century, the 20th-century Aga hides the entrance to a Reformation priesthole. The stone courtyard and the gardens are of the same period and '1630' is carved into the lintel of the porch. Carvings abound inside too. The whole house is elegant, peaceful and welcoming with old furniture and lots of books. Sarah makes her own bread and serves cream teas in the bakery in summer. Lush countryside and a gem of a village.

Rooms: 1 twin, en suite (shower), 1 double, en suite (bath) and 1 single with shared bathroom.

Price: Twin/double £20-£22.50 p.p.; single £20.

Breakfast: Until 8.30am.

Meals: Available locally.

Closed: Christmas.

A367 Wells Rd from Bath through Radstock. After 3 miles at large roundabout B3139 towards Trowbridge. After 1.1 miles, right up drive. Melon Cottage is at top, visible from road.

Map Ref No: 3

Virginia & Hugh Pountney
Melon Cottage Vineyard
Charlton, Radstock
Nr. Bath
Bath & N.E. Somerset BA3 5TN
Tel: 01761 435090

From Bath A367 Exeter road. Left opposite Burnt House Inn at sign for Wellow (3 miles). Once in Wellow turn left. House is 85m down on left-hand corner of crossroads diagonally opposite village school.

Map Ref No: 4

Sarah Danny
The Manor House
Wellow
Bath & N.E. Somerset BA2 8QQ
Tel: 01225 832027
Fax: 01225 832027

Combe Down is the landscape equivalent of Bath's Royal Crescent - stunning. Bath stone was discovered here (by Ralph Allen, who consequently made his fortune) and trundled down the hill to build all that celebrated Regency elegance. Staggering views - the Sticklands even installed a full-height window to take it all in. The garden is gorgeous and the breakfasts, with organic eggs and 'proper' bacon, a real treat. Fluffy towels, herb, fruit and flower teas in your room. A warm, kind and likeable family.

Rooms: 2 twins/doubles and 1 family room, all en suite (shower).

Price: From £27.50 p.p. Single occ. £35.

Breakfast: 7.9.30am.

Meals: Dinner, 3 courses, £15 p.p.

Closed: Christmas.

200 years ago, it wasn't so much 'messing about in boats', more a way of life - canals were arteries of the burgeoning Industrial Revolution. This lock-keeper's cottage was built in 1801 by the Somerset Coal Canal Company. The Wheeldon's honeysuckle- and rose-clad home has the restored canal running through the garden carrying brightly-coloured narrow boats (hire an electric launch for a days pootling) and there are peaceful towpath walks into Bath. The cottage has kept its character, and added log-burning - and personal - warmth. The Wheeldons have 'fed and watered' guests for years.

Rooms: 1 twin/double, 1 double and 1 single, all with private bathrooms.

Price: Double from £23.50 p.p. Single £23.50.

Breakfast: Until 9am.

Meals: Available nearby.

Closed: Christmas & New Year.

From A36 take uphill road by traffic lights and Viaduct Inn. Take 1st turn left, signed Monkton Combe. After village (0.5 miles on) Grey Lodge is first house on left.

Map Ref No: 4

Jane & Anthony Stickland
Grey Lodge
Summer Lane
Combe Down, Bath
Bath & N.E. Somerset BA2 7EU
Tel: 01225 832069
Fax: 01225 832069

5 miles south of Bath just off the A36, 50 yds north of BP garage. (The entrance is at an oblique angle so it is wise to turn in the garage and approach the entrance from the south.)

Map Ref No: 4

Tim & Wendy Wheeldon
Dundas Lock Cottage
Monkton Combe
Bath
Bath & N.E. Somerset BA2 7BN
Tel: 01225 723890
Fax: 01225 722292

The urban exterior of this early Georgian house conceals half an acre of superb garden and magical 180° views of the city. Inside, it's comfortable and uncluttered, the welcome professional. David and Annie tend the garden, with its rose pergola, fishpond and trim lawns and show designer talent in a successful mix of contemporary and trad. The pretty sitting room has Liberty prints and the breakfast room feels French with parquet floor, heavy lace at the windows and geraniums outside. Only seven minutes' walk from the centre.

Rooms: 8 twins/doubles, all en suite (some shower, some bath).

Price: £36-£39 p.p. Single occ. £57-£63.

Breakfast: Flexible.

Meals: An easy walk to all Bath's restaurants.

Closed: Christmas week.

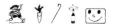

Understated elegance and huge comfort are yours right here in the middle of Bath. John Wood built this as a private house for the Marquess of Queensberry in 1772. Penny has given a boost to classical Regency architecture with her own contemporary style. Her confidence and flair for interior design enable her to combine period furniture, bold colour, polished wood and sumptuous carpets. Bedrooms are perfectly lit and fresh flowers are everywhere; the restaurant is extremely popular. The whole place is professionally run with a personal touch.

Rooms: 29 doubles and twins, all en suite.

Price: £120-£195 per room.

Breakfast: 7.30-9.30am (week). 8-10am (Sunday). Continental included. Full English £7.50 p.p.

Meals: Dinner from £25 p.p. Lunch £11.50-£13.50 p.p.

Closed: Christmas.

From Bath train station follow one-way system to Churchill Bridge. Take A367 exit from r'bout up hill. After 0.75 miles turn left at 'Day and Pierce'. Left down hill into cul-de-sac. On left.

Map Ref No: 4

David & Annie Lanz
Paradise House
Holloway
Bath
Bath & N.E. Somerset BA2 4PX
Tel: 01225 317723
Fax: 01225 482005
e-mail: paradise@apsleyhouse.co.uk

From London, follow London Rd (A4) until it becomes Paragon. First right into Lansdown, second left into Bennett St, then first right into Russel St.

Map Ref No: 4

Penny & Stephen Ross
The Queensberry Hotel &
Olive Tree Restaurant
Russel Street, Bath
Bath & N.E. Somerset BA1 2QF
Tel: 01225 447928
Fax: 01225 446065
e-mail: queensberry@dial.pipex.com

The Georgian and the Victorian blend seamlessly in this lovingly-restored house that was built by a Bath merchant in 1778. Bath-born Derek and Hungarian-born Maria, a psychologist, have decorated the rooms with colours authentic to the era and cleverly amassed period furniture that fits perfectly. After their painstaking renovation on the veranda on this handsome house is back to its former glory. Fires, a mahogany four-poster, garden ponds, canal-side walks and memorably charming, relaxed hosts. All this a 15-minute stroll from the wonders of Bath.

Rooms: 2 doubles, en suite (shower); 1 twin with private bathroom.

Price: £25-£35 p.p. Single occ. £40-£50.

Breakfast: Flexible.

Meals: None - restaurants in Bath.

Closed: Sometimes at Christmas.

Near junction with A46 on A4, towards city centre, opposite Bath Rugby Club training ground.

Map Ref No: 4

Derek & Maria Beckett
Cedar Lodge
13 Lambridge
Bath
Bath & N.E. Somerset BA1 6BJ
Tel: 01225 423468

A grand, listed, Georgian hotel built in 1750 by John Wood the Elder, but it feels like a happy family home. There are toys scattered about, a welcome absence of ceremony, and simple, unimposing bedrooms (pine and prints), some cottagey and some Georgian. At the heart of the house is a large, comfortable sitting room, afternoon sunlight flooding through the shuttered windows. Tea can be taken looking onto the garden (with tennis court) and overseen by court paintings of Charles I and II. Long, lush views - and the walled garden cottage is very special.

Rooms: 3 twins and 5 doubles, all en suite.

Price: £22-£36 p.p. Single occ. £34-£42.

Breakfast: Usually 8-10am. Sunday (child-free late breakfast) until 10.30am. £2.80 extra for full breakfast.

Meals: Available locally.

Closed: 20-30 December.

M4, junc 18, A46 (Bath) for 9 miles. A4 Chippenham for 2 miles. Ignore A4 Bath sign. Right onto A363 (Bradford on Avon) for 150 yds, fork left (Bathford Hill). 1st right into Church St. House 200 yds on right with iron gates.

Map Ref No: 4

Rosamund & John Napier
Eagle House
Church Street
Bathford
Bath & N.E. Somerset BA1 7RS
Tel: 01225 859946
Fax: 01225 859430
e-mail: jonapepsionworld.net

Nice people in an equally nice house; "take us as you find us" - a refreshing change from anxious hostesses making a lip-stiffening effort. It is all large, open, warm and friendly. One cosy and very private bedroom is up its own spiral staircase - a lovely conversion and sure winner of 1st prize in any Loo With A View competition. Sheep graze in the fields around the house and barn, bees slave to make your breakfast honey... this is a proper working farm, with both crops and sheep. Perfectly quiet, yet so close to Cambridge.

Rooms: 1 double and 1 family room, both en suite (shower).

Price: £20 p.p. Single occ. £24.

Breakfast: Until 9.30am.

Meals: Not available, good local pubs.

Closed: 22 December-2 January.

Cambridgeshire

Turn off the A1198 at Longstowe. The house is exactly 3 miles along the B1046, between Little Gransden and Longstowe.

Map Ref No: 11

Sue Barlow
Model Farm
Little Gransden
Cambridgeshire SG19 3EA
Tel: 01767 677361
Fax: 01767 677361
e-mail: modelfm@globalnet.co.uk

Cathedral views from the walled garden and lots of ancient, narrow streets and medieval buildings to discover in this bustling market town. Sheila runs her large, peaceful 17th-century house with care; she serves locally-baked bread and homemade marmalade at the long mahogany dining table. The feel is traditional English. The neatly-furnished bedrooms have floral wallpaper and bedspreads and all face south with lovely garden views. The sublime Cathedral is a mere 5 minutes' walk away and Cambridge 15 miles.

Rooms: 1 double with private bathroom and 1 twin, en suite (bath).

Price: £22 p.p. Single supp. £6.

Breakfast: Until 9.30am.

Meals: Available locally.

Closed: 20 December-2 January and for annual holiday.

A Grade II listed house whose period elegance clearly encourages long stays - only three owners since a doctor built it in the 1800s. Lots of original features: high ceilings, tall windows, wood floors, cast-iron baths, an enormous log-burning fireplace. Yet it all feels open and light - the colour white prevails, fresh and bright. Breakfast at the old pine farmhouse table where the food is "brilliant". Robin and Jenny slipped the leash, left London for the Isle of Ely, where everything, everybody, slows down. Join them, and see one of England's loveliest cathedrals.

Rooms: 1 double suite, 1 family suite and 1 twin, all en suite (bath).

Price: From £25 p.p. Single occ. from £35. Short break rates available.

Breakfast: 8-9am.

Meals: Available nearby.

Closed: Christmas & New Year.

Entering Ely from Cambridge on A10, turn left at lights by Lamb Hotel. Left again at next lights after 200 metres into Egremont Street. House is last on left with off-street parking just beyond.

Map Ref No: 11

Sheila Friend-Smith
Old Egremont House
31 Egremont Street
Ely
Cambridgeshire CB6 1AE
Tel: 01353 663118
Fax: 01353 663118

Cathedral House is 75 yards down from Cromwell House (Tourist Information Centre), in the centre of Ely, near the Cathedral.

Map Ref No: 11

Robin & Jenny Farndale
Cathedral House
17 St Mary's Street
Ely
Cambridgeshire CB7 4ER
Tel: 01353 662124
Fax: 01353 662124

A 1780s Adam-style house tucked quietly away at the edge of the village and with a lovely garden and water features. The sitting room, with Tudor brick walls, drain-brick floors, fireplace and old velvet sofas is the former coach-house, and Sally and Phil add thoughtful touches to make you feel at home, newspapers and soft drinks among them. It is a beautifully kept house, with a grand piano, deeply comfortable chairs and a specially designed kitchen to enable Sally to produce those mouthwateringly inventive meals; she cures her own salmon and uses organic ingredients.

Rooms: 2 doubles, both with en suite (shower).

Price: £30-£35 p.p. Single occ. £45.

Breakfast: 8-9.30am.

Meals: Dinner £25 p.p. Supper £15 p.p. Picnics £10 p.p. B.Y.O. wine.

Closed: Never!

Off A14 north of Cambridge take A10 towards Ely. Right into Waterbeach. Bear left at village green. House is last at end of High Street before bend. Opposite 2 white houses, through white gates.

Map Ref No: 11

Phil & Sally Myburgh
Berry House
High Street
Waterbeach
Cambridgeshire CB5 9JU
Tel: 01223 860702
Fax: 01223 860702
e-mail: sal@berryhouse.demon.co.uk

It's a racing cert - you'll find an engaging style running alongside the most delicious of breakfasts here in the wistful *Waterland* world of Graham Swift's novel. (Malcolm's a buff on matters equine). We cannot possibly overstate the quality of the breakfast: home cooking, locally sourced fresh produce, soft cheeses, hams, black puddings, kippers, haddock. Jan, formerly an illustrator, cooks and attends to the decor - old pine, white linen, huge cushions, handsome wallpapers and fresh flowers. A Georgian home, log fires, croquet lawn and Victorian conservatory - a winner!

Rooms: 1 twin/double with private bathroom and 1 double, en suite (bath). 1 single available for families.

Price: Double £22.50-£25 p.p. Single occ. £30-£35.

Breakfast: Flexible.

Meals: Dinner from £15 p.p. by arrangement.

Closed: Christmas.

Take A142 Newmarket to Ely road, through Fordham and turn right at Murfitts Lane; at the end, right into Carter St and Queensbury is 500m on left next to Fordham Moor Rd.

Map Ref No: 11

Jan & Malcom Roper
Queensberry
196 Carter Street
Fordham, Ely
Cambridgeshire CB7 5JU
Tel: 01638 720916
Fax: 01638 720223

A large, elegant 1840 Regency-style house nestles in the bend of a river at the end of the quiet, historic village of Linton. Rooms are elegant and country squire-ish, with glass doors overlooking the gardens. Some have river views. The lovely conservatory, draped with mimosa and with red and black tile floors and park-bench furniture, is for summer breakfasts, while in winter one repairs to the dark-green dining room. Bedrooms are comfortable and well-equipped, and stocked with books. Judith Rossiter looks after all this and two teenage children, and still finds time to be a charming and helpful hostess.

Rooms: 2 doubles, 1 en suite (bath), 1 with private bathroom.

Price: £19 p.p. Single supp. £22-£25.

Breakfast: Until 9.30am.

Meals: Available locally.

Closed: Never!

Just 10 minutes' walk from Kings College Chapel - services during term time - No 46 is, among the whooshing bicycles and swishing gowns, an oasis of peace, good taste and good conversation. Once home to college staff, the cottage has been lovingly converted and has a wonderful collection of paintings. Pride of place goes to one of the eccentric professor weaving his way on a bike through the oh-so-recognisable streets. It is by Ophelia Redpath, who did the painting, too, of the house. Alice is a marvellous hostess and a fount of information. *Children over 12 welcome.*

Rooms: 1 twin/double with private bathroom and 1 double, en suite (shower).

Price: £30 p.p. Single occ. £50.

Breakfast: Until 9am.

Meals: Available locally.

Closed: Never!

A1307 from Cambridge, left into High Street. First right after The Crown (on left) into Horn Lane with Barclays on corner. House on right next to chapel and before ford.

Map Ref No: 11

Judith Rossiter
Springfield House
14-16 Horn Lane
Linton
Cambridgeshire CB1 6HT
Tel: 01223 891383

Follow signs for city centre, BR station & Botanical Gardens. Panton St is one-way and should be approached via Bateman St from either Hills Rd or Trumpington Rd.

Map Ref No: 11

Alice Percival
46 Panton Street
Cambridge
Cambridgeshire CB2 1HS
Tel: 01223 365285/568305
Fax: 01223 461142

"Small, sweet world of wave-encompassed wonder", wrote Swinburne of Sark. The tiny community of 500 people lives under a spell, governed feudally and sharing this magic with horses, sheep, cattle and pigs, carpets of wild flowers, and birds. There are wild cliff walks, thick woodland, sandy coves, deep rock pools. No cars, only bikes, horse-carriages and the odd tractor. In the hotel there is no TV, no radio, no trouser press... just a dreamy peace, kindness, starched cotton sheets, woollen blankets and food to die for. It is almost self-sufficient, 400 years old... and perfect.

Rooms: 14, en suite, 8 sharing bathrooms.

Price: Dinner, B&B, £59.50-£75.50 p.p.

Breakfast: Flexible.

Meals: Gourmet dinner included.

Closed: 2nd Mon in October-Wed before Easter.

Channel Islands

Take ferry to Sark and ask!

Map Ref No: 1

Elizabeth Perrée
La Sablonnerie
Little Sark
Sark
Channel Islands GY9 0SD
Tel: 01481 832061
Fax: 01481 832408

Ducks, geese, chickens and a Guernsey goat strut about, and the house is semi self-sufficient for fruit and veg. The surroundings are what you come for: 27 vergees (sic) of land, red deer in the park, handsome gardens, woods and wild flower water meadow then steep paths to the sea 15 minutes' walk away, wild garlic everywhere. Gorgeous. The house is comfortable, with thick patterned carpets in huge rooms, white timbered walls, net curtains, ornate hinges and door handles. The top floor has the sea views and there's a balcony for summer. Jackie is a treasure. *Children over 12 welcome.*

Rooms: 1 triple with 3 single beds, 1 double with 1 extra single bed, 1 double, 2 twins, all en suite (bath).

Price: From £25 p.p. Single supp. £10.

Breakfast: Usually 8-9am.

Meals: Snacks & packed lunches available. Tea garden (closed in winter).

Closed: December-mid-January.

From the airport exit turn left into Forest Road, go straight across lights and Tudor Lodge is on right. Beware of narrow entrance!

Map Ref No: 1

Jackie Gallienne
Tudor Lodge Deer Farm
Forest Road, Forest
Guernsey
Channel Islands GY8 0AG
Tel: 01481 37849
Fax: 01481 35662

Burland is a large dairy farm in the process of organic conversion and in Michael's family for 250 years. It produces gourmet frozen yoghurt and has a mid-Victorian farmhouse with unique hexagonal windows. Sandra is warm, chatty and a vegetarian. She has furnished her guestrooms with old country furniture (and a couple of lovely lion's-foot armchairs). Bathrooms are functional, while sitting and dining rooms have big, comfortable pieces, books, maps and games. There's also a very large dog but guest areas are theoretically out of bounds to it. *Babies and over-10s welcome.*

Rooms: 1 double and 1 twin, all en suite (bath/shower).

Price: From £22.50 p.p. Single supp. £2.50.

Breakfast: From 8.30am.

Meals: Dinner available nearby. Packed lunch from £4 p.p.

Closed: Christmas & New Year.

Cheshire & South Wirrall

From Nantwich (A534) enter Burland and cross humpback bridge. Burland Farm is on left 1 mile from the bridge.

Map Ref No: 9

Sandra & Michael Allwood
Burland Farm
Wrexham Road
Burland, Nantwich
Cheshire CW5 8ND
Tel: 01270 524210
Fax: 01270 524419
e-mail: sandy@netcentral.co.uk

"Our guests seem to oversleep". This is peace indeed. A haven for garden buffs, walkers, birdwatchers - Britain at its best with rare trees planted in 1860, flowers everywhere, a pond, a fruitful vegetable garden and a warm welcome from Rachel, a passionate gardener. She also embroiders her own designs which can be seen around the house. It is furnished in elegant, traditional style and the proportions of the light-filled drawing room and the big, high-ceilinged dining room feel just right. The bedrooms are light and large and your hosts like to treat their visitors as guests of the family.

Rooms: 1 double and 1 twin/double, both en suite (bath).

Price: £23 p.p. Single supp. £4.

Breakfast: Before 10am.

Meals: Dinner, £16 p.p., on request. B.Y.O. wine. Good village pubs within walking distance.

Closed: Christmas week-3 January.

You quickly get the feel of Roughlow, planted as it is in the very hillside - it is simple, solid, authentic, and greatly loved. The cobbled entrance yard is a treasure box of carefully-nurtured natural textures and materials, flowering trees and shrubs; the terrace looks out over the Welsh border (40 miles on a clear day); there's also a tennis court. Bedrooms are big and furnished with artistic flair; the suite is vast. Sally was once an interior designer and has an eye for colour and the ability to create a calming, uncluttered space. They both collect art - you will enjoy discovering it all.

Rooms: 3 twins/doubles all with private bathrooms and 1 with sitting room.

Price: £25-£35 p.p. Single supp. £10.

Breakfast: 8-9am.

Meals: Dinner £20 p.p. on request for minimum of 4 people. Good pubs & hotels nearby.

Closed: Never!

From Chester, A55 west. Then A5104 to Broughton, left at roundabout to Pennyffordd on A5104. Through Broughton & over A55. First left to Kinnerton down Lesters Lane. House on right.

Map Ref No: 9

A51 from Chester. Cross roundabout at Tarvin & take A54 to Manchester (not Tarporley). Pass Elf garage. Take second right & follow signs to Willington. Straight over crossroads & up Chapel Lane. Farm on right.

Map Ref No: 9

Jonathan & Rachel Major
The Mount
Higher Kinnerton
Chester
Cheshire CH4 9BQ
Tel: 01244 660275
Fax: 01244 660275

Sally Sutcliffe
Roughlow Farm
Willington
Tarporley
Cheshire CW6 0PG
Tel: 01829 751199
Fax: 01829 751199

Looking like a Regency Indian villa from the long, beautifully kept garden, it is at the end of a drive off a peaceful little lane. Built in 1820 by Charles Monk, a sea captain, it is idiosyncratic, unexpected, a house of different levels, with Gothic arched window frames... a hidden treasure. The hall is flagstoned, an old railway clock ticks solidly, there are seascapes on the walls and from the verandah you can see across the Dee estuary to Wales. They keep chickens, so your eggs are fresh. A warm welcome from two very friendly people.

Rooms: 1 twin with private bathroom. Self-contained cottage sleeps 4.

Price: £19 p.p. Single supp. by arrangement. Cottage £20 p.p.

Breakfast: Until 9.30am.

Meals: Dinner, 3 courses, £15 p.p. Light supper £10 p.p. By arrangement.

Closed: Never!

From A540 to Neston. Right at T-junction, left at the cross, next left and immediately left again down Church Lane. House on right after 20m, hidden down long drive, but signed.

Map Ref No: 9

Mrs Jennifer Legge
The Hermitage
Church Lane
Neston
South Wirrall L64 9US
Tel: 0151 336 5171

A lovely little guest house on a quiet country lane with the village pub at the end of the drive, Dunham Massey Deer Park five minutes' walk away, and only six miles from Manchester. The rooms are modern and almost sumptuous (TV and video hidden in wooden cabinets) and have great country views. David designed the furniture. One bed is vast enough to deserve nine pillows. Janice is a trained cook, specialising in vegetable dishes. David, the 'Silver Fox', was a professional snooker player. Marvellous value so close to the city yet so rural. *Children over 12 welcome.*

Rooms: One 7ft 6in bed, en suite (shower); 1 four-poster, en suite (bath and shower) and 1 double with large, private bathroom.

Price: £26-£32 p.p. Single occ. £39-£46.

Breakfast: Until 9.30am.

Meals: Dinner, 3 courses, from £17.50 p.p. Private dinner parties available on request.

Closed: Christmas & New Year.

Take A556 NE to Manchester, then left on A56 towards Lymm. At first pub turn right down Park Lane. House is next to The Swan With Two Nicks.

Map Ref No: 14

David & Janice Taylor
Ash Farm Country Guest House
Park Lane
Little Bollington, Nr. Altrincham
Cheshire WA14 4TJ
Tel: 0161 929 9290
Fax: 0161 928 5002

A thoroughly unpretentious and completely relaxing house full of the sound of laughter. Sally enjoys entertaining and the arts and receives guests with vivacious good humour in her large, rambling, supremely comfortable family house with big rooms. Nothing sumptuous, all entirely natural. Old toys lie around for new children to play with and a barbecue is set up in the garden for fine weather, otherwise Sally will cook for you with garden produce in her farmhouse kitchen. Bedrooms have high beds, warm rugs and views of the wooded valley.

Rooms: 1 twin, en suite (shower); 1 double, en suite (bath); 2 cottage suites for 2-4 people.

Price: £20-£25 p.p. Cottage suite £25-£27.50 p.p. Under 5s £5, 5-15 yrs £10.

Breakfast: Until 9am.

Meals: Dinner £12.50 p.p. Children £6.

Closed: Christmas & New Year. Cottage suites available all year.

Cornwall

Take Penzance bypass for Land's End. Right at r'bout to Heamoor. Through village, right at x-roads into Josephs Lane, 1st left signed Bone Valley/New Mill. House on right after 0.5 miles.

Map Ref No: 1

Sally Adams
Tremearne
Bone Valley
Penzance
Cornwall TR20 8UJ
Tel: 01736 364576
Fax: 01736 350957

A position to die for: on the wild side, the cliff faces the live blue bay while a secluded garden with a path to the beach has *chaises longues* for the lazy; on the (largely) civilised side, there is St Ives itself with all the finer delights that this ancient-and-modern village has to offer. The Shearns have been running their guest house for years and Jan has a reputation as an excellent cook. The rooms are simply, comfortably furnished; ask for one with a view - your heart will leap with each fresh glimpse. The master suite has a telescope and balcony.

Rooms: 1 master suite, 1 twin and 3 doubles, all en suite. 2 doubles and 2 singles sharing 2 bathrooms.

Price: From £29-£45 p.p. Special rates for weekly bookings.

Breakfast: Until 9.15am.

Meals: Dinner £16.50 p.p.

Closed: Mid-October-mid-March.

In balmy Cornwall, this farm grows salad crops in summer and flowers in winter. The 18th-century house was originally home to a copper-mine captain. The area's fine beaches, villages and art galleries are all close by. Bedrooms are comfortably functional with some good furniture; there's a red telephone box outside and a heated pool inside but the star is the ancient stone fireplace and bread oven in the elegant, mahogany-tabled, high-chaired dining room. Breakfast is usually at separate tables in the sunny conservatory. The garden is lovely too. *Children over 6 welcome.*

Rooms: 2 family, 2 doubles and 1 twin, all en suite. Campsite.

Price: £21-£24 p.p. Single occ. £26.

Breakfast: 8.30-9am.

Meals: Available locally.

Closed: November.

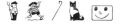

From A30 take A3074 & continue through Lelant and Carbis Bay. Entering St. Ives along Trelyon Avenue, Blue Hayes is prominent on right.

Map Ref No: 1

Jan & John Shearn
Blue Hayes
Trelyon Avenue
St. Ives
Cornwall TR26 2AD
Tel: 01736 797129
Fax: 01736 797129

Take signs for Hayle at roundabout on A30. Take 1st left into Guildford Rd, under railway bridge. The road then becomes Wheal Alfred Rd. Treglisson is 0.5 miles on left.

Map Ref No: 1

Chris & Carole Runnalls
Treglisson
Hayle
Cornwall TR27 5JT
Tel: 01736 753141
Fax: 01736 753141

Windswept walks are within easy reach; seabird acrobatics will dazzle and magical Prussia Cove will enchant you. The road ends at Ennys, so the rural bliss is entirely yours. Woods rise on one side, fields stretch out on the other. Return spellbound to a house full of wood and warmth. Gill has responded to the existing magic of the house and added a dash of her own. Stone floors lead you to a sumptuous log-fired sitting room; afternoon tea is laid out in the kitchen; bedrooms have great views. You can play tennis or swim in the pool. *Children over 5 welcome.*

Rooms: 1 twin, en suite (bath) and 2 four-posters, en suite (shower). 1 luxury self-catering studio for 2.

Price: £25-£33 p.p. Single supp. £7.50. Studio £200-£400 per week.

Breakfast: Until 9.15am.

Meals: Available locally.

Closed: December & January.

Roomy, artistic interior and stunning coastal location - a heaven-sent combination. Set foot in the slate-flagged hallway, and immediately all feels fresh and inviting with natural hues in granite walls and honey-coloured timbers.The antique prints, richly-coloured rugs and tapestries are a crafted counterpoint. Liberty sofas piled high with cushions coax you into comfortable decline. Bedrooms have a deft touch, with fresh flowers and more embroidery. Outside, the wild blue yonder and views across the sea to St. Michael's Mount. Christine plays classical guitar, musically complementing her gentle presence.

Rooms: 3 doubles, all en suite (2 bath and 1 shower).

Price: £20-30 p.p. Single occ. £20-£40.

Breakfast: 8.30-9am

Meals: Available locally.

Closed: Never!

2 miles east of Marazion on B3280 look for sign leading down Trewhella Lane. Keep going to Ennys.

Map Ref No: 1

From A30 after Crowlas roundabout take A394 to Helston. 0.25 miles after next roundabout take 1st right towards Perranuthnoe. Ednovean Farm drive on left and signed.

Map Ref No: 1

Gill Charlton
Ennys
St. Hilary
Penzance
Cornwall TR20 9BZ
Tel: 01736 740262
Fax: 01736 740055
e-mail: ennys@zetnet.co.uk

Christine & Charles Taylor
Ednovean Farm
Perranuthnoe
Nr. Penzance
Cornwall TR20 9LZ
Tel: 01736 711883

Marked on the first-ever map of Cornwall, Crasken is found today hidden behind oak gates and a courtyard that's a riot of colour. Bold red walls and a stone floor in the hall; gorgeous Bergère chairs and lots of books in the sitting room. Bedrooms fuse style and simplicity - one is deep yellow with candles, a nice touch. You're surrounded by fields sodden with history; one conceals an Iron Age settlement, but is there also a Roman villa...? Careful professional excavations started in August 98. Fascinating. *Children over 14 and pets by arrangement.*

Rooms: 2 doubles and 1 twin, all sharing 2 bathrooms.

Price: £19.50-£27.50 p.p. Single occ. from £22.50.

Breakfast: Until 9.30am.

Meals: Available locally.

Closed: November-February.

The view of garden to church to sea to headland is heart-stopping and the ever-changing light casts a spell over the landscape. The dining room is illuminated by fire and candle; the yellow drawing room, with wooden floors and deep sofas, is perfect. Cascading drapes, immaculate linen, a regal four-poster and a luxurious half-tester - the bedrooms are exquisite. Marion speaks with passion and humour of her piece of England. Her garden is a delight - breathe deeply of the clean Cornish air while walking the three minutes to the sea. Irresistible.

Rooms: 1 four-poster, 1 half-tester, 1 twin/double, all en suite (bath and shower).

Price: £38-£42 p.p. Single supp. £10.

Breakfast: Until 9.30am.

Meals: Dinner, 3 courses, £22.95 p.p. by arrangement.

Closed: Christmas.

A394 to Helston. Crasken Farm is signed left just before 'Welcome to Helston' sign. House at end of bumpy lane, behind oak gates.

Map Ref No: 1

Jenny Ingram
Crasken Farm
Falmouth Road
Helston
Cornwall TR13 0PF
Tel: 01326 572670

From Helston A3083, south. Just before Lizard, left to Church Cove. Follow signs for about 0.75 miles. House on left behind blue gates.

Map Ref No: 1

Peter & Marion Stanley
Landewednack House
Church Cove
The Lizard
Cornwall TR12 7PQ
Tel: 01326 290909
Fax: 01326 290192

'Best Free House of the Year', and it is everything you'd want from a country inn. An old farmhouse, it is in a deep rural setting, the ales are honourable, the settles are wooden and the bar meals good. There is a jazzy restaurant - pastel blues and pale yellows - with a good local reputation, a no-smoking conservatory and a beer garden, too. The hotel sitting room is as cosy as you could wish with lots of books - cricket and political biographies - and an open fire. The bedrooms have valley views, simple old pine beds, some Laura Ashley, others white-washed.

Rooms: 4 doubles, 1 twin and 2 family rooms, all en suite (bath or shower); 1 twin with private bathroom.

Price: £33-£40 p.p. Single occ. £44.

Breakfast: Until 9.30am.

Meals: Restaurant dinner, 2 courses, £18.50 p.p., 3 courses, £22.50 p.p. Bar meals, lunch & dinner £3-£11 p.p.

Closed: Never!

Approaching Falmouth on A39, follow Constantine signs. After about 7 miles, as you approach village, inn is clearly signed left, then right.

Map Ref No: 1

Helen & Michael Maguire &
Nigel & Isabel Logan
Trengilly Wartha Inn
Nancenoy, Constantine, Nr. Falmouth
Cornwall TR11 5RP
Tel: 01326 340332
Fax: 01326 340332
e-mail: trengilly@compuserve.com

Begun in the 13th century, 'modernised' in the 16th century, the house has sweeping views to open country and the distant Helford river. Country house elegance entwines with a higgledy piggledy lived-in feel, warm woods, warm kitchen, lots of antiques, dark oak, open fireplace, granite-walled, deep green, candle-lit dining room... all in perfect taste. Bedrooms are cosy and stocked with good books, jugs of fresh water and homemade biscuits. Judy makes her own bread and preserves; both she and Mike are easy hosts.

Rooms: 1 twin with private bathroom; 2 doubles, both en suite (bath).

Price: £22-£27 p.p. Single supp. in high season, £10.

Breakfast: Until 10am.

Meals: Dinner, 4 courses, with wine £18 p.p.

Closed: Christmas.

From Truro, take Falmouth Rd (A39). At Hillhead roundabout follow sign to Constantine. 0.5 miles after High Cross garage turn left to Port Navas. House is opposite the granite mushrooms.

Map Ref No: 1

Judy Ford
Treviades Barton
High Cross
Constantine, Nr. Falmouth
Cornwall TR11 5RG
Tel: 01326 340524
Fax: 01326 340524
e-mail: treviades.barton@btinternet.com

Tidy gardeners avaunt! The 12 acres at Carwinion are a natural, unmanicured Victorian valley garden with a superb collection of bamboos, ferns and other sub-tropical plants. The rambling manor has the faded grandeur and collections of oddities (corkscrews, penknives, magnifying glasses) that successive generations hand on. Your charmingly eccentric host will introduce you to his ancestors, his antiques, his fine big old bedrooms - and serve "a breakfast to be reckoned with". The self-catering wing has a fenced garden to keep your children in and Carwinion dogs out.

Rooms: 1 double and 2 twins/doubles, all en suite (bath). Self-catering wing: 1 large bed/sitting room with kitchen, bathroom and private garden.

Price: £28.50 p.p. Self-catering wing £125-£275 per week.

Breakfast: Until 10am.

Meals: Dinner, 3 courses, with cheese & coffee, £18 p.p.

Closed: Never!

A39 south from Truro; at 4th r'bout after Truro keep left to Falmouth. At 2nd r'bout, follow sign to Mawnan Smith. In village, left past Red Lion and house is 400 yards up hill on right.

Map Ref No: 1

Anthony Rogers
Carwinion
Mawnan Smith
Nr. Falmouth
Cornwall TR11 5JA
Tel: 01326 250258
Fax: 01326 250903

Sitting on the slopes of its own wooded valley, the farm is sheltered and peaceful. The land falls away in front of the house, only to rise up again to meet the distant horizon: look carefully and you might spot deer. The Holts have put armchairs by the bedroom windows so you can take in all the glorious countryside that surrounds this Duchy of Cornwall farm. Their home is solidly comfortable and Barbara prepares splendid, fresh, English food. She is the fourth generation of her family to welcome guests and she does so with true generosity.

Rooms: 1 double, en suite (bath), 1 double and 1 twin, en suite (shower).

Price: £22-£24 p.p. Single supp. by arrangement.

Breakfast: Until 9am.

Meals: Available locally.

Closed: 1 November-31 January.

A30 west; about 6 miles after Bodmin pass Indian Queens/Fraddon (ignore Ladock exit). Pass McDonalds, take 2nd exit (marked Summercourt/Chapel Town), then right immediately. House signed opp. garage.

Map Ref No: 2

Ian & Barbara Holt
Arrallas
Ladock
Nr. Truro
Cornwall TR2 4NP
Tel: 01872 510379
Fax: 01872 510200

A lovely Queen Anne manor house with the elegance and warmth of old-time country-house hospitality. Afternoon tea if you arrive in time. No packed lunches but great hampers; no simple suppers but candlelit dinner parties in the panelled dining room then coffee in the drawing room under the eye of Admiral Sir Arthur Kemp, reputed to haunt Crugsillick. He was responsible for the magnificent plaster ceiling moulded by his French Napoleonic prisoners. The bedrooms are stylish and comfortable. A smugglers' path takes you to the sea three-quarters of a mile away. *Children over 12 welcome.*

Rooms: 1 twin, en suite (shower), 1 twin/double, en suite (bath), 1 four-poster with private bathroom. 3 self-catering cottages (4-7 people). One suitable for wheelchair users.

Price: £40-£48 p.p. Single occ. £60.

Breakfast: Until 9.30am.

Meals: Dinner £25 p.p. Hampers £15. By arrangement.

Closed: Never!

Take A390 from St Austell, left on B2387 to Tregony. A3078 through Ruan High Lanes. Sharp first left towards Veryan, right after 180 metres.

Map Ref No: 2

Oliver & Rosemary Barstow
Crugsillick Manor
Ruan High Lanes
Nr. St. Mawes, Truro
Cornwall TR2 5LJ
Tel: 01872 501214
Fax: 01872 501228
e-mail: barstow_crugsillick@csi.com

More cottage than farm house, Treworga is built on history. A Roman villa stood here once and after its demise Cornish saints arrived. Alison, an artist, will show you the hidden marvels of her home: primitively carved wood from the 8th century, beams from a battle-blown Tudor galleon and a 1570 barrel-vaulted, plaster-moulded ceiling in one of the generous bedrooms. On the landing there is a *chaise longue* and a wall of books; in the sitting room French windows lead out to the garden. But amid all this, it is Alison with her utterly unpretentious spirit that shines out. *Children over 10 and pets by arrangement.*

Rooms: 1 twin, en suite (shower) and 1 double with private bath.

Price: £24-£25.50 p.p. Single occ. £30.

Breakfast: Until 9.30am.

Meals: Available locally.

Closed: Christmas & New Year.

A3078 south to Ruan High Lanes. Treworga Village is signed right, then right again. Keep straight. In village, house is on left past tiny green triangle.

Map Ref No: 2

Mrs Alison Crowther
Treworga Farm House
Ruan High Lanes
Nr. Truro
Cornwall TR2 5NP
Tel: 01872 501423

A classical late Regency English country house with the occasional hint of Eastern promise. In the drawing room where tea is served, a beautiful Chinese cabinet occupies one wall and pale yellows and light blues sit comfortably together. In the dining room, a mahogany oval table is surrounded by exquisite furniture and a Malaysian inscribed tapestry - a thank-you present from the days of Empire. Upstairs, the comfortable bedrooms have antique furniture, garden views and generous baths. The garden is Alison's first love; you'll see why. *Children and pets by arrangement.*

Rooms: 1 double and 1 twin, both en suite (bath); 1 double with private bath.

Price: £30-£37 p.p. Single supp. £10.

Breakfast: Until 9.30am.

Meals: Dinner, 4 courses, £21.50 p.p. by arrangement. B.Y.O. wine.

Closed: Christmas & Easter.

A30 towards Truro, then left for Grampound Rd. After 3 miles, right onto A390 towards Truro. House 200 yds on right by reflector posts, down private lane.

Map Ref No: 2

Alison O'Connor
Tregoose
Grampound
Truro
Cornwall TR2 4DB
Tel: 01726 882460
Fax: 01872 222427

In Lally and William's garden, a sense that all is well in England's green and pleasant land takes you over. St. Crida's church rises on tip-toes above treetops while the murmur of a lazy stream reaches your ears. Inside the 1730s house, shimmering wooden floors are covered with rugs and light pours into every elegant corner. Breakfast at the mahogany table has a habit of turning into an early-morning house party, such is Lally's sense of fun and spontaneity. The big guestrooms exude taste and simplicity. *Children over 8 welcome.*

Rooms: 3 twins/doubles, 1 en suite (bath/shower), 2 with private bathrooms.

Price: £30-£35 p.p. Single supp. by arrangement.

Breakfast: Until 9.30am.

Meals: Available locally.

Closed: Christmas & New Year.

From St Austell, A390 to Grampound. Just beyond the clock tower turn left into Creed Lane. After 1 mile turn left at grass triangle opposite church. House is behind 2nd white gate on left.

Map Ref No: 2

Lally & William Croggon
Creed House
Creed
Grampound, Truro
Cornwall TR2 4SL
Tel: 01872 530372

Your children will love the Vietnamese pot-bellied pigs, the horses and the large dogs. You will appreciate the traditional farmhouse hospitality and the quiet nights in this solid old house. Jacqui used to be head chef for the National Trust, so cooks well; her homemade soups and breads are delicious. You can enjoy carriage rides and even learn to harness and drive a horse and carriage. This is cosy but not twee, with a certain elegance (four-posters, big bathrooms, good china) and kind and welcoming hosts.

Rooms: 2 doubles and 1 family room, all en suite (1 shower and 2 bath/shower).

Price: £22-£25 p.p. Single supp. by arrangement.

Breakfast. 8 8.30am.

Meals: Dinner from £12 p.p.

Closed: Never!

The grandeur is so soft, and Sarah and her family so natural, that you'll feel at home immediately. The Empire sofa, good oils on the walls, faded rugs on wooden floors, lovely lamps and an oak chest are just what you might hope for. They, and Sydney the polar bear, all sit beautifully in the 1780s, creeper-clad vicarage. Good period furniture, fresh flowers and quilted bedspreads in the bedrooms; in one a Napoleonic four-poster. The children's room, off the twin, with its miniature beds is utterly charming. *Children over 5 and pets by arrangement.*

Rooms: 1 four-poster, 1 twin with children's room and 1 suite, all en suite (bath).

Price: £20-£27 p.p. Single supp. £5.

Breakfast: Until 10.30am

Meals: Available locally.

Closed: Christmas Day.

Take A3059 west to Newquay. In 0.5 miles follow signs to Tregaswith. Farm is second on right.

Map Ref No: 2

John & Jacqui Elsom
Tregaswith Farmhouse
Tregaswith
Nr. Newquay
Cornwall TR8 4HY
Tel: 01637 881181
Fax: 01637 881181

From Wadebridge, B3314 towards Rock and Polzeath. After 3.5 miles, left, signed St. Minver. In village, left into cul-de-sac just before Four Ways Inn. House at bottom on left.

Map Ref No: 2

Mrs Sarah Tyson
The Old Vicarage
St. Minver
Nr. Rock
Cornwall PL27 6QH
Tel: 01208 862951
Fax: 01208 863578

CORNWALL

As one visitor said, 'Some barn!' Lovingly converted with original beams and exposed granite walls, it hunkers down in its own secluded valley and a path leads you through the woods to Epphaven Cove. The inside is elegantly uncluttered and cool; seagrass contrasts strikingly with old oak and the downstairs bedrooms have good period furniture, fresh flowers and quilted bedspreads. The shower room - a mixture of rusty reds and Italian marble - is quite magnificent. *Children over 12 welcome.*

Rooms: 1 double and 2 twins sharing 1 bathroom and 1 shower room.

Price: £25 p.p. Single supp. £5.

Breakfast: Until 9.30am.

Meals: Available locally.

Closed: Christmas.

Settling into the snug smoking room with your tea, you will effortlessly obey the central canon of Trebrea, which is 'relax'. It is hard to do otherwise among its oil paintings and wall tapestries, enveloped by its soft grandeur and lulled by a few drinks from the honesty bar. Dinner is in an oak-panelled dining room, deliciously. Between Trebrea and the sea there are nothing but fields, so the views are uplifting. From the yellow-walled and blue-sofaed, energy-sapping drawing room, you can see Tintagel church. It is a dreamy place. *Children over 12 welcome.*

Rooms: 3 twins, all en suite (bath); 4 doubles, all en suite (bath/shower).

Price: £35-£45 p.p. Single occ. £57.50-£62.50.

Breakfast: Until 9.30am.

Meals: Dinner, 4 courses, £22 p.p. Packed lunches by arrangement.

Closed: January-mid February.

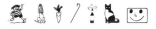

A39 to Wadebridge. At r'bout follow signs to Polzeath, then to the Porteath Bee Centre. Go through the Bee Centre shop car park, down farm track; house signed on right after 150 yards.

Map Ref No: 2

Jo Bloor
Porteath Barn
St. Minver
Wadebridge
Cornwall PL27 6RA
Tel: 01208 863605
Fax: 01208 863954

From Tintagel, turn into Trenale Lane beside R.C. church. Once in Trenale village, turn towards Trewarmett. Hotel is 0.25 miles on left.

Map Ref No: 2

John Charlick & Sean Devlin
Trebrea Lodge
Trenale
Tintagel
Cornwall PL34 0HR
Tel: 01840 770410
Fax: 01840 770092

Here's a farming family with a natural concern for the environment; they can even take you badger-watching. In this stunning coastal setting, you too will fall under the spell of Cornwall's abundant flora and fauna. Trevigue nestles in a hollow, an athletic stone's-throw from the cliffs, round a cobbled courtyard; it's a historic mix, with oak staircase, stone mullions and flagstones - and a solid, honest period feel. Log fires are sometimes essential, but, whatever the season, you can stoke up on hearty, farmhouse fare - home laid eggs, farm bacon and sausages.

Rooms: 2 twins and 2 doubles, all en suite (bath or shower).

Price: £26-£35 p.p. Single occ. from £35.

Breakfast: From 8.30-9am.

Meals: Dinner, 3 courses, £19 p.p.

Closed: Never!

From Crackington Haven follow the coastal road keeping the sea on your right. Up hill and turn right signed Trevigue.

Map Ref No: 2

The Crocker Family
Trevigue
Crackington Haven
Bude
Cornwall EX23 0LQ
Tel: 01840 230418
Fax: 01840 230418

Considered one of the loveliest houses in the area, Manor Farm was the Domesday-listed property of Duke William's half brother. Ancient stone, manicured lawns and rolling countryside outside, sober luxury inside where your hostess, who runs the house with irreproachable efficiency, knows well how to look after visitors. If you stay in to eat, you change for dinner and meet fellow guests for drinks before dining in dinner-party style. There are fine paintings, stone-silled windows onto garden views, carefully-decorated rooms. It is a house of character, totally English, elegant and wonderfully peaceful.

Rooms: 4 twins/doubles, en suite (2 baths, 2 showers).

Price: £30 p.p. Single occ. £35.

Breakfast: At 8.30am.

Meals: Dinner £16 p.p.

Closed: Christmas Day.

From Wainhouse Corner on A39, follow sign to Crackington Haven. At beach turn inland for 1 mile and left into Church Park Road and then first right into lane.

Map Ref No: 2

Muriel Knight
Manor Farm
Crackington Haven
Bude
Cornwall EX23 0JW
Tel: 01840 230304

The road twists and turns, the driveway falls through the spring-fed wooded valley and, suddenly, the secret is yours. The former vicarage - part 16th-century with Georgian and Edwardian additions - is beautiful and within its intriguing garden you are neighbour only to sea, coastal path and fields; nearby are sandy beaches. Lots of light, sea views, seagrass matting, paintings, comfy sofas, pretty fabrics and the feel of a family home. Perfect. Bedrooms are fresh and restful, bathrooms pretty. What's more, Jane and Anthony share their house without fuss. *Children over 5 welcome.*

Rooms: 1 double and 1 twin, each with basin and private bathroom and 1 other twin let to members of same party. Small single for child.

Price: £20-£28 p.p. Single supp. £10.

Breakfast: Flexible.

Meals: Simple supper or 3-course dinner, by arrangement, from £12. Packed lunch from £2 p.p.

Closed: Christmas & New Year.

Leave A39 at Wainhouse Corner south of Bude, to Crackington Haven/St. Gennys Church. 2 miles, fork right by white cottage signed St. Gennys Church. Before church, right into lane/drive.

Map Ref No: 2

Anthony & Jane Farquhar
St. Gennys House
St. Gennys
Bude
Cornwall EX23 0NW
Tel: 01840 230384
Fax: 01840 230537

Close by are clean sands and clear seas, yet this 230-acre farm, built in 1871 for the Duke of Bedford, sits peacefully in an undiscovered pocket. Five generations of Griffins have lived here and Valerie, smiling and kind, will bring you tea and then prepare a fine supper, maybe Devon beef or Cornish lamb followed by local cheeses. She has made every drape, swag and tail herself and rooms are fully colour co-ordinated. For children: climbing area, pony rides, playroom, snooker and farm tours. Well-equipped cottages, too - Valerie puts out fresh flowers and homemade biscuits for you.

Rooms: 2 doubles, 1 twin & 1 family room, all en suite (shower). 1 four-poster, en suite (bath). One cottage sleeps 7, the other sleeps 4/5, some bedrooms en suite.

Price: From £16 p.p. Cottages from £120-£575 per week.

Breakfast: Flexible.

Meals: Dinner, 3 courses, from £13 p.p.

Closed: From October-February. Cottages open all year.

From A39 at Wainhouse Corner follow signs to Canworthy Water for approx. 4 miles. At T-junction left; after 1.5 miles, left for Wheatley Farm, up hill. 1st farm on left 0.25 miles up.

Map Ref No: 2

Raymond & Valerie Griffin
Wheatley Farm
Maxworthy
Launceston
Cornwall PL15 8LY
Tel: 01566 781232
Fax: 01566 781232
e-mail: wheatleyfrm@compuserve.com

The house is named after the hill and the peace within is as deep as the valley. You have utter privacy; a private entrance to your own fresh, elegant suite: a twin-bedded room and a large, square, high sitting room with double doors giving onto the wooded valley. There's a CD player, plus music, chocolates and magazines and you can have tea in the rambling garden that wraps itself around the house. Jos and Mary-Anne really want you to enjoy your stay; you will. Butcher's sausages and free-range eggs for breakfast. Perfect.

Rooms: 1 twin, en suite (bath/shower) with sitting room and adjoining single for child if needed.

Price: £28 p.p. Single supp. £10.

Breakfast: Flexible.

Meals: Dinner, 3 courses, £16 p.p. by prior arrangement. B.Y.O wine.

Closed: Christmas & New Year.

From Launceston, B3254 towards Liskeard. Go through Daw's House and South Petherwin, down steep hill and turn last left before little bridge. House is first on left.

Map Ref No: 2

Jos & Mary-Anne Otway-Ruthven
Hornacott
South Petherwin
Launceston
Cornwall PL15 7LH
Tel: 01566 782461
Fax: 01566 782461

Two hundred years ago the Navy used to test cannons in the creek at the bottom of the garden, but now you hear only the sound of wildlife. Clive and Button have lovingly tended their 1744 house and created a peaceful, comfortable home. They'll bring you scones in a sitting room alive with colour and light and you eat your morning kippers and free-range eggs from a walnut table that cleverly conceals a snooker table. Cranberry covers on the old oak beds, wonderful views from a high brass bed and from the antique four-poster in the large Oyster Room.

Rooms: 1 four-poster, 1 twin/double, both en suite (shower); 1 double with private bath.

Price: £25-£45 p.p. Single person/single night supp. from £10. Special tariff for 'eclipse week'.

Breakfast: Until 10.30am.

Meals: Available locally.

Closed: Never!

A38 over Tamar Bridge. After 7 miles, A374 left towards Torpoint at Ring O'Bells pub in Antony, turn right round back of pub, then 1st left to St. John. Left at small green, house 1st on right.

Map Ref No: 2

Clive & Button Poole
The Old Rectory
St John-in-Cornwall
Nr. Torpoint
Cornwall PL11 3AW
Tel: 01752 822275
Fax: 01752 823322

Bring your own music... there's a boudoir grand to be played as well as a music centre you can use. Ann is fun and a natural entertainer, the sort of person who giggles. Wonderfully comfortable house with touches of luxury and matchless views over Plymouth Sound. It is at the top of a steep hill overlooking a charming village of 600 souls. Ann cooks superb meals with wholefood ingredients and local produce. She also makes her own muesli, bread, yoghurt and ice-cream and can even cater for vegans.

Rooms: 1 twin/double and 1 twin, both en suite (shower); 1 double, en suite (bath).

Price: £21-£24 p.p. Single supp. by arrangement.

Breakfast: Until 9.30am.

Meals: Dinner £20 p.p. Light supper £9.

Closed: Never!

B3247 towards Mount Edgcumbe. Turn right before the school, signposted Kingsand. Down hill to right, left fork on bend into Kingsand, 2nd left, then left again. House on left with yellow door. Avoid single track road.

Map Ref No: 2

Ann Heasman
Cliff House
Devonport Hill
Kingsand
Cornwall PL10 1NJ
Tel: 01752 823110
Fax: 01752 822595

Very special and intriguing, surrounded by tidal estuaries on three sides, Erth Barton is a Grade II listed manor house that has its own chapel in which a 14th-century fresco clings to the walls. Its many rooms are filled with thousands of books and pictures. Guy is eccentric, often very funny and passionate about horses - bring your own, or some may be available to competent riders. Rooms, reached via the wooden spiral staircase, are simple and bright with old rugs, scattered books and fine views. "Fantastic views, fantastic house," said our inspector. *Children over 12 welcome.*

Rooms: 1 twin with separate private bathroom; 2 doubles, both en suite.

Price: £34 p.p. Single supp. £5.

Breakfast: Until 9.30am.

Meals: Dinner £18.50 p.p.

Closed: Never!

Take A38 from Plymouth & cross Tamar Bridge. Through by-pass tunnel over r'bout. On top of next hill left to Trematon; through village to Elmgate. Take middle of 3 roads marked 'dead end'.

Map Ref No: 2

Guy Bentinck
Erth Barton
Saltash
Cornwall PL12 4QY
Tel: 01752 842127
Fax: 01752 842127

An old corn mill with the original water wheel now in the kitchen, immobile, with views down the garden to the river from the bedrooms. Richard is a keen fly fisherman and can set you up. Mariebel is a trained artist and has taught for many years, still happy to teach individuals or groups. Bicton is informal, comfortable and relaxed. Meals are eaten in the huge farmhouse kitchen or in the impressive slate-floored dining room. The Lynher Valley is unspoilt and enchanting, with lovely walks through woodland and over nearby Bodmin Moor.

Rooms: 1 double, en suite (shower and w.c.) and 1 double with private, adjacent bathroom and w.c.

Price: £25 p.p. Single supp. by arrangement.

Breakfast: Flexible.

Meals: Dinner, £18 p.p. & packed lunch, £6 p.p. both by arrangement.

Closed: Never!

14th-century, with the original smoke-blackened trusses that held the thatched roof, it is a wonderful old building with a Grade II* listing. The double bedroom was once part of the main hall which had an open hearth and earthen floor. (It provides, charmingly, three dressing gowns in descending order of size.) The guest sitting room is in the 17th-century wing with a wood-burning stove. The Macartneys are breathing new life into it, with passion and style; they have achieved much. There are ground-floor facilities for parents travelling with a disabled child.

Rooms: 1 double and 1 single with shared use of private bathroom and sitting room.

Price: £25-£30 p.p.

Breakfast: Flexible

Meals: Dinner, £17 p.p., by arrangement.

Closed: Never!

On A388 Callington-Launceston, left at Kelly Bray (opp. garage) to Maders. 400 yds after Maders, left to Golberdon and left at x-roads. After 400 yds, right down unmarked lane. Mill 0.75 miles by bridge.

Map Ref No: 2

A387 through Looe and approx 3 miles beyond, then B3359 signed Pelynt. Just less than a mile on, 2nd left signed Penellick. After 0.5 miles, left at T-junction then fork left signed Penellick.

Map Ref No: 2

Richard & Mariebel Allerton
Bicton Mill
Bicton
Nr. Liskeard
Cornwall PL14 5RF
Tel: 01579 383577
Fax: 01579 383577

Michael & Ann Macartney
Penellick
Pelynt
Nr. Looe
Cornwall PL13 2LX
Tel: 01503 272372
Fax: 01503 272372

Richard breeds Charolais bulls, and there are ducks, doves, a goat and a cat; it is a big, happy extended-family place up a wild-flowered drive in a hidden fold in the Cornish countryside. Helen, an aromatherapist and reflexologist (you can book a treatment), is young, enthusiastic and gentle. Tea and homemade biscuits at the scrubbed pine table, fabulous breakfasts and fresh fish a dinner speciality. Bedrooms are up a private winding staircase, with lovely brass beds, crisp linen, fluffy towels - simplicity and charm. Botelet is a treasure house, highly original.

Rooms: 1 double with extra single and 1 twin (small double with single), both with basins and shared use of private bathroom.

Price: £20-£25 p.p. Single supp. by arrangement.

Breakfast: Flexible.

Meals: Dinner, maybe Thai or Italian, £12-£20 p.p. Packed lunch, cream teas and drinks are also available.

Closed: Occasionally.

Leave Liskeard on the A38. At Dobwalls take left fork, A390 signed St. Austell. After East Taphouse, turn left onto B3359 signed Looe. After 2 miles, turn right signed Botelet.

Map Ref No: 2

Mrs Richard Tamblyn
Botelet
Herodsfoot
Liskeard
Cornwall PL14 4RD
Tel: 01503 220225
Fax: 01503 220225

A tall Georgian 18th-century farmhouse with intriguing round windows and an unspoilt farmyard; the buildings are still used for sheep and cattle. Chickens strut, scratch and lay eggs. Very much a working farm with all the family involved. One son is a sculptor and one is at art school. Iain is passionate about his farm; Anne, too. Huge bunches of dried flowers hang in the kitchen above the Aga - Anne sells them all over the country. The bedrooms are on the second floor, with fine views, and the bathroom on the floor below.

Rooms: 2 twins sharing a bathroom.

Price: £25 p.p. No single supp.

Breakfast: Flexible.

Meals: Lots of places nearby.

Closed: Never!

From Plymouth, A38 then A390 west. One mile before Lostwithiel take 2nd left after garage to Lerryn. Turn left for Couch's Mill. Before bridge, 1st left into cul-de-sac, up hill for 0.25 miles.

Map Ref No: 2

Anne & Iain Mackie
Collon Barton
Lerryn
Nr. Lostwithiel
Cornwall PL22 0NX
Tel: 01208 872908
Fax: 01208 873812

The road up is steep, but the reward is a breathtaking view of the River Fowey flowing through a wooded landscape. Boats tug on their moorings and birds glide lazily over the water; it is a very English paradise. The Cormorant is very much a hotel - large windows and all those mod cons in the bedrooms - but it is run with massive family devotion and is superbly comfortable. There is even a great log fire. The heated pool has the best views and you can walk deep into the countryside from the door. Those views fill every room. *Children by arrangement.*

Rooms: 11 twins or doubles, all with views and en suite baths.

Price: From £39-£46 p.p. Single supp. £12.50.

Breakfast: Until 9.30am.

Meals: Dinner, 4 courses, from £18 p.p. Lunch from £2-£9 p.p.

Closed: Never!

A390 west towards St Austell, then B3269 to Fowey. After 6 miles, left to Golant. Continue into village, along quay and hotel signed right, up hill.

Map Ref No: 2

Estel & George Elworthy
The Cormorant Hotel
Golant
Nr. Fowey
Cornwall PL23 1LL
Tel: 01726 833426
Fax: 01726 833026

See the world in writer/explorer Robin's 18th/19th-century manor house, chock-a-block with exotic artefacts and the sumptuous craftwork of Louella's hand-stencilled fabrics and furniture. Rich, dark colours, wonderful fabrics, quilts, cushions and rugs, old beams and books floor-to-ceiling. A sensuous mix of old-English country life, the 'global village' and atelier - with comfort that swaddles you. Here on the edge of Bodmin Moor, red deer roam; closer to home there are elegant lawns, gardens, a tennis court - and an opera house in a converted barn at the bottom of the garden. That's all.

Rooms: 3 doubles: 1 en suite (bath) and 2 with private bathrooms.

Price: £30 p.p. No single supp.

Breakfast: Flexible.

Meals: Dinner £18 p.p. by arrangement.

Closed: Christmas & New Year.

6 miles after Jamaica Inn on A30, left signed Cardinham Mount. Straight on, ignore Cardigan sign. After 2.5 miles, left to Maidenwell. House is 400 yards on right, after cattle grid.

Map Ref No: 2

Robin & Louella Hanbury-Tenison
Cabilla Manor
Nr. Mount
Bodmin
Cornwall PL30 4DW
Tel: 01208 821224
Fax: 01208 821267
e-mail: RobinHT@Compuserve.com

An elegant 16th-century manor house, generous in size and full of light, Nanscawen sits in five lush acres in the wooded Luxulyan valley. There is utter peace and the views are marvellous. The Martins' hospitality is lavish in modern luxuries such as hot tub, swimming pool, ruffled towels and bathtime goodies and they care deeply that you should be comfortable, however unobtrusive they may be. Lots of peaches and pinks, elaborate drapes and even teddies on the beds. And, moreover... smoked salmon for breakfast.

Rooms: 1 twin/double, 1 four-poster and 1 double - all en suite (bath).

Price: £37-£39 p.p. Single supp. by arrangement.

Breakfast: Until 9am.

Meals: Available locally.

Closed: Christmas & Boxing Day.

Over 23 acres of woodland walks, 60 acres of pasture, an orchard, sheep and cattle, and the winding Ruthern river and Whitehay itself. It is a beautiful 350-year-old farm, in total seclusion, with views across the Ruthern valley. Maxine, in true American style, gives you both elegance and luxury; large, light rooms bring old and new together with exuberant confidence. The sitting room has sofas, antiques and a great stone fireplace. You dine in the hall on a glass table. The bedrooms, too, are generous and attractive, with crisp linen and fine views. Stylish, and just right.

Rooms: 1 double, en suite (bath). 1 twin with private bathroom.

Price: £40 p.p. Single supp. £10.

Breakfast: Until 9.30am.

Meals: Dinner £22 p.p. weekdays only.

Closed: Christmas & New Year. Self-catering always open.

A390 south towards St. Austell. In St. Blazey take right immed. after railway. House is 0.75 miles on right.

Map Ref No: 2

Map Ref No: 2

Keith & Fiona Martin
Nanscawen House
Prideaux Road
Luxulyan Valley
Cornwall PL24 2SR
Tel: 01726 814488
Fax: 01726 814488
e-mail: keithmartin@compuserve.com

STOP PRESS!
House sold.

Judith wants you to treat her wisteria-clad farmhouse as if it were your home; you are free to come and go, to enjoy privacy or to share in their farming life. There are farmyard animals to admire, walks in the countryside or hikes along the coastal path; log fires at night, hearty breakfasts, cooked or with fruit and cheese, served in generous Cornish portions, and pretty bedrooms with floral papers and utter quiet. Four self-catering cottages, individually decorated and with beams and stone walls, also available.

Rooms: Original farmhouse: 1 family suite (1 twin, 1 double and private sitting room) and 1 double, both en suite (bath). Main farmhouse: 1 twin with private bath; 2 doubles, en suite. (shower).

Price: Family room £65. Double £22 p.p. Single occ. £25. Self-catering cottages £100-£555 p.w. Short breaks available.

Breakfast: 8-9am.

Meals: Available locally.

Closed: Christmas.

In St Austell follow signs to Truro on A390. Pass Tesco and Texaco garage on left, climb long hill, just after brow of hill turn right at St Mewan school. After 0.5 miles, 2nd farmhouse on left.

Map Ref No: 2

Judith Nancarrow
Poltarrow Farm
St. Mewan
St. Austell
Cornwall PL26 7DR
Tel: 01726 67111
Fax: 01726 67111

Charles and Mally live *on* the estate of the Lost Gardens of Heligan! Where better for a botanical illustrator and a garden photographer to set up home? This is an 80-acre living museum of 19th-century horticulture: valleys, lakes, jungle, walled gardens, walkways. With the gardens and the coastal path right on your doorstep, you don't need your car; Charles and Mally will collect you from the station for free. There is comfortable furniture and light floods in through the huge windows. Bedrooms are simply decorated and the bathroom is spotless.

Rooms: 2 twins, sharing a bathroom.

Price: £27.50 p.p. Single supp. £5.

Breakfast: Until 9.30am.

Meals: Available locally.

Closed: Christmas & New Year.

From St Austell, B3273 south. Follow signs to Lost Gardens. Approaching gardens, 1st left signed 'Heligan House, Strictly Private'. After 0.25 miles, left at gateposts, past cottages and sharp left. Follow track.

Map Ref No: 2

Charles & Mally Francis
The Wagon House
Heligan Manor
St. Ewe, St. Austell
Cornwall PL26 6EW
Tel: 01726 844505
Fax: 01726 844525

Come to where the stream meanders and the wild deer roam. The Smiths settled here on the fringe of the Forest of Bowland in the Ribble Valley over 20 years ago. They are easy and comfortable to be with, and their house is a converted 18th-century tithe barn. The guest sitting room has a pitched roof of old church rafters, log fires on chillier evenings, plump sofas, antiques, some lace and flounces. Guests have the whole top floor and their own entrance. The light-filled open-plan living area has lots of big potted plants, rugs, wood, original stone and big armchairs.

Rooms: 1 twin/double, en suite (shower) and 1 double, en suite (bath/shower); 1 double with private bath.

Price: £19.50-£22 p.p. Single occ. £26.

Breakfast: Flexible.

Meals: Available locally.

Closed: Christmas & New Year.

Cumbria & Lancashire

M6 juntion 31, A59 to Skipton, turning left to Clitheroe. Through Clitheroe and Waddington, further 0.5 miles, turn left up Cross Lane. 0.75 miles past Colthust Hall. Peter Barn is on the left.

Map Ref No: 14

Jean & Gordon Smith
Peter Barn Country House
Cross Lane/Rabbit Lane
Waddington, Clitheroe
Lancashire BB7 3JH
Tel: 01200 428585

They have got it just right, neatly mixing informality with style. The house is a remnant of a 15th-century hamlet; the ancient well is now in the conservatory and you dine at one table in the Great Hall, not far from the school attended by the Brontë sisters. The style is 'country house': breakfast at separate tables, three acres of garden, majestic countryside, freshly-prepared food, good wines, sleep-inducing comfort and an honesty bar. Perfect for private parties and self-indulgent walkers; a footpath leads out over Leck Fell and into Barbondale. *Children over 12 welcome.*

Rooms: 2 twins and 3 doubles, all en suite (bath). 1 double, en suite (shower). 2 cottage suites.

Price: £44-£51 p.p. Single occ. £72.

Breakfast: Until 9.30am.

Meals: Dinner £25 p.p. Packed lunches, by arrangement, from £7 p.p.

Closed: 1 November-28 February (private parties by arrangement).

Cartmel, still thriving, grew around its famous 12th-century Priory, still magnificent. The Manor is run with easy professionalism by a very nice family. The bedrooms are simple and comfortable, the food is good and history hovers everywhere: a fine tongue-and-ball ceiling, a cantilevered spiral staircase, an Adams-style marble fireplace, a melodious grandfather clock, and carved oak panels in the hall. Newspapers hang from poles in the drawing room and the views across the meadows to the Priory are almost mediaeval. No under fives in the restaurant.

Rooms: 4 twins, 5 doubles, 1 four-poster, 2 family, all en suite (bath).

Price: Dinner, B&B £46.50-£56 p.p. Single supp. £9.

Breakfast: Until 9.30am.

Meals: Dinner included.

Closed: January.

Leave M6 at junction 36 and follow A65 2.5 miles past Kirkby Lonsdale. House is on left 8.5 miles from M6.

Map Ref No: 14

Ian & Jocelyn Bryant
Hipping Hall
Cowan Bridge
Kirkby Lonsdale
Cumbria LA6 2JJ
Tel: 015242 71187
Fax: 015242 72452

Leave A590 (M6 - Barrow road) at top of Lindale Hill. Follow signs to Cartmel. Hotel on right 3 miles from A590.

Map Ref No: 14

Andrea & Chris Varley
Aynsome Manor Hotel
Cartmel
Cumbria LA11 6HH
Tel: 015395 36653
Fax: 015395 36016

Heaven-sent and down-to-earth, the Old Vicarage is in the Winster valley with Yewbarrow Fell ('The Noddle') just behind. A 10-minute walk to the top brings spectacular views. The main house has rooms of simple, stylish luxury and garden views. The Orchard House - in farmhouse style - has bigger rooms and is utterly secluded. From here you walk up through the damson trees, past the tennis court and join the fun. Your hosts are dedicated but easy-going, keen for you to enjoy yourself. They provide maps and routes for walkers, high teas and high chairs for children. The restaurant is not to be missed.

Rooms: 1 family, 1 four-poster, 7 doubles, 4 twins, all en suite (11 baths, 3 showers).

Price: Dinner, B&B £60-£100 p.p. Single supp. £15.

Breakfast: Until 9.30am.

Meals: Included. Non-residents £29.50 p.p.

Closed: Never!

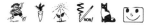

M6 junction 36, then A590 towards Barrow. After 6 miles, right signed 'Witherslack'. In village, left after phone box. House on left just before church.

Map Ref No: 14

Irene & Stanley Reeve &
Jill & Roger Brown
The Old Vicarage
Church Road, Witherslack
Cumbria LA11 6RS
Tel: 015395 52381
Fax: 015395 52373
e-mail: hotel@old-vic.demon.co.uk

The Broughtons throw open their fine 1900s Lakeland gentleman's residence and welcome guests without a hint of stuffiness. They are always around to help you plan your local trips (their knowledge is deep), to run you to restaurants if it's raining, to pour you a glass of wine or to chat. The skylit family suite in the loft is a delicious private hideaway - if you want to, you can even have your breakfast brought up. Bedrooms are comfortable and there is lots of attention to detail. Walk off a splendid cooked breakfast - the village, lake and fells are a mere five-minute stroll away.

Rooms: 1 family suite, en suite (bath) and with breakfast room; 1 twin, en suite (shower).

Price: £26 p.p. Single supp. £8. Children, half price.

Breakfast: Usually 8.30-9.30am.

Meals: Available locally.

Closed: 1 December-4 January.

From Kendal take A591 to Windermere and then follow signs to Bowness. There bear left at bottom of hill; take first left opposite church. Follow road past garage on left. House is 50 yards on right.

Map Ref No: 14

Louise Broughton
Lowfell
Ferney Green
Bowness-on-Windermere
Cumbria LA23 3ES
Tel: 015394 45612
Fax: 015394 48411
e-mail: louiseb@lakes-pages.co.uk

Tea is a carnival of scones, banana cake and shortbread - all homemade. In summer this feast goes *al fresco* with elderflower cordial, croquet and a hammock. Walk off the excess in their 36 acres; you'll find Highland cattle, views and a Vietnamese pot-bellied pig. Robin and Dany provide enthusiasm, heart-shaped cushions on beds, a purple *chaise longue*, vanity units, light and bright bedrooms; downstairs a deep-pink carpet, electric fire, open fire in winter, trinkets, dried and fresh flowers. Walks start at the front door.

Rooms: 1 double, en suite (bath/shower). 1 twin, en suite (shower). 1 twin with private bathroom.

Price: £25-£32.50 p.p. Single supp. £10.

Breakfast: Until 9am.

Meals: Dinner from £17.50 p.p. Packed lunches £5 p.p.

Closed: Christmas & New Year.

Exit 36 off M6, A591 NW. B5284 through Crook village, with Sun Inn on right. Past village hall. 0.5 miles on right after church turn right. Entrance ahead.

Map Ref No: 14

Robin & Dany Brown
Birksey Brow
Crook
Kendal
Cumbria LA8 8LQ
Tel: 015394 43380

Bonnie Prince Charlie rested here. The River Rothay (you cross it on a private bridge to reach the house) flows by and the scenery is glorious. The house, more guest-house than private home, has simple country cottage comforts, with stone-flagged floors wrapped in rugs, beamed ceilings, a clothes-drying room for walkers, a small sitting room and small dining room too. The pastel and chintz rooms are modest but comfortable and all have views of the river. Alan and Gillian are sweet and down-to-earth.

Rooms: 1 family, 1 twin and 2 doubles, all en suite (bath); 1 double, en suite (shower).

Price: £23-£32 p.p. No singles.

Breakfast: Until 9am.

Meals: Available locally.

Closed: 24-26 December.

From Ambleside A593 Coniston road to Rothay Bridge (approx 500 yards). Cross bridge and turn immediately into house entrance.

Map Ref No: 14

Alan & Gillian Rhone
Riverside Lodge
Nr. Rothay Bridge
Ambleside
Cumbria LA22 OEH
Tel: 015394 34208
Fax: 015394 31884

This is a favourite of those hardy mountaineers and it comes as no surprise to learn that Hillary and Tenzing stayed here; the hotel is at the head of the valley, surrounded by spectacular peaks - a hikers' and climbers' heaven. The scenery is breathtaking, and this is a solid and genuine base...as unpretentious as can be. The fire roars comfortingly in the sitting room (dark red patterned carpet), the food is home-cooked and the bedrooms eclectically-decorated (patchwork quilts, floral paper and patterned carpet). Those who enjoy a song with their ale will revel in the Hikers' bar next door.

Rooms: 3 twins/doubles and 1 twin, all en suite (shower); 3 singles, 4 doubles, 1 twin, 2 family, all sharing 4 baths & 1 shower.

Price: £28-£35 p.p.

Breakfast: Until 9.30am.

Meals: Dinner £18.50 p.p. Bar snacks from £5 p.p. Packed lunches £3.50 p.p. Special diets by arrangement.

Closed: 24-26 December.

On A593 from Ambleside towards Coniston, turn right onto B5343. In Great Langdale, hotel is on right.

Map Ref No: 14

Jane & Neil Walmsley
Old Dungeon Ghyll
Great Langdale
Ambleside
Cumbria LA22 9JY
Tel: 015394 37272
Fax: 015394 37272

In an utterly brilliant position under the ridge of Blencathra looking out towards Hellvelyn (John says you get used to the views but it must take years), this rambling Cumbrian farmhouse with its crooked beams has been sumptuously done up; and it is heated by their own stream-operated turbine. A friendly, knowledgeable couple, the Knowles have an impressive library of local walks and mountaineering books. You couldn't find a better place in the mountains - log fires, open, practical hospitality, great comfort and half a mile to the village pub. *Children over 12 welcome.*

Rooms: 2 doubles, en suite (shower) and 1 twin, all en suite (shower and bath).

Price: £28 p.p. Single occ. £33.

Breakfast: 8.30am or earlier.

Meals: Dinner £18 p.p.

Closed: Hardly ever!

Leave M6 junction 40 and head towards Keswick on A66. Turn into Threlkeld and turn right into Blease Road, after pub. Blease Farm is 0.3 miles on right.

Map Ref No: 19

John & Ruth Knowles
Blease Farm
Blease Road, Threlkeld
Nr. Keswick
Cumbria CA12 4SF
Tel: 017687 79087
Fax: 017687 79087

A delightful Victorian Lakeland house, all set about with gables and chimney stacks and light-filtering bay windows, in three peaceful acres on the edge of much-visited Grasmere. After thorough research, your friendly, helpful hosts have redecorated Ryelands in proper period style and the rooms are big and comfortable. You can walk from the house into the beautiful countryside, relax as you row round the lake or make a pilgrimage to Wordsworth's cottage and grave. There is even a boot-and-drying room for when you return. *Children over 10 welcome.*

Rooms: 1 four poster, en suite (bath) and 2 doubles, en suite (1 bath and 1 shower). Self-catering cottage also available.

Price: £30 p.p. Single occ. £45.

Breakfast: 8.30-8.45am.

Meals: Available nearby

Closed: November-February.

On the quiet side of town, the Archway is a restful oasis in which to shake off the bustle of Windermere. Its inside is much prettier than its outside and it is imbued from top to bottom with a wholesome air. There's a cosy sitting room with good books and a pine-tabled dining room with a big old pine dresser. The bedrooms are snug with Welsh country quilts, those at the front have pretty views and the bathrooms - quite small - all boast generous comforts. There are good prints on the walls, fresh flowers and an open fireplace. Anthony is an acupuncturist, Aurea loves cooking and her homemade bread is excellent. *Children over 10 welcome.*

Rooms: 1 twin, 2 doubles, all en suite (shower); 1 twin, en suite (bath & shower).

Price: £23-£29 p.p. Single supp. £15.

Breakfast: Until 9am.

Meals: Dinner £13.50 p.p.

Closed: 2 weeks mid-January.

Enter Grasmere village from A591 and take the turn opposite St Oswald's church. After 100m, turn right into Langdale road. Ryelands is on the left.

Map Ref No: 14

Lyn & John Kirkbride
Ryelands
Grasmere
Cumbria LA22 9SU
Tel: 015394 35076
Fax: 015394 35076

Entering Windermere village from the A591 the Archway is on College Road, first right off Elleray Road.

Map Ref No: 14

Anthony & Aurea Greenhalgh
The Archway
College Road
Windermere
Cumbria LA23 1BU
Tel: 015394 45613
e-mail: Archway@BTinternet.com

Although newish the cottage throbs with homeliness. Guests are immediately wrapped in the Midwinters' cheerful enthusiasm, just as Low Jock Scar itself is folded into the comforting slopes of the valley. From the conservatory you are lured out to ramble in the flourishing gardens, the pride of your green-fingered hosts. Listen out for the burbling beck and rest on its banks in the evening to recover from the five-course feast at dinner.

Rooms: 1 twin and 2 doubles, en suite (2 with bath and 1 with shower) and 1 twin and 1 double sharing bathroom.

Price: £22.50-£27.50 p.p. Single supp. £8.

Breakfast: Until 9am.

Meals: Dinner, 5 courses, £16 p.p. Packed lunch, by arrangement, £3.50.

Closed: 31 October-mid-March.

A touch of formality in the moors: once summoned from the richly-panelled sitting room we were waited on by Janet and Graham. You even ring a bell to announce your readiness for the next course (traditional English cooking). This cosy old farmhouse has fine original features such as the old spice cupboard, the love symbols carved into doors, and the deep shimmering oak - polished to perfection - downstairs. The bedrooms are snug and comfortable. If you are walkers you can be dropped off and picked up; packed lunches are on offer, too.

Rooms: 1 twin, 1 double and 1 single, all sharing bathroom.

Price: £18 p.p.

Breakfast: Until 9.30am.

Meals: Dinner £12 p.p. Packed lunch available on request.

Closed: 31 October-1 March.

Leave Kendal on A6 to Penrith. After 5 miles you see the Plough Inn on left. Turn into lane on left after 1 mile.

Map Ref No: 14

Alison & Philip Midwinter
Low Jock Scar
Selside
Kendal
Cumbria LA8 9LE
Tel: 01539 823259
Fax: 01539 823259

From M6 take A685 towards Kirkby Stephen. After 5.5 miles left to Kelleth/Great Asby. Immediately left again. House 3rd on left with yew trees in front.

Map Ref No: 14

Janet & Graham Paxman
Low Lane House
Newbiggin-on-Lune
Kirkby Stephen
Cumbria CA17 4NB
Tel: 01539 623269

Paradise in the Eden Valley. In her restoration Anne has given sweet voice to the echoes of the past; there has been little external alteration since modernisation in 1719. From the superb, 1740-panelled dining room to the glorious four-poster with sloping floor and working gramophone, the house is a box of delights. Flagstones, wooden floors with good rugs, some pale yellow walls, oak everywhere, a great rug tumbling down a wall, superb furniture and stacks of character... it is a dream. One bathroom was once a stage-set for an Alan Ayckbourn play.

Rooms: 1 four-poster, en suite (shower); 1 twin/double, en suite (bath).

Price: £23 p.p. Single supp. £7.

Breakfast: Until 9.15am.

Meals: Dinner £12 p.p. Packed lunch available on request.

Closed: Christmas & New Year.

In Kirkby Stephen 100m north of main square, left to Soulby & Crosby Garrett. After 3 miles left to Crosby Garrett. After 0.75 miles left again. First left in village, and immediate left through gates into Rectory.

Map Ref No: 14

Anne McCrickard
The Old Rectory
Crosby Garrett
Kirkby Stephen
Cumbria CA17 4PW
Tel: 017683 72074

This is a Victorian folly. Walk through the panelled hall to the vast drawing room and wonder at the courage of Simon and Wendy in re-kindling the magic. Here are a grand piano, great tumbling curtains and rugs galore on wooden floors. The meals at the huge dining room table are informal feasts. The bold, south-facing bedrooms elaborate the fantasy. As for the wardrobes - look in the turrets. And do take in the gilded, vaulted ceilings, the oak panelling, the soaring stained-glass windows. Perhaps, in summer, you may carry your dinner across the field to sit beside the pond, with the ducks.

Rooms: 1 four-poster, 1 double, 4 twins/doubles, all en suite (bath & shower).

Price: £30-£45 p.p. Single supp, £10.

Breakfast: Until 12 noon.

Meals: Dinner, inc. wine, £22.50 p.p. by arrangement. Picnics £10 p.p.

Closed: Never!

M6 junction 38, then A685 through Kirkby Stephen. Just before Brough, right signed South Stainmore and house signed on left after 1 mile.

Map Ref No: 19

Simon & Wendy Bennett
Augill Castle
Brough
Kirkby Stephen
Cumbria CA17 4DE
Tel: 017683 41937
Fax: 017683 41936
e-mail: augill@aol.com

The gardens, open each year for the National Gardens Scheme, are a lovely counterpoint to the awesome grandeur of the Pennines. The house is a careful reflection of Catherine's long career as an interior designer, much of it in the 'rich and thick' mould: elegant drapes, high-backed armchairs, wall tapestries, some deep gold brocade and shimmering eiderdown, heavy ruched curtains, oils everywhere. The bathrooms are wickedly indulgent, a hedonist's Heaven; the views are inescapable. You breakfast in the Orangery, looking over those gardens.

Rooms: 2 doubles and 1 twin, all en suite (bath).

Price: £35 p.p. Single supp. £5.

Breakfast: Until 9am.

Meals: Available locally.

Closed: 24 December-2 January.

M6 junction 40, then A66 east through Kirkby Thore. After 2 miles, left to Long Marton. Follow brown signs to house for 2 miles. Under bridge and 2nd entrance.

Map Ref No: 19

Catherine & Maurice Hardy-Bishop
Marton House
Long Marton
Nr. Appleby-in-Westmorland
Cumbria CA16 6BU
Tel: 01768 361183
Fax: 01768 361183
hardy-bishop@martonhouse.demon.co.uk

Wordsworth's brother-in-law lived here and the great man came over frequently. The views that he enjoyed over to Barton Fell are as glorious as ever. The mood is genuine, simple, country hospitality at its best, with communal dining and no ceremony. Much of the atmosphere comes from Mary herself; she is great fun, down to earth and friendly, a real farmer's wife. The homemade biscuits in the rooms are a typical gesture. The bedrooms are simple and unfussy, and with those views. There are 300 acres, 850 sheep and a lovely walled garden... all in the National Park.

Rooms: 2 twins/doubles, both en suite (shower). Another bathroom also available.

Price: £20 p.p. Single supp. £1.

Breakfast: Until 8.30am.

Meals: Available locally.

Closed: 1 November-31 March.

M6 junction 40, then A66 west. At roundabout left on A592. Follow signs to Dalemain house, go through car park into courtyard ignoring 'No car' signs. Then right for 0.5 miles and right again, at farm building.

Map Ref No: 19

Mrs Mary Milburn
Park House Farm
Dalemain
Penrith
Cumbria CA11 0HB
Tel: 01768 486212

A short stroll takes you to the edge of Derwentwater. Immediately behind, the fells rise and spirits soar. Graham has sculpted a small-scale paradigm of English elegance: reception rooms are crisp and fresh with fine period furniture offset by pastel blues and yellows. In the bold dining room deep reds combine with lots of lamps... formal yet very relaxed. There is an eclectic range of books in the snug and the bedrooms, some of them small, are entirely adequate. The food is honest, and delicious: perhaps carrot and coriander soup, lamb, warm chocolate mousse.

Rooms: 2 twins & 4 doubles, all en suite (bath); 1 double, en suite (shower).

Price: £39-£52.50 p.p. Single supp. £9.

Breakfast: Until 9.30am.

Meals: Dinner, 4 courses, £25 p.p. by arrangement. B.Y.O. wine.

Closed: December & January.

M6 junction 40, then A66 west past Keswick. Over roundabout, then 2nd left signed Portinscale & Grange. Follow signs to Grange for 2 miles. House signed on right.

Map Ref No: 19

Graham Taylor
Swinside Lodge
Grange Road
Newlands, Keswick
Cumbria CA12 5UE
Tel: 017687 72948
Fax: 017687 72948

From the wilds of Soho to the peace of Cumbria - Mike gave up designing for 'something different'. We can understand why he and Janet chose this wood-enfolded, stream-fed garden with its views of Hope Gill Head and its 300-year-old cottage; they have snugly converted it, with new pine and old beams. Angles, corners, thick walls, cunningly-fitted white-tiled bathrooms, gingham curtains, log fire, brilliant breakfast and wonderful hosts, walks in the exhilarating hills then an excellent dinner - it is a delicious country B&B. *Children over 5 welcome.*

Rooms: 1 family, en suite (Continental bath) and 1 double, en suite (shower); 1 single sharing bathroom with double.

Price: From £18.50 p.p. Single supp. £6.

Breakfast: Flexible.

Meals: Dinner from £13.50 p.p. Packed lunches available on request.

Closed: Never!

From A66 take A5086, signed to Egremont, at r'bout just outside Cockermouth. After 1 mile turn left at crossroads by school. Then 1st right signed Brandlingill. House is on the right after 1 mile.

Map Ref No: 19

Mike & Janet Wright
Toddell Cottage
Brandlingill
Nr. Cockermouth
Cumbria CA13 0RB
Tel: 01900 828696
Fax: 01900 828696

It is a real cosy/comfy picture-book cottage, far prettier than you expect. There is a cottage garden with sweet peas, herbs, veg and flowers, perfectly rambling. They kept most of the original features (old farming tools remain on idiosyncratic display), and there is wood everywhere. There are dried flowers, cast-iron tubs, antique linen and patchwork quilts, all against a background of wooden floor boards, high bedroom ceilings and a palpable keenness to make it work. Television is delightfully absent, classical music plays, there are home-laid eggs for a walker's breakfast, and you can see Skiddaw from the house.

Rooms: 1 double, en suite (bath) and 1 twin, en suite (cast-iron bath).

Price: £20-22.50 p.p. Single supp. £10.

Breakfast: Until 9am.

Meals: Available locally.

Closed: 18-28 December.

The setting of this lovely old house could hardly be more beautiful. Many of its rooms face south and have superb views of peaceful countryside with the mountains and fells of Lakeland beyond. The house dates from c.1360 but bedrooms are sumptuous and spacious and the mood is of a tranquil, elegant, country way of living almost forgotten. Anthony, a tenor soloist, and Kathleen love sharing their home. Their food is legendary and, with a list of over sixty fine wines, dining in the 17th-century oak-beamed dining room is a memorable experience.

Rooms: 3 doubles: 2 en suite (shower) and 1 with private bath.

Price: £36-£37 p.p. Single supp. by arrangement.

Breakfast: 8.30-9am.

Meals: Dinner £23.50 p.p.

Closed: Christmas & New Year.

A591 from Keswick to Carlisle (approx 6.5 miles). Right at Bassenthwaite Chapel into village (0.5 miles). Straight on at village green for 170m.

Map Ref No: 19

Roy & Chris Beaty
Willow Cottage
Bassenthwaite
Keswick
Cumbria CA12 4QP
Tel: 017687 76440

From the Keswick bypass take A591. Turn right for Ireby at the Castle Inn. Drive through Ireby to Boltongate (1.5 miles). The Rectory is the first house on right as you come up the hill.

Map Ref No: 19

Anthony & Kathleen Peacock
Boltongate Old Rectory
Nr. Ireby
Cumbria CA5 1DA
Tel: 016973 71647
Fax: 016973 71798

A splash of flamboyancy in an old Victorian house - Philip sparkles in the kitchen, *à la* Floyd. He has his own 'smokee' for the trout and salmon caught that day. He bakes the bread, stuffs the sausages and boils up the marmalade too. He and Judith are experienced hoteliers, with high modern standards in a splendid town house. In the hall a fine mirror, Greek architectural prints and a newspaper rack; sofas in the drawing room, perhaps a leather armchair... all in a tree-lined avenue in the centre of an historic town.

Rooms: 1 twin/double, 2 doubles, all en suite (bath/shower).

Price: £30-£40 p.p. Single supp. £10.

Breakfast: Until 9am.

Meals: Dinner £18 p.p. by arrangement. Packed lunches £5 p.p.

Closed: 1 December-28 February.

From M6 go for city centre on A69 along Warwick Road. Pass 5 sets of traffic lights, then large church on right. Next right after pedestrian crossing into Howard Place. House at far end on left.

Map Ref No: 19

Judith & Philip Parker
Number Thirty One
31 Howard Place
Carlisle
Cumbria CA1 1HR
Tel: 01228 597080
Fax: 01228 597080
e-mail: bestpep@aol.com

Mineral water from the crystal-clear spring, lavish breakfasts with eggs and fruit from the farm, local sausages, oat cakes and homemade preserves - this is farmhouse life at its luxurious best in the heady surroundings of the Peak District. The farmhouse was built by the family in 1880 and is traditionally decorated throughout - antler horns on the landings, grand piano, marble fireplaces. Bedrooms are homely and one has wonderful views across the Derbyshire Peaks. Pam serves homemade cake and tea on arrival and will instantly put you at your ease.

Rooms: 1 double, en suite (shower) and 1 family room, en suite (bath/shower).

Price: £20-25 p.p. No single supp.

Breakfast: Flexible.

Meals: Plenty of local pubs & restaurants.

Closed: December, January & February.

Derbyshire

From A6 follow Chinley signs. At Squirrels Hotel leave B6062, go over bridge, left into Stubbins Lane. After 0.25 miles take left fork onto farm road, over cattle grid and almost 0.5 miles into farmyard.

Map Ref No: 15

Pamela & Nick Broadhurst
Cote Bank Farm
Buxworth
High Peak
Derbyshire SK23 7NP
Tel: 01663 750566
Fax: 01663 750566
e-mail: cotebank@btinternet.com.

People come from far away for the glory of the countryside and the magic of this beautifully-restored farmhouse. It is deeply cared for, from the yellow-walled hall with ticking grandfather clock to the pretty drawing room with sky-blue walls and clouds of cream damask at the windows. Flowers everywhere, dark oak furniture, lots of rugs, fine ancestral bits and pieces, Chippendale chairs. The terraced garden will delight gardeners. Drink, bathe in, pure spring water; it is delicious. Lovely, welcoming owners, deep peace and breathtaking views.

Rooms: 1 double, en suite (shower) and 1 four-poster, en suite (shower).

Price: From £25 p.p. Single occ. from £35.

Breakfast: Until 9am.

Meals: Dinner available locally.

Closed: Christmas.

A beautiful 17th-century stone house restored with intelligence and individuality, Hucklow Hall is a real home where everyone joins in - a very special atmosphere. Bedrooms are lovely, bathrooms delightfully cosy and the deep pink sitting room has a large stone fireplace and rush matting. Antiques mix well with country furniture, stone floors and exposed beams. The Whatleys are warm, interesting people, keen gardeners - the large garden proves their skilful attentions - and providers of wonderful, inventive food. No television and masses of books round off the civilised feel of this house.

Rooms: 1 twin, 1 double and 1 single, sharing 2 bathrooms.

Price: Twin/double £22 p.p. Single £20.

Breakfast: Flexible.

Meals: Dinner, 3-course set menu, £16.

Closed: December & January.

A625 from Sheffield into Hathersage. Right into School Lane. After 100 yards left fork up 'Church Bank'. 50 yards on, right fork, then 0.5 miles. Over cattle grid. Signed.

Map Ref No: 15

Mary Bailey
Carrhead Farm
Hathersage
Hope Valley
Derbyshire S32 1BR
Tel: 01433 650383
Fax: 01433 651441

Great Hucklow is 2.5 miles north east of Tideswell and signed from A623. Follow signs to village, pass Queen Anne pub on right and continue for 500m. Hall is last house on left of village (converted barn next door).

Map Ref No: 15

John & Angela Whatley
Hucklow Hall
Great Hucklow
Tideswell, Buxton
Derbyshire SK17 8RG
Tel: 01298 871175
Fax: 01298 873801

If you love gardens you'll wallow in this one. Within the two acres are herbaceous beds, a lily-pool and a lovely terraced garden of stone walls, hidden patios, even hidden sculptures and streams... exquisitely planned and unfussy. Hens, ponies and doves embellish a charming, old stableyard. The house is elegant yet relaxed and full of antique country furniture and subtle colours. It's O.K. to switch off here; Margaret is easy and welcoming. Breakfast is served in the old schoolroom, and is a carefully-prepared feast - organic eggs, honey, homemade jams and garden fruit. Glorious setting... and place. *Children over 5 welcome.*

Rooms: 1 double, en suite (bath/shower); 1 family and 1 twin sharing bathroom & w.c.

Price: £19.50-£22.50 p.p. Single occ. £25.

Breakfast: Flexible.

Meals: Available locally.

Closed: 23 December-4 January.

Leave the M1 at junction 29 and take the A617 to Chesterfield, then the B6051 to Millthorpe. Horsleygate Lane is 1 mile on, on right.

Map Ref No: 15

Margaret Ford
Horsleygate Hall
Horsleygate Lane
Holmesfield
Derbyshire SI8 7WD
Tel: 0114 289 0333

A deluxe cottage in a tiny hamlet, Mary Everard's house has modern, cosy bedrooms and bathroom with excellent beds and linen, a wood-panelled hall and a large sitting room with views of her lovely garden. Mary, an ex-champion golfer who has turned her hand to tennis, will discover the things you like doing and guide you in the right direction. The peace here is profound and it is only 10 minutes' walk up to Longstone Edge for the best views of Derbyshire.

Rooms: 1 twin and 1 double sharing bath/shower with separate w.c.

Price: From £20 p.p.

Breakfast: Flexible, but usually 8.30-9 am.

Meals: Available locally.

Closed: November & December.

From Bakewell, A619 over bridge - turn left onto B6001 to Hassop. Left up hill & then 1st right (Rowland only sign). Continue through hamlet around 2 sharp bends. Holly Cottage is on right.

Map Ref No: 15

Mrs Mary Everard
Holly Cottage
Rowland
Bakewell
Derbyshire DE45 1NR
Tel: 01629 640624

A magnificent William IV property built on the precipice of a spectacular limestone gorge. Beyond the formal gardens and 30 acres of parkland there are panoramic views over the River Wye and to the green hillside of Brushfield beyond. Inside, sympathetic renovation is complete - you'll marvel at the ornate, delicate plasterwork on the ceilings. Imposing though it is, this former mill owner's house today buzzes with family life. Four generations of Hull-Baileys live here. Bobby cares for guests and family alike with efficient kindness.

Rooms: 2 doubles and 1 twin, all en suite (bath and shower).

Price: From £32-£45 p.p.

Breakfast: Flexible.

Meals: Dinner & packed lunch by arrangement.

Closed: Christmas & New Year.

A 300-million-year old Tufa rockface guards this Grade II listed home, once part of the Duke of Rutland's estate. Rural delights of the Peak National Park start at the gate, so bring walking boots. Trout laze in the gin-clear waters of twin rivers nearby. Jan works very hard to make you happy - it's all spotless, elegant and comfortable. Books, magazines, smellies in the bathroom, guide books, electric blankets and wine glasses add to your comfort. A stone-flagged, beamed hall-sitting room gives you space to read or chat. Breakfast changes daily and includes home baked muffins.

Rooms: 1 double and 1 twin, each with private bathroom; 1 twin, en suite (shower) and separate w.c.

Price: £20-£22.50 p.p. Single occ £25.

Breakfast: Until 9am.

Meals: Not available. Jan can advise you of good places to go and will book a table for you.

Closed: Never!

From Ashford-in-the-Water take B6465 to Monsal Head. Left at Monsal Head Hotel, follow valley to The Old Mill, fork left. Left, at lodge building with white fence and 'Private Drive' sign.

Map Ref No: 15

Bobby & Len Hull-Bailey
Cressbrook Hall
Cressbrook
Nr. Buxton
Derbyshire SK17 8SY
Tel: 01298 871289
Fax: 01298 871845

A6 E of Bakewell, right onto B5056 to Ashbourne. Follow signs to Youlgrave and Alport, 1.75 miles. House is first on right in hamlet - sign at gateway.

Map Ref No: 10

Jan Statham
Rock House
Alport
Bakewell
Derbyshire DE45 1LG
Tel: 01629 636736

DERBYSHIRE

Set at 1,000 feet in the White Peak District, 17th-century Grade II* listed Biggin Hall has been sympathetically restored, keeping its fine old character - outbuildings in local stone, arched mullioned windows, leaded lights - while giving house room to contemporary comforts. James, courteous, gently-spoken and humorous, knows his patch of England well. You will breathe peace and clean air here - the only sound is the wind in the trees. Breakfasts are hearty and the smells emanating from the kitchen are mouth-watering. The River Dove is less than a mile away. *Children over 12 welcome.*

Rooms: 8 rooms in main house and 9 in outbuildings, all en suite. Luxurious master suite available.

Price: £24.50-£55 p.p.

Breakfast: Until 9am. (Full English £3.50 p.p. extra.)

Meals: Dinner, 3 courses with cheese/ fruit & coffee & mints, £14.50 p.p. Afternoon teas & packed lunches also available.

Closed: Never!

From A515 take turning to Biggin between Ashbourne and Buxton. Turn right just after Waterloo pub up drive to Biggin Hall.

Map Ref No: 10

James Moffett
Biggin Hall
Biggin by Hartington
Buxton
Derbyshire SK17 0DH
Tel: 01298 84451
Fax: 01298 84681

Standing on a steep hillside between the Dales and the Peaks, it has enormous views. The top floor is open-plan, loft style with huge leaded windows with distinctive coloured panels around the edges. You dine at two long pine tables, set up so you can gaze in wonder at the surrounding countryside. The feel is contemporary - wrought iron bed, light fittings and candelabra; walls are colour washed. Outside there's wooden decking, a terraced garden and a small lily pond. It's easy, fun and completely without pretension.

Rooms: 1 double, en suite (shower), 1 twin/double, en suite (bath and shower).

Price: £21-£25 p.p. Single occ. £25.

Breakfast: Flexible.

Meals: Dinner, 3 courses, £15 p.p.

Closed: Christmas & New Year.

At junc 26 on M1 take A610 towards Ripley/ Matlock. At Sawmills, right under railway bridge, signposted Crich/ National Tramway. Right at market place onto Bowns Hill. Chapel is 200m on the right.

Map Ref No: 10

Fay & Steve Whitehead
Mount Tabor House
Bowns Hill
Crich
Derbyshire DE4 5DG
Tel: 01773 857008
e-mail: mountabor@email.msn.com.

A solid Victorian farmhouse and the only place to stay in the area, it has its name because it looks over the Kedleston Hall estate, now a National Trust house. From the gardens of Park View you gaze across fields to the Robert Adam masterpiece. Back at the farm, you are received in a drawing room with yellow walls, pale blue ruching and darker blue curtains, blue sofas and an Adam fireplace. You have your own sitting room on the top floor, a homely room with books, chintz sofa and chairs. Beds are antique four-posters. Perfect peace in 370 acres. *Children over 8 welcome.*

Rooms: 2 doubles, en suite (1 bath/shower and 1 shower) and 1 double with private bathroom.

Price: £25 p.p. Single supp. £10.

Breakfast: Flexible.

Meals: Good food available locally.

Closed: Christmas Eve & Day.

From A52/A38 roundabout west of Derby, take A38 north. 1st left for Kedleston Hall. House is 1.5 miles past Park on crossroads in Weston Underwood.

Map Ref No: 10

Linda & Michael Adams
Park View Farm
Weston Underwood
Ashbourne
Derbyshire DE6 4PA
Tel: 01335 360352
Fax: 01335 360352

Gateposts topped with stone pineapples (symbols of hospitality) and huge copper beeches lead to a glorious Georgian house set in 50 acres with grass terraces leading to the River Dove. Polished floors and attractive carpets, but still very much a family home; one bedroom has a four-poster with golden coverlet from another *fin de siècle*. French beds and pale peach walls. Your host is a keen country sportsman and can arrange fly-fishing. Perfect for all that the Dales have to offer. A magnificent house with the kindest of hosts.

Rooms: 1 twin and 1 four-poster, both with separate private bathrooms.

Price: £35 p.p. Single occ. £40. Two nights' minimum stay at weekends.

Breakfast: Flexible.

Meals: Dinner not available. Many good local pubs & restaurants.

Closed: 1 December-1 January.

From Derby on A52, or Litchfield on A515, take Ashbourne by-pass, direction A52 Leek. Turn right after Queen's Arms to Okeover/Mappleton. Through park, over bridge and turn left out of village. House on right with white gate.

Map Ref No: 10

Cedric & Rosemaré Stevenson
Hinchley Wood
Mappleton
Nr. Ashbourne
Derbyshire DE6 2AB
Tel: 01335 350219
Fax: 01335 350580

DERBYSHIRE

Dinner at the Old Rectory has a formal candlelit house party atmosphere, with guests joining their hosts for pre-dinner drinks in the drawing room before proceeding to the silver and crystal settings of the elegant dining room. Then back to the drawing room for port and coffee around a roaring log fire. You're expected to 'dress for dinner', but ties can be provided if necessary. The luxury continues in the bedrooms with their draperies and thick, soft bathrobes. Even the views maintain the high standards, and the countryside all around is a walker's paradise.

Rooms: 2 doubles, both en suite (1 shower, 1 bath); 1 twin with private bathroom.

Price: £39 p.p. Single supp. £5-£12.50.

Breakfast: 8.30-9.15am (week); 8.30-9.45am (Sunday).

Meals: Dinner, 4 courses, £22 p.p.

Closed: Christmas.

From Ashbourne, A52 towards Leek. After 1.5 miles cross into Staffordshire. After 250 yards turn right signed Ilam. At end of Okeover Park, turn left. In 1.5 miles, after Blore Hall, left at x-roads. Pass church; entrance on right.

Map Ref No: 10

Stuart & Geraldine Worthington
The Old Rectory
Blore
Nr. Ashbourne
Derbyshire DE6 2BS
Tel: 01335 350287
Fax: 01335 350287

There are long views over the Dove Valley towards Alton Towers (a comfortable five miles away!) and the house is up a tiny country lane in a fine garden. An ancestor of Peter was Lord Mayor of London, hence the memorabilia. Cynthia is Australian; is that why they are such a delightful and friendly couple? Although elegant, the house is a home and guests really are treated as friends. The hall sets the tone: white tiles, Indian rugs, wood-burning stove and ancestral paintings. There is a small, book-lined sitting room for you, and the bedrooms are impeccable.

Rooms: 2 doubles: 1 en suite and 1 with private bathroom.

Price: £22.50-£24 p.p. Single occ. £30.

Breakfast: Flexible.

Meals: Not available. Good local pubs & restaurants.

Closed: Christmas.

From Ashbourne, A515 Lichfield road. After 4 miles, right onto B5033. After 1 mile right past Queen Adelaide Inn (set back in field). Rose Cottage is about 0.5 miles on right (cream coloured).

Map Ref No: 10

Cynthia Moore
Rose Cottage
Snelston
Ashbourne
Derbyshire DE6 2DL
Tel: 01335 324230
Fax: 01335 324230

Beeches is an ancient farmhouse-turned-restaurant with intertwining nooked and crannied dining rooms, beams, galleries, and a log-fired bar. Add some kittens, dogs, rabbits, Gloucestershire Old Spot pigs, free range hens, the three-acre garden and walks from the doorstep and you might not want to leave. Bedrooms are good-sized with modern pine furniture. Paul runs the 40-acre farm while Barbara cooks using only the best English ingredients and absolutely no 'fast' or processed food.

Rooms: 1 twin, 2 doubles and 7 family suites, all en suite.

Price: £28-£42 p.p. Single occ. £42. Children under 15 £7.50.

Breakfast: Flexible.

Meals: Dinner, à la carte, £18-£22 p.p. Stable supper Sun-Thurs, 2 courses, £12.50 p.p. Sunday lunch, 4 courses, £13.50 p.p.

Closed: Christmas.

From M6 (junc 15) or M1 (junc 24) take A50 and turn off at Doveridge. North to Waldley for 2 miles. At Waldley first right, then first left to Beeches.

Map Ref No: 10

Barbara & Paul Tunnicliffe
Beeches Farmhouse
Waldley
Doveridge, Nr. Ashbourne
Derbyshire DE6 5LR
Tel: 01889 590288
Fax: 01889 590559
e-mail: beeches@aol.com

Le Patron races vintage cars, Madame cooks beautifully and both are gracious and supremely welcoming hosts. Their splendid Georgian mansion, listed by Pevsner, was 'improved' in 1850 with some pillars and later with a high Victorian conservatory where breakfast, overlooking the beautiful garden, is not to be missed. The house has the elegance of Georgian proportions with shutters, antique furniture and fine country or garden views. The bedrooms are in keeping, with excellent bathrooms. Welcoming and most interesting hosts. *Children over 14 welcome.*

Rooms: 1 twin, en suite (shower) and 2 doubles, en suite (bath/shower).

Price: £27.50-£30 p.p. Single occ. Mon-Thurs only, £35.

Breakfast: Until 9.15am.

Meals: Dinner, 3 courses, £20 p.p. available on request.

Closed: Christmas Day & Boxing Day.

Leave M1 at junc 23a. Past airport. Right to Melbourne. Out of village on Ashby road. Right at Melbourne Arms on to Robinsons Hill. Or leave A/M42 at junc 13, follow signs to Calke Abbey. House is on right.

Map Ref No: 10

Robert & Patricia Heelis
Shaw House
Robinsons Hill
Melbourne
Derbyshire DE73 1DJ
Tel: 01332 863827

A former monastery, this Grade II rambling family house dating from 1644 is set in 18 acres of rolling lakeside gardens and is as welcoming as the Wilkins themselves. Rooms are large but cosy, spotless, and flower-filled. Two rooms have lakeside views, and bathrooms with original claw-footed baths. The third occupies the former nursery wing and has its own sitting room. Meals are eaten in the linen-fold-panelled dining room overlooking the garden. Guests can enjoy the gardens, play croquet on the lawns or just relax. Can you resist ...? Plenty of places to visit, too. *Children over 12 welcome.*

Rooms: 1 twin with private bathroom; 1 double and 1 single, both en suite (bath).

Price: Twin/double from £25-£27.50 p.p; single from £27.50-£32.

Breakfast: Flexible.

Meals: Dinner, £15 p.p. & packed lunch available on request.

Closed: Christmas & New Year.

From M42 take A444 towards Burton on Trent for approx. 2 miles, then left immediately before Cricketts Inn. Turn left. The house is 0.5 miles from Cricketts, second house on right and before church.

Map Ref No: 10

Clemency Wilkins
The Old Hall
Netherseal
Swadlincote
Derbyshire DE12 8DF
Tel: 01283 760258
Fax: 01283 762991

What a fascinating place! The tide of the Tamar is magnetic and there's an old mine count house from the days when lead and silver were mined here. Trish, energetic, enthusiastic and immensely warm, is winning the battle against nature, using a reluctant donkey that prefers to have its front feet in the kitchen. Home-grown veg and free-range eggs depend on the rabbits and the fox. You can sail off down the Tamar; there are moorings and a jetty for visiting boats. It's glorious; not frilly, flouncy or luxurious but loaded with character and fun, and real quality.

Rooms: 1 double, en suite (bath) and 1 twin with private bathroom.

Price: £20 p.p. No single supp.

Breakfast: Flexible.

Meals: Dinner, £15 p.p. & packed lunch, £5 p.p. both by arrangement.

Closed: Never!

Devon

Into Bere Alston on B3257, turn left for Weir Quay. Over x-roads. Follow Hole's Hole sign, then right for Hooe. Fork left for South Hooe Farm. 300 yds on, turn sharply back to your left and down track.

Map Ref No: 2

Trish Dugmore
South Hooe Mine
Hole's Hole
Bere Alston, Yelverton
Devon PL20 7BW
Tel: 01822 840329
Fax: 01822 841320

Luxury touches at every turn - as if the rare solitary stream-side setting of this longhouse wasn't enough. Maureen pampers you, spoils you imaginatively: champagne on occasions, toiletries, bedside bags of truffles, soft towels and robes in huge bedrooms - even a jacuzzi! Outdoors, a suntrap-heated swimming pool is colourfully lit at night. Renowned for inspired vegetarian and traditional cooking, Maureen serves breakfast in the (fountained) sunroom. She is gregarious yet unobtrusive, a soothing, easy-going hostess. Moors, not fairies, at the bottom of the wonderful gardens. But there is magic here... Excellent value.

Rooms: 3 garden rooms: 2 doubles, 1 twin/double, all en suite (bath or shower); 1 double, in house with en suite (bath).

Price: £38 p.p. No single supp.

Breakfast: Flexible.

Meals: Dinner, twice weekly, 7 courses, £25 p.p. Tray suppers £7.50 p.p.

Closed: Christmas & New Year.

In Chillaton village keep pub and P.O. on your left, up hill towards Tavistock. After 300 yds, right turn (Bridlepath sign). Cottage at end of lane.

Map Ref No: 2

Maureen Rowlatt
Tor Cottage
Chillaton
Lifton
Devon PL16 0JE
Tel: 01822 860248
Fax: 01822 860126
e-mail: info@torcottage.demon.co.uk

Walk, ride, sail (on Roadford Reservoir) to your heart's content from your base in this lovely, converted mill in the heart of Devon. The Archers have lived all over the world (Hong Kong, Canada, India...) and have chosen to settle among the natural treasures of this delectable region. It is perfect for Sonia's landscape painting and she hopes other painters will join her. They offer you glasses of wine in their large, homely kitchen, fold you in human warmth, advise you how to explore the area, and practise their Cantonese on you if you wish. *Children and pets by arrangement.*

Rooms: 1 twin, en suite (bath and shower) with sitting room.

Price: £25 p.p. Infants free, 7 years & under £2.50. Ask about single supp.

Breakfast: Flexible.

Meals: Dinner £13 p.p. (not on Sundays).

Closed: Christmas & New Year.

Follow signs out of Ashwater to Clawton/Holsworthy. After 1 mile, just by Thorney Cross, mill entrance is inside Renson Farm driveway.

Map Ref No: 2

Geoffrey & Sonia Archer
Renson Mill
Ashwater
Devon EX21 5ER
Tel: 01409 211665
Fax: 01409 211665

The Langtons are warm, grandmotherly (sorry Jack!) types - their smiles are utterly genuine, they really are pleased to see you. Elizabeth David adept, Jean loves cooking and cares greatly about using organic ingredients; everything is homemade. The same attention to detail is apparent in the fresh, bright guestrooms where fruit, mints and sherry await you. Climb all over the cobbled streets of Clovelly, then come back exhausted, but with the delight of knowing that you will be spoilt.

Rooms: 2 twins/doubles (1 en suite bath and 1 with private shower); 1 double, en suite (shower).

Price: £37.50-£40 p.p. Single occ. £50-£55.

Breakfast: 8-9am generally, but can be flexible.

Meals: Dinner £23 p.p.

Closed: 1 November-1 March, but please ask.

Horwood is a 30-acre beef and sheep farm on the edge of a small hamlet, but you'd never know. Pure peace. Gill is a working interior designer so the house was always off to a flying start... with the help of three acres of lovely gardens, including a walled kitchen garden and a lake. There are long southerly views over open countryside and the Grade II listed Georgian house has some wonderful rooms: big hall, library, both dining room and sitting room. The bedrooms are big, the wallpaper and drapes co-ordinated, with tremendous bathrooms.

Rooms: 1 double (5ft four-poster) and 1 twin, both en suite (bath).

Price: £30-£35 p.p. Single occ. £40.

Breakfast: Until 9am.

Meals: Available locally

Closed: Never!

Leave the A39 at Horn's Cross beyond Bideford. Follow signs for Parkham. Take first left into Rectory Lane after church on right. Old Rectory is around next corner after Rectory.

Map Ref No: 2

Jean & Jack Langton
The Old Rectory
Parkham
Bideford
Devon EX39 5PL
Tel: 01237 451443

M5 junction 27 Barnstaple exit. At r'bout turn to Bideford. At second r'bout left to Newton Tracey. After about 2.5 miles right towards Horwood. After 0.25 miles house sign & 2 white entrance pillars on left over cattlegrid.

Map Ref No: 2

Gill Barriball
Horwood House
Horwood
Nr. Bideford
Devon EX39 4PD
Tel: 01271 858231

You can't keep the tea trays upstairs for there is little furniture straight enough to put them on! The house is a creaky, lived-in, 17th-century barn conversion with good country taste. There is a bathroom with a huge bath under a long sloping ceiling, views of a hilltop crowned with trees, a handsome main bedroom with wiggly walls and wicker furniture, a fire in the elegant-but-homely drawing room and a drying area for wet walkers. The flower garden and lawn stretch up the hill. Very nice, easy and unstuffy people.

Rooms: 2 doubles, 1 twin and 1 single, all with basins and sharing bathroom and shower room.

Price: £15-£17 p.p. No single supp.

Breakfast: Flexible.

Meals: Good pubs nearby.

Closed: Christmas & New Year.

The renovation has been beautifully done. They overhauled the house, added a wing and some of the most luxurious bedrooms on Exmoor, all with a keen sympathy for the dignity of the old house. The kitchen/dining room is a feast of beams, flagstones and hidden modern ideas, the heart of the house. A meadowed, wooded valley falls away - sheep grazing - to distant Arlington Court. Cows, dogs, cats and Exmoor ponies play their part in the atmosphere and there are lovely old slate-roofed barns with a pond. Utter silence, and fun, too.

Rooms: 3 doubles, all en suite (bath and/or shower).

Price: £45 p.p. Single occ. £50.

Breakfast: Flexible.

Meals: Dinner, £25 p.p., by arrangement.

Closed: Never!

From Barnstaple, A361 towards Braunton. At 2nd set of lights, turn right signed Bradiford. Next T-junction, sharp left, over bridge, up hill for 50m, 2nd lane to right. House 1st on left.

Map Ref No: 2

Jane & Tony Hare
Bradiford Cottage
Halls Mill Lane
Bradiford, Barnstaple
Devon EX31 4DP
Tel: 01271 345039
Fax: 01271 345039

From Barnstaple A39, Lynmouth road. Second left after Shirwell, signed Upcott; up hill for 1.5 miles. Follow sign to Churchill. Farm next on right.

Map Ref No: 2

Tom & Erica McClenaghan
Ashelford Farm
East Down
Nr. Barnstaple
Devon EX31 4LU
Tel: 01271 850469
Fax: 01271 850862

Snug in the tiny harbour, boats rise and fall with the tide only yards from the bedroom windows. Hugo has wrought a small miracle, squeezing luxury and a wonderful dining room into a tiny head-ducking building. The staff are attentive and cheerful, Hugo effervesces, the sea-breeze sweeps clear your addled brain, the superb food gilds the lily, the walks up the wooded valley or along the coast are as lovely as any in the country and the village is tourist-stuffed, yet magical. Dare I say 'picturesque'...?

Rooms: 2 twins, 12 doubles, 1 single and 1 cottage suite, all en suite.

Price: From £44 p.p. Dinner, B&B, from £76.50 p.p.

Breakfast: Until 9.30am.

Meals: Dinner from £27.50 p.p.

Closed: Never!

You eventually come to a deep, 'secret' valley to discover the rambling Georgian farmhouse of artist John and wife Penny. Crisp and white outside, it's homely and informal inside, with an oak-panelled dining room, antiques and paintings everywhere. Long views down the wooded valley from the rooms across the gardens, a haven with tree houses. A well-travelled and musical family (Penny sings, her daughter's a harpist), they stage four concerts here each year. Moors, woodland and coastal walking, music, comfort and warmth.

Rooms: 1 twin and 1 double with basins, sharing bathroom; 1 kingsize, en suite (bath/shower).

Price: £20-£25 p.p. Single occ. £26-£30.

Breakfast: 8.30am.

Meals: Dinner, 3 courses, £16 p.p.

Closed: Christmas.

From A39, turn into town centre and follow sign to harbour. Hotel overlooks harbour at the end on left.

Map Ref No: 2

Hugo Jeune
The Rising Sun Hotel
Harbourside
Lynmouth
Devon EX35 6EQ
Tel: 01598 753223
Fax: 01598 753480

A361 to Barnstaple. Right at junction of South/North Molton. Through N. Molton, over bridge, onto moor signed Sandyway. After 3.5 miles left at x-roads to Simonsbath; after 400yds right down lane, signed.

Map Ref No: 2

John & Penny Adie
Barkham
Sandyway
South Molton
Devon EX36 3LU
Tel: 01643 831370
Fax: 01643 831370
e-mail: adie.exmoor@btinternet.com

This 14th-century, Grade II listed, thatched Dartmoor longhouse, within Dartmoor National Park, was recently home of author Doris Lessing. Its history goes on and on... enchantingly pervasive in the architecture, interiors, gardens - and atmosphere. Sleep resplendent in four-posters in low-ceilinged, beamy rooms, all with views of the very English country garden, whence come copious fresh flowers. Your hosts are adventurously well-travelled and interesting. Just one field away lies the moor with all its wild treasures. *Children over 14 welcome.*

Rooms: 3 four-posters, 1 en suite (shower), 1 en suite (bath) and 1 with private shower room.

Price: £30 p.p. Single occ. £40.

Breakfast: Flexible, until 9.30am.

Meals: Dinner, 3 courses, £22.50 p.p. by arrangement. B.Y.O. wine.

Closed: Christmas & New Year.

Only 900 years old and still humming with life: there's a goat in love with a goose, a pony in the rambling gardens, dogs, cats, guinea fowl, rabbits and foxes. Sally-Anne is artistic, slightly zany, adventurous and utterly lovable, as are her family. The farm is in the Domesday Book and is steeped in history with huge flagstone fireplaces, interesting contemporary art, books, pianos and wellies by the front door where you leave your stress on arrival. Not a road in sight, perfect quiet and sweeping views.

Rooms: 1 twin and 1 double, sharing bathroom.

Price: £25 p.p. Single occ. £30.

Breakfast: Flexible.

Meals: Available nearby.

Closed: Christmas & New Year.

From M5 take A30 for Okehampton. After 23 miles exit to Okehampton/Belstone. Left, pass garage & immediately right opp. layby into lane. After 1 mile, left at T-junc. Gate on right after 50 yards.

Map Ref No: 2

A30 to Okehampton. After 10 miles left exit into Cheriton Bishop, second left between 2 cottages. Go down & up hill. Road turns sharp left. Go down lane; farm signed.

Map Ref No: 2

John & Maureen Pakenham
Tor Down House
Belstone
Okehampton
Devon EX20 1QY
Tel: 01837 840731

Sally-Anne Carter-Johnson
Higher Eggbeer Farm
Cheriton Bishop
Nr. Exeter
Devon EX6 6JQ
Tel: 01647 24427

A stunning house, in bohemian good taste, faded but intriguing, in a most beautiful part of England. The high ceilings and windows absorb the bustle of an active and artistic family. Stephen, an architect, has a special interest in historic buildings; Lucinda runs an antiques centre. There are pictures, a talking parrot, a dog called Murphy - this is very much a real home, so don't come here for hotelly perfection. Each lovely bedroom, in the less interesting wing, has its own personality. It is all alive, intelligent and welcoming. A wonderful place for dreaming and for art-lovers, and for walks.

Rooms: 1 twin with private bathroom and 1 double, en suite (bath/shower).

Price: £24 p.p. first night; £18 for subsequent nights. No single supp.

Breakfast: Flexible.

Meals: Dinner locally available.

Closed: Christmas & New Year.

There are few traces of its 13th-century origins but the house is listed and there are pieces of fine old oak and granite everywhere, to which the Merchants have added their own antiques and old photographs. The age of this magnificent house (tiny corridors and doorways) has yielded to modern comfort and warmth in a most sensitive way. The bedrooms, particularly, are wondrously cosy, with thick carpets and wooden furniture. Enjoy a Devon farmhouse dinner with home-grown meat and vegetables in the pretty little dining room. This is a working Dartmoor farm, with 50 milking cows.

Rooms: 1 twin, 1 double and 1 four poster, all en suite (shower).

Price: £21-£22 p.p. Single supp. by arrangement.

Breakfast: Flexible.

Meals: Dinner £12 p.p.

Closed: Never!

Leave A30 between Exeter and Okehampton at Cheriton Bishop exit. Go through Crockernwell, immediate left to Drewsteignton. Cross village square, turn left. The Old Rectory is on right after 50m (avoid The Rectory!).

Map Ref No: 2

Lucinda & Stephen Emanuel
The Old Rectory
Drewsteignton
Exeter
Devon EX6 6QT
Tel: 01647 281269
Fax: 01647 281269

Take A382 from Bovey Tracey. After Moretonhamstead, look for signs to Farm.

Map Ref No: 2

Trudie Merchant
Great Sloncombe Farm
Moretonhampstead
Devon TQ13 8QF
Tel: 01647 440595

Through the reigns of 25 English monarchs, Gate House has stood in solid granite on this beautiful corner of Dartmoor; generations have lived out births and deaths, betrayals and betrothals by the light of its hearth. The log fire still blazes in winter and candles light the dining table. It is solid yet soft, quaint yet elegant, tough yet welcoming - a special place much loved by its lovable owners. You are treated to fine table linen, soft towels, pastel colours and a (summer) heated pool. *Riding, golf and fishing can be arranged.*

Rooms: 2 twins/doubles, both en suite (1 bath/shower and 1 shower); 1 double with private bath.

Price: £25 p.p. Single supp. £7.

Breakfast: Flexible.

Meals: Dinner, 4 courses, £15 p.p. by arrangement .

Closed: Never!

Walks from the house (a 17th-century ex-wool-mill) are reason enough to come here. On the edge of one of Dartmoor's prettiest villages, lawned gardens run down to the Bovey river. The bedrooms have superb views over woodland and the river, and the delightful owners - they are SO nice - provide superb organic and local produce. Typically, they don't call the dining room a 'restaurant'; it is informal, welcoming and just four tables. Stretch out on the riverside lawn, or at the tiny 'dipper' bar - magical. Peter spins wool, makes honey, plays the sitar and - rare among hoteliers - they are both modest.

Rooms: 3 doubles, en suite (bath); 1 double, en suite (shower) and 1 single with private bathroom.

Price: £30-£36 p.p.

Breakfast: 8.30-9am.

Meals: Dinner £21 p.p., not Sunday or Monday.

Closed: January & February.

From M5, A30 to Okehampton. Look for Marsh Barton sign onto B3212 to Moretonhampstead. There, take Princetown road, turn left at newsagent for North Bovey.

Map Ref No: 2

The Gate house is 25 yards off North Bovey's village green, down Lower Hill past the village Inn.

Map Ref No: 2

John & Sheila Williams
The Gate House
North Bovey
Devon TQ13 8RB
Tel: 01647 440479
Fax: 01647 440479

Peter Hunt & Hazel Phillips
Black Aller
North Bovey
Moretonhampstead
Devon TQ13 8QY
Tel: 01647 440322
Fax: 01647 440322

An oasis in the middle of High Dartmoor with views down a rugged valley to the River East Dart burbling through Lydgate's 37 acres. It can be an idyll: dry stone walls, grazing sheep, splashes of yellow from the gorse among the heather. In harsh weather it is a blasted wilderness, but Hilary and Judy are well set-up to help you make the most of it. They are very friendly and keen on their delicious organic and vegetarian food, served in the conservatory. The bedrooms are simple, no frills - but you have come for other things.

Rooms: 6 doubles and 1 single, all en suite (5 baths, 3 showers); 1 double with private bathroom.

Price: £28.50-£31.50 p.p. Single supp. £8.

Breakfast: 8.30-9am.

Meals: Dinner £16.50 p.p. Packed lunches £4.50 p.p.

Closed: January & February.

Pure ancient magic! Ann is wiry, twinkly and kind. She has restored this listed Devon longhouse with its Bronze Age foundation, keeping the shippon end (where her gentle giant shire horses live) and creating a snug, welcoming haven for innumerable furry friends and the B&B guests she so enjoys. Small cottagey bedrooms, one with a four-poster. Her shire horses will pull you in a wagon to discover the secret lanes and picnic spots of the Dartmoor she knows and loves so deeply. The house is right by the Two Moors Way footpath. *Children over 10 welcome.*

Rooms: 1 four-poster and 1 twin, sharing a bathroom.

Price: £17.50 p.p. No single supp.

Breakfast: Flexible.

Meals: Packed lunch available.

Closed: Christmas.

From Moretonhampstead, take B3212, signed Postbridge across the moor. Hotel signed in Postbridge to left.

Map Ref No: 2

Hilary Townsend & Judy Gordon Jones
Lydgate Hotel
Postbridge
Devon PL20 6TJ
Tel: 01822 880209
Fax: 01822 880202

From A38 take 2nd Ashburton turning towards Dartmeet & Princetown. In Poundsgate pass pub on left & take 3rd signposted turning right towards Corndon. Straight over crossroads, 0.5 miles further & farm is on left.

Map Ref No: 2

Ann Williams
Corndonford Farm
Poundsgate
Newton Abbot
Devon TQ13 7PP
Tel: 01364 631595

"Very special people and a lovely place to stay in the middle of nowhere" says our inspector. The Hendersons' 17th-century longhouse has a gorgeous cobbled yard, a bridge across to the island (shades of Monet), goats and a lovely family atmosphere. They produce their own moorland water, all their fruit and vegetables and even make cheese. The rooms are simply country-style, the attitude very 'green' (hedge-laying, stone wall-mending, humane lamb-rearing) and the conversation fascinating.

Rooms: 2 twins and 2 singles, all with basins and sharing 1 bathroom.

Price: Twins £18-£18.50 p.p; single £17-£17.50. Under 2s free, under 5s half-price in parents' room.

Breakfast: Flexible.

Meals: Evening meal occasionally available, £10 p.p; also good pub.

Closed: Christmas.

Leave A38 at second Ashburton turning; follow signs for Dartmeet. After 2 miles fork left to Holne. Pass church and inn on right. After 240m, right; after another 150m, left to Michelcombe. Left at foot of hill.

Map Ref No: 2

John & Judy Henderson
Dodbrooke Farm
Michelcombe
Holne
Devon TQ13 7SP
Tel: 01364 631461

The woodpecker comes at 8.10 every morning; this is a haven for wildlife. Even the cat enters the mood, keen to join you in your room if that is its latest chosen spot, and the goat wouldn't want to be forgotten. The house used to be part of the Flete estate, and has big, bright bedrooms with cheerful colours and all the comfort you need. They are unusual, too, with floor-length windows... and velux. There are things like luggage stands and TVs but your friendly and kind hosts aren't in the least bit hotelly; they couldn't be nicer. There is a drying room for walkers. *Children over 10 welcome.*

Rooms: 1 double, with private shower; 1 double and 1 twin/double, both en suite (bath).

Price: £20-£25 p.p. No single supp. Reductions for longer stays.

Breakfast: Flexible.

Meals: Dinner, £12.50 p.p., by arrangement.

Closed: Never!

From Modbury take A379 towards Plymouth. After 1.5 miles, take left to Orcheton. Right after 50m (Flete estate sign). Cottage, 2nd on right.

Map Ref No: 2

Carol Farrand
Goutsford
Modbury
Nr. Ivybridge
Devon PL21 9NY
Tel: 01548 831299
Fax: 01752 268516

They are new to B&B but you can tell that they will be brilliant at it. They are immensely caring people, which is reflected in the relaxed atmosphere. You approach the house up a long drive to a mini-hamlet on top of a hill, four houses surrounded by hills and fields with views to the Avon estuary and a wedge of blue sea. The house is an ancient monument recorded in the Domesday Book, yet there is stacks of comfort, thick carpets, big rooms with big views, whitewashed walls and wonderful food. Guests can be free-range. *Children over 14 welcome.*

Rooms: 2 twins, both en suite (1 bath, 1 shower). Separate w.c. and 1 twin/double, en suite (bath).

Price: £18-£20 p.p. Single supp. from £5.

Breakfast: Flexible.

Meals: Dinner, 3 courses, from £10 p.p.

Closed: Never!

Within walking distance of Salcombe and only a mile from the beach, this is a 1675 farmhouse, thatched, with curved window seats, wooden floorboards and two huge inglenook fireplaces. Michelle and Barry are a lovely couple, and put a lot of effort into the B&B. The comfortable bedrooms have views of the hidden, enchanting valley in front of the house. On their land are a bluebell wood and a cider orchard. The view to Salcombe, over distant housetops, is marvellous. Guests can help themselves to pre-dinner sherry.

Rooms: 2 doubles, 1 twin/double, all en suite (bath or shower).

Price: £25-£35 p.p. Single occ. low season only.

Breakfast: 8.30-10am.

Meals: Dinner, 3 courses, £17.50 p.p., 2 courses £15 p.p. (Mon, Wed, Fri).

Closed: August.

From Kingsbridge, take A379 towards Plymouth for 4 miles. At top of hill, turn left immediately before gradient sign marked Stadbury (before Aveton Gifford). Long private road; take top fork and house is on right.

Map Ref No: 2

Lesley Dawson & Anne Kinning
Lower Stadbury
Averton Gifford
Kingsbridge
Devon TQ7 4BD
Tel: 01548 852159
Fax: 01548 852159

From Kingsbridge take A379 to Malborough. At Shell garage, take Collaton road opposite, then 1st lane left signed Collaton. 1st fork left, house at end of road.

Map Ref No: 2

Barry and Michelle Sames
The Yeoman's House
Collaton
Salcombe
Devon TQ7 3DJ
Tel: 01548 560084
Fax: 01548 560084

An owl is cleverly etched from a piece of wood, a sculpted bench has two figures linking hands, candle-holders stand at the head of the bath, a deep sofa shelters your partner while you chat to him/her from the bath. The eye-catching and often-humorous gestures add much to an already beautiful house in a natural idyll. There is a lovely walled garden with magnolia, a croquet lawn, honeysuckle... an orgy of colour with heart-stopping valley views. There are thoughtful touches everywhere, and hostesses who really do seem to enjoy seeing their guests unwind.

Rooms: 2 doubles & 1 single, both with private bathrooms.

Price: £26 p.p. No single supp.

Breakfast: 8-10am.

Meals: Many good pubs & restaurants within 2 miles.

Closed: Christmas & New Year.

From Kingsbridge, take A381 towards Salcombe, through Malborough. House signed 1 mile to right down lane.

Map Ref No: 2

Sue Fish & Ann David
Maryknowle
Malborough
Salcombe
Devon TQ7 3DB
Tel: 01548 842159
Fax: 01548 842159

Wadstray, a solid, early Georgian country house, has an air of substance. The bedrooms have balconies, or canopied beds, or sea views. There are open fires in the dining room and a fine library for rainier days. But if the interior of the house is enticing, try the outside. The garden is an ever-improving Eden with wonderful sub-tropical plants encouraged by the climate, and a walled garden. There is a self-catering orangery with its own creeper-clad ruin and the mood of a secret garden... and behind it all a long valley view bridged by a distant strip of sea.

Rooms: 2 twins and 1 double, both en suite (bath/shower). 2 self-catering apartments, each suitable for 2.

Price: £27.50-£30 p.p. Single supp. £15.

Breakfast: Usually 8-9.30am.

Meals: Good pub in lovely village, 3 miles away.

Closed: Christmas Day & Boxing Day.

House is on A3122 Dartmouth to Totnes road, 0.5 miles from the Dittisham turn and the Sportsman's Arms. But don't go into Blackawton village. 1 mile from Dartmouth Golf & Country Club.

Map Ref No: 3

Philip & Merilyn Smith
Wadstray House
Wadstray
Blackawton
Devon TQ9 7DE
Tel: 01803 712539
Fax: 01803 712539

The house is old but the Coopers have unleashed their arty, bohemian taste to create an impressionistic ancient-and-modern interior that is a heady mix of laid-back informality and surprising touches of luxury. They are interesting people, green-leaning farmers who produce horses, poultry and organic food. (Diana is modest about her cooking; it is first-rate.) The house is lovely, the outdoor pool is heated, some rooms have distant sea views and Jason runs courses in coppicing and woodwork. Come for a wonderful time rather than hotelly perfection.

Rooms: 2 king-size beds, and 1 double, all en suite (bath/shower); 1 twin with basin and private jacuzzi bath.

Price: £30-£40 p.p. Children in same room as parents, £5. No single supp

Breakfast: Flexible.

Meals: Dinner £22.50 p.p.

Closed: Christmas.

An extravagant nature hide, it is a converted summer house built and originally thatched for grand Sharpham House and feels like a 'garden with a room'. Your room has a balcony that catches the morning sun and gazes over huge rhododendrons, magnolia, fuchsia, a lily-strewn pond and down to a bend in the River Dart far below. The two Richards are gifted gardeners (open to the public) and the gardener's modesty and calm have penetrated to the house itself. It is uncluttered, serene... and very comfortable, with a huge bath, thick rugs, a fine bedroom, and birdsong to wake you. *Pets by arrangement.*

Rooms: 1 twin, en suite (bath).

Price: £25 p.p. Single supp. £5.

Breakfast: Flexible.

Meals: Excellent pub in village

Closed: Never!

Follow A3122 to Forces Tavern, then follow signpost to Cornworthy. At Tideford Cross turn right, and then left over cattle grid.

Map Ref No: 3

Diana Cooper
Higher Tideford
Cornworthy
Totnes
Devon TQ9 7HL
Tel: 01803 712387
Fax: 01803 712388

From Totnes follow signs to Kingsbridge (A381) for 0.5 miles. Left, signed Ashsprington. Into village then left by pub (Dead End sign). House 0.25 miles.

Map Ref No: 3

Richard Soans & Richard Pitts
Avenue Cottage
Ashsprington
Totnes
Devon TQ9 7UT
Tel: 01803 732769

Tiny lanes twist down steep hills, suddenly giving onto great views of the Dart as it approaches the sea. Little villages are somehow built into the slopes. Gillie's house is, at the time of writing, also the village store, which is completely in keeping with the *bijou* nature of this bit of Devon. The surprisingly large house goes up and up, twisting and turning. Gillie was a landscape architect and costume designer - her flair is visible. Great brass beds, fat duvets and electric blankets add comfort to lovely, snug bedrooms. This is great value for a bright welcome in a special area of England.

Rooms: 1 twin, en suite (shower), 1 double, en suite (bath) and 1 double sharing bathroom.

Price: £15-£20 p.p. No single supp.

Breakfast: Flexible.

Meals: Good food in local pubs.

Closed: January & February.

From Totness, take A381 south for 1 mile; left, for Tuckenhay. After village, head for Cornworthy. Left at Hunter's Lodge sign; house opposite inn.

Map Ref No: 3

Gillie Brock
Hall House
Cornworthy
Totnes
Devon TQ9 7ES
Tel: 01803 732325

Come for those views of valley and hill, and the setting - ineffable. The old farm buildings form three sides of a quadrangle around a courtyard tucked into a south-facing hill. The views of rounded hills and grassy valleys are lovely. Breakfasts are in a huge open kitchen. The bedrooms are warm and thick-carpeted. There's a winter lounge with open fire and a bright and sunny garden lounge that leads through the conservatory and onto the terrace. Your hosts are friendly and relaxed, busy and welcoming.

Rooms: 2 doubles, en suite (bath/shower) and 1 double, en suite (shower).

Price: From £30 p.p. Single supp. from £5.

Breakfast: Flexible.

Meals: Dinner, £17.50 p.p., by prior arrangement. Light supper also available.

Closed: Never!

From Dartmouth take Totnes road for 1.5 miles. House signed to left up Venn Lane.

Map Ref No: 3

Ms Jan Bird
Broome Court
Broomhill
Dartmouth
Devon TQ6 0LD
Tel: 01803 834275
Fax: 01803 833260

A stunning little Regency townhouse, just 'off the flat', yet overlooking the sights and sound of the famous naval town of Dartmouth. It is full of light, with elegant but homely rooms, a romantic first-floor balcony wrapped in vines and a walled garden. Richard Turner loves to cook and may also play the pianola in the drawing room to amuse you. Right in the heart of town, but village-quiet at night. All the assets of a hotel but with the intimacy of a private house.

Rooms: 2 twins/doubles and 1 double, all en suite (bath/shower) and 1 double with private bathroom.

Price: £25-£40 p.p. Single occ. £35-£80.

Breakfast: 8.30-noon!

Meals: Dinner £15-£25 p.p. by prior arrangement.

Closed: 1 November-1 March.

In Dartmouth town centre turn left in front of the NatWest bank onto Victoria Road. House is first up the hill on the right.

Map Ref No: 3

Richard Turner
Ford House
44 Victoria Road
Dartmouth
Devon TQ6 9DX
Tel: 01803 834047

The Gunfield will soon be an institution in Dartmouth. At the heart are young, enthusiastic owners and staff, so it's lively and fun. Then there's the position right on the water and the Devon coastal path; the lower deck for breakfasts and BBQs in fine weather; the pontoon for boat taxis to Dartmouth and for motor boat trips to beaches. There's the bistro, the restaurant, the lovely carved wooden bar; great rooms look straight onto the water. In all ways this is a special place. *Bikes, watersports, golf deals and babysitting available.*

Rooms: 6 doubles, 4 twins/doubles, all en suite (bath or shower), except one Victorian bathroom.

Price: £30-£45 p.p. Single supp. £10-£15.

Breakfast: 8.30-10am (week); 9-11am (Sunday).

Meals: Restaurant dinner, 3 courses, for around £20 p.p. Lunches available, too, & BBQs in summer.

Closed: Never!

Into Dartmouth and follow signs to The Castle. Hotel 200 yds before Castle on left.

Map Ref No: 3

Mike & Lucy Swash
The Gunfield Hotel
Castle Road
Dartmouth
Devon TQ6 OJN
Tel: 01803 834571/834843
Fax: 01803 834772
e-mail: enquiry@gunfield.co.uk

DEVON

The view from Nonsuch is staggering. From your wicker seats in the conservatory you can spy the whole of Dartmouth below, a thousand yachts at their moorings (and marinas). To your left the mouth of the Dart is guarded on both points by ancient castles. But Nonsuch does not rest on its natural laurels; everything about it is captivating. The guests' sitting room has its own balcony and each room has one too. Great fresh breakfasts, large and extremely comfortable beds in big airy bedrooms, top quality bathrooms, views and more views. *Children over 10 welcome.*

Rooms: 5 twins/doubles, with 2 en suite (bath), 1 with private bathroom, with 2 en suite (shower).

Price: £30-£40 p.p. Single supp. £10.

Breakfast: Flexible.

Meals: Dinner, 3 courses, £15 p.p. Cheese course, £3.50 p.p.

Closed: Never!

From Exeter take A38 towards Torquay then A380 (Torquay). Follow for 20 miles, Kingswear signed on right. Down hill, fork up (Higher Contour Rd), up hill, down, round bend, 1st house on seaward side.

Map Ref No: 3

Christopher Noble
Nonsuch House
Church Hill
Kingswear
Devon TQ6 0BX
Tel: 01803 752829
Fax: 01803 752829

Quintessential Devon congregates at the Linhay - tiny lanes with high hedges, the smell of fresh coffee and homemade rolls, and clotted cream. Captivating smells waft from the kitchen as you step inside Clare Shaw's brilliant home. She has brought a rare warmth to this Victorian converted barn. Only two rooms to stay in, but absolutely top marks for style: one rather Mexican with rugs, the other romantic with Swedish sleigh beds. Over the hills and the sea is not far away....

Rooms: 1 twin and 1 single with private bathrooms, 1 double, en suite (shower).

Price: £20-£25 p.p. No single supp.

Breakfast: Flexible.

Meals: Dinner £17.50 p.p. available on request. Picnics £8.50 p.p.

Closed: Never!

Take A3122 towards Dartmouth. Turn left at Sportsman Inn signed to Dittisham. After 2 miles Bozomzeal is signed on right. Linhay is second drive on left.

Map Ref No: 3

Clare Shaw
The Linhay
Bozomzeal
Dittisham, Dartmouth
Devon TQ6 0JQ
Tel: 01803 722457
Fax: 01803 722503

Don't come if you are stuffy. But I challenge any of you with an open mind and sense of fun to fail to enjoy Fingals. Is it a home or is it a hotel? Beautiful and stuffed with all the bits and pieces to make you happy and comfortable (inside pool, jacuzzi, sauna, grass tennis court, library, superbly comfortable rooms, etc) it throbs with the vitality and enthusiasm of both Richard and Sheila. Conversation, good food and wine flow loosely round the family dinner table and throughout the house. A smashing place... and there's even a stream flowing through the garden.

Rooms: 1 family/twin/double, 1 twin, 7 doubles, all en suite. Self-catering barn of rare beauty with 1 twin and 1 double, sharing bathroom.

Price: £35-£50 p.p. Variable single supplement.

Breakfast: Flexible, any time after 9 am.

Meals: Dinner £25 p.p.

Closed: 2 January-26 March.

A381 south from Totnes, up hill, left towards Cornworthy/Ashsprington. Turn right at ruined gatehouse by Cornworthy to Dittisham. Descend steep hill. Hotel is signed on right after the bridge and up the hill.

Map Ref No: 3

Richard Johnston
Fingals at Old Coombe Manor Farm
Dittisham
Dartmouth
Devon TQ6 0JA
Tel: 01803 722398
Fax: 01803 722401
e-mail: Richard@fingals.demon.co.uk

Clough Williams-Ellis (of Portmeirion) designed this elegant country house, set in five acres of wooded gardens in the Dartmoor National Park; test his genius yourself. It works: the spaces, the light and the soft, warm colours, the all-embracing atmosphere of elegant homeliness. There's comfort at every turn, antiques and heirlooms, and chats with well-travelled Madeleine and Mike are full of fun and a broad perspective. Enjoy the views of the Devon hills from the enchanting gardens and play tennis on the all-weather court.

Rooms: 1 twin/double with private bath; 1 double with private shower.

Price: £23-£25 p.p. Single supp. by arrangement.

Breakfast: Flexible.

Meals: Available by arrangement.

Closed: Never!

A38 west to Plymouth. Take A382 turn-off, and 3rd turning off r'bout, signed Bickington. Through village, right at junction (to Plymouth), right again (to Sigford/Widecombe). Over top of A38. Penpark is 1st entrance on right.

Map Ref No: 3

Madeleine & Michael Gregson
Penpark
Bickington
Newton Abbot
Devon TQ12 6LH
Tel: 01626 821314
Fax: 01626 821101

DEVON

It isn't easy to make people feel at home while still giving them space to be alone; the Rooths succeed. The comfortable rooms and bathroom are in their own private 'wing', but once you come downstairs in the morning you will be warmly greeted by Gina and her black labrador. Breakfast is delicious, only early if you ask for it to be so. There are huge roses in the dining room window, a swimming pool, tennis court and green green fields beyond. Gina, by the way, is very knowledgeable about the nearby gardens to be visited.

Rooms: 1 twin and 1 double, let only to members of the same party willing to share bathroom.

Price: £25 p.p. Single occ. £27.50.

Breakfast: Flexible.

Meals: Excellent food available locally.

Closed: Christmas & Easter.

Definitely for lovers of The Great Outdoors; an impressive 18th-century stone farmhouse hiding in the Teign valley. The converted barn has mighty bedrooms with stunning views, unplastered stone walls and exposed beams, true to the original building. Little touches enhance the comfort and there are more treats than the standard. Unfussy, delicious food with dashes of exotica using bounty from the home farm. 170 acres on which to walk, fish, relish flora and fauna. Also clay pigeon shooting and, back home, snooker.

Rooms: 1 twin and 3 doubles, all en suite (bath/shower), 1 double, with en suite (shower).

Price: £30 p.p. Single supp. £10.

Breakfast: Cooked breakfast: until 9.15am.

Meals: Dinner, £20 p.p., by arrangement.

Closed: Never!

Turn off A38, going south to Chudleigh Knighton. Turn right just before village, and right at white thatched cottage. House is signed.

Map Ref No: 3

Chris & Gina Rooth
Culver Combe
Chudleigh
Newton Abbot
Devon TQ13 0EL
Tel: 01626 853204
Fax: 01626 854458

A38 exit at Chudleigh Knighton. Turn right; right again to Teign Valley. After approx. 5 miles right at crossroads into Ashton. Before post office sharply left. After 1 mile, house signed on left.

Map Ref No: 3

Maria Cochrane &
Angela & Colin Edwards
Great Leigh Guesthouse
Doddiscombsleigh
Nr. Exeter
Devon EX6 7RF
Tel: 01647 253008
Fax: 01647 252058

Richard's eccentric grandmother built the house in 1934. So, apart from having the second longest, single-ridged thatched roof in the county, it is unusual and fascinating (more doors than you'd think possible). Richard is a Savoy-trained cook and Lynne has the most beguilingly long Welsh vowels, softly spoken; they are a sweet-tempered couple. They love entertaining and do so informally, in the nicest possible way. You are wrapped in the peace and beauty of Dartmoor.

Rooms: 1 twin and 2 doubles, all en suite (bath).

Price: £30 p.p. Single occ. £37.50.

Breakfast: 8-9.30am (usually served in your room).

Meals: Dinner £25 p.p. on request.

Closed: Never!

Their great love in life is horses, breeding and racing. There are 180 acres of farm and park land around a 300-year-old house in lovely grounds. There is a gorgeous magnolia tree guarding the front door and a grand horse-chestnut on parade in the park land - the big attraction here. The house is neat and tidy, with bedrooms which are plain but charmingly furnished - all with timbered walls and good views. Breakfast is served in the dining room which has an adjoining conservatory. Within a short walk is a very picturesque lake for coarse fishing and walks.

Rooms: 1 twin and 1 double, both en suite (shower); 1 double, en suite (bath). Another bath & shower available.

Price: £18-£25 p.p. Single supp. £2.

Breakfast: 7.30-9am.

Meals: Great pubs within 2 miles.

Closed: Christmas.

Take B3212 from Exeter, then second turn to Christow on left. Go over humpback bridge, up the hill and look for signs.

Map Ref No: 3

Richard & Lynne Hutt
Rock House
Dunsford
Exeter
Devon EX6 7EP
Tel: 01647 252514

M5, junction 28, head for Cullompton, then left for Exeter. Through town and left at Sports Centre sign. Right at T-junction and cross over motorway bridge. Next left (signed Plymtree). House is next lane on left.

Map Ref No: 3

Fay Down
Upton
Cullompton
Devon EX15 1RA
Tel: 01884 33097
Fax: 01884 33097

Recently moved to Appledore, Joan, who ran a jewellery shop and Bruce, a lawyer, have chosen to live in an exquisite Grade II listed townhouse (1800) built around its main feature - a wide spiralling staircase with wrought-iron bannisters. A long elegant window runs from top to bottom and floods the house with light. Bigger than it looks, it has big bedrooms (wooden floors, bold colours) looking across the Bay of Appledore. The split-level garden is a good place to have breakfast. Lovely.

Rooms: 3 doubles, all with private bathrooms.

Price: £25-£30 p.p. Single supp. £5.

Breakfast: Flexible.

Meals: Pub food available locally.

Closed: Never!

The top of a steep hill seems an odd place for a coaching inn - the horses must have toiled. Now reap the panoramic rewards over the Exe valley and Tiverton (better as twinkling nightscape!). High ceilings, large windows framing the views, bring light and space to this refreshingly unpretentious, bustling family house. Barbara is a kind, chatty, no fuss hostess. Dining room, with beautiful dresser, and drawing room with antiques, have a subdued grandness. One room has a Victorian four-poster; another on the ground floor opens onto the gardens, beyond which lies the family farmland.

Rooms: 2 doubles (1 en suite and 1 with private bathroom) and 1 twin with private bathroom.

Price: From £20 p.p. Single occ. £24.

Breakfast: Anytime before 9am.

Meals: Supper, £12 p.p., by arrangement.

Closed: Never!

From Bideford follow signs to Appledore, go down the hill round to the quay front, house on left.

Map Ref No: 3

Joan Harkness
Bradbourne House
Marine Parade
Appledore
Devon EX39 1PJ
Tel: 01237 474395
Fax: 01237 422626

At junction 27 (M5) take A361 for approx 4.5 miles. Turn off at Gornway Cross, for Grand Western Canal. At Canal Hill take 1st right into Exeter Hill. House is at top on left.

Map Ref No: 3

Barbara Pugsley
Hornhill
Exeter Hill
Tiverton
Devon EX16 4PL
Tel: 01884 253352
Fax: 01884 253352

Unusual, remote, relaxed and hugely entertaining. Few conventional frills but a lot of unconventional ones: an 'honesty' bar, a relaxed young staff who don't hover, Victorian baths and some real fireplaces in the bathrooms, perhaps a piano (or two) in the bedroom, memorable communal dinners and the easiest-going owners in England. Toss logs on the fire, choose your own records, play snooker - but don't expect hotel service; this is much more fun. One of our favourite hotels, unpretentious yet stately... and not for the stuffy. A great place for a private party.

Rooms: 11 twins/doubles and 3 family rooms, all en suite.

Price: From £65-£70 p.p. Single occ. £60-£90.

Breakfast: Flexible.

Meals: Dinner £35 p.p.

Closed: Never!

You fish? This is the place for you. A homely cottage with well-furnished, good-bedded, patchwork-quilted bedrooms, bountiful breakfasts cooked on the Aga (fresh tomatoes baked with parsley, rhubarb and yoghurt, homemade marmalade...), linen table napkins and a vast lake in the midst of the rolling peace of the Devon hills. You can play tennis, but swimming is not recommended, because of the large fish! Cross a ford to get there, and a stream wanders through the garden. Water everywhere - and a most friendly welcome.

Rooms: 1 twin and 1 double, both en suite (bath/shower); 2 singles sharing bath, shower & w.c. Self-catering fishing lodge available.

Price: £25 p.p.

Breakfast: Flexible.

Meals: Good pub nearby.

Closed: Never!

From M5 junction 27, turn sharp right on bridge in Sampford Peverell. Continue 2 miles to Uplowman and then for 4 miles to Huntsham.

Map Ref No: 3

Mogens & Andrea Bolwig
Huntsham Court
Huntsham
Nr. Bampton
Devon EX16 7NA
Tel: 01398 361365
Fax: 01398 361456

A373 east towards Honiton and follow signs for Kentisbeare. Right after post office in village, and after about 200m right again and cross ford to Millhayes.

Map Ref No: 3

Jackie Howe
Millhayes
Kentisbeare
Cullompton
Devon EX15 2AF
Tel: 01884 266412
Fax: 01884 266412

Devon cream teas are world famous but they rarely come complete with an enormous 18th-century longhouse, a kitchen so big you can scarcely spot the Aga, and sparkling, comfortable bedrooms. After a farmhouse-quiet night there follows a farmhouse-generous breakfast (porridge in winter). And here in the middle of nowhere, your hosts have a (licensed) selection of French wines and great whiskies! Other surprises include expert golf tuition nearby and painting courses. There are wonderful walks in the surrounding area and superb scenery north and south.

Rooms: 1 family, 1 double and 1 twin, all en suite (shower).

Price: £17.50-£25.00 p.p. Single occ. £19-£25.

Breakfast: Flexible.

Meals: By prior arrangement.

Closed: Christmas.

From your free-standing bath you can look straight onto the church, a fine view from a fine bathroom. Upstairs, the sloping of the floors is part of the fun, but the overall mood is one of utter quiet. It is part of the Combe estate (Grade II*) with magnificent thatch and cruck beams, a 1600 date-stone and a 17th-century extension. South-facing, it still has quantities of wood visible and is known as a 'cross-passage' house. You have your breakfast in the old dairy and there is a very pretty drawing room with bright colours, shutters and leaded windows.

Rooms: 1 double & 1 twin, sharing bathroom.

Price: £20 p.p. No single supp.

Breakfast: Flexible.

Meals: Supper, £10 p.p., by arrangement.

Closed: Christmas.

At M5 junction 25 take A358 to Ilminster then A303 towards Honiton. After A30 merges from left, Courtmoor Farm is 0.5 miles ahead on the right.

Map Ref No: 3

Rosalind & Bob Buxton
Courtmoor Farm
Upottery
Nr. Honiton
Devon EX14 9QA
Tel: 01404 861565
Fax: 01404 861474
e-mail: courtmoor.farm@btinternet.com

From A30 towards Exeter from Honiton, turn left after 1.5 miles (signed Gittisham). In village, turn right over bridge - large house last on left.

Map Ref No: 3

Mr Andrew Hill
Town House
Gittisham
Honiton
Devon EX14 0AJ
Tel: 01404 851041
Fax: 01404 851041

They are lovely, artistic people, like their house. It is very much a family home in the middle of the village in a lovely part of Devon. Ali has a flair for interiors and the rooms are full of surprises. She works hard at not being like other B&Bs, much to her credit; breakfast, for example, is special. They have bought paintings by local artists to put in the self-contained cottage which is charmingly done, with split levels, wood beams and its own garden. This is a house with a heart; Ali is lovely and will look after you brilliantly.

Rooms: 1 twin and 1 double, both en suite (shower). 1 cottage sleeps 5.

Price: £20-£35 p.p. Single supp. £5.

Breakfast: Flexible.

Meals: Good pub nearby.

Closed: Never!

From Chard take A30 signed Honiton. Turn left signed Stockland and 3rd left off straight road down hill into village. Pass King's Arms on left, turn next left. House 200 yards up hill on left.

Map Ref No: 3

Nick & Ali Smith
Mannings
Chard Road
Stockland
Devon EX14 9DS
Tel: 01404 881473
Fax: 01404 881885
e-mail: 106222.2247@compuserve.com

The nine-acre gardens, full of nooks and crannies, are wonderful. The orchard has damsons and cherries, there are trees galore (ghinkos, meta sequoia, magnolia, jacaranda and Chinese shrubs). There are even three ponds and a bamboo valley, ewes, lambs, ponies, geese and free-range hens - and the setting on a hill is memorable. The cottages and suites have stripped pine, Laura Ashley-style linen and curtains and oak kitchens. But it is for the gardens that you come, and for the food: organic and local, traditional and delicious. Up to 16 can eat at separate tables.

Rooms: 1 twin/double, en suite (bath). In the cottages: 2 doubles.

Price: £26-£29 p.p. Single supp. £3.50-£5.

Breakfast: Until 8.45am.

Meals: Dinner, inc. aperitif, £19.50 p.p.

Closed: Mid-November-Christmas Eve. Early January-mid-February.

From Chard, A30 Honiton road for 0.25 miles. Fork left for Wambrook and Stockland. After 3 miles, right after animal sanctuary. Follow signs for Furley/Membury. At T-junc, left to Ford, then bear right. House on left.

Map Ref No: 3

Robert & Pat Spencer
Goodmans House
Furley
Membury
Devon EX13 7TU
Tel: 01404 881690

I could look at this view for hours: clear across Lyme Bay and along the Dorset coast for 30 miles - it is spectacular. Behind me is the Normans' large 1920s house where years of travel and naval lifestyle lie behind their meticulous and old-fashioned hospitality. The rooms are thoroughly comfortable and the dining room refurbished in Art Deco style in keeping with the period of the house itself. Two of the guestrooms are large with wonderful coastal views, the third more cottagey; all have chairs, a writing desk and fresh flowers. *Children over 8 welcome.*

Rooms: 1 family room and 2 twins, all en suite (bath).

Price: £20-£25 p.p. Single occ. £30-£37.50.

Breakfast: Until 9am.

Meals: Supper tray on first night, ordered in advance, £7.50 p.p.

Closed: Mid-November-early March.

Into Lyme from A3052, house is 1st left after 'Welcome to Lyme' sign on right. From Lyme up Sidmouth Rd, past Morgan's Grave & Somers Rd, then enter first driveway on right. Opposite junction sign.

Map Ref No: 3

Tony & Vicky Norman
The Red House
Sidmouth Road
Lyme Regis
Dorset DT7 3ES
Tel: 01297 442055
Fax: 01297 442055

Dorset

You can hire a rod and catch your own trout supper though you may not recognise it when Katie's worked her Paris-trained, *Cordon Bleu* magic on it. Guests join a house-party atmosphere in this 1900s house, moving from the stunning oak-panelled lounge with its garden views to the beamed dining room. Let go and relax in the engaging company of your hosts and the peace of their large estate in the lake-dotted Devon/Dorset countryside. Great walks, abundant wildlife, seaside over the hills and 30 single malt whiskies at the bar.

Rooms: 2 double, both en suite (bath); 2 twins/singles, both en suite (1 shower, 1 bath). Cottage sleeps 5.

Price: £20-£38 p.p. Single supp. by arrangement. Cottage £180-£495 p.w.

Breakfast: Cooked: 8.30-9am; Continental: flexible.

Meals: Dinner, 2-3 courses, sometimes available, £13-£22 p.p.

Closed: Christmas.

From A35 take Hunter's Lodge pub turning onto B3165 towards Lyme Regis. After 1.4 miles, right down lane, signed Cathole/ Amherst. Follow lane to right and to house.

Map Ref No: 3

Andrew & Katie Bryceson
Amherst Lodge Farm
Uplyme
Nr. Lyme Regis
Dorset DT7 3XH
Tel: 01297 442773
Fax: 01297 442625
e-mail: stay@amherstlodge.com

A fabulous getaway surrounded by 10 acres of orchard, valleys and wooded hills. Guests have absolute privacy in their own converted 17th-century wing. The rooms are thoroughly French in flavour with antique French beds, French furniture and bold colours. Add to this the Englishness of exposed beams and a snug open log fire, stone walls and soft, deep chairs. Irresistible. The food and wine is excellent; breakfast may be of cured ham, 100% meat sausages, local kippers - to give you an idea. To-die-for sunsets and lovely, lovely people. Do you need more?

Rooms: 1 twin and 3 doubles, all en suite (bath).

Price: £29-£32.50 p.p. Single supp. £16.

Breakfast: Until 9.30am.

Meals: Dinner, 3 courses, £14.50 p.p. Hot supper tray £11.50 p.p.

Closed: 24 December-2 January.

From Dorchester on A35, after 13 miles take second road sign posted left to Shipton Gorge and Burton Bradstock. First left to farmhouse.

Map Ref No: 3

Sydney & Jayne Davies
Innsacre Farmhouse
Shipston Gorge
Nr. Bridport
Dorset DT6 4LJ
Tel: 01308 456137
Fax: 01308 456137

An unstuffy farming household, never too busy to share their visible and audible enjoyment with guests. Rural seclusion, down a long, quiet lane, tucked away in the green folds of west Dorset, with views of farmland and hills. A stone farmhouse, recently built - though you'd scarcely realise - with rambling character, beams, big log-fired drawing room, dark period furniture, loads of space, and a large kitchen - the hub of the home. There are fresh, cosy, clean warm-red rooms with big beds, fabulous, filling farmhouse fare, fishing and country pursuits.

Thomas Hardy called this flagstoned inn The Sow and Acorn. Now ancient, and a Grade II listed building, it echoes to the merry chink of cutlery, glass and skittles and is a favourite hostelry for locals and visitors. The first-floor bedrooms are very stylish with antiques and crisp white bed linen, two canopied four-posters and in another bedroom an Edwardian six-foot inlaid mahogany bed. Great food in the restaurant (smoking or non-smoking), an impressive wine list and a British menu using produce from local farms and the fishing port of West Bay. Log fires and beams in the bars.

Rooms: 3 doubles: 2 en suite (1 shower, 1 bath) and 1 sharing bathroom. 1 room has its own sitting room and can be self-catering.

Rooms: 5 doubles, 2 twins, 2 four-posters, all en suite.

Price: £18-£22 p.p. Single supp. by arrangement.

Price: £40-£60 p.p. Single occ. £55.

Breakfast: Flexible.

Breakfast: Until 9.30am.

Meals: Dinner £10-£12 p.p.

Meals: British menu in restaurant or bar.

Closed: Christmas & New Year.

Closed: Never!

A303 from Crewkerne, take A356 to Dorchester for 7 miles, then take 3rd right to Beaminster (B3163) down hill and up. At top turn right signed 'Langdon: no through road'.

On A37 Yeovil-Dorchester road, in centre of Evershot village.

Map Ref No: 3

Map Ref No: 3

Judy Thompson
Higher Langdon
Beaminster
Dorset DT8 3NN
Tel: 01308 862537

Susie & Martyn Lee
The Acorn Inn
Evershot
Dorchester
Dorset DT2 0JW
Tel: 01935 83228
Fax: 01935 891330

You are deeply in 'Hardy' country here; the bedrooms are traditionally pretty and beamy with fresh flowers everywhere. There is an inglenook fireplace in the dining room with log fires that are coaxed into flame at the faintest hint of cold. Anita and André have travelled widely and Anita is very knowledgeable about health food. She loves this work and can produce almost anything you want for breakfast. There is a small sitting area in the dining room if you want to be private, with ample books, or a very pretty garden to sit in.

Rooms: 1 twin and 1 double, both en suite (bath); 2 singles, sharing bathroom. Cot bed & extra bed available on request.

Price: Twin/double £22 p.p. Single £17 p.p.

Breakfast: 8-9.30am

Meals: No, except occasionally by special request.

Closed: 20 December-3 January.

From Holywell Cross (midway between Yeovil & Dorchester on A37) turn to Batcombe & Minterne Magna; 50 yards, left into small lane to Chetnole. Follow for 0.75 miles. Brambles on right.

Map Ref No: 3

André & Anita Millorit
Brambles
Woolcombe
Melbury Bubb, Nr. Dorchester
Dorset DT2 0NJ
Tel: 01935 83672
Fax: 01935 83003

You could scarcely find a more picture-book 'English cottage'. A lovely village, fields and hills all around, a 400-year lifespan, a thatched roof, a stream to cross, a pretty flowery garden, a stone-flagged hall. The bedrooms are basic - nothing fancy at all - and have simple pine furniture. No sitting room, but a huge stone fireplace dominates the dining room. Nicky is independent, enthusiastic and most knowledgeable about walks and visits in Hardy Country though she will leave you to your own devices once you are properly advised. *Children over 8 welcome.*

Rooms: 2 doubles (1 with room for extra bed) and 1 twin, all with basins and sharing 2 bathrooms.

Price: £20 p.p. Single supp. £5.

Breakfast: Until 9.30am.

Meals: No, but good food locally available.

Closed: Christmas.

From Dorchester A37/ north. After 5 miles, in Grimstone, right under railway bridge to Sydling St. Nicholas. Lamperts is first thatched cottage on right in village.

Map Ref No: 3

Nicky Willis
Lamperts Cottage
Sydling St. Nicholas
Dorchester
Dorset DT2 9NU
Tel: 01300 341659
Fax: 01300 341699

The family labrador, Holly, will greet you to this warm and friendly country house with owners to match. There is a walled half-acre garden and herbaceous border (Tia's passion). All rooms are beautifully decorated and have stunning views. After a day out or a good walk feel at home and hunker down with a pile of their books in front of a blazing log fire. And in the morning enjoy a memorable breakfast with free range eggs and homemade jams and marmalades in the elegant dining room (again with log fire in winter). On a quiet road, this is a lovely old house, comfortable and easy.

Rooms: 1 twin/double, 1 double and 1 single, sharing 2 bathrooms.

Price: £20-£22 p.p.

Breakfast: Until 9am.

Meals: Dinner £10 p.p. by prior arrangement. Many good pubs within 3 miles.

Closed: 23-27 December.

A great escape from the usual Dorset tourist routes into this magical wooded valley and the quaint little village of Old Upwey. The Scotts have laboured devotedly to transform the 17th-century buildings of Friars Way - their own (Grade II listed) cottage and a separate barn. Cottage rooms live up to all one's expectations: low ceilings, beams, pretty cottage florals. The barn has its own sitting room and patio terrace onto the beautiful garden. An enthusiastic welcome and if you're superstitious you can throw a coin into the village wishing well.

Rooms: In cottage: 1 twin/double with private bathroom. In annexe cottage: 2 doubles, both en suite.

Price: From £23 p.p. No single supp.

Breakfast: Until 8.45am.

Meals: Good pub in walking distance. Packed lunches £3 p.p. if you ask in advance.

Closed: Never!

From Dorchester, B3143 into Buckland Newton over crossroads, Holyleas on the right opposite village cricket pitch.

Map Ref No: 3

Tia Bunkall
Holyleas House
Buckland Newton
Dorchester
Dorset DT2 7DP
Tel: 01300 345214
Fax: 01305 264488

On B3159 between Martinstown and Weymouth and signed opposite St. Laurence parish church car park.

Map Ref No: 3

Christina & Les Scott
Friars Way
Church Street
Upwey
Dorset DT3 5QE
Tel: 01305 813243
Fax: 01305 813243

The most striking thing about this Georgianised, high-chimney-stacked Victorian house, set in 3 acres of garden and trees, is the grand and very light hall. As you step in you are greeted by fine oak panelling, an impressive staircase, royal seals, a tall clock, rustic style furniture and academic portraits. It all smacks of an elegance and a grace echoed in the delicately coloured, big, stone-mullioned bedrooms and in the panel-ceilinged, ornate-fireplaced dining room. Threading through all this is a warm welcome from your very nice host, and the pub is very close. *Children over 12 welcome.*

Rooms: 1 twin, en suite (shower); 2 doubles: 1 en suite (bath) & 1 with adj. private bathroom.

Price: £23 p.p. Single supp. £3.

Breakfast: Flexible.

Meals: Within walking distance.

Closed: Christmas.

Your welcome begins as you step through the door to find an antique-type stove in a hall full of intriguing curios. Enjoy both Tony's collection and Rose-Marie's cooking (she's also fluent in Spanish, French and Italian) in this elegant, 18th-century listed house. The house is palpably 'English', a perfect Thomas Hardy setting, at ease with itself and its guests and comfortable in a delectable village, half a mile's stroll from the old town of Shaftesbury. You may well opt to stay put, for the Old Rectory's walled garden offers quiet seclusion, with views to the Dorset hills beyond.

Rooms: 1 double and 2 twins/doubles, all en suite (bath).

Price: £31-£33 p.p. Single occ. £40.

Breakfast: Flexible.

Meals: Dinner, 4 courses, £22 p.p. by arrangement.

Closed: Christmas.

From Shaftesbury A30 to Sherborne. Left onto B3092. 4 miles to Marnhull church, right down Church Hill. After 0.75 miles house on left just past village shops, before Blackmore Vale Inn.

Map Ref No: 4

Mary-Ann & Peter Newson-Smith
Lovells Court
Marnhull
Dorset DT10 1JJ
Tel: 01258 820652
Fax: 01258 820487

From Shaftesbury take B3091 towards Sturminster Newton. After 0.5 miles down St John's Hill the Old Rectory is on right at bottom of hill, with parking on left.

Map Ref No: 4

Rose-Marie & Tony Haines
The Old Rectory
St. James
Shaftesbury
Dorset SP7 8HG
Tel: 01747 853658
Fax: 01747 854276

The sounds linger: the raucous babble of early morning birds, the gentler sound of running water, the creaking of the great iron wheel as it responds to the rush of water from the pond. The visual memories are equally intense: the mill-pond at dusk, the setting and views, the beamed bedrooms, and even a kingfisher. Some bedrooms are in the main house, others in the more recently-done mill house and grain loft. Guests have a sitting room with a window over the pond. Dinner is good home fare in a no-nonsense dining room with separate tables.

Rooms: 3 twins/doubles, all en suite (1 bath, 2 shower).

Price: From £25 p.p. Single occ. £35.

Breakfast: Until 9am.

Meals: Dinner, 3 courses, £15 p.p. (only Thursday, Friday & Saturday). 24 hours' notice required. B.Y.O. wine.

Closed: Never!

From Blandford Forum take A350 and take sign for Melbury Abbas. At bottom of hill left for West Melbury. Just before village hall turn right, down hill, house on left, 10 metres after forking left.

Map Ref No: 4

Richard & Tavy Bradley-Watson
Melbury Mill
Melbury Abbas
Shaftesbury
Dorset SP7 0PD
Tel: 01747 852163

So close to the centre of town and so quiet, thanks to the massive walls and walled garden - open to the public once a year. The house is a Regency gem, of which there are many in this impressive little historic town. Inside the hall there is a marvellously odd statue of a man, made from motorbike parts, and an intricate model of a navy craft... not entirely predictable. Neither is the breakfast: kippers, homemade jams (the garden is rich with fruit), eggs every way... One bedroom has views of the church and hills beyond, a vast and luxurious bathroom and a desk. A complete delight.

Rooms: 2 twins, both en suite (bath).

Price: £25 p.p. Single occ. £35.

Breakfast: Until 9.30am.

Meals: Good restaurants locally.

Closed: Christmas Day.

From Shaftesbury take the B3091 towards Sturminster Newton. After 0.25 miles down St John's Hill, Cliff House is first on the right with parking by their garage.

Map Ref No: 4

Diana Pow
Cliff House
Breach Lane
Shaftesbury
Dorset SP7 8LF
Tel: 01747 852548
Fax: 01747 852548
e-mail: xhv79@dial.pipex.com

A perfect spot for an untroubled retreat. Ella is well-travelled, friendly and very keen for you to settle easily into her soft, green corner of Dorset. She keeps a four-acre garden, immaculately, and has a small vineyard of German grapes; the peace and the birdsong find their way into the house through the French doors. There are bold colours - apple green in the bedroom, sunny yellow in the sitting room and red in the bathroom - books, family portraits and paintings. Breakfast is Aga-cooked; if you can stir yourself afterwards there are lots of walks from the house.

Rooms: 1 twin/double with private bathroom.

Price: £20 p.p. Single occ. £25.

Breakfast: Until 9.30am.

Meals: Meals available locally.

Closed: Never!

Tim, a post-war classic car restorer, Lucy, a nurse, and their four very civilised children all enjoy entertaining guests. They restored their beloved cottage and wheelwright's workshop with their own hands, turning the forge into a museum of Dorset blacksmithing - a fabulous array of farrier's tools. The attic bedrooms are snug, with Lucy's quilts, country antiques and sparkling bathrooms. Breakfasts may include organic sausages or eggs from the Kerrridges' free-ranging chickens. The Downs beckon keen walkers, warm corners invite readers, overflow children can camp - what a setting! What a lovely family!

Rooms: 1 double/family room, en suite (shower); 1 double and 1 single (let to same party) sharing adjacent bathroom. 1 self-catering cottage to sleep 2/3.

Price: £20-£22.50 p.p. Single £25. Extra £2.50 p.p. for bookings of one night only.

Breakfast: Until 9am.

Meals: Good food available locally.

Closed: Never!

From A30 between Shaftesbury and Salisbury, turn right at Berwick St John & Alverdiston sign, then along for 0.5 miles. Turn right and continue until you see drive directly in front of you. House is white cottage on left.

Map Ref No: 4

Mrs Ella Humphreys
Ferne Park Cottage
Ferne
Shaftesbury
Dorset SP7 0EU
Tel: 01747 828767

From Shaftesbury take A350 to Compton Abbas. The Old Forge is the first property on left before C. Abbas sign. Turn immediately left there off main road. Entrance on left through five-bar gate.

Map Ref No: 4

Tim & Lucy Kerridge
The Old Forge, Fanners Yard
Compton Abbas
Shaftesbury
Dorset SP7 0NQ
Tel: 01747 811881
Fax: 01747 811881

General Pitt-Rivers, of famously eclectic tastes, lived here. Across the road the water meadows descend to the river that winds round Sturminster Newton. Australian Margie is fun and easy-going; the house is the same, with a huge fireplace in the hall and a smaller one in the snug sitting room. Bedrooms are big and unpretentiously attractive with plain Wilton carpets. Breakfasts, served from the vast and friendly kitchens, are feasts of local sausage, homemade marmalade and fruit salad, etc. A wonderful house.

Rooms: 1 double, en suite (bath), 1 double with private bathroom; 1 twin and 2 singles sharing 1 bathroom and another w.c.

Price: From £23 p.p.

Breakfast: Flexible.

Meals: Not available. Good pub within walking distance.

Closed: Christmas.

A magical place. Complete peace: the garden runs down to the river Stour and has uninterrupted views over the water meadows. The millhouse, 16th-century and Grade I listed, is as warm and interesting as the owners. The inside is no surprise: an original moulded plaster ceiling, half-tester bed in one room, a real four-poster in another, rich decoration and large table in the dining room. There is no sitting room for guests but the rooms are big and who cares when the house is so magnificent? *Children over 12 welcome.*

Rooms: 1 double, en suite (bath); 1 double and 1 four-poster sharing bathroom.

Price: £20-£30 p.p. Single occ. £30.

Breakfast: Flexible.

Meals: Available locally.

Closed: Never!

On A357 Sherborne to Blandford road. House is 0.25 miles west of Sturminster Newton Bridge, on south side of road.

Map Ref No: 4

Charles & Margie Fraser
Newton House
Sturminster Newton
Dorset DT10 2DQ
Tel: 01258 472783

House is on A357 between Sturminster Newton and Blandford. Look for well-marked turning on north side between Lydlinch and Fiddleford.

Map Ref No: 4

Mr & Mrs A & J Ingleton
Fiddleford Mill
Fiddleford
Sturminster Newton
Dorset DT10 2BX
Tel: 01258 472786

Ian, a retired surgeon, wishes he had played cricket for England; half the pictures in the house are of cricket. The Bishops are affable and helpful but will leave you largely to your own devices. You can use the conservatory; it has a ruched tent-type canopy and views of the Purbeck Hills. The house is part of an old farm complex, the rest occupied by families and children. Their own garden, small but perfectly tended, is at the bottom of an escarpment but you can climb to the top to take in amazing views. The cottage is *bijou*, with smallish rooms, but every inch is well used and it is very comfortable.

Rooms: 1 double and 1 twin, both en suite.

Price: £25 p.p.

Breakfast: Usually from 8.30am.

Meals: Available locally.

Closed: Never!

You can see across the Corfe valley and the Purbeck hills, for you are only three miles from the sea, in total peace and seclusion. You can walk to the coast, or visit the local pub. This is a Victorian Gothic mansion on a grand scale, with high ceilings, beams, stone and wooden floors and, unusually for the period, extremely large windows through which the light generously pours - especially into the big bedrooms which have lovely views. The decoration, not unlike Richard and Sara, is individual, with nods to classical influences. The dining room has deep blue wallpaper - striking, formal yet unusual.

Rooms: 1 double and 1 twin, en suite (bath) and 1 double, en suite (shower).

Price: £25 p.p. Single supp. £12.50.

Breakfast: Until 9am.

Meals: Good food at pub or restaurant, both 0.5 miles away.

Closed: Christmas Day & Boxing Day

On Wareham-Swanage road, turn right immediately before Corfe Castle to Church Knowle. Through village. 1 mile from New Inn on left is White Way Farm. Down drive, over cattle grid and cottage is on right.

Map Ref No: 4

Ian & Jane Bishop
Cartshed Cottage
Whiteway Farm
Church Knowle
Dorset BH20 5NX
Tel: 01929 480801

Take the A351 from Wareham to Swanage. Turn right at Corfe Castle, signposted to Church Knowle. After 0.5 miles take track to the left, signposted Bucknowle House.

Map Ref No: 4

Sara & Richard Harvey
Bucknowle House
Bucknowle
Nr. Wareham
Dorset BH20 5PQ
Tel: 01929 480352
Fax: 01929 481275
e-mail: harvey@lds.co.uk

If you ever stayed with the Hipwells in Affpuddle you will want to spoil yourself again. Their new house, rebuilt in 1762 after the great fire, on the foundations of a 13th-century goldsmith's house, is just as lovely as the old one. It is in the square of this attractive town and the views are soft and lush. The mood is of restrained luxury, uncluttered, often beautiful good taste. Bedrooms are cream with old mahogany furniture and beams. There's a large drawing room and good paintings are all around. The Hipwells are easy; the house, and the garden, are a refuge. *Children over 10 welcome.*

Rooms: 3 twins/doubles, each with private bathroom.

Price: £22.50 p.p. Single occ. £28.

Breakfast: Flexible.

Meals: Dinner sometimes available in winter, £10-£12 p.p.; otherwise, many good restaurants nearby.

Closed: Christmas-New Year.

From A35 take A351 to Wareham. Follow signs to town centre. In North St, go over traffic lights into South St. 1st left into St John's Hill and house on S.W. side.

Map Ref No: 4

Anthea & Michael Hipwell
Gold Court House
St. John's Hill
Wareham
Dorset BH20 4LZ
Tel: 01929 553320
Fax: 01929 553320

The house takes its name from the place where fishermen brought their craft ashore, in the unspoilt upper reaches of Poole Harbour. The lowland heath, reed beds and sea form a spectrum of bio-diversity - including dawn visits by deer to the large garden. Here, Elizabeth's green fingers conjure up a mass of flowers and exotic plants, as well as home-grown produce - jams, eggs, vegetables, herbs and fruit; the food is apparently 'fabulous'. Rooms have south-facing sea views; there are log fires and a lovely, huggable grey dog, a weimaraner called Tess.

Rooms: 1 twin, 1 double and 1 kingsize four-poster suite, all en suite (bath, shower and a bath/shower respectively).

Price: £20-£32 p.p. No single supp.

Breakfast: Flexible.

Meals: Dinner £10-£15 p.p. by arrangement

Closed: Hardly ever!

From Upton crossroads (0.5 miles S E of A35/A350 interchange) turn west into Dorchester Rd, second left into Seaview Rd, cross junction over Sandy Lane into Slough Lane, then first left into Beach Rd. House 150 yards on right.

Map Ref No: 4

David & Elizabeth Collinson
Lytchett Hard
Beach Road
Upton, Poole
Dorset BH16 5NA
Tel: 01202 622297
Fax: 01202 632716

'Twixt sea and New Forest - definitely; 'twixt town and country - so it seems, for this rambling Georgian townhouse is so countrified. The garden's broad-shouldered trees shrug off urban intrusions so all you sense is peace. Retire to the elegant interior with its fresh flowers, flag-stoned hall, elegant drawing room with portraits and period pieces. Retreat to your comfortable, more simply-styled room: the twin overlooking the (quiet at night) road, or the double looking into the gardens. Deborah plainly enjoys her home - and sharing it.

Rooms: 1 double with private bathroom and 1 twin, en suite (bath).

Price: £20 p.p. Single occ. £30.

Breakfast: Flexible.

Meals: Available locally.

Closed: Christmas.

The Turnbulls are as thoroughly English as their 1930s thatched house and their huge and engaging country garden. Sara keeps a large, welcoming home with an impeccable mix of family portraits, landscape paintings and some silk paintings from Hong Kong, and she successfully mixes antique and modern furniture, whites and pastels. She also pays attention to detail such as a new toothbrush for the forgetful, linen table napkins and two sorts of tea. Every view is into green 'Thomas Hardy' countryside. Bring your racquets - there's a tennis court in the garden.

Rooms: 1 double, 1 twin and 1 single sharing 2 bathrooms. Possible use of private bathroom.

Price: From £20 p.p.

Breakfast: Until 9.30am.

Meals: None, but good food available locally.

Closed: Never!

From Wimborne town square go up West Borough to 1st set of traffic lights Old Merchant's House is first on right opposite the Town Hall.

Map Ref No: 4

Deborah Stevenson
Old Merchant's House
44 West Borough
Wimborne Minster
Dorset BH21 1NQ
Tel: 01202 841955

B3078 from Wimborne to Cranborne. Turn right to Holt. After 2 miles Thornhill is on the right, 200 metres beyond Old Inn.

Map Ref No: 4

John & Sara Turnbull
Thornhill
Holt
Wimborne
Dorset BH21 7DJ
Tel: 01202 889434

Your relaxed and friendly hosts are intelligent, involved citizens who live in a dream thatched cottage in a very pretty hidden village set in rolling farmland. Their one, cosy, stripped-pine-furnished guestroom is reached by a near-perpendicular staircase, with adjoining small, private sitting room. The claw-footed bath and chain-pull loo are on the ground floor - all strictly for the nimble. The Paceys love their listed historic home - it has been used recently for a film - and have furnished it for the comfort of body and soul. You will find a sense of timeless peace here.

Rooms: 1 double with private bathroom (downstairs) and use of own sitting room.

Price: £22.50-£25 p.p. Single occ. £25.

Breakfast: Flexible.

Meals: Available locally.

Closed: Christmas.

From the M27, A31 to Ringwood. Turn onto B3081, through Verwood and left onto B3078. 4.5 miles along, left at Hinton Martell sign and, 0.5 miles on, house is first thatched one on left, after phone box.

Map Ref No: 4

Christine & Christopher Pacey
Hinton Cottage
Hinton Martel
Wimborne
Dorset BH21 7HE
Tel: 01258 840569

Once you have discovered the area and this old house (dated 1741 with recent award-winning renovation), you are seduced. Walk straight from the garden into the old town, into the countryside or down to the River Tees. Your quiet, secluded suite at the back of the house is in 'New England Style' with antiques, quilts over bed and chairs, white walls, lots of cotton. Philip and Judy, who specialise in Staffordshire china animals, are friendly, helpful and attentive. Eat continental breakfast here or splurge on full English at 'The Old Well' across the road.

Rooms: 1 large twin/double with sitting room & private bathroom.

Price: £20 p.p. Single occ. £35.

Breakfast: Flexible.

Meals: Available locally.

Closed: End January-end March, & June.

From A1 Scotch Corner take A66 to Barnard Castle over Egglestone bridge, past Bowes Museum to Butter market straight ahead of you. Turn left half way down The Bank.

Map Ref No: 15

Durham

Philip & Judy Brown
Brown's Antiques
No. 34 The Bank
Barnard Castle
Durham DL12 8PN
Tel: 01833 637891
Fax: 01833 637891

Drive for two miles through the forest to get here; there are 5000 acres of mixed woodland, moors and becks, a valley with two small rivers, old oaks and beeches... fabulous. It is a walker's paradise, with pure air, birds aplenty, deer, and woodpeckers in the garden. The Georgian shooting lodge is in an open glade with views of the moors, almost Swiss in its prettiness. Helene has lived here all her life. There are comfy sofas, big downstairs rooms, open fires, books and games. Dine among oils and Art-Nouveau fittings, sleep well in comfortable bedrooms. An enchanted spot. *Children over 8 welcome.*

Rooms: 2 doubles, en suite (bath & shower). 1 twin, en suite (shower).

Price: £20-£27 p.p. Single supp. (June-Aug) £10.

Breakfast: Until 9am.

Meals: Dinner £16.50 p.p. Packed lunch £4 p.p.

Closed: 14 December-14 January.

A68 from Darlington, left to Hamsterley village. Continue for 2 miles (ignore forest signs), then right, signed The Grove, then left. Take right, signed Hamsterley Forest. After 3 miles, over stone bridge, house faces you.

Map Ref No: 20

Helene Close
Grove House
Hamsterley Forest
Bishop Auckland
Durham DL13 3NL
Tel: 01388 488203
Fax: 01388 488174
e-mail: x047@dial.pipex.com

Just 12 miles from Durham, one of England's jewels, and one of only 20 similarly listed farmhouses in the county. It is way off the beaten track in magical scenery, a Grade II* early 17th-century building with later additions, with huge charm. The kitchen has the original bread oven and in it Marguerite produces mouth-watering meals, and enjoys doing so. It is also sybaritically comfortable, with deep sofa and armchairs below beams and before the open fire in the drawing room. Higgledy piggledy and comfortable - perfect.

Rooms: 1 twin with adjacent private bathroom.

Price: £28 p.p. Single occ. £34.

Breakfast: Flexible.

Meals: Dinner, 4 courses, £18 p.p.

Closed: Never!

Going east on A689, approx 1 mile west of Wolsingham, turn left opposite brown caravan sign. Over bridge, sharp left over disused railway line. 0.5 miles up track, fork right through ford. House 200 yards further on.

Map Ref No: 20

Anthony & Marguerite Todd
Coves House Farm
Wolsingham
Weardale
Durham DL13 3BG
Tel: 01388 527375
Fax: 01388 526157

Irresistible for lovers of horses; there are over 60 of them about. The Booths are mad about them and you can learn to ride, or to do so more elegantly. Once a hunting lodge, Ivesley is at the end of an avenue of beech trees planted in the 1350s to commemorate the end of the Black Death. Half the house is new, discreetly so; the floorboards that creak are in the old part. The big bedrooms are very much 'country house', with antiques, and the grandeur of the dining room and drawing room belie their recent birth. Only 15 minutes from the centre of Durham. *Children over 8 welcome.*

Rooms: 2 twins, en suite (shower); 1 double, en suite (bath). Bathroom also available.

Price: £28.50 p.p. Single supp. from £10.

Breakfast: Until 9am.

Meals: Dinner £17.50 p.p. by arrangement.

Closed: Christmas Day.

A1, then A68 to Tow Law. Right onto B6301, signed Lanchester. After 3.7 miles, turn right. House drive is 0.7 miles up hill on left.

Map Ref No: 20

Roger & Pauline Booth
Ivesley Equestrian Centre
Waterhouses
Durham DH7 9HB
Tel: 0191 373 4324
Fax: 0191 373 4757
e-mail: ivesley@msn.com

Patricia Mitchell is a knowledgeable guide to the history of this wonderful, Grade II listed 14th-century family house on the Essex Way. The 'new wing' is 15th-century, and here you have breakfast in front of the log fire. The bedrooms are colourful, cosy and welcoming, with exposed beams, uneven wooden floors and 'museum corners' which enshrine original features of the house. There are three pubs within 100 metres, or a two-acre garden providing refuge from the hum of village life; and in the courtyard Patricia's hobby, a second-hand clothes shop, is famous for miles around.

Rooms: 1 double/family room, en suite (bath), 1 twin with own bathroom and 1 single with separate shower room & w.c.

Price: Family room £40-45, with £5 supp. for camp bed. Twin £17.50-£20 p.p. Single £25-£30.

Breakfast: Flexible.

Meals: No, but available locally.

Closed: Never - except in a crisis!

Essex

On A1124, 2.5 miles west of A12 junction. House is on left beyond the Cooper's Arms and opposite Queens Head.

Map Ref No: 11

Patricia & Richard Mitchell
Old House
Fordstreet
Aldham, Colchester
Essex CO6 3PH
Tel: 01206 240456
Fax: 01206 240456

ESSEX

"Truly lovely people," wrote our inspector. "Individual, authentic and unusual". Peter is a cabinet-maker (clavichords, furniture, dolls' houses) and his work is all over the house... including a chair carved from a tree. Noël is a writer on art and antiques; the house has a stimulating scatter of pictures. Even a loo is plastered with Victorian narrative scenes. The garden is fun, too; it rambles down to a brook, with a wild copse and a tennis lawn. The bedrooms are big, stylish and solidly comfortable, with interesting old furniture and good garden views.

Rooms: 2 doubles with shared bathroom and 1 single, en suite.

Price: £20 p.p.

Breakfast: Flexible.

Meals: Supper, £10 p.p., by arrangement.

Closed: Occasionally.

Enter village on A131 from Sudbury, pass pub and after 50 yards turn right. House at bottom of drive.

Map Ref No: 11

Noël & Peter Owen
Bulmer Tye House
Bulmer Tye
Nr. Sudbury
Essex CO10 7ED
Tel: 01787 269315
Fax: 01787 269315

There's the quality of an old Constable-country house inside - ancestral portraits and antiques - belying the external appearance of this almost colonial-style 1950s bungalow in Dedham Vale. This much-loved AONB provides the wider setting; the gardens - with pond, lush greenery and tennis court - provide a relaxed focus within the rolling valley scenery. Jeremy, whose parents lived in the local manor house, is a character, a 'spade's a spade' man. Play the baby grand piano, enjoy conversation with widely-travelled people of wide-ranging interests and considerable charm.

Rooms: 1 family and 1 twin, both en suite (bath/shower); 1 double with private bathroom.

Price: £21-£25 p.p. Single occ. £28.

Breakfast: Flexible.

Meals: Dinner £16 p.p. by prior arrangement.

Closed: Never!

From A134 (Colchester/Sudbury Road), at Great Horkesley take Boxted Church Road for 2 miles east. House is 200 yds beyond turning to church.

Map Ref No: 12

Jeremy & Mary Carter
Round Hill House
Parsonage Hill
Boxted, Colchester
Essex CO4 5ST
Tel: 01206 272392
Fax: 01206 272392

Behind that gorgeous 1700s house, close to the Suffolk border, is an equally gorgeous garden. There is light, and space and air and silence, both in and out. The house has been renovated in Lutyens style. The first thing you see is the hall decorated with painted panels. The drawing room has a grand piano, fireplace and big windows onto the rose garden; croquet on the lawn, midge-swatting by the hidden pond, then Coral's afternoon tea complete the picture. Bedrooms are bright and full of goodies; bathrooms have all you could wish for and one of the longest baths we know.

Rooms: 1 double and 1 twin with private bathroom; 1 single/twin with separate bathroom.

Price: £20 p.p. Single occ. £30.

Breakfast: Until 9.30am.

Meals: Available locally.

Closed: 22 December-2 January.

Listen to the sea. It murmurs across the saltings where the Brent geese wheel and the great Constable skies stretch. The house is minutes from wild walking; this island of Mersea is secluded, surprising. The house began in 1343, a hall house nearly as old as the exquisite church. The Georgians added their bit but the venerable beams and uneven old construction shine through. It is a sunny, comfortable, beautiful house. There is a snug, book-filled, sitting room and a terracotta-floored conservatory gazing over the large garden. It is a privilege to stay here, among such nice people.

Rooms: 1 twin with private bathroom; 2 twins sharing a bathroom.

Price: £20 p.p. Single occ. £25.

Breakfast: Until 9am.

Meals: Available locally: good restaurant 2 miles away & pub within walking distance.

Closed: Never!

From A12 north of Colchester follow A120 towards Harwich for approx 7.5 miles. Turn left to Lt Bromley & follow for 2.9 miles. House set back on right.

Map Ref No: 12

Christopher & Coral McEwen
Aldhams
Bromley Road
Lawford, Manningtree
Essex CO11 2NE
Tel: 01206 393210
Fax: 01206 393210
e-mail: coral.mcewen3@which.net

Take B1025 from Colchester, over causeway then bear left and follow brown & white signs to the farm.

Map Ref No: 12

Ruth Dence
Bromans Farm
East Mersea
Essex CO5 8UE
Tel: 01206 383235

Boyts is ravishing, a 16th-century stone farmhouse in landscaped gardens. There is a huge fireplace in the sitting room, stone-flagged floors, window seats, wooden (sic) mullions, leaded windows around which climb a magnolia. The vast dining room has a fireplace, oil paintings, mahogany table. The bedrooms are just as lovely. The Italianate-style gardens have a canal and ornamental ponds, crested newts, ha-has and paddocks beyond, and open farmland beyond that. John, ex-Army, has a keen, wry sense of humour; Sally is lovely, and keeps a cockatiel in the kitchen.

Rooms: 1 double and 1 twin, both en suite (bath).

Price: £30 p.p. No single supp.

Breakfast: Until 9.30am.

Meals: Available locally; a 3-minute walk to local pub with restaurant.

Closed: 21 December-2 January.

Gloucestershire

At M5 junc. 16 take A38 for Gloucester. After 6 miles, take Tytherington turn. From north, leave M5 at exit 14 and south on A38 towards Bristol. Tytherington turning after 3 miles. Farm is off Baden Hill Road.

Map Ref No: 3

Mr & Mrs Eyre
Boyts Farm
Tytherington
Wotton-under-Edge
Gloucestershire GL12 8UG
Tel: 01454 412220
Fax: 01454 412220

A treat: utterly delightful people of exquisite manners and wide-ranging interests (ex-British Council and college lecturing; arts, travel, gardening...) in a manor-type house full of beautiful furniture. The house was born of the Arts and Crafts movement and remains fascinating: wood panels painted green and log-fired drawing-room for guests, quarry tiles on window-sills, handsome old furniture, comfortable proportions... elegant but human. The garden's massive clipped hedges and great lawn are impressive, as is the whole place. Refined but easy.

Rooms: 2 twins and 1 double: 1 with private bath/shower & 2 with shared bathroom.

Price: £28 p.p. Single supp. £5.

Breakfast: Until 9.15am.

Meals: Dinner £17.50 p.p. B.Y.O wine.

Closed: December & January.

The solid walls of this farmhouse have sheltered the King family for 75 years and, for friends, family and neighbours alike, it is a welcoming, bustling meeting place. The son works the arable and dairy farm with his father, and the daughter and son-in-law's own nearby farm sends fresh produce for your breakfast - some of it organic. This is an honest value B&B - Sonja knows her stuff and there's no standing on ceremony: come here to enjoy a slice of real working farming life. The famous Westonbirt Arboretum - breathtaking whatever the season - is a stroll away across the field.

Rooms: 2 twins and 1 double, all en suite (shower); 3 separate w.c.s.

Price: From £17.50 p.p.

Breakfast: Flexible.

Meals: No, but locally available.

Closed: Never!

Take B4060 from Stinchcombe to Wotton-under-Edge. Go up long hill, house is at top on left - the gateway is marked.

Map Ref No: 4

Hugh & Crystal St John Mildmay
Drakestone House
Stinchcombe
Dursley
Gloucestershire GL11 6AS
Tel: 01453 542140

A433 from Tetbury for 5 miles. On entering Knockdown, farm on right before crossroads.

Map Ref No: 4

Sonja King
Avenue Farm
Knockdown
Tetbury
Gloucestershire GL8 8QY
Tel: 01454 238207
Fax: 01454 423 8033

Steep honey-coloured gables, mullioned windows and weathered stone tiles enclose this lovely 17th-century house on a quiet village lane. It is English to the core - and to the bottom of its lovely garden (the house sits in six acres). Caroline is a competent hostess with a cool, gentle manner and a talent for understated high-class interior decor. The two ample, airy guestrooms are furnished with antiques and the bathrooms are modern. Caroline can organise local bike hire and delivery.

In a little-visited but lovely area of the Cotswolds, this attractive long stone house sits in splendid, peaceful isolation. Lovely high windows in the central part give onto the views and from the bright green-painted conservatory you can admire the garden that the Barrys have so lovingly tended. Inside, the decor is fresh - so are the flowers - the furniture and books old, the delightful owners happy and proud to have you in their home. Beds are incredibly comfortable with excellent sheets and pillows.

Rooms: 1 twin and 1 double, both en suite (bath and shower).

Rooms: 1 double, en suite (bath); 1 twin and 1 double sharing bathroom.

Price: £24-£35 p.p. Sing supp. £10.

Price: £29-£32 p.p. Single supp. by arrangement.

Breakfast: Flexible.

Breakfast: 8-9am.

Meals: Excellent pub nearby.

Meals: Excellent pubs nearby.

Closed: December & January.

Closed: Christmas, New Year & Easter.

South through village from A417. Turn right after Masons Arms. House is 200m on left.

From Cirencester A417 towards Lechlade. At Meysey Hampton crossroads left to Sun Hill. After 1 mile left at cottage. Hampton Fields is 400 yards down drive.

Map Ref No: 4

Map Ref No: 4

Roger & Caroline Carne
The Old Rectory
Meysey Hampton
Nr. Cirencester
Gloucestershire GL7 5JX
Tel: 01285 851200
Fax: 01285 850452

Richard & Jill Barry
Hampton Fields
Meysey Hampton
Cirencester
Gloucestershire GL7 5JL
Tel: 01285 850070
Fax: 01285 850070

A fine Elizabethan coaching inn in a sleepy Cotswold village, it is far, far from the 'pseudo-inn-chain' style. This is old-fashioned hospitality at its best. The New Inn is Brian and Sandra-Anne's life - you sense this in their relaxed, personal welcome. They and their staff take the time to talk you through a local walk, the ales on tap, the wonderful menu. Chef Stephen Morey's food is "divine". All the bedrooms are different - a four-poster here, a half-tester there, a romantic floral theme brilliantly developed; she is an interior designer, he a charming ex-publisher.

Rooms: 1 twin, 1 single, 2 twins/doubles and 10 doubles, all en suite.

Price: Twins/doubles £93-£110 per room; single £65.

Breakfast: 8-9.30am.

Meals: Dinner, 2 courses, £23.50 p.p.; 3 courses, £26.50 p.p.

Closed: Never!

The large lake at the side of the house is at windowsill level, giving you a strange feeling of being underwater! The lake, the mill race and Judy - who's down-to-earth and friendly - make this place special. The independent will like having their own wing and front door. Bedrooms are newly and simply decorated and have modern furniture. With lots of space to sit outside, hills to climb and a genuinely warm welcome from Judy, you really should bring the family.

Rooms: 1 twin/double (extra single if needed) and 1 twin, both en suite (shower).

Price: £19-£22 p.p. Single supp. £3-£6.

Breakfast: Flexible.

Meals: Good pubs nearby.

Closed: Christmas Day.

Leave A40 soon after Burford, taking B4425 towards Bibury. Turn left, after Aldsworth, to Coln St-Aldwyns.

Map Ref No: 4

Brian & Sandra-Anne Evans
The New Inn at Coln
Coln St-Aldwyns
Nr. Cirencester
Gloucestershire GL7 5AN
Tel: 01285 750651
Fax: 01285 750657
e-mail: stay@new-inn.co.uk

From Stroud take A46 towards Bath. After 2 miles turn right to North Woodchester then 2nd left, down the hill, sharp right up short drive.

Map Ref No: 9

Mrs Judy Sutch
Southfield Mill
Southfield Road
Woodchester, Nr. Stroud
Gloucestershire GL5 5PA
Tel: 01453 872896
Fax: 01452 872896

American sculptress Carol settled in this historic wool town and restored the 15th-century listed house with gusto. Her sure touch has unleashed all its ancient beauty. The Jacobean staircases and the huge stone fireplace, the mellow Cotswold stone, the colours and Carol's vibrancy are intoxicating. Themed rooms have been created with huge flair. You can dine by an open fire *and* there's a Thai restaurant. *Children over 9 welcome.*

Rooms: 1 huge 4-poster family room, en suite (bath); 2 doubles/triples with 4-posters, en suite (shower); 3 4-posters, all en suite (shower) and 1 deluxe 4-poster room with open fire.

Price: £27.50-£45 p.p. Single supp. £15.

Breakfast: Usually 8-9.30am.

Meals: Dinner, 4-course set menu Thai meal, £16.50 p.p.

Closed: Christmas Eve & Day.

A46 from Stroud to Cheltenham. In Painswick go past churchyard then 1st right (Victoria St). Turn left at top, March Hare rest. straight ahead, house round left hand corner.

Map Ref No: 9

Carol Keyes
Cardynham House
The Cross
Painswick
Gloucestershire GL6 6XA
Tel: 01452 814006
Fax: 01452 812321

A superb Grade I listed house, without pretension to modern luxury, in a fascinating village. The family has lived at Frampton since the 11th century. The house speaks the elegant language of Vanburgh, is beautifully crafted (do study the stonework outside, the carving and panelling inside) and has a Strawberry Hill Gothic orangery (self-catering). Choose between two large rooms: one with Flemish tapestry, double-tester bed with hand-embroidered curtains and own dressing-room; the other a twin with views, antiques and panelling. Dutch ornamental canal, water lilies, lake, superb views... gorgeous!

Rooms: 1 double, en suite, 1 double with tester bed with dressing room and single bed.

Price: £40 p.p.

Breakfast: Flexible.

Meals: Good restaurant opposite & 2 pubs on the village green.

Closed: Never!

From M5 junction 13 west, then B4071. Turn left through village green, then just look to the left! Entrance is between two large chestnut trees 200 yds on left, behind long brick wall.

Map Ref No: 9

Mrs Henriette Clifford
Frampton Court
Frampton-on-Severn
Gloucestershire GL2 7EU
Tel: 01452 740267

Frampton is special, its elongated village green (the longest in England?) flanked by a goodly lesson in English architecture-through-the-ages, duck ponds and a tiny cricket pitch. The Old School House is built of warm Frampton brick and Carol's welcome is just as warm. The large rooms are pleasing to look at, the garden is full of colour, the world outside consists of fields and footpaths. A restful stay is guaranteed. *Children over 10 welcome.*

Rooms: 2 twins, both en suite (bath and shower).

Price: £25 p.p. No single supp.

Breakfast: Until 9am.

Meals: No, but locally available.

Closed: 21 December-1 January

Petrina is a natural and imaginative cook. Eating here is something special; both she and James thrive on the bustle and conversation of guests, young and old. You'll feel at ease - very early risers can help themselves to tea and coffee, having let the dogs out! Bedrooms are large and airy; the beds are huge. Large gardens with rolling lawns and sweeping views - an attractive and elegant house (since this photo it's had its beard shaved and now sports a v. smart Georgian porch) with a real sense of fun. Petrina loves young children.

Rooms: 2 king-size/twins: 1 en suite (sep. shower & w.c.) and 1 with adj. bathroom shared with 1 double (good for families).

Price: £25-£30 p.p. Single supp. by arrangement.

Breakfast: Flexible.

Meals: Dinner £17.50 p.p. Gourmet dinner £22.50 p.p.

Closed: Never!

From A38 turn west onto B4071. Take first left, drive the length of village green. 300 yards after it finishes, right into Whittles Lane. House is the last on right.

Map Ref No: 9

Carol Alexander
The Old School House
Whittles Lane
Frampton-on-Severn
Gloucestershire GL2 7EB
Tel: 01452 740457
Fax: 01452 740457

Take A40 from Gloucester towards Ross-on-Wye, then B4215 towards Highnam. 2 miles on left is Whitehall Lane. House is approx. 0.5 miles down lane on right behind laurel hedge.

Map Ref No: 9

James & Petrina Pugh
Whitelands
Whitehall Lane
Rudford
Gloucestershire GL2 8ED
Tel: 01452 790406
Fax: 01452 790676

Sit on the terrace - which is candlelit in the evenings - and take in the views of undulating hills and vineyards. Michael and Jo will bring you a glass of wine and supper. They are genuine, kind and so settled into their corner of England that you will relax immediately. Michael loves old cars - the Puma racing car was made right here - and is a guide at the vineyard. He also delivers organic bread to the neighbours. Jo makes excellent flapjacks and caters for special diets. The pretty and immaculate bedrooms are in a converted grain barn and have a soaring A-frame ceiling. You'll be very comfortable.

Rooms: 1 twin, en suite (bath), 1 double with private bath/shower. In cottage, 1 twin.

Price: £25 p.p. No single supp.

Breakfast: Flexible.

Meals: Dinner, 3 courses, inc. glass of wine, £15 p p. Snack from £5 p.p.

Closed: Never!

A magnificent Georgian manor in 15 acres, a delightful marriage of the formal and the wild, with mill and dovecote recorded in the Domesday Book. The two-acre lake is always active with visiting and resident wild-fowl. Life here is elegant, comfortable and peaceful. The delightful owners have filled the house with gorgeous things. It stands behind the parish church. An excellent pub is a two-minute walk up the lane and there are attractive self-catering cottages in the old coaching yard.

Rooms: 4 four-posters, all en suite (1 with shower, 1 with bath and shower and 2 with bath); 1 twin and 1 twin/double, both en suite (bath).

Price: £37.50-£47.50 p.p. Single occ. up to £65.

Breakfast: 8.30-9.45am, or by arrangement.

Meals: Dinner, from £25 p.p., by arrangement.

Closed: Christmas.

A40 from Gloucester to Ross-on-Wye, right onto B4215 signed Newent. After 7 miles, take last right before M50 (signed Dymock). Right after 3 Choirs Vineyard, house 1 mile on right.

Map Ref No: 9

Jo & Michael Kingham
The Old Winery
Welsh House Lane
Newent
Gloucestershire GL18 1LR
Tel: 01531 890824

A435 north from Cheltenham, then B4079. About 1 mile after A438 crossroads, sign to Kemerton on right. Leave road at War Memorial. House is behind parish church.

Map Ref No: 9

Bill & Diana Herford
Upper Court
Kemerton
Tewkesbury
Gloucestershire GL20 7HY
Tel: 01386 725351
Fax: 01386 725472

Tucked away at the end of a lane opposite an 11th-century church, this idyllic spot has as its backdrop the Cotswold hills. A heavily-laden mulberry tree gives fruit at summer's end for breakfast served in the dining room, which has a palpable Georgian elegance and a blazing log fire on cold days. This is a period house to which the glossiest magazine couldn't do justice. What's more there are many walks that start from the house; Liz will give you maps and a picnic. A period self-catering cottage with log fires and wonderful walled garden also available. *Children over 8 welcome.*

Rooms: 5 doubles, 1 twin and 2 family rooms. 6 bedrooms are en suite and 2 have private bathrooms.

Price: From £32.50 p.p. Cottage, sleeps 4 + cot, from £300 per week.

Breakfast: Between 8.15-9.15 am.

Meals: Available locally, or supper trays in winter. Packed lunch also available.

Closed: 22-27 December.

Immediately enticing, this stunning 1435 townhouse will engage all your senses; delicious aromas float from the restaurant kitchen, wonderful views hold the eye and real warmth envelops you. A wrought-iron spiral staircase disappears through the beamed ceiling and leads to the cosy rooms - one has its own terrace overlooking rooftops in the town. More beamed ceilings, leaded windows, exposed walls and firm beds: you'll relish the idea of retreating here after dinner. *Children over 7 welcome.*

Rooms: 5 doubles, all en suite (shower).

Price: £37.50 p.p. No single supp.

Breakfast: Until 10am.

Meals: Dinner, 3 courses, £28.50 p.p.; lunch, 3 courses, £16.50 p.p.

Closed: 14 January-10 February.

From Broadway take B4632 (Stratford road) for 1.5 miles. At Willersey right into Church Street. The Old Rectory is at end of lane opposite church. Car park at the rear of the house.

Map Ref No: 9

Mrs Liz Beauvoisin
The Old Rectory
Church Street
Willersey, Broadway
Gloucestershire WR12 7PN
Tel: 01386 853729
Fax: 01386 858061
e-mail: beauvoisin@btinternet.com

From Cheltenham take B4632 to Winchcombe. Wesley House is on the High Street.

Map Ref No: 9

Matthew Brown
Wesley House
High Street
Winchcombe
Gloucestershire GL54 5LJ
Tel: 01242 602366
Fax: 01242 602405

Clapton is, indeed, perched high on a hill and the views beyond the walled garden are magnificent. This 16th- and 17th-century manor house has a flagstoned hall, huge fireplaces, sit-in inglenooks and Cotswold stone mullioned windows. One of the bedrooms has a secret door that leads to a stunning, surprising fuchsia-pink bathroom. The other is smaller with garden views. Homemade jams for breakfast, which can be eaten outside in fine weather.

Rooms: 1 double, en suite (bath/shower); 1 twin/double, en suite (bath).

Price: £28 p.p. Single supp. £15.

Breakfast: Usually 8-9.30am.

Meals: Menus available for local pubs & restaurants.

Closed: Christmas.

In one of the most tourist-visited villages in England but away from the hubbub, this B&B is a welcome harbour. The house is repro. Cotswolds, the furnishing pretty and unfussy as is the garden - Diana is an avid gardener who talks to her plants. There's a roof terrace for an evening drink with a view (Coombe is licensed); rooms are smallish with superb new beds. Your hosts care for their guests to the extent of applying an 11pm closing time so that sleep is guaranteed for all, and a daytime exeat of 10.30-4pm so that you don't miss any of the local treasures.

Rooms: 4 doubles and 2 twins, all en suite; 1 double with private bath.

Price: £31-£38 p.p. Single occ. £48.

Breakfast: From 8-8.40am.

Meals: Available locally.

Closed: Christmas Eve, Christmas Day, & New Year's Eve.

From Cirencester, A429 towards Stow. Turn right at Bourton Lodge Hotel, signed Clapton. Follow signs. In village, down hill and left at green-doored 3-storey house. Manor is left of the church.

Map Ref No: 10

Karin & James Bolton
Clapton Manor
Clapton-on-the-Hill
Nr. Bourton-on-the-Water
Gloucestershire GL54 2LG
Tel: 01451 810202
Fax: 01451 821804

From the centre of Bourton the model village is on your left and Birdland is on your right. Coombe House is 400 yards further on the left.

Map Ref No: 10

Diana & Graham Ellis
Coombe House
Rissington Road
Bourton-on-the-Water
Gloucestershire GL54 2DT
Tel: 01451 821966
Fax: 01451 810477

The owners call it "a townhouse in the country". It is a Victorian manor whose Englishness is lightly spiced with a North American touch in the decor. Bedrooms are large and two look across the wide Dikler valley, green as far as the eye can see. You can walk for miles and come back for a sauna or, in summer, a swim. The house is renowned for its home-baked bread and Frank can also organise personally-guided tours of famous local gardens. You really feel nothing is too much trouble. *Children over 12 welcome.*

Rooms: 1 queen-size, 2 doubles and 1 king-size, all en suite (2 with bath/shower, 1 with bath and 1 with shower).

Price: £34 p.p. Single supp. £10.

Breakfast: 8-10am.

Meals: Dinner, £25 p.p., by arrangement.

Closed: January.

The house was originally a church on the site of an extinct medieval village mentioned in the Domesday Book and converted in 1610 with Georgian additions. (Moseley and Mitford hid here during the war.) The gardens are glorious, with a lake and wonderful views. The hall and ground floor are stone-flagged with rugs laid on top for colour and there are delightful touches of exotica everywhere. One bedroom is massive, with bathroom across the corridor. A wonderful place; John and Camilla are easy-going and entertaining. Our inspector didn't want to come home. *Children over 7 welcome.*

Rooms: 2 doubles, both en suite (bath). 1 single with private bathroom.

Price: £38 p.p.

Breakfast: Until 9.30am.

Meals: Supper by arrangement. Food also available at fantastic local pub or nearby restaurant.

Closed: Never!

From Stow take B4068 to Lower Swell. House is on left, driveway entrance opposite Unicorn Hotel.

Map Ref No: 10

Frank Simonetti
Crestow House
Lower Swell
Stow-on-the-Wold
Gloucestershire GL54 1JX
Tel: 01451 830969
Fax: 01451 832129
e-mail: fjsimon@compuserve.com

4 miles north of Moreton-in-Marsh on A429 turn left to Aston Magna. At church turn immediately right & Neighbrook is 0.75 miles on the right.

Map Ref No: 10

John & Camilla Playfair
Neighbrook
Aston Magna
Moreton-in-Marsh
Gloucestershire GL56 9QP
Tel: 01386 593232
Fax: 01386 593500

It's homely and comforting, yet stylish, too. There's huge attention to detail and much to recommend the home of the Knotts, not least the captivating view up the stairs of a complex forest of beams, timber posts and bannisters. Interesting shapes everywhere, a split-level bathroom, honey-coloured stone windows with seats, tudor bricks and hand-made furniture crafted by Robin in his workshop. You'll feel at ease with this small family.

Rooms: 2 doubles, 1 en suite (bath) and 1 with private bathroom.

Price: £25 p.p. (less for longer stays). Single supp. £5.

Breakfast: Flexible.

Meals: Available at acclaimed Churchill across the road.

Closed: Christmas & New Year.

In centre of Paxford opposite church.

Map Ref No: 10

Lisa & Robin Knott
Wells Farmhouse
Paxford
Chipping Campden
Gloucestershire GL55 6XH
Tel: 01386 593429

It seems that all local roads lead to the Churchill Arms. Everyone seems to have been there, eaten there - and been thoroughly impressed. There is something genuine about the place. It is owner-managed, staff are natural and friendly and the food is of high quality - not as formal (or expensive) as its sister restaurant in Moreton, the Marsh Goose. The bedrooms are compact and well designed, with shiny little bathrooms slotted into limited space. The feeling here is lively and fun, and those looking for sustenance are given as much personal attention as demand allows.

Rooms: 2 doubles, en suite (bath/shower) and 2 twins/doubles, en suite (bath).

Price: £30 p.p. Single supp £10.

Breakfast: Flexible.

Meals: Dinner £20 p.p. Lunch £12 p.p.

Closed: Christmas Day.

From Moreton in the Marsh, take A44 towards Worcester/Evesham. Through Bourton-on-the-Hill, take right at end to Paxford. Straight through Brockley, over railway track and tiny bridge into Paxford and Inn is in village on right.

Map Ref No: 10

Sonia Kidney & Leo Brooke-Little
The Churchill Inn
Paxford
Chipping Campden
Gloucestershire GL55 6XH
Tel: 01386 594000
Fax: 01386 594005

Fascinating conjecture: the Kettle may be the oldest continuous business premises in Britain. The Kettle refers to the Blacksmith's trade, but it has been a coaching inn, brewery, grocer's and pottery. Susie now runs an antiques shop downstairs and the mood is set by stripped wooden doors, coir carpets, beams, leaded windows and white linen. Guests go through a little alleyway and up an iron staircase onto a platform that overlooks Cotswold rooftops to the church. You could almost be in France. You can breakfast on the platform and there's a dear little sitting room too.

Rooms: 2 doubles, en suite (shower), 2 twins sharing bathroom. Guests share sitting room.

Price: £25 p.p. Single occ. £27.50.

Breakfast: Until 9am (week). Until 10am (weekend).

Meals: Not available, but plenty of excellent restaurants nearby.

Closed: Mid-January-mid-February.

Take A44 (Oxford-Evesham Rd). Turn off to B4018 for Chipping Campden, approx. 2 miles. The house is at the top of the village on the right-hand side heading towards Stratford-on-Avon.

Map Ref No: 10

Charles & Susie Holdsworth-Hunt
The Kettle
High Street
Chipping Campden
Gloucestershire GL55 6HN
Tel: 01386 840328
Fax: 01386 841740
e-mail: bed&breakfast@kettlehouse.co.uk

Lindy and Tony have transformed their 200-year-old barn into a light and sunny space, kept simple with plain walls and seagrass flooring. Moroccan rugs, antiques, and a wood-burning stove add warmth and theatre to the drawing room. Lindy, who speaks French, organises garden tours and the bookshelves reflect her interest in garden design. Visitors can unwind in the peace of the terrace overlooking her own flower-laden garden and the cornfields beyond, play a round of croquet or fish in the trout/duck pond (rare breeds). *Children over 12 welcome. Golf and fishing nearby.*

Rooms: 1 double, en suite (shower) and 1 twin with private bathroom.

Price: Double £30 p.p. Twin £25 p.p. Single supp. £8-£10.

Breakfast: Flexible.

Meals: Good food available locally.

Closed: Christmas & New Year.

Hampshire & Isle of Wight

From Salisbury, A354 towards Blandford, through Coombe Bissett. After 1.5 miles, left on bend to Rockbourne. There, 200 yards after 30 mph zone, house drive signed to left. After 50 yards take right fork to house.

Map Ref No: 4

Lindy & Tony Ball
Marsh Barn
Rockbourne
Fordingbridge
Hampshire SP6 3NF
Tel: 01725 518768
Fax: 01725 518380

The warmth of Carole Hayles's welcome is matched by the lushness of the stunning garden with its weeping willow and rhododendrons. There are two aging spaniels, two cats, welcome signs on the door knobs, sherry decanters and lots of china. Comfortable bedrooms are full of little extras, with lots of minute detail. You can walk across a buttercup meadow into 15 miles of unspoilt New Forest. Or you could hire a bike (or stable your horse), play golf on the local course, fish in the lakes, sail on the Solent or relax on the sandy beaches only 15 minutes away.

Rooms: 2 doubles, en suite (shower); 1 double, en suite (bath).

Price: £25-£28 p.p. Single supp. £5.

Breakfast: Until 9am.

Meals: Dinner £15 p.p. by arrangement.

Closed: Christmas.

It was built for Siemens in 1897 to be the most luxurious house on the South Coast; a fortune was lavished on the wood alone. It is still vibrant with oak and exquisite stained glass. The Mechems, generous and open-minded, deserve this magnificent house. What else could they do to make it unforgettable? Well, there are exemplary bedrooms, six of which look out to sea and the Isle of Wight. The whole place indulges you in massive luxury; a first-floor conservatory, wonderful food, an unexpected family atmosphere, some modern art. Only 200 yards from the beach, it is uplifting - and remarkable.

Rooms: 15, all en suite (bath), 6 have sea views.

Price: £55-£65 p.p. Dinner, B&B £70-£85 p.p.

Breakfast: 7.30-9am.

Meals: Dinner £23.50 p.p. Light Italian lunches £3.50-£10 p.p.

Closed: Never!

From London, M3, then M27 and A31. Burley is signed approx. 5 miles before Ringwood. In centre of Burley take right into Pound Lane. Large sign at top of drive.

Map Ref No: 4

Carol Hayles
Burbush Farm
Pound Lane
Burley, Nr. Ringwood
Hampshire BH24 4EF
Tel: 01425 403238
Fax: 01425 403238

From Lyminghton take signs for Milford-on-Sea (B3058), turn right along Park Lane in village, house on left up hill.

Map Ref No: 4

Nicola & Stewart Mechem
Westover Hall
Park Lane
Milford-on-Sea, Lymington
Hampshire SO41 0PJ
Tel: 01590 643044
Fax: 01590 644490

In a quiet cul-de-sac, this elegant house is only five minutes' walk from the Quay and the centre of Lymington; coach and train stations are both within easy walking distance, too. It is easy to explore the ancient beauty of the New Forest from here. The huge drawing room has five large windows and overlooks lawns and herbaceous borders; in the garden there's a heated swimming pool for summer use. Bedrooms are large and well furnished. Self-contained one-bedroom flat on first floor of house with garden views also available. *Children over 12 welcome.*

Rooms: 1 double and 1 twin, both en suite (bath). 1 single, en suite (shower). Self-catering flat.

Price: £25-£29 p.p. Flat from £175-£245 per week, all inclusive

Breakfast: Between 8-9am, unless by prior arrangement.

Meals: Good restaurants & pubs within walking distance.

Closed: Christmas & New Year.

Beware the bear in the corner if you pass in the dark. He is just one of the antiques and heirlooms that fill this elegantly-proportioned Edwardian townhouse. There are ancestors and a rocking horse too. The Jeffcocks are cultured, travelled and welcoming. A perfect central position for visiting pretty Beaulieu and the New Forest.

Rooms: 1 double en suite (shower). 1 double with private bathroom. 1 single sharing bathroom with owners.

Price: £24 p.p.

Breakfast: Flexible.

Meals: Available nearby.

Closed: Christmas & New Year.

Jan will send a map when you book, along with instructions on how to avoid Lyndhurst which can be a bottleneck in high season.

Map Ref No: 4

From Brockenhurst take the A337. Continue into Lymington. At lights on corner of Southampton Road and Avenue Road turn right into Avenue Road. There is a short drive, first left.

Map Ref No: 4

Jan Messenger
Mulberries
6 West Hayes
Lymington
Hampshire SO41 3RL
Tel: 01590 679549

Josephine and David Jeffcock
40 Southampton Road
Lymington
Hampshire SO41 9GG
Tel: 01590 672237
Fax: 01590 673592

One of the best. A beautiful old house, full of history, with panelling, antiques, nooks and crannies, odd steps and low corners living in partnership with gardens that lead into each other from terrace to lawn to apple orchard to lily pond. A Victorian dining room balances a silvery damask and turquoise sitting room. Great bedrooms too. Anthea is a dynamo doing B&B for the fun of it... and to pay for ever better furnishings.

Rooms: 3 twins/doubles: 1 en suite and 2 with separate, private bathrooms.

Price: £23-25 p.p. Single supp. £10.

Breakfast: Flexible.

Meals: Dinner £15 p.p. Mon-Thurs.

Closed: Christmas & New Year.

You can't see the join! - between the Victorian schoolhouse and the well-designed additions, invisibly united within the period original. Through the arched wooden door is the big hallway and an instantly welcoming sense of family life. And it gets better. The kitchen is a pure country-life retreat, all old oak and terracotta, the nerve centre of the vivacious Susie's cooking and entertaining - plainly a matter of great pride to her. The garden is expansive, with croquet lawn where two adorable dogs rumble and play. One word summed up this house for our inspector: "sublime".

Rooms: 1 double and 1 twin, each with private bathroom.

Price: £23 p.p. Single occ. £25.

Breakfast: Flexible.

Meals: Dinner, 3 courses, £16 p.p. by arrangement.

Closed: Never!

Between Romsey and White Parish on the A27, 0.75 miles from the Romsey turning towards Salisbury. The driveway to the house is directly off the A27.

Map Ref No: 4

Anthea & Bill Hughes
Spursholt House
Salisbury Road
Romsey
Hampshire SO51 6DJ
Tel: 01794 512229
Fax: 01794 523142

M3, exit 9, take A272 to Petersfield. After 2 miles fork right to Warnford and Preshaw, over crossroads. House is 2nd on left after 300 yards.

Map Ref No: 4

Susie & Christopher Church
The Old School House
Lane End
Longwood, Nr. Winchester
Hampshire SO21 1JZ
Tel: 01962 777248
Fax: 01962 777744

Design flair and high standards in an easy atmosphere... a rare find. Every tiny detail has been thought of, exquisitely. Old wooden floors and tables in the Bistro, big wooden windows onto the lovely garden (*al fresco* dining in summer), a mirrored champagne bar in gold and blue, sweeping expanses of cream walls hung with prints and oils, and some very handsome furniture. In the bedrooms: power showers, deep baths, decor such as coloured cushions on white bedspreads... all perfect. Good food and the best wines. Nice staff, too, and perfect peace in the garden rooms.

Rooms: 22 doubles, en suite (bath). 1 double, en suite (shower).

Price: Room rate from £85-£115. Suite: £165 per night.

Breakfast: 7-9.30am (week), 8-10am (weekend) £6.50-£9.50 p.p.

Meals: Lunch & dinner, 3 courses & bottle of house wine, approx. £30 p.p. in Bistro.

Closed: Never!

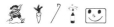

In the heart of medieval Winchester, this beautifully converted Victorian guardhouse is distinctly more welcoming than it once was. Visitors can satisfy both spiritual and secular needs, being close to the Cathedral and Water Meadows, and right next door to the superb restaurant of the Hotel du Vin. The style is bright and uncluttered, with wooden floors, and guests eat breakfast at a long, communal table, seated on an old church pew. The two guest rooms are elegantly furnished, each with a power shower; one has French windows onto a private, flower-filled courtyard. *Children over 12 welcome.*

Rooms: 1 twin, en suite (shower); 1 twin with private shower.

Price: £30 p.p. Single supp. £20.

Breakfast: Flexible.

Meals: Many restaurants in Winchester, and one next door!

Closed: Christmas.

From M3 jct 11 signed Winchester South. At first roundabout follow signs to St Cross & Winchester. After 2 miles Hotel du Vin is on the left.

Map Ref No: 4

Michael Warren
Hotel du Vin and Bistro
Southgate Street
Winchester
Hampshire SO23 9EF
Tel: 01962 841414
Fax: 01962 842458
admin@winchester.hotelduvin.col.uk

M3, junction 11, signed to St. Cross/Winchester. St. Cross Rd becomes Southgate St. House on left just past church at entrance to Archery Lane.

Map Ref No: 4

Mary & Andrew Dolman
The Guard House
Southgate Street
Winchester
Hampshire SO23 9EF
Tel: 01962 861514

Luxuriating in your wonderful bedroom, you might think you're in a five-star hotel. But this is a Georgian coaching inn run with an unerring sense of hospitality. The inn has two bars dripping with 'collectables', a restaurant and a pretty, not prissy, breakfast room. Then, across the narrow Cathedral-shaded street is a medieval townhouse with your own post office, classy 'corner shop' leading to a plump-chaired, log-fired 'snug' then into a courtyard. Above, more rooms of quality and character. Menus are inviting. Excellent value.

Rooms: 1 single, 3 twins, 1 suite and 8 doubles, all en suite.

Price: £45-£117.50.

Breakfast: 7.30-9am (week); 8-10am (weekend).

Meals: Dinner, 2-courses, from £13 p.p. Lunch £5-£7 p.p. Packed lunch by arrangement.

Closed: Christmas Day.

Privacy in a B&B is rare. Here you have it, just 12 minutes walk from the centre of town, Cathedral and water meadows, in your own half of a Victorian townhouse beautifully furnished and decorated and immensely welcoming. Fizzy serves sumptuous breakfasts (she is Constance Spry trained) and keeps the flowers fresh. You are also left with an 'honesty box' so you may help yourselves to drinks. The rooms are small and cosy and there is a log fire in the sitting room. *Children over 7 welcome.*

Rooms: 1 twin and 1 double, both en suite (shower & bath).

Price: £22.50-£25 p.p. Single occ. £40.

Breakfast: Flexible.

Meals: Available nearby.

Closed: Christmas.

Immediately south of Cathedral between Winchester College and Cathedral. Access via south gate, Canon Street.

Map Ref No: 4

Timothy Manktelow-Gray
The Wykeham Arms
75 Kingsgate Street
Winchester
Hampshire SO23 9PE
Tel: 01962 853834
Fax: 01962 854411

Leave M3 at junction 9 and follow signs for Winchester Park & Ride. Under motorway, straight on at roundabout signed to St. Cross. Left at T-junction. St. Faith's Road about 200m ahead.

Map Ref No: 4

Guy & Fizzy Warren
Brymer House
29/30 St. Faith's Road
St. Cross, Winchester
Hampshire SO23 9QD
Tel: 01962 867428
Fax: 01962 868624

Scarcely a cottage! A good big English house built about 250 years ago in a sensational six-acre English garden which boasts a trout stream, lake and a collection of unusual shrubs. Patsy and Richard work together as garden designers. The guestrooms have all been re-done so everything is fresh and immaculate. It is all light and airy, richly carpeted and very well decorated. The Masons will collect you from the airport, organise hire cars and light summer barbecues.

Rooms: 1 double and 1 twin/double, both en suite (shower); 1 twin with private bathroom.

Price: £20-£40 p.p.

Breakfast: Flexible.

Meals. Evening barbecues - weather permitting.

Closed: Never!

A once-plain cottage transformed by designer Julie into a very special place in its superb setting by a tributary of the River Test. The blue-green flash of kingfisher tells you this is an unspoiled river. Julie has come to know it and its fish. Friends and neighbours (one and the same!) include gillies with whom she can arrange a day's fishing. The cottage now sparkles with her taste and imagination - flowers, riverside terrace, comfortable, elegant bedrooms, all overlooking the river, two in what she calls 'The Bothy': smart, purpose-built, reed-thatched. A very special place.

Rooms: 1 twin with private bathroom, 1 double, en suite (shower) and 1 suite with bath and shower.

Price: £25 p.p. Single occ. £35-40.

Breakfast: Flexible.

Meals: Dinner £25 p.p. B.Y.O. wine. Special picnic £15 p.p. by arrangement.

Closed: Christmas & New Year.

From A303 take A3057 towards Stockbridge, then take 1st right and 1st left. Right at T-junction. Malt Cottage is at bottom of lane opposite Crook & Shears pub.

Map Ref No: 4

Patsy & Richard Mason
Malt Cottage
Upper Clatford
Andover
Hampshire SP11 7QL
Tel: 01264 323469
Fax: 01264 334100
maltcottage.accommodation@virgin.net

From Andover take A3057 towards Stockbridge. Turn right to Upper Clatford, about 5 minutes out of Andover. After farm on left, over white bridge, house on left.

Map Ref No: 4

Julie Maffe
Fishing Cottage
Upper Clatford
Andover
Hampshire SP11 7HB
Tel: 01264 364214
Fax: 01264 364214

Ada immediately feels like someone you've known forever and there's no standing on ceremony - just come and join in. The house is beguilingly, artistically disordered. Works of art are everywhere and portraits reveal some intriguing ancestry: the aunt who married George Bernard Shaw, the step-mother who wrote *The Far Pavilions*. The kitchen is a riot of belongings and pets; the large bedrooms are traditional. There are a few modern houses nearby but you are insulated by lawns, a lake and a tennis court. *Children over 12 welcome.*

Rooms: 1 twin with basin and private bathroom.

Price: £25 p.p. Single supp. £5.

Breakfast: Until 10am.

Meals: Good restaurants nearby.

Closed: Christmas.

From A30 at Hartley Witney, take A327 north to Eversley, go straight over roundabout. Left into Warbrook Lane, bear right at fork to Lower Common. After phone box, house on right with green conservatory.

Map Ref No: 5

Mrs Ada Dawnay
Fleet House
Eversley
Hampshire RG27 0QU
Tel: 0118 973 2130

A 400-year-old farmhouse, an unpretentious, practical place to stay... great for families who would enjoy splashing in the heated outdoor swimming pool (so rare for England) and for cyclists, for whom a lock-up is provided. Brick-and-beam hall, fat velvet chairs, log fire, big farmhouse kitchen with Aga and intriguing vaulted ceiling, Russell Flint prints, bright and cheerful rooms, three children, a hearty breakfast, glorious rolling downland countryside all around. The house sits end on to the nearby road so the bedrooms are quiet. Great value.

Rooms: 1 twin, en suite (bath) and 1 twin, en suite (shower); 1 twin with private bath.

Price: £17-£22.50 p.p. Single supp. by arrangement.

Breakfast: 7.30-9am (week); 8.30-9.30am (weekend).

Meals: Dinner £15 p.p. Packed lunch £3.50 p.p. Snack supper £3.50 p.p.

Closed: Never!

From M3 junct.5 take B3349 to South Warnborough. There, pass pub on left, go over x- roads and farmhouse is 50 yards on right, opposite phone box.

Map Ref No: 5

Colin & Wendy Turner
Street Farmhouse
The Street
South Warnborough, Hook
Hampshire RG29 1RS
Tel: 01256 862225
Fax: 01256 862225

Its quayside setting, wooden panelling, big fireplace and flagstoned hall make this 17th-century former Governor's residence an attractive base. All the big bedrooms are wood panelled, one with a huge four-poster and two with timber balconies and views out to sea. Meals can be served outside in the garden bar. You also eat well in the buzzy, cheerful yellow and wood Brasserie overlooking the garden, or in the sumptuous burgundy dining room. A very welcoming hotel and it shares a wall with the castle. Locals reckon The George has put the island back on the map.

Rooms: 15 twins/doubles and 1 single, all en suite (bath).

Price: £65-£85 p.p. Single supp. £25. Dinner, B&B rates available.

Breakfast: 8-10am (week); 8.30-10.30am (weekend).

Meals: Dinner £36.75 p.p. Brasserie à la carte from £17.50 p.p. Lunch available.

Closed: Never!

From Lymington ferry to Yarmouth. Follow signs to town centre.

Map Ref No: 4

Jackie Everest
The George
Yarmouth
Isle of Wight PO41 0PE
Tel: 01983 760331
Fax: 01983 760425

In the loveliest part of the island, with high ground, great walks on the Downs and in an Area Of Outstanding Natural Beauty. Newtown Nature Reserve is down the road too, with all its migrant birds and wild flowers. The house is lovely, next to the church. Guests are given a self-contained flat, which we confess to not having seen. But judging from the house itself it should be right for this book; apparently there is a mix of modern furniture and some old pieces. The very friendly Sheila takes in your breakfast: fresh fruit, free-range eggs, croissants, the full works.

Rooms: 1 self-contained flat with twin beds.

Price: £25 p.p. Single supp. £2.50.

Breakfast: Flexible.

Meals: Available locally.

Closed: Christmas Day.

From Yarmouth take road to Shalfleet through village. After 0.5 miles turn right for Calbourne. The house is by the church across the green.

Map Ref No: 4

Sheila & Oliver Mathews
The Old Rectory
Calbourne
Isle of Wight PO30 4JE
Tel: 01983 531247
Fax: 01983 531253

The Harrisons bought this stunning Jacobean pile for its matchless gardens: 15 acres of pathed wilderness, exotic and sub-tropical flowers. A stroll is an adventure; you come across an old swimming pool cascading with plants, a bench on a lofty vantage point, a crystal clear stream banked with bamboo, a smooth lawn, a walled garden, a sunken rose garden and a grass tennis court. The massive house has lovely rooms and acres of space, so much that it is hard to furnish fully without a small fortune to spend. Come to the Isle of Wight if only to see the garden.

Rooms: 3 doubles and 3 twins, en suite (bath).

Price: £20-£27.50 p.p. Single supp. £10.

Breakfast: 8-9.15am.

Meals: Light meals available if ordered in advance.

Closed: Christmas.

Coming from Newport drive into Shorwell, go down a steep hill, under a rustic bridge and turn right opposite a thatched cottage. Signed.

Map Ref No: 4

John & Christine Harrison
North Court
Shorwell
Isle of Wight PO30 3JG
Tel: 01983 740415
Fax: 01983 740409

The front is Georgian, the back Victorian. Inside, thick, thick walls and stone flags speak of a more ancient history. Valerie and Carol are active within the community and clearly content in their uncontrived home. The pretty, traditional bedrooms have marvellous views of the richly-wooded countryside. Their grandchildren are regular visitors: your children may share toys in the house and garden, and you also have your own large piece of the 2.5 acre garden and use of the tennis court. There's a small library; music appreciation is high on the agenda.

Rooms: 1 twin with private bath, shower & w.c.; 2 doubles sharing bathroom, shower & w.c.

Price: £18.50 p.p. From Easter '99, £20 p.p. Single supp. £1.50. Under 5s, £5; 5-12, £13.50.

Breakfast: Flexible.

Meals: Packed lunch on request.

Closed: Never!

Herefordshire

East on A40 from Ross-on-Wye towards Gloucester. Turn right to Hope Mansell & Pontshill. Take 3rd lane on left opposite Gallery. After 1 mile, house is on left between lane sign-posted 'village hall' and the church.

Map Ref No: 9

Mrs Carol Ouvry & Mrs Valerie Godson
The Old Rectory
Hope Mansell
Ross-on-Wye
Herefordshire HR9 5TL
Tel: 01989 750382
Fax: 01989 750382

Bill always remembers guests' names and looks after them well at dinner. Christine heads up the kitchen, using as much fresh, organic, local produce as possible. All the rooms are individual - "it's not a decorate-by-numbers hotel," says Christine. Fat beds, hand-crafted quilts, deep sofas and fluffy towels; this feels like a cross between one's own dream sitting room and a good London club. The centre of the house is early Georgian, the wings Victorian, the central semi-circular sweeping staircase sensational. Views to Ross over the wooded valley revive the spirit.

Rooms: 6 doubles and 1 single, all en suite (bath and/or shower).

Price: £33-£50 p.p. Single supp. £15. Ask for bargain break discounts.

Breakfast: Until 9.45am.

Meals: Dinner in restaurant approx. £25 p.p. Bar Bistro menu £2.95-£12.75.

Closed: 25-27 December.

The Knights Templar, then the Knights of St John, once owned Garway church; it is a Norman gem. The house is late Victorian and filled with warmth and charm, with a long plank table at which to eat Aga-cooked breakfasts and dinners. There are fine views from both house and garden across the Monnow Valley to the Brecon Beacons and the Black Mountains. Somehow, the tranquillity and assurance of the church have communicated themselves to this house. *Children over 8 welcome.*

Rooms: 1 double (four-poster) and 1 twin, each with basin, sharing bathroom. Separate shower & w.c.

Price: £20-£22.50 p.p. Single supp. £5-£10.

Breakfast: Until 9.30am.

Meals: Dinner £16 p.p. by prior arrangement.

Closed: Never!

From the A40 Ross-Monmouth road, take A4137 and turn at sign for Glewstone. Hotel signed on right in hamlet.

Map Ref No: 9

Christine & William Reeve-Tucker
Glewstone Court
Glewstone
Ross-on-Wye
Herefordshire HR9 6AW
Tel: 01989 770367
Fax: 01989 770282

A466 towards Monmouth. After 7 miles, B4521 towards Abergavenney. At Broad Oak, right towards Garway. First right past school, signposted Garway Hill. Old Rectory is 150 yards on right.

Map Ref No: 9

Caroline Ailesbury
The Old Rectory
Garway
Herefordshire HR2 8RH
Tel: 01600 750363
Fax: 01600 750364

An authentic old longhouse that looks as if its builders dismantled HMS Victory - so many ancient oak beams, panels and stairs, such an overwhelming sense of history. It is homely and full of space - the kitchen was the dairy - neither grand nor stuffy. Antony makes his own bread and marmalade! He adds a gentlemanly, ex-army elegance, and is kind and easy-going too. There's a happy yellow labrador to match. Inside, there is an African mood for one guestroom; elsewhere, it's old oil paintings, portraits, books and inglenook fireplace. Outside, there are ducks, geese, chickens and guinea fowl. It is robust, unaffected - come not to be spoiled but to enjoy the experience.

Rooms: 2 doubles and 1 single, sharing bathroom.

Price: £18-£20 p.p.

Breakfast: Flexible.

Meals: Available locally.

Closed: Never!

From Abergavenny, take Hereford road (A465). Left (signed Longtown) after 5 miles. Fork right at entrance to Longtown at sign with no arms. After 2.5 miles, house signed on left on low stone wall. House 600 yards up drive.

Map Ref No: 9

Antony Egremont-Lee
Middle Trewern
Longtown
Herefordshire HR2 0LN
Tel: 01873 860670

Such an unusual place, miles from nowhere on the Welsh borders. Built in the 17th century as a grain barn, lovingly renovated with weatherboarding and stone tiling, it has a vast open threshing bay which frames the woods and hills like an old-time idyll of rural England. The double-aspect dining room is above this bay. The cattle byres round the yard, perfect in their ancient curviness, house the conservatory/greenhouse where guests sit. The bedrooms have simple modern furniture and share a small shower-room. Honest value and superb views.

Rooms: 1 family room (double and a single) and 1 single, sharing shower & w.c.

Price: £18 p.p. Children under 12 £14.

Breakfast: Until 8.30am unless by special arrangement.

Meals: Dinner £12 p.p. B.Y.O. wine. Packed lunch also available.

Closed: Never!

Take B4350 from Hay to Clifford. Pass Castle & turn right to Bredwardine. Take third left at top of hill. Pass between chapel & small playing field. Castleton Barn is ahead on right.

Map Ref No: 9

Ann & Ron Tong
Castleton Barn
Clifford
Nr. Hay-on-Wye
Herefordshire HR3 5HF
Tel: 01497 831690

The staircase, mentioned in Pevsner's Guide to Historic Houses, is 17th-century. Most of the house was built in 1520 and is breath-taking in its ancient dignity, its undulating floors, two-foot thick walls and great oak beams sagging under the weight of Jackie's cup collection. Take a book from the small library and settle into a window seat looking over the gardens. There is a guest sitting room, too, festooned with work by local artists. Candles feature all over the house. The two beamed and four-postered bedrooms verge on the luxurious; so does the other one. Gorgeous.

Rooms: 1 double, en suite (bath), 1 four-poster with private adjacent bathroom and 1 suite with kingsize four-poster, en suite (bath).

Price: Double £23.50 p.p. Four-poster £24.50 p.p. Suite £32 p.p. Single supp. £15.

Breakfast: Until 10am.

Meals: Available locally.

Closed: Christmas.

From Hereford, A438 into village. House on left with a large green sign and iron gates.

Map Ref No: 9

Jackie Kingdon
Winforton Court
Winforton
Herefordshire HR3 6EA
Tel: 01544 328498

Deep in the middle of nowhere, this is an unpretentious, modernised mill house. Rooms are small and cosy, with exposed beams and slate window sills, and only the old mill itself interrupts the view of the surrounding greenness. Best of all, though, is sinking into downy sleep to the sound of the Arrow River burbling away - a real tonic for frazzled city-dwellers. Grace is chatty and informal and though guests have the run of the cottage the lovely kitchen tends to be the gravitational centre of this home.

Rooms: 1 double, en suite (shower), 1 double sharing bathroom & w.c. with extra twin.

Price: £18-£20 p.p. No single supp.

Breakfast: Until 9am.

Meals: Dinner, from £12 p.p, by arrangement.

Closed: Christmas & New Year.

Take A438 from Hereford. After Winforton & Whitney-on-Wye, sharp right for Brilley after toll bridge on left. Left fork to Huntington, over x-roads and next right to Huntington. Right into 'No through' road, then 1st right.

Map Ref No: 9

Grace Watson
Hall's Mill House
Huntington
Kington
Herefordshire HR5 3QA
Tel: 01497 831409

Devoted restoration over 20 years has breathed new life into this Hereford manor (rather grander than typical) complete with stone barn, clapboard cow byre and puddleduck pond. Martin and Daphne are rightly proud of their work and greet guests like visiting friends. The bedrooms, named after birds, have immense character, the best fabrics, antiques, nice pine. Upstairs views to hills, downstairs French doors onto a pretty garden. Magnificent cruck hall with gallery and fire. Totally organic food (they are registered with the Soil Association), served with panache. A heavenly experience.

Rooms: 12 rooms (twins or doubles or suites), all en suite.

Price: From £37.50-£60 p.p. Single occ. from £55.

Breakfast: Until 9.30am.

Meals: Dinner from £25 p.p.

Closed: January.

Wisteria-clad Church House has all the advantages of being in a small town, with a rural atmosphere thrown in. A church on one side, a large garden which disappears into rolling hills on the other. Much of the house is Shaker in style: refreshingly simple bare boards and flat paint. Andrew (a wine merchant; Liz is a concert singer) hires out mountain bikes. The whole family makes super company; you can't fail to relax. Cotton sheets, flowers, homemade jams and a delightfully chubby bath.

Rooms: 1 twin with basin and 1 double sharing bathroom.

Price: From £20 p.p. Single supp. by arrangement.

Breakfast: Until 9.30am.

Meals: Dinner available locally.

Closed: Christmas.

Off A44 Leominster to Kington road, 1 mile east of Kington on the right. Hotel is signposted 200m down a smooth track.

Map Ref No: 9

Martin Griffiths & Daphne Lambert
Penrhos Court Hotel
Kington
Herefordshire HR5 3LH
Tel: 01544 230720
Fax: 01544 230754
e-mail: martin@penrhos.kc3ltd.co.uk

Coming into Kington, follow signs for the town centre. Go through middle of town and up long steady hill to St. Mary's church. House is on left opposite church.

Map Ref No: 9

Andrew & Lis Darwin
Church House
Church Road
Kington
Herefordshire HR5 3AG
Tel: 01544 230534
Fax: 01544 231100

The Gillelands rescued the flooded, 14th-century hall house from dereliction in 1988 and now it is a mini Dorchester, such is the comfort, splendour and attention to detail. A newspaper and pot of tea can be brought to your door in the morning, and there is crisp white linen on the dining table. In the garden, 30 varieties of herbs flourish along with fruit trees, vegetables, a large pool and a stream. Jacqueline has made every drape and cushion cover and does all the cooking.

Rooms: 1 twin, 1 twin/double, 1 double and 1 four-poster, all en suite.

Price: £60 p.p. Sun-Thurs; £65 p.p. Fri & Sat.

Breakfast: Usually 8.30-9.30am.

Meals: Available in restaurant.

Closed: Last 3 weeks of January.

From north, A49 to Leominster. After the level crossing, right onto the B4361 signed Richards Castle. After 0.75 miles, left to Eyton & Lucton. Hotel on right of the common.

Map Ref No: 9

Jacqueline & Martin Gilleland
The Marsh Country Hotel
Eyton
Leominster
Herefordshire HR6 0AG
Tel: 01568 613952
e-mail: meg@themarsh.kc3ltd.co.uk

Quite breathtaking. This Georgian gentleman's residence overlooks one of the finest views in England - the Malvern Hills to the east and the Black Mountains to the west. Gracious rooms, log fires, modern bathrooms, and central heating. The 14th-century barn, once the original house, is now a splendid party hall. The four acres of garden include terracing, ponds, a motte and bailey, a 12th-century chapel and a magnificent walled garden with major plans for parterres and rills for the Millennium. Come and stay; Stephanie's cooking is worth a detour.

Rooms: 1 double and 1 twin, both with private bathroom.

Price: £23 p.p. No single supp.

Breakfast: Flexible.

Meals: Dinner by prior arrangement. Packed lunches on request.

Closed: Christmas.

From A438 Hereford/Brecon road turn right on A4111 through Eardisley village. Bollingham House is 2.5 miles up hill on left, behind a long line of conifers.

Map Ref No: 9

Stephanie & John Grant
Bollingham House
Eardisley
Herefordshire HR5 3LE
Tel: 01544 327326
Fax: 01544 327880

This is one of only three remaining 'tranquil' areas of England (says the CPRE), the hills of North Herefordshire, 18 acres of which are the grounds and gardens of this 17th-century farmhouse. Victorian additions brought generous, high-ceilinged spaces. Antiques, old paintings and large, high beds with crisp white linen add to the comfort. Guy grows the fruit and veg and bakes the bread; Amanda loves cooking and sharing meals with guests around the huge dining table. Wonderful, and in a very lovely, surprisingly undiscovered, corner of England. Tennis too.

Rooms: 1 twin, en suite (bath) and 1 double, en suite (bath and shower).

Price: £32 p.p. Single supp. £5.

Breakfast: Flexible.

Meals: Dinner, 3 courses, £19 p.p.

Closed: Christmas.

An utterly fascinating place. The 17th-century farmhouse, cider house, dairy, granary and 14-acre private nature reserve are perched at the top of a small valley; the views are tremendous. In the huge dining room is the old cider mill, and dinner may feature the Wiles' home-smoked fish or meat and homemade bread. Much of what they serve is organic - all the wines are. One room is across the courtyard, the other three in the granary annexe; they are all timber-framed, compact and well thought out and have their own sitting rooms. *Children over 8 welcome.*

Rooms: 4 suites, each with own bathroom.

Price: £26.50 p.p. Single occ. £31.50.

Breakfast: Until 9.30am.

Meals: Dinner £12.50-£18.50 p.p.

Closed: Never!

House 1 mile south of A4112 between Tenbury Wells and Leominster. On entering Leysters from Tenbury Wells left at crossroads in village. Ignore sign to Leysters church. House on left, through white gate (after post box in wall).

Map Ref No: 9

Guy & Amanda Griffiths
The Old Vicarage
Leysters
Leominster
Herefordshire HR6 0HS
Tel: 01568 750208
Fax: 01568 750208
e-mail: guy.griffiths@virgin.net

From Leominster, take A49 north but turning right onto A4122, signed Leysters. Lower Bache is then signed.

Map Ref No: 9

Rose & Leslie Wiles
Lower Bache House
Kimbolton
Nr.Leominster
Herefordshire HR6 0ER
Tel: 01568 750304

Super people with humour and most hospitable instincts, the Daltons call their house "rambling, romantic, ancient, silent". It is a big old manor with gardens and croquet lawn just beside the lovely 12th-century church. You may breakfast beside the great log fire in the Tudor dining room on chilly mornings or under the spreading chestnut tree on warmer days; relax after dinner in the cosy, little oak-panelled sitting room. Rooms are big, family-style, with books, flowers and garden views. Easy, unstuffy - wonderful value. Two excellent pubs within walking distance, too.

Rooms: 1 twin and 1 twin/double, both en suite (bath/shower); 1 double with private bathroom.

Price: £20-£23.50 p.p. Single supp. £5.

Breakfast: Flexible.

Meals: Dinner £18 p.p. Available on request, as is a packed lunch.

Closed: Never!

From A417 travelling south, left to Ullingswick at x-roads. Continue through village. Turn left then right at signs to Ullingswick church. Drive is on right before church lychgate.

Map Ref No: 9

Christopher & Susan Dalton
Upper Court
Ullingswick
Herefordshire HR1 3JQ
Tel: 01432 820295
Fax: 01432 820174

Moor Court is an active, traditional livestock and hop farm which still dries its own hops - you can watch their oast house at work. The buildings, about 500 years old, ramble and enfold both gardens and guests in a homely, traditional way. Inside, all the ancient ingredients are there - timbers, stones, inglenook - as well as contemporary delights such as stripped pine doors, fresh cotton sheets, red velvet curtains. Bedrooms are big and sunny, furniture is traditional, afternoon tea comes with homemade cakes and lace cloths. A comfortably informal place.

Rooms: 1 twin, en suite (bath/shower) and 1 twin and 1 double, en suite (bath).

Price: £17.50 p.p. Single occ. £25.

Breakfast: Flexible.

Meals: Dinner, 3 courses, £12.50 p.p.

Closed: Never!

From Hereford east on A438. Take A417 into Stretton Grandison. First right past village sign, through Holmend Park. Veer left past phone box. Moor Court is on the left, exactly 1 mile from Stretton turnoff.

Map Ref No: 9

Elizabeth Godsall
Moor Court Farm
Stretton Grandison
Nr. Ledbury
Herefordshire HR8 2TP
Tel: 01531 670408

The Domesday-mentioned farm and former cider mill has its own stream and lake, ducks, dogs and cat. Virtually every guest comments on the warm welcome and peacefulness. There are high beamed ceilings to its big rooms, antique and modern farmhouse furniture (one bedroom has a fine half-tester), and good views. The Youngs will drive you to nearby restaurants for dinner and collect you by 11pm, then serve you breakfast with homemade breads and jams next morning. Service indeed.

Rooms: 1 double, en suite (bath); 1 family room (double and single) and 1 double, each with private bathroom.

Price: £22 p.p. Single supp. £3.

Breakfast: Until 9am.

Meals: None, but free taxi service to local pub!

Closed: Never!

Forests must have fallen to build this house; the 1612 barn behind the Georgian façade is a soaring tangle of timbers, a paean to carpentry. The hall, open to the roof, is beautiful, with a graceful staircase. Heavy oak beams are on bold display, and part of the timber cruck can be seen. Guests have a sitting room and breakfast is served in the beamed dining room. The bedrooms are pleasantly comfortable; in some Judi provides towelling robes for the quick flit to the antique bath. A delightfully unexpected house with a charming hostess, and there is a lovely garden to enjoy too... all this in the centre of luscious Ledbury.

Rooms: 1 double, en suite (shower) and 1 double and 1 twin, both with basin, sharing bathroom.

Price: £24-£27 p.p.

Breakfast: Until 9.30am.

Meals: Dinner & packed lunch sometimes available by request - otherwise, lots of places in town.

Closed: Christmas Day & Boxing Day.

Going north on A4172, pass Little Marcle church. Sign for house is on right. Priors Court is up a long drive (about 0.25 miles) just after Newbridge Farm Park on left.

Map Ref No: 9

Roger & Judy Young
Priors Court
Aylton
Nr. Ledbury
Herefordshire HR8 2QE
Tel: 01531 670748
Fax: 01531 670860

From Ledbury bypass, take A449 signed Worcester/town centre. Barn House on left just past Somerfields but before central town crossroads.

Map Ref No: 9

Judi Holland
The Barn House
New Street
Ledbury
Herefordshire HR8 2DX
Tel: 01531 632825

Wisteria wraps itself around the warm brick walls, sheep bleat behind the stable, a pond shimmers... and you play tennis, swim in the neighbour's outdoor pool or walk the Malvern Hills. The guests' drawing room is elegant; there are books by the fire and plump armchairs and sofas to sink into. Half-timbered bedrooms with window-seats, ornately-carved canopied beds, Jacobean panelling, and an upstairs drawing room all seem like icing on the cake. Michael is an excellent cook and dinner is a special occasion, so do eat in.

Rooms: 3 doubles, 2 four-posters and 1 twin/double, all en suite.

Price: £34.50 p.p. Single supp. £15. Small children free.

Breakfast: Flexible.

Meals: Dinner £22 p.p.

Closed: Christmas & New Year.

Leave M50 at Junc. 2, towards Ledbury. Take first left to Bromsberrow Heath. Right by post office in village and go up hill. House is on right.

Map Ref No: 9

Michael & Ellen Ross
The Grove House
Bromsberrow Heath
Ledbury
Herefordshire HR8 1PE
Tel: 01531 650584

'I would like to return; they are lovely and the Mill represents everything that a good B&B should,' said our inspector. Only three miles from Sissinghurst, this is an enchanted watery place; the large, light drawing room even straddles the mill race. It is a deliciously welcoming place - the tea tray is laid with fine china, towels are fluffy and baths old-fashioned. Kenneth will carefully choose a wine from his cellar to go with Heather's much-praised cooking, and you'll all eat together in the beamed dining room. *Too much water for children under 12.*

Rooms: 1 twin/double and 1 four-poster en suite (bath); 1 twin with private adjacent bathroom.

Price: £29-35 p.p. Single supp. £10.

Breakfast: Until 9am.

Meals: Dinner £20 p.p.

Closed: Christmas - New Year.

From Maidstone, A229 south through Staplehurst and left to Frittenden. In about 1 mile take narrow lane right opposite white house. Right again at end - house is first on right, through wood.

Map Ref No: 6

Kent

Kenneth & Heather Parker
Maplehurst Mill
Frittenden
Kent TN17 2DT
Tel: 01580 852203
Fax: 01580 852117
e-mail: maplehurst@clara.net

A working farm and in the family since 900, with views that glue you to the spot; not a road, railway line or telegraph pole in sight. Comfort and elegance go hand in hand: large rooms, high ceilings, beautiful mahogany furniture and an enormous dining table. Rosemary Piper pampers her guests - she'll bring you hot drinks in the sitting room and, on request at weekends, a seasonal dinner using local produce. Bedrooms are huge and light, never fussy, have superb bathrooms... and those views! *Children over 12 welcome.*

Rooms: 2 twins: 1 en suite and 1 with separate private bathroom; 1 double with separate private bathroom.

Price: £24.00-£27.50 p.p. Single occ. variable.

Breakfast: Until 8.45am.

Meals: Supper, from £11 p.p., by arrangement; available most nights.

Closed: 1 December-31 January.

At traffic lights in centre of Hawkhurst, A268 towards Rye. At Shell garage 1.5 miles after lights, immediately right into Conghurst Lane. After 1.25 miles on left is signed driveway.

Map Ref No: 6

Rosemary Piper
Conghurst Farm
Hawkhurst
Kent TN18 4RW
Tel: 01580 753331
Fax: 01580 754579

In a unique English village on the Isle of Oxney, this is a house with a history. King Canute gave a house on the present site to the Church in 1032. The charming, friendly Watsons have years of experience entertaining and cosseting guests. There are big, thick towels on heated towel rails, superb white linen on the beds plus super goodies in the bathrooms. Electric blankets and log fires if needed, maps etc in the bedrooms... and a sense of English comfort in this lovely home. Breakfast can be eaten in the garden in summer; dinner, in the main dining room, is a special treat.

Rooms: 1 twin and 1 double with private bathrooms; 1 double, en suite (shower).

Price: From £35 p.p. Single supp. £15.

Breakfast: Until 9am.

Meals: Dinner, £20 p.p., by arrangement.

Closed: Christmas & New Year.

Take B2082 from Tenterden, signed Wittersham & Rye. Turn right at War Memorial, go for 275 yards, entrance on left just past school sign & before church.

Map Ref No: 6

Ian & Mim Watson
Wittersham Court
Wittersham
Tenterden
Kent TN30 7EA
Tel: 01797 270425
Fax: 01797 270425

Designed by Clough Williams-Ellis (creator of Portmeirion) for American star Hedda Hopper, this is a 1920s atmospheric dreamscape. Charming, efficient Helmut and kind, ever-busy Jennifer now run it as a laid-back, pampering, house-party-style luxury hotel in its charming original decor where the 1920s 'flapper' feel for high living still pervades. There are delicious corners, a look-out room with telescope, utterly elegant bedrooms with deluxe bathrooms - varying in size and price. Excellent dinners too. A special place... worth the price for a special occasion.

Rooms: 8 doubles, 2 twins and 1 single, all en suite.

Price: £45-£110 p.p.

Breakfast: Flexible

Meals. Dinner £28 p.p. Snacks £8 p.p. Cream teas £3.50 p.p.

Closed: Christmas & mid-June. Restaurant closed some evenings.

Let the occasional thwack of willow on leather on the neighbouring village green set the tempo. This restful listed house bears the gentle stamp of your delightful, well-travelled hostess. Rooms are soft pastel shades, there are gorgeous fabrics, fresh flowers and watercolours. After a glass of sherry, dinner is served on fine china at a big polished table. Prospect House has a very pretty garden, a reminder, as if one were needed in this setting, that you're at the very heart of the 'Garden of England'. *Children over 8 welcome.*

Rooms: 2 twins with shared bathroom.

Price: £26 p.p. Single occ. £36.

Breakfast: Flexible.

Meals: Dinner, 3 courses, £20 p.p.

Closed: Occasionally.

Take exit 10 off M20, to Brenzet and Lydd. Through New Romney to Littlestone. Turn left and continue for 1 mile.

Map Ref No: 6

Helmut & Jennifer Gorlich
Romney Bay House
Coast Road
Littlestone, New Romney
Kent TN28 8QY
Tel: 01797 364747
Fax: 01797 367156

M20 junc. 9, follow A28 west for 5 miles then left for Woodchurch. Pass the 'Bonny Cravat' pub; village green is on right. House is halfway along green on left, with a 30 mph sign near garage.

Map Ref No: 6

Fiona Adams-Cairns
Prospect House
Woodchurch
Ashford
Kent TN26 3PF
Tel: 01233 860285
Fax: 01233 860285

You'll find a friend for life in Harvey the basset and he'll paddle along with you while you explore this marvellous oast house. In the big, comfy sitting room are albums of compelling photos from World War I taken by Iain's grandfather - a stretcher-bearer in the French army. In the dining room is the original bench from Headcorn station, complete with carved graffiti. You can eat outside or play croquet on a lawn surrounded by a wild flower garden and overlooking fields of sheep. Bedrooms are comfortable and homely and have king-sized beds. *Children over 10 welcome.*

Rooms: 3 twins/doubles, 1 en suite (bath), 1 en suite (shower) and one with private bath.

Price: £25-£30 p.p. Single occ. £45.

Breakfast: Until 9am.

Meals: Dinner £19 p.p. B.Y.O. wine.

Closed: Christmas.

Take B2163 from junc. 8 of M20. Left onto A274, through Biddenden then first right (signposted Benenden). Left at Castletons pub. After 0.25 miles, turn right on sharp left-hand bend. After 200m, gate on left.

Map Ref No: 6

Iain & Jane Drysdale
Bishopsdale Oast
Biddenden
Ashford
Kent TN27 8DR
Tel: 01580 291027/292065
Fax: 01580 292321

This is fairyland and Erica is the Queen. The 500-year-old cottage is impossibly pretty; the garden, with floodlit fountains and ornamental pond, is magical. Attention to detail is Erica's thing: what could be fussy details are emboldened and swept along by strong colours used with her characteristic panache. There's a peach and a lilac bedroom, and a four-poster room - the latter with two single beds tucked away in the gallery. Erica - demure one moment, razor-sharp the next - is solicitous and eccentric. When she cooks supper, the evening will be something special. *Children and vegetarian food by arrangement.*

Rooms: 1 triple, en suite (shower); 1 twin/double, en suite (bath) and 1 four-poster family, en suite (bath).

Price: £33.50-£36.50 p.p. Single supp. £10.

Breakfast: Flexible.

Meals: Simple supper by arrangement, £14.50 p.p.

Closed: 1 September-mid-March.

From Tenterden, A28 in direction of Ashford. At Bull pub in Bethersden, turn off towards Smarden. Beamed yellow house on right after 2 miles.

Map Ref No: 6

Erica Wallace
Little Hodgeham
Smarden Road
Bethersden
Kent TN26 3HE
Tel: 01233 850323

There has been a house here since the Domesday Book. The old part, built of Kentish ragstone, has massive white-painted (medieval?) beams; the 19th-century extension continued the low ceilings. Two inviting bedrooms have white broderie duvet covers and fresh flowers. Meals are taken in the elegant dining room while kingfishers and herons find their dinner in the spring-fed pond outside. Denise is quietly welcoming and loves children, gardening, her two ginger cats and black spaniel. Superb for ferry and tunnel.

Rooms: 2 twins, sharing bathroom.

Price: From £20 p.p. Single occ. £25.

Breakfast: Flexible.

Meals: Dinner, 3 courses, £15 p.p. Packed lunch £5 p.p.

Closed: Christmas.

The Lathams are well-travelled, friendly and active. The house is a mixture of styles: Tudor, Georgian and modern co-exist in harmony. High ceilings and a conservatory with terracotta-tiled floor brimming with greenery conjure up images of the decadent 20s. It is gloriously homely with comfortable bedrooms, green and yellow baths and the odd beam to be ducked. Guests have their own log-fired drawing room with wonderful views. All this only 10 minutes from the Chunnel and in lush countryside. *Children over 10 welcome.*

Rooms: 3 twins: 2, en suite (bath) and 1 let only to members of same party willing to share bathroom.

Price: £25 p.p. Single occ. £37.50.

Breakfast: Until 9.30am.

Meals: Dinner, £20 p.p., by arrangement.

Closed: Christmas & New Year.

Exit at M20 junc. 9. At second r'bout take A20 to Charing. After 1 mile left at Godinton Lane. After 2 miles pass cottages on left. Worten House is second turning on right. Red postbox by gate. House at end of drive.

Map Ref No: 6

Charles & Denise Wilkinson
Worten House
Great Chart
Ashford
Kent TN23 3BU
Tel: 01233 622944
Fax: 01233 662249

From M20 junc. 1 take B2068 north. After 4.6 miles left opposite B.P. garage. House is at bottom of hill on left after 1.7 miles. Turn left into drive.

Map Ref No: 6

Richard & Virginia Latham
Stowting Hill House
Stowting
Nr. Ashford
Kent TN25 6BE
Tel: 01303 862881
Fax: 01303 863433

Deep in woodland and with views across a small valley, the Victorian vicarage has been lovingly renovated and welcomes children: they can enjoy the space in the old cellars - now a large den. Upstairs has been decorated and finely furnished with great attention to detail: the large, blue drawing room is packed with mementos from travels abroad and has an oriental grandfather clock. The dining room has a huge mahogany table and seascapes on the walls. Bedrooms are large, light and comfortable. On the quiet, Bryan is quite a card...

Rooms: 1 double, en suite (shower); 1 twin/double with private shower and separate w.c.; 1 family with private bathroom.

Price: £27.50-£30 p.p. Single occ. £40.

Breakfast: Flexible.

Meals: Dinner, £20 p.p., by arrangement.

Closed: Christmas.

When the Oakleys began renovating in 1975, this Norman, Jacobean-restored house gave up long-held secrets. From a ceiling fell 16th-century tobacco pipes; in a hidden passageway hung 16th-century pictures. The Oakleys' passion, commitment and care have paid off. Rooms in the main house are full of character; those in the barn are simpler but more peaceful. The drawing room is refreshingly uncluttered, allowing the house its own elegance. Breakfasts and dinners are cooked with real care. The indoor swimming pool, sauna, steam room and spa are now open.

Rooms: 13 doubles and 2 family rooms in main house. Stables, barn and cottage, all en suite.

Price: £32.50-£45 p.p. Single supp. £22.50-£30.

Breakfast: Until 9.30am (week), 10am (weekends).

Meals: In restaurant.

Closed: 24-28 December.

From Dover, B2011 Folkestone Rd. Pass train station, right into Elms Vale Rd, signposted Hougham. After 1 mile, keep right and Old Vicarage is on right after 200 yards.

Map Ref No: 6

Bryan & Judy
Old Vicarage
Chilverton Elms
Hougham, Dover
Kent CT15 7AS
Tel: 01304 210668
Fax: 01304 225118

From A2/A20 follow signs to Deal on A258. Turn right to St Margaret's at Cliffe. Wallett's Court is 1 mile on right, signed.

Map Ref No: 6

Lea & Chris Oakley
Wallett's Court Country House Hotel & Restaurant
Westcliffe, Dover
Kent CT15 6EW
Tel: 01304 852424
Fax: 01304 853430
e-mail: wallettscourt@compuserve.com

If you enter by the back door you will miss the dazzling effect of the hall on first sight. It beckons you into the rest of the house. When house and garden are gorgeous, hosts enchanting and the area hums with history, what more can one ask? Fine bedrooms, good furniture, a big, cast-iron bath that will diminish you. Katie arranges flowers beautifully and is generous with them amid the Georgian elegance; both she and Neil are very present to enjoy your company. *Children by arrangement.*

Rooms: 2 twins/doubles, both with basins, sharing 1 bathroom.

Price: £28 p.p. Single supp. £10.

Breakfast: Until 9.30am. Weekends by arrangement.

Meals: Dinner, £20 p.p. inc. wine, by arrangement. Light suppers can be organised.

Closed: Christmas & New Year.

Take A25 from Canterbury. Go through Wingham. Continue on Ash by-pass for 2 miles. Take 4th turn left on by-pass signposted Weddington. House 200m on left.

Map Ref No: 6

Katie & Neil Gunn
Great Weddington
Ash
Nr. Canterbury
Kent CT3 2AR
Tel: 01304 813407
Fax: 01304 812531

Step out of your car (or Jac's if she's collected you from the station) and walk into the friendliest of welcomes. Everything was twice as good as we'd expected - even the beam-laden 1650s house started as two, and the main sitting room has two inglenooks. You're part of the family here, yet, with your own entrance and book-filled sitting room, you are free to do as you please and can help yourself to tea or coffee. She even does a snacks 'room service'. Comfortable, clean and simple bedrooms, good modern bathrooms, gardens for cavorting kids.

Rooms: 1 double, en suite (shower) and 1 double with adjoining twin, en suite (bath).

Price: £20 p.p. Children £5-£15, according to age.

Breakfast: Flexible

Meals: Dinner £10 p.p. Lunch/supper £5 p.p.

Closed: Never!

From M20 exit 11, take B2068 for Canterbury. After crossing A2, house is about 100 yards on right. White with post box in wall.

Map Ref No: 6

Chris & Jac Bray
Sylvan Cottage
Nackington Road
Canterbury
Kent CT4 7AY
Tel: 01227 765307

The Harrises farm 50 acres high on the North Downs. They have a tennis court, so play is surrounded by grazing sheep and fine views. Nicola is immensely kind and keen for her guests to feel at home. You eat in the light and large garden room, or more formally around the oak refectory table in the dining room. There is a panelled sitting room and a formal drawing room with a bay window and garden views. The bedroom with own basin has some fine period furniture and the private bathroom has both Victorian cast-iron bath and power shower. Home-grown, free-range eggs for breakfast, too.

Rooms: 1 twin with private bathroom. One further twin and single for members of the same party willing to share bathroom.

Price: £25 p.p.

Breakfast: Until 9.30am.

Meals: Dinner, £17 p.p., by arrangement.

Closed: 31 October-28 February.

From M20, junc. 8, A20 east towards Ashford. After 4.5 miles, left to Warren St. Continue for 1 mile. Harrow pub on right. Bear left. After 300 yards, 3-way junction, sharp left. House is third on left after 0.5 miles.

Map Ref No: 6

Mrs Nicola Harris
Bunkers Hill
Lenham
Kent ME17 2EE
Tel: 01622 858259

Come and marvel at the pot-bellied pig - the Yerburghs are very fond it it. This beautiful, porticoed, brick house has a gorgeous drawing room, some fabulous antiques and family portraits. There's a secret garden within the grounds and an arbour and a pond. The front bedroom has fine views and an open fire in winter. John is calm and unflappable, with a touch of mischief; Gillian is full of energy and they continue to provide a genuine welcome. *Pets by arrangement. Children over 12 welcome.*

Rooms: 3 doubles: 1 en suite (bath) and 2 with private bathrooms.

Price: £35 p.p. Single supp. £5.

Breakfast: Until noon!

Meals: Dinner £25 p.p.

Closed: Christmas & New Year.

From Dover M2 to Pavillion Services. Drive into station, continue on road past pumps. Ignore exit signs. Left at T-junc. first left & continue for 200m. Left at next T-junc. House is third on left.

Map Ref No: 6

Gillian & John Yerburgh
Hartlip Place
Place Lane
Nr. Sittingbourne
Kent ME9 7TR
Tel: 01795 842583
Fax: 01795 842673

There's a 350-year-old lime in the acres of garden. Valerie has her own bluebell and rhododendron wood; all around, there is a near-overwhelming 'chorus' of woodland in the midst of this AONB. No wonder local wildlife congregates in this haven - squirrels and rabbits, occasional basking foxes. The garden is the magnetic focus of views from your comfy and warm, unfussily decorated rooms. The dining room has a delightfully crafted dresser, built with the house in 1900; enjoy Valerie's homemade jams and her elderflower cordial.

Rooms: 1 double and 1 single, both en suite (shower) and 1 twin with private bathroom.

Price: £25-£27.50 p.p. No single supp.

Breakfast: Flexible.

Meals: Dinner, 4 courses, £17.50 p.p.

Closed: Never!

Built in 1762 as a private residence, it used to receive Queen Victoria. Today, informality reigns and you'll immediately feel part of a well-kept secret. The Burgundy Bar buzzes with local life, staff and customers are on first-name terms and the facing sofas and open fires encourage everyone to linger. The Bistro - sunny yellow contrasted with dark wooden furniture - serves simply-cooked food made with the freshest ingredients. The sound of chatter and billiards may draw you to take coffee in the Havana Room. Elegant bedrooms have CD players - and huge beds. You'll sleep on Egyptian cotton, nothing less.

Rooms: 25 doubles, all en suite.

Price: £34.50-£49.50 p.p. Singles pay double occ. rate.

Breakfast: 7-9.30am (week); 8-10 am (weekend).

Meals: Dinner, 3 courses, £27.50-£30 p.p., house wine included.

Closed: Never!

From A2 take Cobham/Shorne exit. Turn right at T junc. Turn right into first gateway 'Puckle Hill House', then turn immediately right down drive to Gardeners Cottage.

Map Ref No: 6

Valerie Peters
Gardeners Cottage
Puckle Hill
Shorne Ridgeway
Kent DA12 3LB
Tel: 01474 823269
Fax: 01474 823269

M25 then A21 south. After 13 miles, exit signed Tunbridge Wells. A264 into town, right at lights into Calverley Rd. At mini roundabout, left into Crescent Road.

Map Ref No: 6

Peter Chittick
Hotel du Vin et Bistro
Crescent Road
Royal Tunbridge Wells
Kent TN1 2LY
Tel: 01892 526455
Fax: 01892 512044

Frank and Judith, known to each other as kitchen scullion and chief chamber maid, are so full of life that it's little surprise that the guest sitting room remains largely unused. You'll find guests in the kitchen with them. Cluttered bookshelves, homemade bread (Judith's) and marmalade (Frank's), good conversation, a charming three-legged dog and ducks and geese on the pond all add up to something special. The bedrooms are stylishly simple and one en suite bathroom is entered through the modern-day equivalent of a priest hole. This is peaceful, so don't worry about the nearby road.

Rooms: 1 double, en suite (shower), 1 twin with private shower and 1 single with shared bathroom.

Price: £22 p.p.

Breakfast: Until 9am.

Meals: Available locally.

Closed: Never!

Leave A21 at Tonbridge North. Take exit to Weald. There, left into Scab Arbour Rd at Forge garage. After about 3 miles, right at T-junc. onto B2027 towards Edenbridge. Jessops is 0.5 miles on left.

Map Ref No: 5

Judith & Frank Stark
Jessops
Tonbridge Road
Bough Beech
Kent TN8 7AU
Tel: 01892 870428

An exquisitely old house of mixed ages, starting with a medieval oak-panelled dining room (where you breakfast). Yet the mood is relaxed and easy, with a well-mannered intelligence and openness. The Streatfeilds have been in Chiddingstone for centuries but carry their history lightly; it is woven into the fabric of the building. Guests sleep in an Edwardian wing, where the style is muted, and can settle into the fireside sofas in the library (once the billiard room). It is authentic, they are real people, it's worth every penny. Book early for weekends.

Rooms: Main house: 1 twin and 1 twin/family room with shared bathroom. Annexe: 1 double, en suite (bath).

Price: Twin/double £22 p.p.; single £25. Minimum 2 nights' at weekends, £20 p.p. per night.

Breakfast: Usually 7-9am.

Meals: Light suppers £9-£14.50 p.p.

Closed: Christmas & New Year.

From A21, N. Tonbridge exit. Follow signs to Penshurst Place, then to vineyard. Pass it, then right at T junc. towards Edenbridge. Through village, bear left (following signs to Edenbridge). House is 0.5 miles on left.

Map Ref No: 5

Mr & Mrs Mervyn Streatfeild
Hoath House
Chiddingstone Hoath
Nr. Edenbridge
Kent TN8 7DB
Tel: 01342 850362

Stamford has been called 'the finest stone town in England' - St George's is one of the many 15th-century churches and Kim is its rector. The Victorian rectory opposite is quiet, cool and elegant with thick stone walls. There are beams, original floor tiles, fireplaces, lots of antique furniture and plasterwork. The Swithinbanks, quiet, intelligent people, have given the bedrooms a William Morris feel; bathrooms are large and well-supplied with fluffy towels.

Rooms: 2 twins with choice of 2 large separate bathrooms.

Price: £15-£19 p.p. Single occ. £15-£17.50.

Breakfast: Flexible.

Meals: Dinner available locally. Packed lunch on request.

Closed: Never!

From A1 take B1081 for Stamford. 1 mile, through lights over bridge and up hill. Turn right onto St. Mary St. At T-junc. right into St. George's Square. House on right with steps up.

Map Ref No: 10

Penelope Swithinbank
St. George's
16 St. George's Square
Stamford
Lincolnshire PE9 2BN
Tel: 01780 482099
Fax: 01780 763351

Lincolnshire

The Domesday-mentioned mill operated until 1910, milling corn for local villages. Today many of the old features are intact and rooms ingeniously organised around them. It's a beautiful, watery place: a footbridge leads over the River Welland to a mill pond and meadow, ducks splash around and one bedroom has its own patio by the pond. Pretty bedrooms all have river views and printed floral bedspreads and curtains and, often, fresh flowers. There are good bathrooms and wooden floors everywhere.

Rooms: 6 twins/doubles, all en suite.

Price: £24-£30 p.p. Single occ. £30-£45.

Breakfast: Flexible.

Meals: Supper by special arrangement. Good local pubs.

Closed: Never!

Drift off to sleep on a cloud of rose scent: Ozric makes the only genuine English rose oil and water, distilled here in an outbuilding. Outside your bedroom lies a bed of roses, 3.5 acres of them: magical. The house is full of intriguing features: two boat-shaped windows that open onto the garden; a vast studio/sitting room built in the 1900s by Gardner of the R.A. and filled with paintings and African carvings; some fearsome fish on the Portuguese tiles round the claw-footed bath. Ozric and Chantal are extremely warm and welcoming.

Rooms: 1 twin with adjoining bathroom; 1 double, en suite (shower).

Price: £25 p.p. Single supp. by arrangement.

Breakfast: Flexible.

Meals: Dinner available locally.

Closed: Christmas & New Year.

From Stamford, A16 to Spalding. At Tallington, Mill Lane is 2nd turning on right before the old village school.

Map Ref No: 11

John & Susan Olver
The Mill
Mill Lane
Tallington
Lincolnshire PE9 4RR
Tel: 01780 740815
Fax: 01780 740280

From Bourne on A15 north towards Sleaford, first hamlet on left signed to Cawthorpe. The house is last on right before road becomes a track.

Map Ref No: 11

Ozric & Chantal Armstrong
Cawthorpe Hall
Bourne
Lincolnshire PE10 0AB
Tel: 01778 423830
Fax: 01778 426620

You can go fen-skating when the ice is in, follow the model steam train round the garden, ride the bikes, watch the birds, admire the myriad spring flowers. Beautiful Georgian Pipwell is lovingly decorated in rich blues and greens, each room with its own character. An attractive country-house clutter of old pine tables, sunflowers in vases, things suspended and perched, makes the house feel human and warm; so does Lesley's friendly but unintrusive welcome. You may be offered tea and homemade cakes when you arrive and you will surely appreciate the log fire in winter.

Rooms: 2 doubles: 1 with private shower room and 1 en suite (bath/shower); 1 twin, en suite (shower).

Price: Double £20 p.p. Single £30.

Breakfast: Between 8-9am.

Meals: Available locally.

Closed: Christmas & New Year.

Another symphony in brick, nuzzling the village church. Penny and Roger are a cheerful and engaging couple; she was once a maths teacher and he ran an art studio. He now races and restores classic cars. The dining room has a wood-burning stove and leads onto a large flower-filled conservatory; the garden is a gem, much-loved and mature. The family room has bare, 300-year-old floorboards and all rooms are floral but modern. Bathrooms are bold - one is orange with hand-printed stencils. Boston was England's second largest port in the Middle Ages whence the Pilgrim Fathers first tried to sail to America.

Rooms: 2 doubles, 1 family room, all en suite (shower).

Price: £18-£25 p.p.

Breakfast: Flexible.

Meals: By arrangement. Good pub nearby.

Closed: Never!

Turn off A17, 1.5 miles NE of Holbeach, into Washway Rd. Go past telephone box, pub and garage and Pipwell Manor is on the left.

Map Ref No: 11

Lesley Honnor
Pipwell Manor
Washway Road
Saracen's Head, Holbeach
Lincolnshire PE12 8AL
Tel: 01406 423119
Fax: 01406 423119

From Spalding take A16 for about 8 miles. At roundabout with Texaco garage take Sutterton exit. 1 mile to village, house on right before church.

Map Ref No: 11

Roger & Penny Fountain
Georgian House
Station Road
Sutterton, Boston
Lincolnshire PE20 2JH
Tel: 01205 460048
Fax: 01205 460048

LINCOLNSHIRE

Built with local hand-made bricks which have mellowed gloriously, this impressive, listed Queen Anne vicarage is in a dream-like village setting. The sitting room is panelled throughout, the typical square Lincolnshire hall with stone flags leads to a red pine staircase with more panelling. Michael, ex-Navy, ex-MP, and Julia both love cooking and have a huge fruit and vegetable garden. Bedrooms and bathrooms are as comfortable as you could wish.

Rooms: 1 twin and 1 double, both with private bathroom.

Price: £22.50 p.p. Single supp. £7.50.

Breakfast: Flexible.

Meals: Dinner, £18.50 p.p. (inc. wine), on request. Packed lunch available.

Closed: Never!

Lincoln is so close, yet you feel entirely cut off from any bustle; rabbits and squirrels may play for you on the croquet lawn while you breakfast. The fine, unusually asymmetrical 18th-century manor is enclosed in the most magnificent walled garden. Jill looks after you well - homemade cake when you arrive and huge breakfasts to set you up for the day. The rooms are of generous proportions with garden views, pale paint and floral curtains. *Children over 10 welcome.*

Rooms: 2 twins: 1 en suite (bath/shower) and 1 with private bath/shower; 1 double, en suite (shower).

Price: From £22 p.p. Single supp. £5.

Breakfast: Flexible.

Meals: Ploughman's supper on request.

Closed: Christmas & New Year.

Wrangle is 9 miles north of Boston on A52. In village follow signs to Angel Inn. Old Vicarage opposite church by War Memorial.

Map Ref No: 11

Michael & Julia Brotherton
The Old Vicarage
Wrangle
Boston
Lincolnshire PE22 9EP
Tel: 01205 870688
Fax: 01205 870688

From Lincoln A15 south. Once in Bracebridge Heath, Manor House is last house on left hidden among trees with walled garden.

Map Ref No: 10

Jill & Michael Scoley
The Manor House
Sleaford Road
Bracebridge Heath
Lincolnshire LN4 2HW
Tel: 01522 520825
Fax: 01522 542418

The farmhouse is 200 years old, the farm is down the road from the house, there is a large lake nearby and Christine Ramsay is one of the most welcoming and helpful people we have met - she also cooks a delicious cake. Guests have their own cosy sitting room with open fire and the dining room is where you'll eat *en famille*. The flower-filled garden is lush, the bedrooms are light, airy and restful. Guests keep coming back. *Children over 5 welcome.*

Rooms: 1 twin and 1 single sharing bathroom; 1 double, en suite (shower).

Price: Double/twin £17-£20 p.p. Single £22.

Breakfast: Flexible.

Meals: Light suppers £8 p.p. Lunch & packed lunch available on request.

Closed: Christmas & New Year.

This is a long low modern house built on the land of a farm run by Stamp Junior. There's lots of interest in the roofline and huge picture windows with views onto rolling fields. It is a warm, generous, bright and light house. Anne is a writer and both she and Richard love doing B&B; they have attracted a loyal following. They offer you space and light, beautiful rooms and divine food and are committed to conservation on their farm. *Children over 8 welcome.*

Rooms: 1 twin and 1 double, both en suite (bath and shower).

Price: £20-£25 p.p. Single occ. £30.

Breakfast: Flexible.

Meals: Light suppers available on request.

Closed: Christmas & New Year.

From Lincoln A15 north. Second left after Scampton RAF station signed to Fillingham & Ingham. First right onto B1398. Second left to Fillingham. First house at bottom of hill on right.

Map Ref No: 16

Christine & Bill Ramsay
Church Farm
Fillingham
Gainsborough
Lincolnshire DN21 5BS
Tel: 01427 668279
Fax: 01427 668025

Turn off A157 in East Barkwith at War Memorial into Torrington Lane. Bodkin Lodge is last property on the right on edge of village.

Map Ref No: 16

Anne & Richard Stamp
Bodkin Lodge
Torrington Lane
East Barkwith
Lincolnshire LN3 5RY
Tel: 01673 858249

Charming and enthusiastic and with easy-going, sporty children, Michael and Clare enjoy getting to know their guests. An ornithologist and a botanist, they are very aware of conservation issues. The house was once a famous stud and the old horse-watering pond is now a wildlife haven. A home beehive gives breakfast honey. Only the tennis net separates the lovely garden from the herd of handsome red cows (calving is Jan-April). The back of the house is 18th-century, the front Victorianised; the guestroom is big and full of character.

Rooms: 1 twin with private bathroom; 1 single with shared bathroom.

Price: £20 p.p.

Breakfast: Flexible.

Meals: Packed lunch available on request.

Closed: Christmas & New Year.

The rolling wolds and flat fens of unsung Lincolnshire go on for ever. The Grange sits beautifully among it all, artistically old-furnished, oak-doored and beamed and with floral curtains. Original tiles and shutters, claw-footed baths and fireplaces create an atmosphere that can only unwind you. Anthony is an interior designer and produces wildflower seed from their 12-acre holding. The kitchen is the sort of place where you want to chat to Anthony while he cooks your Lincolnshire sausages. *Children over 7 welcome.*

Rooms: 1 double, en suite (bath & shower); 1 twin/double with private bath & shower and, occasionally, 1 extra single.

Price: £18-£22 p.p. Single supp. £4.

Breakfast: Flexible.

Meals: Available locally.

Closed: Christmas & New Year.

From Baumber take road signed Bardney & Wispington. After 0.25 miles, house is on right down a long drive.

Map Ref No: 16

Michael & Clare Harrison
Baumber Park
Baumber
Nr. Horncastle
Lincolnshire LN9 5NE
Tel: 01507 578235
Fax: 01507 578417

From Spilsby take A16 north for 1 mile. In Partney bear left at church, signed A16 Grimsby. Partney Grange drive is 60 yards on left.

Map Ref No: 16

Anthony & Frances Collard
The Grange
Partney
Spilsby
Lincolnshire PE23 4PH
Tel: 01790 753151
Fax: 01790 753151

Wonderful accommodation in a Kensington 1860s Victorian town house. The newly-decorated bedrooms are on the ground floor and you have your own key and entrance. The rest of the house is still the family home. The mood is of elegance - pale yellows, light flooding in through the big windows - and easy formality, with mahogany table, dresser with dry flowers and silver, antique chairs and floral fabrics. Breakfast is served in the dining room overlooking the charming, secluded garden. Nanette really enjoys people. *Children over 12 welcome.*

Rooms: 2 twins, en suite (bath & shower). 1 double, en suite (shower).

Price: £37.50-£40 p.p. Single occ. £55.

Breakfast. 8.30 9am.

Meals: Available locally.

Closed: Never!

London

Most London B&Bs and hotels have a strict cancellation policy - make sure you discuss the issue before booking.

Left out of Earls Court Rd station, over Cromwell Rd then left into Pembroke Rd. Warwick Gardens is 3rd turning right off this road.

Map Ref No: 5

Nanette Stylianou
47 Warwick Gardens
London W14 8PL
Tel: 0171 603 7614
Fax: 0171 602 5473

Just off the King's Road, so perfectly central. The house is Georgian, set back from the road, strewn with wisteria, looking over a sports ground. And inside, a real family home. Jane does large Continental breakfasts, not fry-ups, in the stunning kitchen-cum-conservatory with its green plants and dashes of pink enamelled glass; a cool friendly space looking onto a lovely London garden. High up, top-floor bedrooms are pretty and atticky with views over the square on one side, and down an alley of gardens on the other. Jane loves cooking, so do eat in if you wish.

Rooms: 1 twin and 1 room with futon bed and an extra single sharing 1 bathroom.

Price: £40-£50 p.p. Single supp. £10.

Breakfast: Continental only, from 8-10am.

Meals: Dinner, £20 p.p., by arrangment. B.Y.O. wine.

Closed: August, Christmas & New Year.

Parallel with King's Road between Smith Street and Royal Avenue.

Map Ref No: 5

Jane Barran
17 St. Leonard's Terrace
London SW3 4QG
Tel: 0171 730 2801
Fax: 0171 730 2801

The nerve centre of Susie's large Victorian house is a wonderful flowered conservatory/eating area with cushioned wicker chairs. It looks onto a ballustraded terrace and a cool green lawn shaded by surrounding trees. It is a very bright space by day, even more attractive over dinner with candles reflected in the windows. Photographs mounted on the kitchen wall are reminders of the 10 years that the Priestleys spent in Asia. The bedrooms are large and beautifully decorated with lots of floor space. Such a welcoming home is a treat... and in London, too!

Rooms: 1 twin/double and 1 double, both with private bathroom.

Price: £42 p.p. Single supp. £10.

Breakfast: Until 9.30am.

Meals: Dinner by arrangement.

Closed: Christmas & New Year.

From Sloane Square drive south across Chelsea Bridge to Clapham Common, turn left at the Common along the north side. Macaulay Rd is on the left opposite the church.

Map Ref No: 5

Susie Priestley
8 Macaulay Road
London SW4 0QX
Tel: 0171 622 9603
Fax: 0171 720 8094

Camberwell animates Jackie - there's a great feeling of community here, and it's a honey-pot for the artistic with its arts week, fair and college. 119 Knatchbull Road must be one of its prime addresses. Guests eat Continental breakfasts in a huge and very unkitcheny kitchen. French windows lead out under a wisteria- and rose-canopied pergola from which you can admire the flower and tree-fringed garden. And upstairs are large bedrooms with sofas, books, the odd oil painting by Jackie's son, an Ethiopian cartoon story... and complete quiet (opposite are the Age Concern centre and public library!). *Children over 12 welcome.*

Rooms: 2 doubles, 1 en suite (bath/shower) and 1 with private shower room.

Price: £30 p p Single occ. £35.

Breakfast: Extensive Continental breakfast, from 7-9.30am.

Meals: Available locally.

Closed: Never!

In the heart of vibrant Camden Town, well set back in a quiet, wide tree-lined street moments from Regent's Park - what a superb central London base! The stunningly spacious kitchen was designed by Peter (an architect and lighting specialist) and every room in the modernist house has had the best brought out of it. All is distinctive and understated with luxurious carpets, cool colours and fresh flowers in the bedrooms. Friendly and welcoming, Peter will happily share his knowledge of London.

Rooms: 1 twin with bunks and 1 twin/double sharing bathroom; 1 small double, en suite (shower & private w.c.)

Price: Twin/double £35 p p. Single supp. £5.

Breakfast: 7 10am.

Meals: Many restaurants within walking distance.

Closed: Never!

Ask when booking, free car parking available.

Map Ref No: 5

Jackie Rokotnitz
119 Knatchbull Road
Camberwell
London SE5 9QY
Tel: 0171 738 7878
Fax: 0171 738 6788

From Camden Town tube station go up Parkway. Albert Street is the second on the left. Number 78 is on the left.

Map Ref No: 5

Joanna Lafeber & Peter Bell
78 Albert Street
London NW1 7NR
Tel: 0171 387 6813
Fax: 0171 387 1704

The flavour of country living in Primrose Hill: the big, colourful, kitchen, complete with Aga, hanging pots and pans, wooden floor and table, is where you take a delicious breakfast and Carole's advice on what's on in London. The gorgeous bedrooms are on the top floor, a mix of brass, sisal flooring, crisp linen, bath robes, wood and contemporary decor. They are bright and very comfortable, grand but not imposing. Carol is very experienced at looking after guests and thoroughly professional.

Rooms: 1 twin, en suite (bath); 2 doubles, both with private bathrooms.

Price: From £40 p.p. Single supp. £20.

Breakfast: Extensive Continental only: 8-9am (week), 8.30-9.30am (weekend) - negotiable!

Meals: Available locally.

Closed: Never!

Leave Chalk Farm tube station, cross Adelaide Rd., turn right for 20 steps, then left into Bridge Approach. Cross bridge, turn right & walk till you reach No. 30 on right-hand side.

Map Ref No: 5

Andrew & Carole Ingram
30 King Henry's Road
Primrose Hill
London NW3 3RP
Tel: 0171 483 2871
Fax: 0171 483 4587

Hampstead Heath starts at the end of the road. This is a beautiful bit of London, a largely untouched Georgian village. The hotel, more like a private home, has a dining room with crisp linen, deep rose walls and big windows overlooking a garden. The bedrooms, all designer-different, are on rambling levels in the Victorian twists of the old house. The service is exquisite (turned-down beds, complimentary sherry) and Diana is a most human manager.

Rooms: 5 singles, 8 twins/doubles, 3 junior suites, all en suite (bath); 2 family rooms sharing bathroom.

Price: £75 p.p. Singles £70-£95. Breakfast extra.

Breakfast: Until 9.30am. (Continental, £6.50 p.p. Full English, £9.50 p.p.)

Meals: Room service provides excellent Italian food from local kitchen. Lots of local restaurants.

Closed: Never!

From Hampstead tube turn right uphill into Heath St. Then 3rd right into Elm Row, which leads to Holford Rd.

Map Ref No: 5

Diana Sparks
Sandringham Hotel
3 Holford Road
Hampstead
London NW3 1AD
Tel: 0171 435 1569
Fax: 0171 431 5932

This tall house (1875) stretches up to lovely large roofscape bedrooms. Quite a climb. The design throughout leaves you plenty of space with sparse, well chosen ornamentation combining with beautifully chosen colours to create different moods. Breakfast healthily in the stunning basement which has French windows onto a small garden. Bedrooms are warm with pale terracotta walls and carpets - colours are paramount here - with big comfortable beds and proper bathrooms.

Rooms: 1 double, with en suite (bath) & small kitchen. 1 twin and 1 single, both sharing bathroom.

Price: Double/twin £30-£35 p.p. Single occ. £15. Single £35.

Breakfast: Until 9.30am.

Meals: Restaurants & cafés nearby.

Closed: Never!

From Chalk Farm tube, cross Adelaide Rd, turn right for short distance before turning left into Bridge Approach. Cross bridge into Regent's Park Rd. Right into Erskine Rd and left at end.

Map Ref No: 5

Jenny Stringer
19 Ainger Road
Primrose Hill
London NW3 3AS
Tel: 0171 586 8835
Fax: 0171 586 8835

Three minutes on foot from Marble Arch, yet the bedrooms at the back are incredibly quiet for central London. It is an 1810 town house in a perfect Georgian square. The 4th-floor room is worth the climb - big blue bedsteads, period furniture, lots of books. Double doors open to the dining room's wooden floor, large rug, huge bookcases beside an ornamental fireplace, gilt mirror and two old oils. Shuttered windows look onto the square, a picture of age and subdued grandeur. Patty is down to earth and easy-going.

Rooms: 2 twins/doubles, one en suite (bath) and one with private bathroom.

Price: £40 p.p. Single supp. £20.

Breakfast: Until 9am.

Meals: Not available, but plenty of restaurants locally.

Closed: Christmas & New Year.

From Marble Arch tube turn right up Edgware Rd, then 1st left into Seymour Rd which runs into Connaught Square. House is situated in northwest corner.

Map Ref No: 5

Mrs Patty Risso-Gill
22 Connaught Square
Marble Arch
London W2 2HG
Tel: 0171 402 9470
Fax: 0171 402 0810

A beautiful home in a quiet, tree-lined street, minutes from Hampstead Heath and Kenwood House. Inside, lovely antique furniture and a breakfast room that overlooks a pretty garden. There is a vaguely Bohemian, unfussy atmosphere here and a rare sense of humour to boot. Jamie prides himself on low cholesterol breakfasts, so expect some innovative touches. There is a patio with chairs whither to repair to sit out the lively Hampstead dance - with its cafés, restaurants and youthful vigour. Bedrooms are in the basement and are attractive, smallish but private. *Children over 12 welcome.*

Rooms: 2 doubles, both en suite (shower).

Price: £30 p.p. Single supp. £10.

Breakfast: 7-8.30am.

Meals: Lots of restaurants in Hampstead.

Closed: Never!

Left out of Hampstead tube station, down Hampstead High St. 2nd left into Willoughby Rd and 1st right into Kemplay Rd. House on right.

Map Ref No: 5

Jamie Wilson
Carlisle House
23 Kemplay Road
Hampstead
London NW3 1TA
Tel: 0171 435 8310
Fax: 0171 794 8843

This is special indeed, and remarkable value for London, so close to Regent's Park. A very modern Japanese-style house built round a courtyard with a peaked glass roof so that it fills with light and air. Wood and glass take pride of place, colours and shapes are subtle and pure, bedrooms have low platform beds, the minimalist-decor living quarters are open-plan, green-planted and ethnic-ornamented with treasures from far-flung holidays. Rodger and Sue are a delightful, articulate couple; Peckham the parrot completes the picture.

Rooms: 1 double and 1 single, sharing bathroom (single room only let to member of same party willing to share bathroom).

Price: Double £35 p.p. Single £35-£40.

Breakfast: Until 10am.

Meals: Available locally.

Closed: Never!

From Camden Town tube station take Camden Rd towards Holloway. Pass Camden Rd BR station and 4th right into Murray St. No 66 is on corner of Murray St and Camden Mews.

Map Ref No: 5

Sue & Rodger Davis
66 Camden Square
London NW1 9XD
Tel: 0171 485 4622
Fax: 0171 485 4622

Totteridge and Limetrees embody all the advantages of the suburban green belt. Not 30 minutes from the heart of the city on the Northern Line, this large modern house is built in an enclave of six detached private houses, a stone's throw from country walks and as quiet as the grave at night. Strike out into the Totteridge and Dollis Valleys and be lost to humanity for hours. Ruth keeps the house and its large rooms immaculate and uncluttered, while she herself is breezily easy to get on with. Also worth particular mention are her excellent and varied home-cooked meals. *Car parking in the forecourt.*

Rooms: 1 double, en suite (shower) and 1 twin, en suite (bath).

Price: £37.50 p.p. Single supp. £10.

Breakfast: Flexible.

Meals: Dinner, £18-£22 p.p., by prior arrangement.

Closed: Christmas & New Year.

From M25 take exit 23 and join A1 towards London. At Sterling Corner roundabout, take A411 to left. Left into Hendon Wood Lane (B552), then join Totteridge Lane (A5109). Alternatively, ask about tube details.

Map Ref No: 5

Ruth Hirsch
Limetrees
140 Totteridge Lane
London N20 8JJ
Tel: 0181 446 0399
Fax: 0181 446 5173

It is fun to meet people of such character as Mrs Garnier. She calls a spade a spade, is devoted to her little terrier and tells colourful stories of her amazing house and her family's long local history. From 1349 until the Dissolution of the Monasteries, it was a college for priests, conveniently sited near to the church. Later, it was saved from ruin and brought back to life. It now has a superb panelled dining room, big bedrooms and great views. The two en suite bathrooms are ingeniously converted from large cupboards. *Children over 7 welcome.*

Rooms: 1 twin and 1 twin/double, both en suite (bath); 1 double with adjacent private bathroom. Also extra shower and w.c.

Price: From £19 p.p.

Breakfast: Flexible.

Meals: Afternoon tea served free of charge. Lunch & evening meal available in local pub.

Closed: Never!

From Thetford take A1075 north towards Watton. After 9 miles turn left to Thompson. After 0.5 miles take second left at red letter box on corner. Turn left again, house is at dead end.

Map Ref No: 11

Mrs Garnier
College Farm
Thompson
Thetford
Norfolk IP24 1QG
Tel: 01953 483318
Fax: 01953 483318

Norfolk

Another lovely Norfolk Georgian house, red-brick and with those gateposts that mark a boundary so stylishly. This is the English home at its grand best, the house that everyone would like to live in. It has the elegant proportions of the late 18th-century country house; the hall, drawing room and dining room are gracious and beautifully furnished. The big-windowed bedrooms look onto the lovely garden and your hostess - sweet, friendly and most helpful - speaks French. *Children by arrangement; dogs and pool similarly.*

Rooms: 2 twins, each with basins and a private bathroom. Sitting room available.

Price: £25 p.p. Ask about single supp. Please book in advance.

Breakfast: Flexible.

Meals: Dinner £17.50 p.p. on request. Reduced for 3 or more.

Closed: Christmas.

Nick may still be in the process of improving his recent purchase, but do go and stay. It is very comfortable and Nick - new to B&B - is architect, cook and a fun host with artistic flair. The rectory is awash with Hills eclectica: stone busts, religious curiosities and architect's drawings. Good-humoured Bohemiana livens up the usual austerity of a rectory. A tangled garden surrounds the house, dinners are candlelit, food and wine excellent. Don't go if you want the finished sterility of a hotel. Do go if you want to explore the Norfolk coast from somewhere memorable.

Rooms: 2 doubles and 1 twin sharing 2 bathrooms.

Price: £22.50 p.p. Single supp. £5.50.

Breakfast: Flexible.

Meals: Dinner, £12.50 p.p., by arrangement.

Closed: Christmas & New Year.

From Swaffham take A1065; turn right to Litcham after 5 miles. House is on left as you come into village. Georgian red brick with stone balls on gatepost.

Map Ref No: 11

John & Hermione Birkbeck
Litcham Hall
Litcham
Nr. Kings Lynn
Norfolk PE32 2QQ
Tel: 01328 701389
Fax: 01328 701164

From Swaffham, take A1065 for 6 miles, turn right at B1145 signed Bawdeswell. In Litcham, left in village, then immediately right to Tittleshall. House at end of High St opposite church.

Map Ref No: 11

Nick Hills
Old Rectory
Church Lane
Tittleshall
Norfolk PE32 2PN
Tel: 01328 700700
Fax: 01328 700030

Two of the bedrooms are huge and high-ceilinged, with chairs where you can enjoy the view through the fine long windows. They are generous with towels, bath-robes and other extras, such as a fridge and sofa. This is a large family farm with plenty of dogs and horses (stabling is available) and delightful hosts - real farmers, their walls bearing the proofs of their successes at point-to-pointing and showing. It is a lived-in, easy-going house, with comfortable touches of elegance such as grand piano, gilt cornicing etc. *Children over 12 by arrangement.*

Rooms: 2 doubles: 1 en suite (shower) and 1 (bath/shower); 1 twin with private bathroom & w.c.

Price: £18-£25 p.p. Single supp. £5.

Breakfast: Flexible.

Meals: Pub within walking distance.

Closed: Christmas week.

Jane calls everyone 'darling' and has a heart of gold. She is a good Yorkshire girl, an excellent cook (all her vegetables are home-grown) who used to be a nurse and who loves having guests. Meanwhile, Michael pours the drinks. The house, a converted barn, is eminently and traditionally comfortable, guests may use the large kitchen and the sitting room and also stable their horses. How much more hospitable can one be? One of the only places in Norfolk properly kitted up for wheelchair users.

Rooms: 2 twins sharing adjacent private bathroom & shower room.

Price: £20 p.p.

Breakfast: Usually 9am, or by arrangement.

Meals: Dinner £10 p.p. by arrangement.

Closed: Christmas.

Take A148 N.E. and second of two turnings right to Harpley (no signpost) opposite Houghton Hall sign. After 200 yds crossroads, straight over. House 400 yds on left, white with copper beeches.

Map Ref No: 11

Amanda Case
Lower Farm
Harpley
Nr. Kings Lynn
Norfolk PE31 6TU
Tel: 01485 520240

From Fakenham A148 towards Kings Lynn. After 4 miles left opposite garage to Tatterford. At white gates turn left, right and then left. The barn is set back on the right.

Map Ref No: 11

Michael & Jane Davidson-Houston
Manor Farm Barn
Tatterford
Nr. Fakenham
Norfolk NR21 7AZ
Tel: 01485 528393

Mary runs a bustling household with good humour; "clean, but not always tidy", which is fine by us. The atmosphere is as welcoming and down-to-earth as it is laid-back and 'family'; children are part of the scene. There is bold design sense, too; everything wooden has been painted in bright, unusual colours, everything draped in brightly-coloured coverings. Upstairs, faded carpets, fresh flowers, good sheets, a lovely bathroom with sequined Indian wall-hanging and wooden floor. In the sitting room there are deep sofas, a log-burner, wooden floor and low-beamed ceilings.

Rooms: 1 double, en suite (bath) and 1 double with private shower. Cot and fold-up bed available.

Price: £17-£22 p.p. Single supp. £5.

Breakfast: Flexible.

Meals: Not available, but Mary will give you the lowdown on local pubs.

Closed: Christmas.

From Burnham Market, follow signs to Fakenham for 2 miles - next village is North Creake. Over bridge, sharp left, house 0.25 miles on right.

Map Ref No: 11

Mary & Jeremy Brettingham
Glebe Farmhouse
Wells Road
North Creake, Fakenham
Norfolk NR21 9LD
Tel: 01328 730133
Fax: 01328 730444
e-mail: jezzab@globalnet.co.uk

Scattered chickens and dogs, and the delightful Rosie, will provide a big welcome. This feels more like a home than a B&B; it is a Georgian vicarage, up an ivy-lined drive in a quiet backwater behind the centre of the rural village of Hindringham. An elegant staircase takes you to two pretty rooms with superb and unspoiled views of the countryside. Breakfasts, prepared by a generous Rosie, are sure to be a feast. Five miles inland from the beautiful, magical north Norfolk coast, known only to a happy minority. *Children and use of tennis court by arrangement.*

Rooms: 1 twin, en suite (bath) and 1 double with private bathroom.

Price: From £20 p.p. Please ask about single supp.

Breakfast: Until 9am.

Meals: Dinner, 3 courses, £12 p.p. by arrangement.

Closed: Christmas.

From Fakenham, follow road signed Cromer for 6 miles. Left at Crawfish pub into Hindringham, down hill and left into Blacksmith's Lane. Follow up hill, house on left.

Map Ref No: 12

Rosie & Robin Waters
The Old Vicarage
Blacksmith's Lane
Hindringham
Norfolk NR21 0QA
Tel: 01328 878223

There is room for everyone in this large 19th-century farmhouse. The friendly Elizabeth has a lovely sense of humour and is one of those people who can cope with anything. Her working farm (arable and beef cattle) has dogs and geese, chicks in spring and a thoroughly lived-in feel. Guests have their own sitting room and dining rooms and large, pleasant bedrooms that give onto the countryside. There is an easy atmosphere and city-dwellers will feel that they have escaped from it all. *Children over 12 welcome.*

Rooms: 2 twins and 1 double: 1 twin en suite and 1 shares bath with double.

Price: From £20 p.p. Single supp. in season, £5.

Breakfast: Flexible.

Meals: Dinner from £14 p.p.

Closed: Christmas & New Year.

A big, easy-going family home on the outskirts of a rural Norfolk village, it is a 17th-century rectory with Victorian additions. The huge drawing/dining room, the wonderful double room with great brass bedstead and canopy, the west-facing garden with croquet lawn... enjoy them all. The Winter children are growing up and moving out, but yours are more than welcome. It may seem untidy but the atmosphere is just utterly relaxed and the family are fun. The coast is very close for swimming, sailing and watching the famous Blakeney seals. *No smoking except in the dining room.*

Rooms: 1 twin with private bath, shower & w.c.; 1 double, en suite (bath).

Price: £20 p.p. Discount for children.

Breakfast: Flexible.

Meals: Dinner £12.50 p.p. Available on request. B.Y.O. wine.

Closed: Christmas & New Year.

From Fakenham B1146 towards East Dereham. After 2 miles turn left to Gt. Ryburgh. In village left up Highfield Lane opposite pink cottage and on for 0.5 miles - house on right.

Map Ref No: 12

Elizabeth Savory
Highfield Farm
Great Ryburgh
Fakenham
Norfolk NR21 7AL
Tel: 01328 829249
Fax: 01328 829422

From Fakenham A1067 towards Norwich. At Guist clock tower turn left; second turning to Wood Norton. House is on right after 100 yards, through white gates, over 2 cattle grids.

Map Ref No: 12

Jo & Giles Winter
The Old Rectory
Wood Norton
Norfolk NR20 5AZ
Tel: 01362 683785

An 18th-century windmill with the river lapping the wall. A magnificent sitting room overlooks the marshes; some bedrooms look over the endless seascape - one has a walk-around balcony. Everything is special here, from the obvious thrill of staying in a windmill to the great welcome and good coffee at breakfast. Jeremy has just taken it over, a guest who fell in love with the place. He upped sticks from his Battersea restaurant and now does wonders with local ingredients: caught-that-day fish or the delicious seamarsh samphire. Bring your binoculars.

Rooms: 2 twins, 1 en suite and 1 with shared bathroom; 3 doubles, 1 en suite and 2 with private bathrooms; 1 single with shared bathroom.

Price: Twins/doubles £25-£34.40 p.p. Singles usually pay double occupancy rate.

Breakfast: 8.30-9am.

Meals: Dinner £15 p.p.

Closed: Never!

From Holt take Cley Road through the narrow - and only - street in Cley. There's a sign to the mill on the left. Drive over the bridge to the car park.

Map Ref No: 12

Jeremy Bolam
Cley Mill
Cley-next-the-Sea
Holt
Norfolk NR25 7RP
Tel: 01263 740209
Fax: 01263 740209

A splendid 18th-century flint-and-brick house for family holidays in North Norfolk, half a mile from that much loved piece of coastline with its swimming, sailing, bird watching and seal watching trips, and stately homes for rainy days. The Lacostes have young children of their own so cots and high chairs are available and children's needs easily dealt with; you can hire bikes, too. The bedrooms are sumptuously comfortable, the furniture traditional, the paintings by local artists. Pauline is a trained chef and the food is excellent.

Rooms: 1 twin and 1 double, en suite (shower); 1 family room, en suite (bath and shower) and 1 double, en suite (bath).

Price: From £25 p.p. Single supp. £10-£15.

Breakfast: 8.30-9.15am.

Meals: Dinner £10.50-£15 p.p. High teas by arrangement.

Closed: Christmas & 13-20 February.

From Holt, leave A148 and go through town centre. Pass B.P. garage, left after corner following sign to Weybourne. Down hill to Weybourne, right at T-junction; entrance opposite church and coast road junction.

Map Ref No: 12

Charles & Pauline Lacoste
Rosedale Farm
Holt Road
Weybourne, Holt
Norfolk NR25 7ST
Tel: 01263 588778

Heydon is one of Norfolk's finest Grade I Elizabethan houses. Sarah has opened up the Georgian Old Laundry beside the house and has kept many original features - white walls, scrubbed tables, stone-flags. Everything else, beds, carpets, etc are new and of high quality. Bedrooms are fresh and light; one has a bathroom with a fireplace and a free-standing bath. With your own courtyard, you feel pretty well self-contained, but great breakfasts are served in the open-plan dining/sitting room downstairs. Visitors can walk in the front park and the swimming pool can be used if you ask beforehand. A rare treat.

Rooms: 2 twins/doubles, 1 en suite (bath) and 1 with private bathroom.

Price: £25-£30 p.p. Single supp. in high season, £5.

Breakfast: Flexible.

Meals: Good pub within walking distance.

Closed: Christmas.

From Norwich, B1149 for 10 miles. 2nd left after bridge, signed Heydon. After 1.5 miles, right into village, straight into park, over cattle grid, past Hall to left and follow signs.

Map Ref No: 12

Sarah Bulwer-Long
The Old Laundry
Heydon Hall
Heydon
Norfolk NR11 6RE
Tel: 01263 587343
Fax: 01263 587805

Pack your bags and head for the Norfolk Broads. This is the sort of lovely old Georgian house one can usually only dream of. It has everything going for it - looks, position and a mass of luxurious detail inside. The owners combine the atmosphere of a private home with impeccable service and food and now you can even book in for beauty treatments! Most bedrooms are large and there are two charming attic rooms. All are stylishly chintzy and the bathrooms are terrific. The River Bure meanders by and there are rowing boats, or you can dock your own.

Rooms: 3 twins, 6 doubles and 1 family suite, all en suite.

Price: £35 p.p. Single occ. £65.

Breakfast: Flexible.

Meals: À la carte lunch & dinner.

Closed: Never!

B1150 north to Coltishall. Over humpback bridge and first right. Turn down drive before church.

Map Ref No: 12

Jill & Don Fleming
The Norfolk Mead Hotel
Coltishall
Norwich
Norfolk NR12 7DN
Tel: 01603 737531
Fax: 01603 737521

Not a room has been left untouched in the Dixons' devoted restoration of this fine Regency house. Rooms are huge, with high ceilings and crowned pelmets. Beds are vast and luxurious; bathrooms ditto. Many thoughtful touches: good lamps for reading, a terrace overlooking the sunken garden for morning coffee and a warm, west-facing spot picked out for evening cocktails. You breakfast on local bacon and sausages in the huge Regency dining room and can have afternoon tea in the conservatory. Cooking is *Cordon Bleu* and the wine list long.

Rooms: 1 double and 1 single, en suite (bath) and 1 double with private bath.

Price: £30-£32 p.p. Single £35.

Breakfast: Until 9am.

Meals: Dinner £18.50 p.p.

Closed: Christmas & New Year.

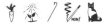

An ancient house - the deeds from 1610 hang in the hall, the moat is star of the garden - with a near-perfect traditional interior where high ceilings, antiques, fine fabrics are set off by original oak floors, hand-painted walls and great pots of dried flowers. Mrs Baxter, a bubbly interior designer who is fluent in French, German and Italian, is eager to get things right: her immaculate, elegant house with its many welcoming details says she does. The dining room is formal, the breakfast room sunnily relaxed; in both you will use fine china and silver cutlery. *Children over 12 welcome.*

Rooms: Main house: 2 doubles, 1 en suite (shower) and 1 with private bathroom. The Barn: 1 twin with private bathroom and sitting room.

Price: £35 p.p.

Breakfast: Flexible.

Meals: Dinner £25 p.p. Lunch & packed lunch by arrangement.

Closed: Christmas & New Year.

From Diss going north on A140. At Newton Flotman, turn right signed Saxlingham Nethergate. Second drive on the left.

Map Ref No: 12

Sally & Roger Dixon
The Lodge
Cargate Lane
Saxlingham Thorpe, Norwich
Norfolk NR15 1TU
Tel: 01508 471422
Fax: 01508 471682

From the centre of Starston (by the bridge) go north along Church Hill (alongside church). Road becomes Hardwick Road. 1.2 miles from junction by church is entrance to Starston Hall. Follow farm track to house.

Map Ref No: 12

Christina Baxter
Starston Hall
Starston
Norfolk IP20 9PU
Tel: 01379 854252
Fax: 01379 852966
e-mail: m.baxter@starstonhall.co.uk

The lawns cascade down Conifer Hill, wisteria perfumes the garden and you look out over hill and farmland. Don't forget your costumes - there's a heated swimming pool. Richard and Patricia are utterly charming and so easy to talk to; their respective passions are fishing and gardening. They'll bring you sherry in the drawing room and light a fire for you. The big bedrooms have thick carpets and the scent of wisteria fills our favourite room - it looks over lawns and a daffodil-covered hill.

Rooms: 1 twin/double, en suite (bath), 1 twin with private bathroom plus 1 double let to same party willing to share bathroom. Extra w.c. and basin available.

Price: £25 p.p. Single supp. by arrangement.

Breakfast: Flexible.

Meals: Good pubs nearby.

Closed: Never!

A143 Diss-Yarmouth for 9 miles. At roundabout turn left towards Harleston, then immediately left to Starston. Over crossroads, into village, over bridge, immediately right. After 0.5 miles, drive on left by white railing.

Map Ref No: 12

Mrs Patricia Lombe Taylor
Conifer Hill
Redenhall Road
Starston, Harleston
Norfolk IP20 9NT
Tel: 01379 852393
Fax: 01379 852393

Traditional Scottish gridle-scones on arrival, plus, perhaps, homemade marmalade, bread, fruit cake and shortbread, a log fire and comfy sofas make this a nourishing haven for pilgrims on St Cuthbert's Way or en route for Holy Island, five miles away. Built from local stone, the Grade II listed manse adjoins the southernmost Church of Scotland, whose stained glass windows can be admired from the garden. The two bedrooms are elegant and restrained in style, with good period furniture. Mrs Huddart, locally born and bred, has a good sense of humour.

Rooms: 1 double and 1 twin, both en suite (bath).

Price: £25 p.p. Single supp. £7.50.

Breakfast: Until 9am.

Meals: Dinner, £17.50 p.p., by arrangement. Packed lunch from £4 p.p.

Closed: 20 December-5 January.

A1 north from Newcastle, then B6353 left to Lowick. In town, left at Post Office, then 1st right, 1st left, signed.

Map Ref No: 20

Mrs Barbara Huddart
The Old Manse
Lowick
Berwick Upon Tweed
Northumberland TD15 2TY
Tel: 01289 388264

Northumberland

A totally surprising house, full of beautiful things. It is far from the modest bungalow it appears to be: an Aladdin's cave, larger than you could imagine. The sitting room is bright and elegant, with fine views to Bamburgh Castle; the dining room has deep red rugs and a mahogany oval table. The garden/breakfast room, the hub of the house, has a country cottage feel to it. In summer the table can be moved outside to the sun-trapping courtyard for breakfast. The bedrooms have fresh flowers and very good books. Mary is kind, discreetly laid back and interesting. A fascinating place.

Rooms: 1 twin & 1 double, sharing private bath & shower.

Price: £25 p.p. Single supp. £5.

Breakfast: At 8.30am.

Meals: Dinner £17.50 p.p. by arrangement.

Closed: Christmas, New Year & occasionally in winter.

This honest farm lies in 400 acres of mixed arable land that sweep down to the coast. The Jacksons are hard-working but still find time to greet and know their guests. The bedrooms are large, bright and well-furnished; there is a conservatory at the back in which to have tea on arrival, and the croquet lawn, with its splendid views to the sea, will draw even the most hapless beginner out to its uneven folds. Breakfast is a feast, but it is the Jacksons and their genuine warmth that make this place so enjoyable.

Rooms: 2 doubles & 1 twin, all en suite (shower). Bathroom also available.

Price: £24 p.p. Ask about single supp.

Breakfast: Until 9am.

Meals: Dinner £13 p.p. by prior arrangement. Packed lunches from £3.50 p.p.

Closed: Christmas & New Year.

North from Newcastle on A1, then right signed Bamburgh on B1341. Continue to village, pass 30 mph sign and hotel, then 1st right, house 400 yards on right.

Map Ref No: 20

Mary Dixon
Broome
22 Ingram Road
Bamburgh
Northumberland NE69 7BT
Tel: 01668 214287

From Alnwick, A1068 to Alnmouth. At Hipsburn r'bout follow signs to station and cross bridge. Straight on to Bilton Barns down first left-hand lane, about 0.5 miles from road.

Map Ref No: 20

Brian & Dorothy Jackson
Bilton Barns
Alnmouth
Alnwick
Northumberland NE66 2TB
Tel: 01665 830427
Fax: 01665 830063

Once the home of Capability Brown's family - even he couldn't improve the tumbling Northumbrian countryside. Stephen and Celia have prettily restored and refurnished Shieldhall with just enough restraint. The oak-filled, dark-beamed, inglenooked dining room is just right for candlelit dinners. His cabinet-making skill is superb - admire the bar concealed in the library. Guest suites have entrance arches (originally the cart park), and are cosily set round a rose-clad courtyard, each in different style and timber. Celia is a cheerful and attentive hostess who enjoys cooking for her guests.

Rooms: 1 family suite and 2 doubles, all en suite (shower) and 1 family suite, en suite (bath).

Price: £21.50-£25.00 p.p. Single supp. £8.50.

Breakfast: Flexible.

Meals: Dinner £14.75 p.p

Closed: 1 November-1 March.

From Newcastle take A696 (signed Jedburgh). On B6342 take right 4 miles north of Belsay and house is on left after 300 yards.

Map Ref No: 20

Celia & Stephen Gay
Shieldhall
Wallington
Morpeth
Northumberland NE61 4AQ
Tel: 01830 540387
Fax: 01830 540387

This is a lovely, wholesome, family place where horses and naturally happy children thrive. Ailsa Speke, welcoming and passionate about horses, runs the immaculate old sprawling farmhouse with great good humour, serving a proper country breakfast with fresh orange juice. Rooms are good-sized, plain-carpeted, bright with cotton prints and views across Northumbria. The dining room has beams, mahogany and, again, great rolling views. Relax here, play tennis on the excellent court, or visit quaint old Corbridge.

Rooms: 1 twin and 1 double, both with private bathrooms.

Price: £25 p.p. No single supp.

Breakfast: Flexible.

Meals: Available locally.

Closed: 1 December-31 January.

From Newcastle, A69 signed Hexham. At A68 roundabout take Corbridge, then 1st right, signed Aydon & Thornbrough. Over dual carriageway to 1st farmhouse on right. On for 50 yards to drive on right, signed.

Map Ref No: 20

Ailsa & Ben Speke
Thornbrough High House
Corbridge
Northumberland NE45 5PR
Tel: 01434 633080

NORTHUMBERLAND

Simplicity at its pure best. Lizzie has somehow done to this 'gentleman's residence' of about 1800 what many of us would like to do with our lives: it is uncluttered, clean, focused, and pays exquisite attention to inherent - rather than added - detail. So there are no frills or flounces, no serried ranks of collected objects to impress you; the eye is drawn to the Georgian details, the doors, windows, waxed floorboards, proportions. Fresh flowers, rugs, comfortable beds and wonderful views enhance this stylish place. Lizzie is a notable cook, too.

Rooms: 2 doubles, en suite (1 bath, 1 shower). 1 single, en suite (shower).

Price: £22.50 p.p. Single £25.

Breakfast: Flexible.

Meals: Dinner, 2 courses, £10 p.p.; 3 courses, £12.50 p.p. By arrangement.

Closed: Never!

Take A69. Signed to Ovington, on left if travelling to Hexham. Through Ovington village, passing 2 pubs. House signposted on the left after sharp corner.

Map Ref No: 20

Liz Pelly
Ovington House
Ovington
Prudhoe
Northumberland NE42 6DH
Tel: 01661 832442
Fax: 01661 832442

The gardens, Mrs Clark's pride and joy, make this place. They are formal, scented and spectacular, moving in a careful, colourful, artfully controlled sweep to a wooded wilderness. A vast orderly vegetable and soft fruit garden supplies the Loughbrow jam-making business; a little canal runs beneath a turfed bridge; bees buzz. The warm and gorgeously 18th-century house has four reception rooms, moulded ceilings and chintzy country house decor. Rooms are big, simple and have magnificent views. Mrs Clark loves cooking for guests.

Rooms: 1 double and 1 twin, both with private bath; 1 twin, en suite (bath) and 2 singles sharing bathroom.

Price: £25 p.p. Single supp. £10.

Breakfast: Between 8-9am, except by prior arrangement.

Meals: Dinner, inc. wine, £18 p.p.

Closed: Occasionally.

From Hexham take B6306 signed Blanchland. After 0.25 miles, fork right. After a further 0.25 miles you will find the lodge gates in middle of road fork. House is 0.5 miles up the drive.

Map Ref No: 20

Patricia Ann Clark
Loughbrow House
Hexham
Northumberland NE46 1RS
Tel: 01434 603351

The views through the many windows are sweepingly glorious. The luxury within is considerable, but understated. Coffee after dinner is served in the yellow drawing room warmed by log fires, family pictures and oil paintings. Breakfast in the kitchen at a huge oak table under a beam festooned with dried flowers. The bedrooms are in country-house chintz-and-lace style, furnished with antiques and those gorgeous views. Tea on the terrace on arrival, in summer. David breeds horses and gladly shows you the stables at evening feed time. Susan cooks superbly, and runs cookery courses.

Rooms: 1 twin & 1 double, both en suite (bath); 1 double with private bath.

Price: £24-£29 p.p. Single supp. £10.

Breakfast: Until 9am.

Meals: Dinner £18.50 p.p. by arrangement.

Closed: 24 December-2 January.

Just two miles from Hadrian's Wall, it is at the end of a long sweeping drive with woodland on one side, pasture on the other, birdsong and the sound of horses' hooves, and the occasional roe deer ambling into view. The house is well lived-in, elegant and comfortable, with old family paintings and some splendid antiques. The bedrooms are crisp, pretty and beautifully furnished. There is a walled garden and breakfast can be taken on the terrace. After many years abroad the Stewarts have returned to Katie's roots; she grew up in this lovely house. *Children over 10 welcome.*

Rooms: 1 double & 1 twin, both en suite (bath); 1 twin with private bathroom.

Price: £25-£30 p.p. No single supp.

Breakfast: Until 9am.

Meals: Available locally.

Closed: October-February.

From Hexham take B6306 south. First right to Witley Chapel to top of hill and into dip. Tree on right with sign to farm. Right down track for 0.75 miles.

Map Ref No: 19

Go 7 miles north of Cordbridge on A68. Turn left on A6079 and after 1 mile turn right through Lodge gates with arch. House 0.5 miles down drive.

Map Ref No: 20

David & Susan Carr
East Peterelfield Farm
Hexham
Northumberland NE46 2JT
Tel: 01434 607209
Fax: 01434 601753

Simon & Katie Stewart
The Hermitage
Swinburne
Nr. Hexham
Northumberland NE48 4DG
Tel: 01434 681248
Fax: 01434 681110

A family house in breathtaking countryside, Mantle Hill has received glowing reports for its 18th-century sobriety and stupendous gardens. There's a pond garden in the hillside, terraced lawns, space and colour, lovely family: pony-mad teenage young, Peter, a land agent/farmer/wine trader, and Charlotte - deeply into organic gardening and maintaining her reputation for good food. Grandmother's silk Shanghai hangings adorn the staircase wall, bedrooms have fresh white linen and good, solid, old furniture, the surrounding Hesleyside estate is wonderful for walking. *Children over 3 welcome.*

Rooms: 1 twin with private bathroom and 1 double, en suite (bath).

Price: £20-£28 p.p. Children, £15. No single supp.

Breakfast: Between 8-9am.

Meals: Dinner £17.50 p.p. by arrangement (minimum 4 people).

Closed: Christmas & New Year.

From the A69, 1 mile west of Hexham, take A6079/6320 north to Bellingham. Just before crossing the North Tyne river at Bellingham, take left to Hesleyside. Mantle Hill is 0.25 miles on left after Hesleyside Hall.

Map Ref No: 19

Peter & Charlotte Loyd
Mantle Hill
Hesleyside
Bellingham, Hexham
Northumberland NE48 2LB
Tel: 01434 220428
Fax: 01434 220113
e-mail: charlotte@mantlehill.demon.co.uk

Nottinghamshire

Southwell's Minster is "the most rural Cathedral in England" and can be seen, floodlit every night, from some of the Olde Forge's bedrooms. Hilary, talkative and kind, has lived in Southwell for 38 years and feels passionately about it; you can walk to the shops and pubs from this house. Pink in front and very pretty, it has a cottagey feel, though it is bigger than it looks. Filled with antiques and interesting things, rooms are small but pretty (pastels) and Hilary's breakfasts are famous. You may eat them in the plant-filled conservatory or, in summer, by the pond.

Rooms: 1 twin and 3 doubles, all en suite; 1 twin with private bathroom.

Price: £25-£28 p.p. Single occ. £35-£40.

Breakfast: 9am (week), 9.30am (weekend).

Meals: Light supper, £10.50 p.p., available on request. Plenty of pubs & restaurants within walking distance.

Closed: Never!

From Nottingham A612 to Southwell. Right into main street & pass the Minster. About 100 yards further on fork right at the library, then turn right almost immed. down an alley beside the Old Forge to a car park at the rear.

Map Ref No: 10

Hilary Marston
The Old Forge
Burgage Lane
Southwell
Nottinghamshire NG25 0ER
Tel: 01636 812809
Fax: 01636 816302

You'll be bowled over by the view. From the generous windows of the majestic red drawing-room, beyond the manicured gardens, the Vale of Belvoir is at your feet. The hill behind is the highest between here and the Urals! The house is not so much grand as loved and lived in - beneath Edwardian grandfather's kindly gaze - and some parts clearly bear the comfortable mark of time. Hilary is a friendly, quiet, intelligent and busy grandmother. The (unheated) swimming pool is for the hardy... in summer.

Rooms: 2 doubles and 1 twin, all with private baths; 1 twin, en suite (shower).

Price: £20-£22 p.p. Single occ. £20-£25.

Breakfast: Flexible.

Meals: Available locally - 3 good pubs within walking distance.

Closed: Christmas.

From Nottingham take A606 to Upper Broughton. Drive to top of hill, then sharp left into Colonel's Lane. Signed.

Map Ref No: 10

Hilary Dowson
Sulney Fields
Colonel's Lane
Upper Broughton, Melton Mowbray
Nottinghamshire LE14 3BD
Tel: 01664 822204
Fax: 01664 823976

"What a welcome! She's really chatty, no hang-ups, I felt completely at home and wanted to stay longer", wrote our first inspector. Practically everyone in Oxfordshire seems to count Deborah as a friend. The 17th-century house hunkers down in an idyllic hamlet with 14th-century church and the low rural hum of an Agatha Christie novel. The river Thames runs through the village. Beams, uneven floors, period furniture, open fire in inglenook, oak doors, local or home-grown food. Attractive and comfortable without any pretension.

Rooms: 1 double, en suite (shower) and 1 double with private bathroom.

Price: £24-£26 p.p. Single supp. £7.

Breakfast: Until 9am (week), flexible at weekends.

Meals: Dinner, 3 courses, from £17 p.p. Supper, 2 courses, from £12 p.p. Packed lunches £5 p.p. All by arrangement. B.Y.O. wine.

Closed: Never!

Oxfordshire

Turn right at T-junction in Little Wittenham. Rooks Orchard is fifth building on right behind a long hedge. Turn right into second gate.

Map Ref No: 4

Jonathan & Deborah Welfare
Rooks Orchard
Little Wittenham
Abingdon
Oxfordshire OX14 4QY
Tel: 01865 407765
Fax: 01865 407765
e-mail: jonathan.welfare@which.net

Unpretentious country B&B at its best: a hard-working Aga, cats and dogs everywhere, piano, books, real fire and views over the 500-acre arable and sheep farm. It's impossible not to feel at ease in this totally solid farmhouse where you're unfussily but genuinely welcomed by Hilary. There are home-laid eggs, homemade marmalade and honey with your breakfast and plenty of tea and coffee. Total seclusion and peace and riverside walks along the Thames Path. *Children over 8 welcome.*

Rooms: 1 double and 1 twin, both en suite (bath).

Price: £24-£25 p.p. Single occ. £5-£10.

Breakfast: Until 9am.

Meals: Meals available locally.

Closed. Christmas & lambing season (ask!).

Refreshingly original (viz the large projected clock on the drawing room wall) as well as ravishingly beautiful - and Anthea and Stephen are fun, too. Clocks are their main business now, with a workshop in the outhouse. They are as laid back as they are efficient... unusual for owners of houses like this. The decor is oak floors, white walls, wood, antique and contemporary simplicity (no chintz), with the odd dash of exotica from extensive long-haul travel. The drawing room has a vast fireplace for winter.

Rooms: 1 twin/double, en suite (shower) and 1 double, en suite (bath); 1 double with private bathroom.

Price: £35 p.p. Single occ. £50.

Breakfast: 9am (week), 10am (weekend).

Meals: Dinner available locally.

Closed: Christmas & New Year.

From Wallingford take A329 signed Shillingford. After 2 miles left through Shillingford Hotel car park just before the river. Follow track for 0.5 miles.

Map Ref No: 4

Hilary Warburton
North Farm
Shillingford Hill
Wallingford
Oxfordshire OX10 8NB
Tel: 01865 858406
Fax: 01865 858519

From M40, A329 towards Wallingford. In Stadhampton take lane immediately after mini-roundabout left across village green. House straight ahead.

Map Ref No: 4

Anthea & Stephen Savage
The Manor
Stadhampton
Oxfordshire OX44 7UL
Tel: 01865 891999
Fax: 01865 891640

OXFORDSHIRE

Strikingly genuine hosts, Miriam and Michael love their house and their intricate garden; it is a honey-pot for birds and guests alike. They want everyone to enjoy their land and point the way to the nature trails that criss-cross the 150 acres of farmland. The house is part 15th-century, part Victorian and has a conservatory brimming with greenery. Tiny staircases and narrow corridors lead to the pretty bedrooms which are dominated by huge beds. Timber-supported walls and floorboards bend and creak with age. An asylum for city refugees.

Rooms: 3 twins/doubles, all en suite (bath).

Price: £25 p.p. Single supp. £5.

Breakfast: Any time!

Meals: None, but many pubs & Le Manoir aux Quatre Saisons nearby!

Closed: Never!

This beautiful farmhouse was once owned by St. John's College, Oxford, and the date stone above the entrance reads 1629, although an original house goes even further back. Small stone-arched and mullioned windows trickle in light, yet both bedrooms are light and airy. There are Tudor fireplaces, timbered and exposed walls. The huge, twin bedroom has ornate plasterwork and views of the garden and church. The green and peach double is cosier and overlooks the garden and open fields. The sitting room/dining room has a woodburning stove where Mary Anne or Robert will bring you homemade shortbread and tea when you arrive.

Rooms: 1 double and 1 twin, each en suite (shower).

Price: £22.50 p.p. Single supp. £10.

Breakfast: Until 9am.

Meals: Good restaurants locally.

Closed: Mid-December-1 February.

From northbound M40 turn off at junction 7 for Milton Common. Left by Three Pigeons pub. After 0.75 miles, and a line of poplars, right down drive.

Map Ref No: 10

Michael & Miriam Hedges
Lower Chilworth Farm
Milton Common
Thame
Oxfordshire OX9 2JS
Tel: 01844 279593

From Oxford take A420 towards Swindon for 8 miles, right at r'bout, signed Witney/ Standlake (A415), over 2 bridges, immediately right by pub car park. At T-junction, right; drive on right, past church.

Map Ref No: 4

Mary Anne & Robert Florey
Rectory Farm
Northmoor
Nr. Witney
Oxfordshire OX8 1SX
Tel: 01865 300207
Fax: 01865 300559

Lord Craven, in love, brought the Queen of Bohemia to the village. In *Tom Brown's School-Days* the house is a "low-lying wayside inn" and it still lies low - you duck to get about the wonderful, beamed, downstairs four-poster room. Upstairs, passages and steps turning all ways, are other beamed rooms, equally attractive... and colourful, too. The beamed sitting room, with log fire in inglenook, has some fine antiques. Carol serves dinner in her huge L-shaped kitchen, or the brick-paved courtyard. Glorious walks from the doorstep, and a shaggy old English sheepdog.

Rooms: 1 four-poster, en suite (bath), 1 half-tester, en suite (shower) and 1 twin sharing bathroom.

Price: £25 £30 p.p. Single supp. by arrangement.

Breakfast: Until 9am.

Meals: Dinner, 3 courses, £15.50 p.p.

Closed: Never!

From M4, junct 14, north on A338. Turn left onto B4001. Through Lambourn & 1 mile north of village, left and after 2.5 miles, in Kingston Lisle, left to Uffington, through village and right after church.

Map Ref No: 4

Carol Wadsworth
The Craven
Fernham Road
Uffington
Oxfordshire SN7 7RD
Tel: 01367 820449

It is good to see the owner of a hotel wiping the sauce off his fingers before shaking your hand. Burford House is small enough for Jane and Simon to influence every corner; this is also their home. It is a delight, small and intensely personal, re-decorated with elegant good taste without any loss of character: oak beams, good fabrics, antiques, plain colours, log fires, luxurious bathrooms, ravishing breakfasts, a little garden... all in this exquisite Cotswold town. And with a subtle sense of fun, too, that avoids any hint of stuffiness. You can unwind here - guests return time after time to do so.

Rooms: 1 twin, 2 doubles and 4 four-posters, all en suite.

Price: From £40-£60 p.p. Single supp. by arrangement.

Breakfast: Light breakfast until 11 am. Cooked: 8-9am (week), 8.30-9.30am (weekend).

Meals: Supper, by prior arrangment. Good restaurants locally. Light lunch & afternoon tea available.

Closed: 2 weeks in January/February.

In the centre of Burford.

Map Ref No: 10

Jane & Simon Henty
Burford House
99 High Street
Burford
Oxfordshire OX18 4QA
Tel: 01993 823151
Fax: 01993 823240

Bridget confides "I used to be solicitous, then realised guests didn't want that". Bridget, gracious and elegant, the house and the setting are intoxicating. Our inspector calls it "a Sawday idyll". This is country elegance with no concession to modernity: furniture and rugs fit beautifully, the kitchen is stone-flagged and wood-boarded. The Coach House has a bedroom, kitchen and sitting room for B&B or self-catering. The River Windrush trickles through the garden, the church and the ruins of Minster Lovell Hall sit beside it.

Rooms: 1 twin with private bathroom; 1 twin in Coach House with bath.

Price: £35 p.p. Single supp. £10.

Breakfast: Until 9.30am.

Meals: Dinner £20 p.p.

Closed: Christmas & New Year & one week at Easter.

Cosseted in the heart of beautifully maintained Ditchley Park, Newbarn Farm is a walkers' - and riders' - paradise. You can stroll straight out across the lawns and into 6,000 acres of grounds and woodland. The Dents themselves have nine acres of fields and lawn, with a small spring-fed lake which further softens the scene. The house (1740 plus discreet extension) is comfort itself and piloted by an easy-going Rosie. There's a large drawing room where the space and lack of clutter let the mind unfurl. Bedrooms are large, not overadorned, pretty with fruit and flowers, and comfortable. It's deeply rural and very friendly.

Rooms: 1 double, en suite (bath) and 1 twin with private bath.

Price: £32-£35 p.p. No single supp.

Breakfast: Flexible.

Meals: Excellent pubs nearby.

Closed: Christmas.

From Burford take A40 towards Oxford. At next roundabout bear left for Minster Lovell. Head for Minster Lovell Hall across bridge. House on right before church.

Map Ref No: 10

Ms Bridget Geddes
The Old Vicarage
Minster Lovell
Oxfordshire OX8 5RR
Tel: 01993 775630
Fax: 01993 772534

From Oxford take A44 north towards Woodstock/Evesham. Through Woodstock and 1 mile later, at Shell garage, left signed Charlbury (B4437). House 2.5 miles on left at end of wood, down track and over cattle grids.

Map Ref No: 10

Rosanagh & Andrew Dent
Newbarn Farm
Ditchley Park
Oxfordshire OX7 4EX
Tel: 01993 898398
Fax: 01993 891100
e-mail: dentcomm@compuserve.com

Outside is the bustle of a county town; inside this Queen Anne house, you are free from the twentieth century's bluster. Built in the early 1700s it has an appealing air of old-fashioned grandeur that has mellowed with age, as if to invite a wider circle of people into enjoyment of what remains pure luxury. Charming Roberto lends sparkle to it all. After running a larger hotel for some years, they have opted for fewer guests, more focused service here; both are warmly enthusiastic about ensuring your happiness.

Rooms: 1 twin/double and 1 double, both with sitting rooms and en suite bathrooms.

Price: From £35 p.p. Single occ. from £55.

Breakfast: Flexible.

Meals: Packed lunch available on request.

Closed: January.

Dating back to 1720, this lovely farmhouse is an excellent base for Blenheim Palace, Oxford and the Cotswolds. Well-furnished bedrooms share a shower room. The rest of the house has generous rooms with good pictures and prints, pleasant country furniture and a happy, relaxed atmosphere. The Stevensons are most welcoming and will suggest good local walks and plenty of places to eat. The double bedroom once featured in a Laura Ashley catalogue; the spiral staircase to the twin is a challenge for the unsprightly.

Rooms: 1 double and 1 twin, sharing shower room.

Price: From £20 p.p. Single occ. from £25.

Breakfast: Flexible.

Meals: Available locally.

Closed: Christmas.

From Oxford take A44 to Woodstock. Turn left into the High Street before pelican crossing. On left opposite Brotherton's brasserie.

Map Ref No: 10

Roberto & Christina Gramellini
Holmwood
6 High Street
Woodstock
Oxfordshire OX20 1TF
Tel: 01993 812266
Fax: 01993 813233
christina@holm-wood.demon.co.uk

Take A44 north from Oxford's ring road. At r'bout 1 mile before Woodstock left onto A4095 into Bladon. Take last left in the village. House is on 2nd bend in road with iron railings.

Map Ref No: 10

Helen Stevenson
Manor Farmhouse
Manor Road
Bladon, Woodstock
Oxfordshire OX20 1RU
Tel: 01993 812168
Fax: 01993 812168

A haven in the middle of Oxford. Clever use of design details and materials have kept the old-house feel and the intimacy of a private club. The splendid bedrooms in smart florals and checks - some in the old part of the hotel with fireplaces and panelling - have glorious marble bathrooms. Entrance hall with bar and winter fire, paintings and prints everywhere, leather chairs in the Parsonage Bar dining room. Hotel guests can use the first floor roof garden, lush with plants, for tea or sundowner. First class service - from real people; staff are hand-picked as much for their personality as for their skill.

Rooms: 30, all en suite.

Price: Double £145-£170 per room. Suite £195. Single £125.

Breakfast: Until 11am.

Meals: Lunch & dinner available.

Closed: 24-27 December.

Lying on a belt of warm-coloured limestone that sweeps from the Cotswolds to Lincolnshire, Great Tew is a model village. And this is a perfect pub; a fire roars, jugs and mugs hang from the low-timbered ceiling and beers are changed weekly. The dining room is tiny and intimate with beamed, stone walls; everything is home-cooked. The bedrooms are snug and newly-decorated and the A-shaped double-aspect room right at the top has views of the pretty garden. All is sparkling and well-cared for; Tim and Anne love this place.

Rooms: 4 doubles and 1 single, all en suite (shower); 1 double, en suite (bath).

Price: Double £32.50 p.p. Single £40.

Breakfast: At 9am.

Meals: Bar meals & dinner in pub.

Closed: 25 December-1 January.

From A40 ring road south at Banbury Road roundabout to Summertown and towards city centre. Hotel on right next to St Giles's church.

Map Ref No: 10

A361 from Chipping Norton, turn right onto B4022; pub is signposted.

Map Ref No: 10

Ian Hamilton
The Old Parsonage
No. 1 Banbury Road
Oxford
Oxfordshire OX2 6NN
Tel: 01865 310210
Fax: 01865 311262
e-mail: old parsonage@dial.pipex.com

Anne & Tim Newman
Falkland Arms
Great Tew
Oxfordshire OX7 4DB
Tel: 01608 683653
Fax: 01608 683656

A thatched cottage, a jigsaw of beams, nooks and crannies, with an old-fashioned cottage garden - climbing roses and wisteria rambling up and over everything, in a quiet Cotswolds village. It is an engagingly relaxed, happy house and is full of music and laughter. The garden is Judith's passion - she has deep knowledge of all things horticultural AND green fingers. She writes on the subject and has produced a guide to garden visits. Artistic and intelligent, she lends her own personality to the house: lived-in elegance, good food, log fires, bright pastel and white bedrooms. Fresh everything...

Rooms: 1 double and 1 twin, both en suite (bath).

Price: £28 p.p. Single occ. £35.50.

Breakfast: Until 9.30am.

Meals: Dinner, 4 courses, £20 p.p., by arrangement.

Closed: Christmas.

Maggie's brisk efficiency is a reflection of her deep desire for guests to enjoy her home as much as she does. South-facing, the sun streams up the valley and penetrates the stone mullion windows, giving a marvellous glow to this painstakingly restored house. Bedrooms are large, light and airy with thick beams and carpets and walk-in wardrobes. Views over the church on one side and the valley on the other improve the higher up you go. The attic houses a games room with full-size snooker table. *Children over 8 welcome.*

Rooms: 2 doubles, one en suite (bath) and 1 with private bathroom.

Price: £25-£30 p.p. Single supp. £10.

Breakfast: Until 8.30am weekdays. Flexible at weekends.

Meals: Dinner £20 p.p.

Closed: Never!

Sibford Gower is 0.5 miles south off B4035 which runs between Banbury and Chipping Camden. House is on main street on same side as church and school.

Map Ref No: 10

Judith Hitching
Gower's Close
Sibford Gower
Nr. Banbury
Oxfordshire OX15 5RW
Tel: 01295 780348

From A422, 7 miles NW of Banbury turn left down hill, then after going up a hill, turn left by church. Follow drive right to end.

Map Ref No: 10

Maggie Hainsworth
Mill House
Shenington
Banbury
Oxfordshire OX15 6NH
Tel: 01295 670642
Fax: 01295 670642

The village is enchantingly English with thatch, wispy smoke and maypole dancing on the green. The Manor is a long low house in soft-gold stone with madly high irregular dormers and mossy old tiles. There are log fire, sofas and cushions in the drawing-room and the pastels are light and fresh in the Winter bedroom, with its fireplace, and in the Crows Nest room where the ceiling slopes and one great beam crosses the floor. The family bustle charms you, animals abound and birds sing; easy and fun, a happy place.

Rooms: 2 doubles: 1 en suite (bath) and 1 with w.c. and private bath (this room, with double and 2 singles, can also be used as family room).

Price: £28.50 p.p. Single occ. £37. Deposit of £10 p.p.

Breakfast: Flexible.

Meals: Dinner, 3 courses, £25 p.p.

Closed: Never!

Leave your hectic life behind, slow down and enjoy the peace of these surroundings and the healthy country food. The Caves will give you a real farmhouse welcome. Their one bedroom is pastel and floral with beams, two windows, old pine furniture, a power shower and a triangular corner bath. (Families are most welcome and can often be squeezed in.) Fresh-laid eggs and black pudding for breakfast if you wish. A very charming, immaculately clean and genuine house.

Rooms: 1 family/twin/double with private bath, shower & w.c.

Price: £18.50 p.p. No single supp.

Breakfast: 7-9.30am.

Meals: No, but available locally.

Closed: Never!

M40, exit 11 to Banbury. Take A422 for Stratford-upon-Avon, through Wroxton village, right to Hornton. There, in centre, right at Round Green. House is 1st on right.

Map Ref No: 10

Malcolm & Vicki Patrick
The Manor House
Hornton
Nr. Banbury
Oxfordshire OX15 6BZ
Tel: 01295 670386
Fax: 01295 670386

B4525 N E from Banbury for 4 miles. Follow signs to Sulgrave Manor. First right into Park Lane. Farm entrance is approx. 170m on right.

Map Ref No: 10

Steven & Libby Cave
Wemyss Farm
Sulgrave
Banbury
Oxfordshire OX17 2RX
Tel: 01295 760323

The deep comfort of this 1770 farmhouse bears witness to Sara's profession - interior design. Cushions, curtains and sofas are adorned with beautiful fabrics - orange and yellow checks here, Colefax and Fowler florals there. The kitchen glows with sunshine yellow and cupboards are hand-stencilled. Stephen and Sara have been here for 25 years and happily share their books, piano, tennis court, gardens, lake and local knowledge. The beds are memorably comfortable and all have excellent linen sheets.

Rooms: 3 twins/doubles, all en suite (1 shower, 1 bath and 1 bath and shower).

Price: £26 p.p. Single supp. £8.

Breakfast: Flexible.

Meals: Dinner, 4 courses, £15 p.p., by arrangement.

Closed: Never!

Low ceilings, exposed beams and stone fireplaces - and the bedrooms, perched above their own staircases like crows' nests, are delightful. The barn room has its own entrance. All rooms are unusual and full of character, old and luxurious; the family's history and travels are evident all over. Your hosts will occasionally dine with guests. They are good listeners, amusing and utterly friendly, as is Ulysses, their large soppy golden retriever. It's all so easy that you may not want to leave.

Rooms: 1 double, en suite (bath) and 1 twin/double, en suite (bath/shower); 1 twin/double with private bathroom.

Price: £26-£29 p.p. Single supp. £8.

Breakfast: 8-9am.

Meals: Dinner £20 p.p.

Closed: Christmas.

In Kings Sutton follow signs to Charlton but, before leaving Kings Sutton, take last turning right, off Astrop Road, opposite a tree with a seat around it. Farmhouse is at the bottom of the lane.

Map Ref No: 10

From the M40, exit 10 and take A43 towards Northampton. After 5 miles, left to Charlton. There, left and house is on the left, 100 yards past the Rose and Crown.

Map Ref No: 10

Sara & Stephen Allday
College Farmhouse
Kings Sutton
Banbury
Oxfordshire OX17 3PS
Tel: 01295 811473
Fax: 01295 812505
e-mail: sallday@compuserve. com

Col & Mrs Nigel &
Rosemary Grove-White
Home Farmhouse
Charlton
Nr. Banbury
Oxfordshire OX17 3DR
Tel: 01295 811683
Fax: 01295 811683

A very English and lived-in, cosy Georgian house with natural charm and elegance. You can dine by the light of candles on a small 18th-century table beneath the painted gaze of Inigo Jones, a forebear of Mr Wallace, or settle by a log fire in the guests' panelled drawing room. In good weather, breakfast and dinner can be served in the garden, under the vines and in a lovely welcoming atmosphere; the Wallaces genuinely enjoy people. There are mature trees and shrubs, old roses and herbs, an acre of garden and superb countryside (AONB).

Rooms: 2 twins/doubles: 1 en suite bath and 1 en suite shower; 1 single with adjacent bathroom.

Price: Double £25 p.p. Single occ. £25.

Breakfast: 7.30-9am.

Meals: Dinner, £15 p.p., by arrangement. Also good pubs nearby.

Closed: Never!

An enthralling house that twists and turns through the ages - an Elizabethan landing, a Georgian panelled hall, a Victorian cast-iron bath. The same family has lived here for five generations. From the spectacular panelled hall with its piano and fireplace, you ramble into the heart of the house. The huge bedrooms are romantic (especially the four-poster) and have lovingly-equipped bathrooms (hangover cures and other essentials). This is a house where tradition is treated with respect and if you stay over the weekend you'll share one - a Sunday breakfast of boiled eggs and kedgeree.

Rooms: 1 four-poster, en suite (bath); 1 double (queen boat bed) with private bathroom; 1 twin, en suite (shower).

Price: From £37.50 p.p. Single supp. £10.

Breakfast: Until 9am (week), 8.30am (Sunday).

Meals: No, but good pub & restaurants within 1 mile.

Closed: December-mid-January.

Close to M40 exits 4 & 5, and M4 exits 8 & 9. Once in Frieth follow road through village & on towards Hambleden & Henley. House is 0.75 miles along on right.

Map Ref No: 5

In Henley centre take Duke St. After 170m right into Greys Rd. After almost 2 miles (as you leave 30 mph zone) take second drive on right, signed 'Hernes Estate. Private Drive'.

Map Ref No: 5

Wynyard & Julia Wallace
Little Parmoor
Frieth
Henley-on-Thames
Oxfordshire RG9 6NL
Tel: 01494 881447
Fax: 01494 883012

Richard & Gillian Ovey
Hernes
Henley-on-Thames
Oxfordshire RG9 4NT
Tel: 01491 573245
Fax: 01491 574645

Holmwood is a large Georgian manor house set in beautiful grounds. The interior is immaculate and exactly right for its period. In the galleried hall a staircase sweeps you regally up to the very large rooms: all except one look onto the garden and far beyond. There's a stately drawing room, woodland to explore, tennis and croquet to play. The real French doors of the dining room and drawing room open onto the grounds. Brian and Wendy are irreproachably efficient and genuinely friendly. *Children over 12 welcome.*

Rooms: 2 twins, 2 doubles and 1 single, all en suite (bath).

Price: Double £27.50 p.p. Single supp. £35.

Breakfast: 7.45-9.45am.

Meals: Available locally.

Closed: Christmas.

A place to remind yourself of the wonders of English country life. So perfectly peaceful; birds make the biggest noise. In the evening, more music to the ears: the crackle of the fire and the sound of easy chatter. It is a lovely house with a sitting room full of Persian rugs and with a baby grand that beckons those who can play. Bedrooms are unmistakably 'country' and low ceilings and uneven floors reveal their 16th- and 17th-century roots. There are eight acres of grounds with all-round views and free-range hens.

Rooms: 2 twins/doubles, en suite (bath); 1 double with private bathroom and 1 twin, en suite (shower).

Price: £22.50-£27.50 p.p. Single occ. £28-£34.

Breakfast: 7.30-9am.

Meals: Good choice of places locally.

Closed: Christmas.

From Henley-on-Thames A4155 towards Reading. After 2.5 miles, College on left & pub on right. Before pub turn into Plough Lane. House is up hill on left.

Map Ref No: 5

Brian & Wendy Talfourd-Cook
Holmwood
Shiplake Row
Binfield Heath, Henley
Oxfordshire RG9 4DP
Tel: 0118 947 8747
Fax: 0118 947 8637

Go NW on Peppard Road from Henley for 3 miles, then right for Shepherds Green. House is on right after 0.3 miles. Please phone to advise time of arrival.

Map Ref No: 5

Sue Fulford-Dobson
Shepherds
Shepherds Green
Rotherfield Greys, Henley-on-Thames
Oxfordshire RG9 4QL
Tel: 01491 628413
Fax: 01491 628413

Staggeringly beautiful scenery surrounds this c.1845 rectory hotel. Easy-going atmosphere and unpretentious comfort: the entrance hall doubles as a bar in the evenings and the dining room has a curtained-off sitting area with plump chairs and a fire. A nice touch is having mineral water, fruit and chocolates laid out on the sideboard for anyone to help themselves. The good-sized bedrooms are thoughtfully decorated, most of them are furnished with antiques and nearly all have spectacular views. Great food to suit all tastes. People come again and again.

Rooms: 4 twins, 5 doubles and 1 family room, all en suite.

Price: £35-£43 p.p. Single occ. £50-£55.

Breakfast: 8-9.30am.

Meals: Dinner, 3 courses, £19 p.p.

Closed: Christmas & 1-14 January.

Shropshire

From A5 head into Oswestry. Leave town on B4580 signed Llansilin. Hotel on left just before Rhydycroesau.

Map Ref No: 9

Miles Hunter
Pen-y-Dyffryn Country Hotel
Rhydycroesau
Nr. Oswestry
Shropshire SY10 7JD
Tel: 01691 653700
Fax: 01691 653700

In this ancient, magpie-gabled house in the village of Knockin - church and pound are 800 years old - you will be treated to strong coffee and croissants, billiards and fresh flowers by a laughing, theatrical Pam and a gently smiling Peter. They create an atmosphere of vitality, warmth, elegance and good taste all at once. Excellent talkers, they are also knowledgeable about local history. There are two pianos, open fires, dark timbers, creaky stairs and a superb breakfast, plus a lovely garden and perhaps a friendly pub for supper.

Rooms: 1 twin and 1 double, en suite (shower) and 1 family room with double and 2 singles, en suite (bath/shower).

Price: £20-£22 p.p. Single occ. from £25.

Breakfast: Usually 7.30-9.30am.

Meals: Packed lunch, by arrangement.

Closed: Never!

Upper Brompton is delightful and down-to-earth, a working farm that combines agricultural bustle with elegant living spaces. The old Georgian farmhouse and outbuildings are solid and warmly russet, the rooms decorated in soft English country style with four-posters and many welcoming touches including a pot of tea and homemade cake on your arrival. Christine, vivacious and easy-going, makes a superb breakfast. George runs his large farm with enthusiasm; they both clearly enjoy making you feel at home.

Rooms: 2 doubles (four-posters), both en suite (bath); 1 kingsize, en suite (shower).

Price: £29-£35 p.p. Single supp. £10. Winter breaks available.

Breakfast: Flexible.

Meals: Available locally.

Closed: Christmas & New Year.

From Shrewsbury take A5 north. Through Nesscliffe, after 2 miles left to Knockin. Through Knockin, past Bradford Arms. Farmhouse 150 yards on left.

Map Ref No: 9

Pam Morrissey
Top Farmhouse
Knockin
Nr. Oswestry
Shropshire SY10 8HN
Tel: 01691 682582
Fax: 01691 682656

Farm is 4 miles south of Shrewsbury on A458. In Cross Houses turn left after petrol station, signed Atcham 1 mile. Down lane and right to Brompton; follow to farm.

Map Ref No: 9

Christine Yates-Roberts
Upper Brompton Farm
Cross Houses
Shrewsbury
Shropshire SY5 6LE
Tel: 01743 761629
Fax: 01743 761679

SHROPSHIRE

You'll probably be greeted by Bertie, the gentle black labrador, when you arrive at this large, comfortable Victorian house. You'll receive a warm welcome from Jackie and Jim too, before being shown to one of the charming bedrooms with uninterrupted views of the Stretton Hills. You can lie in bed in the morning, with the sun streaming in, and gaze over beautiful countryside, or enjoy it all from the conservatory downstairs. Then eat a good breakfast before exploring the gardens or venturing further afield, on horseback perhaps. Stabling provided and horses can be hired locally. *Children over 12 welcome.*

Rooms: 1 double with private bath and 1 twin/double, en suite (bath).

Price: £22-£25 p.p. Single supp. £5. Special breaks also available.

Breakfast: Flexible.

Meals: Good pubs nearby. Packed lunch from £2.50 p.p.

Closed: Christmas-New Year.

From Shrewsbury, go south on A49. In Dorrington turn right to Smethcott. After 3 miles, left at crossroads (signed Smethcott). House is 0.5 miles on.

Map Ref No: 9

Jackie & Jim Scarratt
Lawley House
Smethcott
Church Stretton
Shropshire SY6 6NX
Tel: 01694 751236
Fax: 01694 751396

Best of all must be the beds - 17th-century French wedding, Gothic brass, 1940s Italian boudoir, and more - but the whole converted crofter's cottage has lovely fabrics, beams, antiques and attention to detail. Run by a mother-and-daughter team, Jinlye sits, old, luxurious and sheltered, at 1,400ft surrounded by ancient hills, rare birds, wild ponies and windswept ridges. The skies are infinite; humanity was here 12,000 years ago and you can walk deep in ancient wildness before returning to superb home cooking and a loo with a view. *Children over 12 welcome.*

Rooms: 4 doubles, 2 twins/doubles and 2 twins, all en suite, except 1 double with private bath.

Price: £27-£40 p.p. Single occ. £42-£57.

Breakfast: 8-8.45am.

Meals: Dinner £15-£17.50 p.p.

Closed: Never!

From Shrewsbury take A49 to Church Stretton past the Little Chef and right towards All Stretton. Turn right, immediately past the phone box, up a winding road, up the hill to Jinlye.

Map Ref No: 9

Jan & Kate Tory
Jinlye
Castle Hill
All Stretton, Church Stretton
Shropshire SY6 6JP
Tel: 01694 723243
Fax: 01694 723243

336

337

On the edge of beautiful Corve Dale (come for the walking), Church House is quaint and comfortable. Margaret, and several centuries, have given the house easygoing manners and atmosphere. Child-friendly, it has a six-acre menagerie; also a soothing garden retreat with ornamental pool for (more adult) contemplative moments. Up the quirky, three-legged stairs, the bedrooms are in simple, cottage style with sloping ceilings. Downstairs, French windows onto the garden, stained glass doors, oak-beamed kitchen, open-plan dining room. Margaret's a whizz on local history.

Rooms: 1 double/family, en suite (shower) and 1 twin with private shower.

Price: £18.50 p.p. Reduction for 4 nights or more.

Breakfast: Until 9am.

Meals: Dinner, 3 courses, £12 p.p. by arrangement.

Closed: 1 November-Easter.

Fields of billowing crops lead up to the pretty farmhouse courtyard full of flowers and labradors. There's a rose-covered pergola and, behind the barns, a kitchen garden. The bedroom, in the converted barn, is large, pastel-coloured and utterly quiet - perfect for those who like their own space. Breakfast in the main house includes home-grown honey; they make beeswax too. Energetic, fun, family-farm feel. *Children over 10 welcome.*

Rooms: 1 twin, en suite (bath).

Price: £20 p.p. Single occ. £40.

Breakfast: Flexible.

Meals: Available locally.

Closed: Never!

From Bridgnorth take A458 to Shrewsbury. After 3 miles, in Morville, fork left onto B4368 to Craven Arms. After 1 mile (Aston Eyre) turn right before church and follow sign to house.

Map Ref No: 9

Margaret Cosh
Church House
Aston Eyre
Bridgnorth
Shropshire WV16 6XD
Tel: 01746 714248
Fax: 01746 714248
e-mail: astoneyre@aol.com

From Bridgnorth, take A458 to Shrewsbury. 0.5 miles after Morville, turn right into a stone road and follow signs to Hannigans Farm.

Map Ref No: 9

Fiona Thompson
Hannigans Farm
Morville
Bridgnorth
Shropshire WV16 4RN
Tel: 01746 714332
Fax: 01746 714332

Your every need is anticipated. The bathroom is packed with goodies, there's stacks of information to browse through, and books to share. The brass beds have crisp, flowery, fresh linen and it's all warm, quiet and very comfortable. Number Twenty Eight is on a beautiful Georgian street of listed and restored buildings, just outside the town walls and only 85 metres from the river (the ducks take their morning stroll past the house). The house is a gem and your hosts are generous, genuine and welcoming.

Rooms: 1 twin, en suite (bath/shower) and 1 double, en suite (shower). Cottage: 1 family and 1 double, both en suite (bath/shower). Westview House: 2 doubles both en suite (bath/shower).

Price: From £30 p.p. Single supp. £10.

Breakfast: Flexible.

Meals: Not available. Good restaurants within walking distance.

Closed: Never!

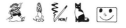

It takes just two minutes to walk into the most beautiful of medieval market towns. Or you can hop over the wall and swim from the river weir. Or just gaze, open-jawed, up at the castle ramparts. But you have come here for the food. They won a Michelin star in their Suffolk restaurant and the feast continues in Ludlow, with local produce if possible. This is a restaurant-with-rooms, the latter small but pretty, almost Shaker in style: simple fabrics, linens, cotton-weaves, king-size beds and views of the river. Good people, and huge commitment.

Rooms: 6 doubles, all en suite.

Price: £32.50-£44 p.p. Single occ. £55-£80.

Breakfast: Until 9.30am.

Meals: Dinner £22.50-£27.50 p.p. Lunch from £8 p.p.

Closed: Never!

House at bottom of Lower Broad Street, between Broadgate and Ludford Bridge.

Map Ref No: 9

Patricia & Philip Ross
Number Twenty Eight
28 Lower Broad Street
Ludlow
Shropshire SY8 1PQ
Tel: 01584 876996
Fax: 01584 876860
e-mail: ross.no28@btinternet.com

Drive into centre of Ludlow, heading for castle. Take road called 'Dinham' to left of castle and follow down short hill turning right at bottom before crossing river. On left, signed.

Map Ref No: 9

Judy & Chris Bradley
Mr Underhills at Dinham Weir
Dinham Bridge
Ludlow
Shropshire SY8 1EH
Tel: 01584 874431

The stupendous site and generous size of this early Georgian house reflect the status of the ancestor who built it in 1740. The present-day Salweys are farmers and Hermione's scrumptious food is based on home-reared beef and lamb and garden vegetables. The large softly-furnished bedrooms have antique chairs and modern bedding and one has a Louis XV bed. The Salweys are lovely, interesting people and the estate even has a Georgian bath house near the trout lake.

Rooms: 1 twin and 1 double, en suite (bath) and 1 double with private bathroom.

Price: £35 p.p. Single supp. £5.

Breakfast: Until 9am.

Meals: Dinner £16 p.p. (£20 p.p. with wine.)

Closed: 31 October-1 April.

From Ludlow over River Teme by traffic lights, 2nd right to Presteigne & Richard's Castle on B4361. After about 100 yards, drive is first right.

Map Ref No: 9

Humphrey & Hermione Salwey
The Lodge
Ludlow
Shropshire SY8 4DU
Tel: 01584 872103
Fax: 01584 876126

Leintwardine was once a Roman garrison; it is still in one of England's best defended, last unspoilt areas. This handsome former farmhouse is part 17th century, off a country lane so quiet that buzzards and deer are often seen close by. Log fires and beams, a sparkling communal dining table, a large garden bursting with colour, an orchard, welcoming hosts, modern comforts plus a certain elegance... all this amid a rare plethora of castles and historic towns. *Children over 10 welcome.*

Rooms: 1 double and 2 twins, en suite (shower); 1 double with private bathroom. Two self-catering cottages.

Price: £24-£27 p.p. Children 10-12 years, £12-£14. No single supp.

Breakfast: Flexible.

Meals: Dinner £17.50 p.p.

Closed: Christmas.

From Leintwardine, cross river, take first right signposted Knighton, first left signposted Hereford, first right up narrow unmarked lane. House is 300 yards on left.

Map Ref No: 9

Hildegard & Graham Cutler
Lower House
Adforton
Leintwardine
Shropshire SY7 0NF
Tel: 01568 770223
Fax: 01568 770592
e-mail: cutler@globalnet.co.uk

Standing in lush gardens that slope down to a millstream and across meadows to the River Teme, this is a gracious house with fine Georgian windows and valley roof. It has a millstream and a weir, a motte and a heronry, a point-to-point course and a ha-ha. Yvonne is a qualified cook and walkers who want to stretch their muscles in the surrounding Welsh border country will do so knowing they can tuck into a first-rate dinner when they return. Good-sized bedrooms with fine furniture, luxurious beds and cotton sheets.

Rooms: 1 double, en suite (shower), 2 twins/doubles with private bath and 1 single sharing bathroom.

Price: £25-£30 p.p. Single supp. £10.

Breakfast: Until 9am.

Meals: Dinner £18 p.p. Book in advance.

Closed: Never!

Deeply rural, but a short walk to one of the last parlour bars in the UK, the Sun Inn. Then walk back to Tanglewood for a memorable dinner; Anna cooks with herbs, spices, garlic and passion... unless you want something more simple. She and her husband Alan are easy hosts, experienced, and interesting. Anna has a most infectious laugh. The house is an architectural hotchpotch, heavily beamed and very old but with modern additions. The big comfy sitting room has piles of books. Near exquisite Ludlow (summer festival, September Food Festival) and they will collect you from the train.

Rooms: 1 twin and 1 double, both en suite (bath/shower).

Price: £23 p.p. Single supp. by arrangement.

Breakfast: Until 9am.

Meals: Dinner £14 p.p., sometimes available.

Closed: Christmas & New Year.

From Ludlow A49 to Shrewsbury. At Bromfield A4113. Right in Walford for Buckton, continue until second farm on left. Look for large sign on building.

Map Ref No: 9

Hayden & Yvonne Lloyd
Upper Buckton
Leintwardine, Craven Arms
Ludlow
Shropshire SY7 0JU
Tel: 01547 540634

From A49, take A4113 signed Leintwardine. After around 5 miles, pass Cottagers Comfort pub on right, take lane on left (unsigned). Through trees and turn right at junction. House on right on bend.

Map Ref No: 9

Anna Ecclestone
Kinton Thatch
Kinton
Leintwardine, Craven Arms
Shropshire SY7 0LT
Tel: 01547 540611
Fax: 01547 540534

"One of the most beautiful houses I've ever been in!" said our inspector. Roger owns a restaurant in Ludlow and two in Chelsea, but this is his *home*. Come to discover the sophisticated comfort and elegance hiding behind the grey stone exterior: stone-flagged floors, wood-burning stoves, polished tables, antiques blended with naïve textiles, vast and luxurious bathrooms, pure cotton sheets and amazing electronics in each bedroom to delight musicians and baffle the over-50s. An unstinting welcome and unequalled value.

Rooms: 1 twin, with sitting room and en suite (bath); 1 double, en suite (bath). Self-catering cottage for 2.

Price: Twin £40 p.p.; double £33 p.p. Single supp. £12.

Breakfast: Until 9.30am.

Meals: By arrangement.

Closed: Never!

Found in a land of fat sheep and ancient hill forts, this 17th-century mill ended Gill and Andrew's search for a refuge from the city. With an absence of fussiness in the house, total seclusion and surrounding natural beauty, this feels like a retreat - just what your hosts (a designer and an illustrator) want. Rooms are quite small but comfortable and decorated with taste: the twin has brass beds, the doubles stripped pine furniture. The River Unk flows through the mill's three acres of meadowland and gardens. *Children over 8 welcome.*

Rooms: 2 doubles and 1 twin, all with basin and sharing 1 bathroom. Separate w.c. on ground floor.

Price: £21-£23.50 p.p. Single supp. £7. Reduction for children.

Breakfast: Until 9am.

Meals: Dinner, £17 p.p., by arrangement.

Closed: From 1 November-Easter weekend.

Take B4368 W to Clun. Left at fork towards Knighton on A488. Over bridge. Cockford is 1 mile from bridge, signed on left. House on right up drive.

Map Ref No: 9

Roger Wren
Cockford Hall
Clun
Shropshire SY7 8LR
Tel: 01588 640327
Fax: 01588 640881

From Clun take A488 towards Bishops Castle. First left signed Bicton. In Bicton, 2nd left signed Mainstone. House is first right after Llananhedric Farm.

Map Ref No: 9

Gill Della Casa & Andrew Farmer
The Birches Mill
Clun
Nr. Craven Arms
Shropshire SY7 8NL
Tel: 01588 640409
Fax: 01588 640409

Snuggling up to the 12th-century parish church of St Mary, Michael and Roma's home is surrounded by National Trust land and infused with peacefulness. Antiques, silver, crystal and fine china are in daily use. Beds and bedrooms are big: one has a small private sitting room. The guests' drawing room has sofas, an elegant fireplace and tall windows that give on to a terrace. You can help yourselves to drinks. Roma makes the breakfast bread and jams - the smell will draw you from your bed. A civilised place.

Rooms: 1 double, 1 twin, 1 twin/double, all en suite (bath).

Price: £35 p.p. No single supp.

Breakfast: Until 9am.

Meals: Dinner £20 p.p.

Closed: Christmas & New Year.

From A49 at Craven Arms turn left onto B4368 signed Aston on Clun. By humpback bridge turn right (signed Hopesay). After 1.5 miles house is on left by church.

Map Ref No: 9

Roma & Michael Villar
Old Rectory
Hopesay
Craven Arms
Shropshire SY7 8HD
Tel: 01588 660245
Fax: 01588 660502

A rambling, old, characterful (even down to the towel rails) pink house, garden-sheltered and tree-protected, Edgcott is a haven on the expansive heath. George Oakes painted those striking Strawberry Hill Gothic murals the full length of the sitting/dining room. Mrs Lamble is a lovely gentle hostess, a dedicated gourmet who cooks with her own garden vegetables. She's also an Exmoor enthusiast - rides, walks, village visits galore will be suggested. And you may play the family piano.

Rooms: 1 twin and 1 double, each with private bathroom; 1 twin/double, en suite (bath/shower).

Price: £20-£23 p.p. No single supp.

Breakfast: Flexible.

Meals: Dinner, 4 courses, £15 p.p by arrangement. B.Y.O. Also, excellent pubs in village.

Closed: Never!

Somerset

Take A358 from Taunton, then left on B3224 to Exford. In Exford take Porlock Lane. Edgcott is 0.25 miles from village.

Map Ref No: 3

Gillian Lamble
Edgcott House
Exford
Somerset TA24 7QG
Tel: 01643 831495
Fax: 01643 831495

It is a place for all seasons, this secluded Yeoman house, with a rare tranquillity, fine scenery and a genuine welcome at the rugged heart of Exmoor. Informal candlelit dinners are just as romantic when the leaves are golden brown as when they are spring green. Wonderful moorland and coastal walks. Bring a rod and your JR Hartley know-how and you can fish in the Durbins' private lake. There are roaring fires for winter breakfasts, beds are big and linen-wrapped - one a carved French four-poster - and the bath towels are 'mammoth'.

Rooms: 2 doubles (1 with four-poster) and 1 twin, all en suite (bath/shower).

Price: £23-£29 p.p. Single supp. £10.

Breakfast: 8.30-9am.

Meals: Dinner, 4 courses, £14 p.p.

Closed: Christmas & New Year.

The picture-book Priory - 'Old' it is, 12th-century old - leans against its church, has a rustic gate, a walled garden, flowers everywhere. Indoors, the old oak tables, flagstones, panelled doors, books and higgledy piggledy corridors sing "there'll always be an England". But a perfect English house in a sweet Somerset village needs a touch of pepper. Cosmopolitan Jane, a red sitting room and some Mexican-style hand-painted wardrobes give it. House and hostess are at once friendly, elegant and homely.

Rooms: 1 twin with private shower and 1 four-poster with private bathroom; 1 twin, en suite (bath). Self-catering cottage also available.

Price: From £22.50-£27.50 p.p. Single supp. by arrangement.

Breakfast: Until 10am.

Meals: Available locally.

Closed: Christmas.

Take B3224 towards Exford. The entrance to the drive is 2.3 miles after Wheddon Cross.

Map Ref No: 3

Ann & Philip Durbin
Cutthorne
Luckwell Bridge
Wheddon Cross
Somerset TA24 7EW
Tel: 01643 831255
Fax: 01643 831255

Turn off A39 into village of Dunster, right at blue sign 'unsuitable for goods vehicles'. Follow until church. House is adjoined.

Map Ref No: 3

Jane Forshaw
The Old Priory
Dunster
Somerset TA24 6RY
Tel: 01643 821540

The hamlet is tiny, tucked into a hidden valley; the house inside is as warm as the pink stone outside, a 17th-century farmhouse full of antiques. There are sofas in the large hall and a separate sitting room, with open fires in both places, books, magazines and pictures. The dining room is elegant, the bedrooms big and comfortable. One has particularly good views and the furnishings are a "delight to the eye". There are lots of thoughtful touches, such as torches. Breakfast is an orgy of fresh eggs, butcher's sausages and bacon and homemade marmalade.

Rooms: 2 twins and 1 double, all en suite (bath).

Price: £28 p.p. Single supp. £7. Children under 14, £14.

Breakfast: Until 8.45am

Meals: Excellent pubs nearby.

Closed: Christmas.

Meet the Wolversons: they'll enjoy meeting you. A friendly, intelligent, well-travelled couple, they have adorned their house with things of interest from their trips. They have settled well into this comfortable village house with its fine terraced garden and croquet lawn. There's a lovely conservatory for breakfast and the generous rooms with period mouldings are decorated in gentle pale colours and furnished with colourful rugs on sea-grass matting and lots of cushions. There are dogs, fine linens and lace, books and plants and masses of atmosphere.

Rooms: 1 double and family/double sharing bathroom, separate shower & w.c.

Price: £22-£25 p.p. Single occ. up to £28.

Breakfast: Until 9.30am.

Meals: Excellent food available locally.

Closed: Christmas & New Year.

From Taunton take A358. Left onto B3224 to Ruleighs Cross etc. After 4.5 miles right to Willet, through Willet, right at T-junction to Higher Vexford & Lower Vexford.

Map Ref No: 3

Nigel & Finny Muers-Raby
Higher Vexford House
Higher Vexford
Lydeard St. Lawrence
Somerset TA4 3QF
Tel: 01984 656267
Fax: 01984 656707
e-mail: 101752.1124@compuserve.com

From M5 exit 25, follow the signs to A358/Minehead. Left to Halse. Rock House is in the middle of the village, 100m from pub.

Map Ref No: 3

Christopher & Deborah Wolverson
Rock House
Halse
Nr. Taunton
Somerset TA4 3AF
Tel: 01823 432956
Fax: 01823 432956

SOMERSET

If you have been to Johannesburg you may know their old Bay Tree Restaurant. Robert is a South African and as easy and interesting as they so often are. Lesley now cooks wonderful meals at the cottage and runs cookery courses, too. It is a delicious place; a perfect Somerset cottage with an apple orchard and view across fields to the lofty church. The interior is utterly in keeping; pine, coir carpets, straw table mats, regular wooden beams on the ceilings and a warm sense of fun. All this, and with such easy access to the M5.

Rooms: 1 twin/double, en suite (bath) and 1 twin, en suite (shower).

Price: £22-£25 p.p. No single supp.

Breakfast: Until 9am.

Meals: Gourmet dinner, £17 p.p. including wine.

Closed: Christmas & New Year.

Leave M5, junc. 26, Wellington turn off and go along West Buckland road for about 0.75 miles. Turn left just before red garage doors. Go down lane and bear right and cottage is 3rd house at the end of the lane below church.

Map Ref No: 3

Lesley & Robert Orr
Causeway Cottage
West Buckland
Wellington
Somerset TA21 9JZ
Tel: 01823 663458
Fax: 01823 663458

The Georgian exterior is impressive, but don't be intimidated, for it is a visual treat inside and out and Jill is immensely welcoming. The rooms are splendid, formal, lovely - as you'd expect, and expense has gone unspared. The bedrooms are luxurious: e.g. cream carpet, pale pastel shades, an old roll-top desk. The garden throbs with fecundity: strawberries, gooseberries, pears, plums, peaches and so on. There are lambs for the table, and armfuls of roses. If you arrange it ahead you may be able to use the tennis court and pool with a carefree, un-Georgian abandon.

Rooms: 2 doubles, both with private bathrooms.

Price: £25 p.p. Single supp. £10.

Breakfast: Until 10am.

Meals: Only by arrangement. Lots of local pubs within a few miles.

Closed: Christmas & New Year.

M5, junc. 25 and take A358 around Taunton and towards Minehead. At Cross Keys r'bout take Bishops Lydeard/Minehead exit. 150 yards past Manor Camp, right into lane signed Fitzroy. House 2nd on left.

Map Ref No: 3

Mrs Jill James
Fitzroy House
Fitzroy
Taunton
Somerset TA2 6PH
Tel: 01823 432027
Fax: 01823 433737

Two local architects poured their talents into this barn conversion, a triumph of sensitive styling in a minute hamlet on the edge of the idyllic Quantocks. There are log fires, slanting ceilings, exposed beams, space and light, all set against various shades of yellow and white. Paintings of landscapes, animals and country sports add to the rural mood. There is a wood-burning stove in the drawing room, and large French doors onto the courtyard. It is all most attractive and friendly, as is the garden - encircled by a stream.

1,000 feet up on the Quantocks - glorious hills known, it seems, to few outside the South West. The views are long and the position beautiful, in 20 acres of fields, birdsong and woodland. The farmhouse has had 300 years to form its character: wooden panelling in the little guest sitting room, flagstone floors, beams, inglenook fireplace with wood-burner, open fires and so on. The house is kept meticulously by the very friendly Pamela. The bedrooms - e.g. brass bedstead, white cover, sloping ceiling and wooden latch door - are as comfortable as they are attractive.

Rooms: 1 twin with private bathroom; 1 double and 1 twin/double, both en suite (shower).

Rooms: 2 doubles and 1 twin, en suite (1 bath, 2 showers).

Price: £22-£25 p.p. Single supp. £5.

Price: £23-£25 p.p. Single occ. £30.

Breakfast: Flexible.

Breakfast: Until 9.30am.

Meals: Dinner, £16-£22 p.p., by arrangement.

Meals: Not available. Pubs within walking distance or short drive.

Closed: Never!

Closed: Never!

Take A358 NW past Bishops Lydeard and under 2 railway bridges keeping on main road. After 1 mile turn left signed Trebles Holford. Follow 'No Through Road' to end. House is on right.

Leave Taunton on A358 north towards Williton & Minehead. After about 7 miles right for West Bagborough. Go through village, up hill for 0.5 miles and Tilbury Farm is on left-hand side.

Map Ref No: 3

Map Ref No: 3

Mrs Phillida Hughes
Redlands House
Trebles Holford
Combe Florey
Somerset TA4 3HA
Tel: 01823 433159

Mrs Pamela Smith
Tilbury Farm
Cothelstone
Taunton
Somerset TA4 3DY
Tel: 01823 432391

In 1992 Charles and Jane Ritchie fled London and headed for Somerset's lovely Quantock Hills to renovate this exquisite 17th-century farmhouse. Their philosophy is simple - why should visitors be any less comfortable on holiday than they are at home? Thus, their place is deliciously welcoming, with very pretty, fresh and large rooms looking over the cobbled courtyard or open fields. Breakfast will include home-baked bread and homemade jams. Try to stay for dinner which Charles and Jane prepare using fresh local ingredients.

Rooms: 1 twin with private bathroom, 1 double with private shower and 1 double, en suite (shower & w.c.).

Price: En suite £22.50 p.p., others £20 p.p. Single supp. £2.50.

Breakfast: Until 9am.

Meals: Dinner £25 p.p. Supper £15 p.p. Fri-Sun, by arrangement.

Closed: Never!

Walk to the top of the Quantocks and gaze across to Wales. Heather-clad moorland, deep tree-lined combes, wild red deer and soaring buzzards add to the scene. Back at the house there is hardly a murmur but for the sound of birds and the trickle of water. The house is snug and pretty, with a cottagey atmosphere, a little sitting room with a small open fire of brick, and floral sofas. Angela is a great home-maker, with Richard in full support, so you are treated with huge kindness. Sit in the lush tree-bound lawn and listen to nightjars and Dartford warblers.

Rooms: 2 doubles and 1 small twin, sharing bathroom and shower room.

Price: £22 p.p. Single supp. at busy times, £3.

Breakfast: Until 9.30am.

Meals: Dinner, 4 courses, £16 p.p.

Closed: End of November-beg. of March.

Leave M5 at junction 25. A358 towards Minehead. Leave A358 at West Bagborough turning. Follow through village for 1.5 miles. Farmhouse third on left past pub.

Map Ref No: 3

Charles & Jane Ritchie
Bashfords Farmhouse
West Bagborough
Taunton
Somerset TA4 3EF
Tel: 01823 432015
Fax: 01823 432520
e-mail: critchie@abling.co.uk.

At Holford turn south off A39 between garage & Plough Inn. Follow signs to Alfoxton Park & at Y-junction fork right. Go into hotel grounds. Leave hotel on left, over 2nd cattle grid. House on left at top of hill.

Map Ref No: 3

Richard & Angela Delderfield
Alfoxton Cottage
Holford
Nr. Bridgwater
Somerset TA5 1SG
Tel: 01278 741418
Fax: 01278 741418

The Quantocks are a treat and from here you have at least 38 square miles of great walking. Wildlife bounds, flits and creeps through the garden, woods and heathland: wild deer, hill ponies, badgers and almost 30 species of birds. Laze on the terrace or by the ornamental pond in the rambling garden and soak in the views to the Mendips and Glastonbury Tor. The rooms are comfortable (old and antique furniture, china and flowers); breakfast in the conservatory and dine by candle-light. Michael and Penny will join you for tea in the guest lounge. You may not want to leave. *Children and horses by arrangement.*

Rooms: 1 twin, en suite (bath) and 1 double with private bathroom.

Price: First-night rates £22-£25 p.p. Single occ. £30.

Breakfast: Flexible.

Meals: Dinner £12-£15 p.p. Light supper, £7 p.p. Packed lunch, £2 p.p. All by arrangement.

Closed: Never!

From Bridgwater, A39 through Cannington. Main road forks right (at Cottage Inn); go straight on and over x-roads to Over Stowey. Turn left after church at green triangle. Left to Friarn. House on right beside bridlepath.

Map Ref No: 3

Michael & Penny Taylor-Young
Friarn Cottage
Over Stowey
Bridgwater
Somerset TA5 1HW
Tel: 01278 732870
Fax: 01278 732870

A house with a history - ancestral home of Robert Blake, Bridgwater's MP in 1640, appointed admiral after 'winning' Cromwell's Civil War at sea virtually single-handed. He captured the Scillies and Jersey and shattered Dutch naval supremacy at the Battle of Portland. Tread the same flagstones in this wonderfully restored 15th-century house. Drink in the atmosphere of the converted Cider Press' enormous four-postered guestroom. Warm colours, fresh linen, period fireplaces, keel-sized timbers, paintings, artefacts and antiques, walled gardens. Commanding views over Bridgwater Bay to Wales on a clear day.

Rooms: In main house: 1 twin and 1 double, both with private bath. In Cider Press: 1 four-poster, en suite (bath) & 1 triple with private shower.

Price: £20-£25 p.p. Single occ. £25-£30.

Breakfast: 7.30-9.30am.

Meals: Dinner £15-£20 p.p. by arrangement.

Closed: Never!

From junc. 25 off M5, follow signs through Taunton to Minehead, follow signs to Kingston St. Mary. Go through KSM and at crossroads take Aisholt and Nether Stowey road. After 3rd sign to Aisholt house is in front of you.

Map Ref No: 3

Nicky & John Thompson
Plainsfield Court
Plainsfield
Over Stowey, Bridgwater
Somerset TA5 1HH
Tel: 01278 671292
Fax: 01278 671292

Familiar with garderobes, piscinas and solars? If not, visit this remarkable Grade I listed 15th-century farmhouse and be enlightened. Explore the West Bedroom with massive-timbered walls, a ceiling open to the beamed roof and a four-poster bed; and don't miss the oak panelled Gallery Bedroom with recently uncovered secret stairway. Feel baronial while seated for breakfast beside the Great Hall's massive fireplace at the 16-ft oak table. Minimum disturbance to fabric and flavour (except suitable washing facilities), and maximum atmosphere.

Rooms: 1 family room, en suite (shower); 3 doubles, all en suite (shower &/or bath).

Price: £20-£28 p.p. Single occ. £30.

Breakfast: Until 9.30am.

Meals: Dinner available locally.

Closed: Never!

The Parrys describe their cosy, comfortable, cottage as 'happy' and they take genuine pleasure in sharing it. Surrounded by beautifully kept (National Gardens Scheme) gardens and a cleverly-planted arboretum, within the folds of the Blackdown Hills, this is a magical and peaceful place. But it is the hospitality that you will remember best. Both your hosts are unpretentiously friendly and cheery people and Pam dishes up generous portions of fresh, delicious, country fare for both breakfast and dinner, either in the snug dining room or the airy conservatory. Simple decor and wonderful value.

Rooms: 1 family suite with up to 4 beds, en suite (bath); 1 double and 1 single (let only to members of same party) with adjacent bath & separate w.c.

Price: By ROOM: family suite, £48; double, £28; single, £22.

Breakfast: Until 9.30am.

Meals: Dinner, 2 courses, £9 p.p., 3 courses, £10 p.p.

Closed: Perhaps Christmas Day.

From Bridgwater A39 west around Cannington. After second roundabout, follow signs to Minehead. Take first left after Yeo Valley creamery. Farm is first house on the right.

Map Ref No: 3

From Taunton south on B3170. Turn west for Churchinford. Follow finger posts for Stapley. Alternative routes via Wellington Hemyock or Upottery for eastbound travellers.

Map Ref No: 3

Ann Dyer
Blackmore Farm
Cannington
Bridgwater
Somerset TA5 2NE
Tel: 01278 653442
Fax: 01278 653427
e-mail: dyerfarm@aol.com

Pam Parry
Pear Tree Cottage
Stapley
Churchstanton, Taunton
Somerset TA3 7QA
Tel: 01823 601224
Fax: 01823 601224
e-mail: colvin.parry@virgin.net

The village is a stone-and-thatch delight. Courtfield, Grade II listed, deep in the village but hidden in a fine, walled, two-acre garden, is very much a family home. Richard, a keen entomologist and painter, has filled the house with art, both his and his daughter's. The house is full of family memorabilia. There is a tennis court (challenges accepted!), and a new conservatory. Valerie, whose Russian father was an hotelier in Cairo, has inherited his flair for cooking and entertaining. The bedrooms are large, and delightful. One of our favourites. *Children over 8 welcome.*

Rooms: 1 twin and 1 double, each with own separate bathroom & w.c.

Price: £25 p.p. No single supp.

Breakfast: Until 9.30am.

Meals: Dinner £15 p.p. B.Y.O. wine.

Closed: Christmas & New Year.

Extremely pretty with its thatched roof and Strawberry Hill Gothic windows, this house will instantly cast its spell on you. Your hosts have created immense comfort; soft, large sofas in the guest sitting room, thick carpeting, easy chairs in the bedrooms and excellent meals using garden produce at house-party dinners. Carved Tudor oak beams in the sitting room and panelled passages speak of the house's history and there are French doors from the dining room onto the sweeping lawns. In a tiny conservation hamlet surrounded by farmland, the peace is deep.

Rooms: 5 twins/doubles, all en suite bath/shower.

Price: £36 p.p. Single supp. £12.

Breakfast: Flexible.

Meals: Dinner, 4 courses, £17.50 p.p. by prior arrangement.

Closed: Never!

Leave A303, to take A356 south towards Crewkerne. Second left to Norton-sub-Hamdon. House in centre of village at foot of Church Lane.

Map Ref No: 3

Richard & Valerie Constable
Courtfield
Norton-sub-Hamdon
Stoke-sub-Hamdon
Somerset TA14 6SG
Tel: 01935 881246

At Horton Cross r'bout at junction of A303 and A358, take A358 towards Chard. After Donyatt, left signed Ilminster. After 1 mile, lane to right signed Cricket Malherbie. House on left after a mile, 200 yards past church.

Map Ref No: 3

Michael Fry-Foley
The Old Rectory
Cricket Malherbie
Ilminster
Somerset TA19 OPW
Tel: 01460 54364
Fax: 01460 54374
e-mail: malherbie@aol.com

In a quiet hamlet sits this lovely square-set Georgian house in local Ham stone with walled gardens - one contains the swimming pool, another the kitchen garden - and long views in all directions. Inside, you find glorious comfort without any pretence - it is all genuine, comfortable and the bathrooms are real rooms with windows. Meals are memorable, with Charmian's homemade bread and marmalade for breakfast while a candlelit dinner may include delicacies such as fresh salmon, vegetables straight from the garden and the freshest raspberries (in season). *Children by arrangement.*

Rooms: 1 twin, en suite (bath); 1 twin and 1 double, each with a private bathroom.

Price: From £27.50 p.p. Single occ. £35.

Breakfast: Until 9.45am.

Meals: Dinner £22 p.p. by prior arrangement. Packed lunch available.

Closed: Christmas & New Year's Eve.

Take either of two lanes off A30. Follow sign for West Chinnock but ignore left turn to West Chinnock itself. House is on right about 100m after Middle Chinnock church on left.

Map Ref No: 3

Guy & Charmian Smith
Chinnock House
Middle Chinnock
Crewkerne
Somerset TA18 7PN
Tel: 01935 881229
Fax: 01935 881229

This 300-year-old thatched farmhouse has, despite its age, every comfort and a marvellous feeling of space. The dining room has a sense of warm Pre-Raphaelite Gothic, with sumptuous colours, wrought-iron, real-candle chandelier, family portraits, long wooden table and high-backed chairs. There's the touch of an artist throughout; and there's luxury, too: crisp linen, fluffy towels, cotton robes and particularly comfortable beds. Jane is happy to cook dinner and there is a wonderful, quiet village pub. The walled garden produces herbs and vegetables, and breakfast includes 'real' meat.

Rooms: 1 twin with private bath; 1 double, en suite (shower).

Price: £22.50 p.p. Single occ. £25-£35.

Breakfast: Flexible.

Meals: Dinner, 3 courses, £15 p.p; 2 courses, £12 p.p. by arrangement.

Closed: Never!

On Somerton to Langport road, just before Halfway Inn, take road signed to Pitney. House is last house but one on right, with dark green railings.

Map Ref No: 3

Peter & Jane Burnham
Estate Farmhouse
Pitney
Langport
Somerset TA10 9AL
Tel: 01458 250210
Fax: 01458 253227

The Somerset Levels, a rare natural wetlands habitat, have unique tranquillity, wildlife and peace. This idyllic state embraces Bere Farm, with its Georgian farmhouse and pretty stone-walled gardens. Inside, all is cosily, traditionally comfortable - Aga, snug bedrooms, with luxury touches in the bathroom. But it's the smiling welcome that generates the real warmth here. Philip and Susan love the countryside; he is keen on country pursuits; she is passionate about gardening, as you can see, and cooking, as you can savour. *Babies and children over 12 welcome.*

Rooms: 1 twin and 1 double, both with private bathrooms.

Price: £26 p.p. No single supp.

Breakfast: Flexible.

Meals: Dinner £13-£17.50 p.p. by prior arrangment.

Closed: Christmas & New Year.

From Langport take A372 through Aller and turn right at left hand bend signed Beer and High Ham. Pass Bere Farm on right and take first lane on left at stone barn to Beer Farm.

Map Ref No: 3

Philip & Susan Morlock
Beer Farm
Bere Aller
Langport
Somerset TA10 0QX
Tel: 01458 250285
Fax: 01458 250285

In the 1740s this was three cottages. When Diane saw the house she fell in love with it, and it shows in the warmth of her welcome. The sitting room has pale green carpet, white walls, both morning and evening sun; it looks over a formal terrace and the walled garden beyond. The flagstoned dining room and breakfast room are all in one with the kitchen where Diane cooks on the Aga while enjoying your company. The two main bedrooms are at the front; double-glazed, cottagey and with old pine furniture, they are elegant. Somerton is a characterful town and this is in the heart of it.

Rooms: 1 double, 1 twin and 1 single, each with basin and sharing 1 bathroom & 2 toilets.

Price: £23 p.p. Single supp. £5.

Breakfast: 8.30-9am, unless by prior arrangement.

Meals: Dinner, 2 courses, £15 p.p. by prior arrangement only. Lots of places locally.

Closed: Christmas & New Year.

From A303 at Podimore roundabout take A372 (Langport road). Follow signs to Somerton and then take left that brings you into North Street.

Map Ref No: 3

Mrs Diane Bearne
Still Cottage
North Street
Somerton
Somerset TA11 7NY
Tel: 01458 272323

The views are of the mystical countryside that surrounds Glastonbury Tor and a more exquisite house would be hard to find. Phoebe, a shepherd, sought the perfect home for her flock and her children: she found it. The antique beds have hand-made mattresses, cotton linen and fat pillows. Terracotta walls, rugs, flagstones and brick - stunning. In the barn there's an indoor swimming pool that gives on to the view. It's all magnificent.

Rooms: Double suite with a drawing and a dining room, plus 3 single rooms. In barn: huge double suite, with dressing room and kitchen/living area.

Price: £130 per suite per night. Single room prices by negotiation.

Breakfast: Flexible.

Meals: Dinner, 3 courses, £25 p.p. by arrangement.

Closed: Never!

From Wells, A39 to Glastonbury. Left at North Wootton sign. Follow signs for West Pennard. At T-junction right onto A361. After 500m, first left. Through tunnel of trees, house on left.

Map Ref No: 3

Ms Phoebe Judah
Pennard Hill Farm
Stickleball Hill
East Pennard, Shepton Mallet
Somerset BA4 6UG
Tel: 01749 890221
Fax: 01749 890665

One of the grandest houses in this book, Pennard has been in Susie's family since the 17th century - the cellars date from then, the superstructure is stately, lofty Georgian - but the Deardens are delightfully unstuffy and welcoming. Guests have the run of the library, formal drawing room, billiards room and six acres of garden with a spring-fed pool to swim in. Or walk in 300 acres of cider orchards, meadows and woods. Multilingual Martin deals in antiques, Susie is a *Cordon Bleu* cook. It is warm, civilised with fairly plain, properly unhotelly bedrooms.

Rooms: 1 double and 1 twin, en suite (bath) and 1 twin with private bathroom.

Price: From £25 p.p. Single occ. £28.

Breakfast: Flexible.

Meals: Dinner, 3 courses, £20 p.p., by arrangement.

Closed: Christmas.

South on A37 from Shepton Mallet, through Pylle and next right to East Pennard. Pass church to T-junction at very top. House on left.

Map Ref No: 3

Martin & Susie Dearden
Pennard House
East Pennard
Shepton Mallet
Somerset BA4 6TP
Tel: 01749 860266
Fax: 01749 860266
e-mail: m.dearden@ukonline.co.uk

Catherine is a Wells Cathedral guide and sings in the choir. Engaging and interested, she'll sit with you over fresh coffee in the cottagey kitchen with pine table and dresser hung with huge cups and saucers, dried flowers and views of fields. Guests have their own pretty sitting room. Upstairs, the bedroom is reached through your bathroom, has French-feel blue-stained bedheads and wardrobe, antique patchwork quilts and books. The cottage is set in eight acres and is superb walking country (there's a special walk to The Old Stores (No 373), and luggage transfer can be arranged). *Dogs welcome, tennis and croquet available.*

Rooms: 1 twin/double, en suite (bath/shower). Further twin available for members of same party willing to share bathroom.

Price: £20 p.p. Single supp. £5.

Breakfast: Flexible.

Meals: Dinner available at village pub or in Wells.

Closed: Christmas & New Year.

A371 to middle of Croscombe. Right at red phone box and then immediately right into lane. House is up hill on left after 0.25 miles. Drive straight ahead into signed field.

Map Ref No: 3

Michael & Catherine Hay
Hillview Cottage
Paradise Lane
Croscombe, Nr. Wells
Somerset BA5 3RL
Tel: 01749 343526
Fax: 01749 676134
e-mail: wells@alderking.co.uk

The endearing intimacy of this 17th-century cottage puts you instantly at ease. The bedrooms are cosy and light; some look onto the busy village street, all have old family books. Naturalists and walkers especially will love it, given the hosts' passion for local natural history. Malcolm has written a guide on walks from the garden gate, leading out onto the Mendip Hills and to the Somerset Levels - one is a gentle day's walk between Hillview Cottage (No 372) and The Old Stores. Malcolm will give you route notes and map and transport your luggage.

Rooms: 1 twin, en suite (shower), 1 double, en suite (bath/shower) and 1 double with shared bathroom.

Price: £18.50-£19.50 p.p. No single supp.

Breakfast: Until 9.30am.

Meals: Good food in pub opposite.

Closed: Christmas.

The house is in the village, on the A371 (Wells to Cheddar road), directly opposite the Westbury Inn.

Map Ref No: 3

Malcolm & Linda Mogford
The Old Stores
Westbury-sub-Mendip
Wells
Somerset BA5 1HA
Tel: 01749 870817
Fax: 01749 870980
e-mail: MOGLIN980@aol.com

The 'young' house (1770s) has fine medieval outbuildings with a museum-worthy clutter of old tools, giant bellows in the forge, bark-clad beams over the threshing floor. The Thompsons have done a superb renovation job, mixing old and new - modern kitchen, stone-flagged floors - and Wendy's fine needlework. The bedrooms have pretty furnishings, country antiques and magnificent views over spring-lamb fields to distant Glastonbury Tor. Round this off with a cottagey garden, a spreading apple tree and friendly cats. *Children over 10 welcome.*

Rooms: 1 double, en suite (shower) and 1 twin, en suite (bath); 1 double with private bath.

Price: From £22 p.p.

Breakfast: 8-9am.

Meals: Available nearby.

Closed: Christmas.

Gracious Jacobean style spills over from this beautiful late-Victorian mansion into its 18-acre parkland setting. Inside, it's just as you would expect: four-poster beds, carved ceilings, walnut panelling, magical hallways filled with ancient furniture and bric-a-brac, plants and flowers everywhere. Hard to believe it's all en-suite - and mod-cons too. Glencot was rescued from a state of dilapidation by Jenny and her husband; she is cultured yet unstuffy. Sculls on the river, steam in the sauna, trout on the line, aces on the table-tennis table, even nurdles on the cricket pitch - enjoy it all!

Rooms: 3 singles, 3 twins and 9 doubles, all en suite.

Price: £40-£48 p.p.

Breakfast: 7-9am (week), 8-10am (weekend).

Meals: Dinner £22-£23.50 p.p. Light & packed lunches available on request.

Closed: Never!

From Wells towards Cheddar on A371, house is 100yds on the left after Westbury-sub-Mendip village stores.

Map Ref No: 3

Tony & Wendy Thompson
Stoneleigh House
Westbury-sub-Mendip
Nr. Wells
Somerset BA5 1HF
Tel: 01749 870668
Fax: 01749 870668

From Wells follow signs to Wookey Hole. Before village, look for pink cottage on left. 100 yards on, sharp left at finger post. House is on right in Glencot Lane.

Map Ref No: 3

Jenny Attia
Glencot House
Glencot Lane
Wookey Hole, Nr. Wells
Somerset BA5 1BH
Tel: 01749 677160
Fax: 01749 670210

Rosalind, cheerful and chatty, will bend over backwards to make you feel welcome. As a geologist and a walking enthusiast, she knows a lot about the area. Animal lovers are especially welcome - there are sheep and goats that respond by name, chickens, ducks and geese. The large Garden Suite, with inglenook fireplace, retains its 17th-century charm and opens onto a secluded walled garden; the other rooms have a more modern feel. Wells Cathedral can be seen in a fold in the hills (and you can walk there to hear evensong).

Rooms: 1 suite (1 twin/double) with private bathroom; 1 double with extra single, en suite (bath), 1 double, en suite (shower).

Price: £19.50-£25 p.p. Single occ. £24-£35.

Breakfast: Until 9am.

Meals: Dinner available locally. Light refreshments by arrangement.

Closed: Never!

From Wells A371 towards Shepton Mallet for 1 mile then left onto B3139. In Dulcote, left at stone fountain. Farmhouse clearly marked 4th on right.

Map Ref No: 3

Rosalind Bufton
Manor Farm
Dulcote
Wells
Somerset BA5 3PZ
Tel: 01749 672125
Fax: 01749 672125

The 14th-century French-style castle casts its spells over the house - you see it from one of the bedrooms and the house's huge stone fireplace probably came from there. In the 16th century the house was a row of weaver's cottages, today it is one thoroughly English home - antique furniture, comfortable sofas, beautiful bits and pieces and paintings with stories to tell. From the drawing room you walk into a garden where birdsong fills the scented air. Jane, charming and flexible, will look after you well. *Cot available for babies.*

Rooms: 1 double and 1 twin, sharing connecting bathroom (separate entrances). Possible extra double sharing bathroom with owner.

Price: £20 p.p. No single supp.

Breakfast: Flexible

Meals: Good pub food a few yards away.

Closed: Christmas.

Nunney is signposted right off the A361 Frome-Shepton Mallet road. Go down hill to market square, left over humpback bridge and immediately left again. House first on right (1 Horn Street).

Map Ref No: 4

Jane Stagg
The Bell House
Nunney
Nr. Frome
Somerset BA11 4NP
Tel: 01373 836309

Guardhouse, moat, turrets: a pink crenellated castle c.1270 awaits you. The interior is Jacobean with vast, oak-panelled drawing and dining rooms, all with massive carved fireplaces. Upstairs, billiards and pool in an immense room; everything here is on a superlative scale. Bedrooms are panelled and romantic, bathrooms excellent. Despite the suit of armour, weapons, art and delicate carved pieces from the East, this is very much a home rather than a museum. A remarkable place; relax into it and let osmosis do its work. There are also two self-catering turrets.

Rooms: 3 four-posters, all en suite (1 bath/shower, 2 bath and shower); 2 self-catering turrets, en suite, for 2/4 persons.

Price: £33-£44 p.p. Singles charged at room rate. Turrets from £60 per night.

Breakfast: Until 9.30am.

Meals: Dinner available locally.

Closed: 1 November-February.

Staffordshire

Travelling on A50 Stoke-on-Trent to Uttoxeter turn left into Caverswall. At T-junction bear right into village. At village square right, then immediately right after first church.

Map Ref No: 9

Yvonne Sargent
Caverswall Castle
Caverswall
Staffordshire ST11 9EA
Tel: 01782 393239
Fax: 01782 394590

A lively, 15th-century, family home opposite Chartley Castle. Once through the black, studded oak door you see panelled walls and heavily-beamed ceilings. In the hall there is a warm, higgledy piggledy feeling with umbrellas, walking sticks, wellies, riding boots and family pictures. In the four-poster bedroom the bathroom is hidden behind a secret panelled door. The floors are uneven, the bedrooms are excellent, the breakfasts hearty and your hosts delightful. *Children over 12 welcome.*

Rooms: 1 four-poster and 1 twin, both en suite (shower).

Price: From £25 p.p. Single supp. £5.

Breakfast: Until 9.30am.

Meals: Good food available locally.

Closed: Christmas & New Year.

An oak-panelled, four-postered Tudor retreat only two miles from Alton Towers. Children are welcome here - cots, high chair and babysitting - and this rambling farmhouse is also enchantingly adult and friendly - Chris was born here. This is the kind of time capsule you can't simulate: oak timbers, stone, tapestry drapes, curios, pewter and books galore. There are gorgeous, almost grand, lawned, formal and herb gardens, pond and summerhouse, plus tennis and croquet. Lovingly renovated 18th-century cottage in private grounds also available.

Rooms: 3 doubles, all en suite (2 with shower and 1 with bath). Self-catering cottage in the grounds, sleeps 4.

Price: £22 p.p. Single supp. £3-£5. Cottage £140-£350 per week.

Breakfast: Until 9.30am.

Meals: Available locally.

Closed: Christmas Eve & Day.

Halfway between Stafford & Uttoxeter on A518, just past Chartley Castle ruin on left and at top of the hill. Farm is on right.

Map Ref No: 9

Sarah Allen
Chartley Manor Farm
Chartley
Nr. Stafford
Staffordshire ST18 0LN
Tel: 01889 270891

From Uttoxeter, B5030 for Rocester & Alton Towers. By JCB factory left onto B5031. At T-junction after church right onto B5032. Right & over bridge. Take 1st lane on left signed Prestwood. Farm is 0.75 miles along lane on right.

Map Ref No: 9

Chris & Margaret Ball
Manor House
Prestwood
Nr. Denstone, Uttoxeter
Staffordshire ST14 5DD
Tel: 01889 590415
Fax: 01335 342198

Our first inspector was so impressed that she popped back for a riding lesson. "Utterly charming people", wrote the second. They are devoted to all things horsey and love eventing and dressage. It is gorgeous riding country, with vast views. The place is full of bird-life, dogs, cats and the ubiquitous horses. It is all you might dream of from a B&B: a 'working' home, dining room with Welsh dresser and grandfather clock, a kitchen with Aga and pine table, fruit from the garden and homemade jam. You pass through the Denstone school grounds to get here.

Rooms: 1 twin, en suite (bath) and 2 doubles sharing private bathroom.

Price: £22.50 p.p. No single supp.

Breakfast: Until 8.30am.

Meals: Pubs & restaurants available locally.

Closed: Christmas.

In village, follow signs to Denstone College and enter grounds. In front of College buildings turn left. Continue for 300 yards to stud.

Map Ref No: 9

Phyl Price
Denstone Stud and Riding Centre
Hall Riddings
Denstone
Staffordshire ST14 5HW
Tel: 01889 591472
Fax: 01889 591472

The Blackbourne river flows gently past the 18th-century pink Dower House in its peaceful 2.5 acres of garden and orchards - all harmonious tranquillity. The black swans and the white fan-tails contrast dramatically. The house has low, beamy ceilings and is charming: woodburning stove in the dining room, coal fire in the drawing room, superb bed linen, soft and pretty colours, flowery curtains against plain walls and carpets, fresh flowers everywhere. Your welcoming, thoughtful hostess is also an imaginative cook. *Dogs by arrangement.*

Rooms: 1 twin/double, en suite (bathroom); 1 twin with private bathroom.

Price: £30 p.p. Single occ. £35.

Breakfast: Flexible.

Meals: Dinner £18 p.p. Supper £13 p.p.

Closed: Christmas.

Suffolk

Take A143 out of Bury St. Edmunds towards Ixworth. Ignore all Pakenham signs until Mill Road, Pakenham, then turn right, take left fork - the house is pink with white gates, on the left.

Map Ref No: 11

Mrs Diana Gurteen
The Dower House
Bailey's Pool
Pakenham, Bury St. Edmunds
Suffolk IP31 2LX
Tel: 01359 230670

Don't be fooled by the plain exterior. Diana was once a stage manager in the London theatre and it shows; she is outgoing, fun, brilliant with people and has a marvellous sense of taste. The bedrooms are perfect, with attractive duvets and curtains, pale walls and lots of nice touches (e.g. bedside torches). The terracotta of the sitting room walls is stunning. The garden is surprisingly large, with a terrace, fishpond, lawn and herbaceous borders - very pretty; sit and enjoy it. To cap all this Diana will cook you mouth-watering dinners.

Rooms: 1 twin and 2 doubles, all en suite (shower or bath).

Price: £22.50 p.p. Single occ. £35.

Breakfast: Flexible.

Meals: Dinner £15 p.p. B.Y.O. wine.

Closed: Christmas & January, but open New Year.

Lavenham's medieval townscape is greatly loved, a jostling half-timbered throng set in its own time. Less is seen of the interiors: one of the finest - the Grade I listed Priory - is now yours to enjoy, whether for its authentic architecture, or its huge comfort. The Great Hall's massive inglenook fireplace warms the heart, too (stone flagstones are heated, so no cold feet!). Ancient oak timbers everywhere, and quirky, hand-crafted irregularities of detail and space. Your hosts are great fun, bringing a relaxed family atmosphere to this magnificent house and gardens. Worth every penny. *Children over 10 welcome.*

Rooms: 2 double and 1 twin/double (one room with Polonaise bed, one with *lit bateau* and one with big four-poster), all en suite.

Price: £35-£45 p.p. Single occ. £50-£60.

Breakfast: Flexible.

Meals: Dinner £20 p.p. by prior arrangement.

Closed: Christmas & New Year.

From Sudbury, take B1115 to Lavenham. Pass Swan Hotel on right, take next right into Market Lane, cross Market Place, turn right, then left. House is on right next to school.

Map Ref No: 11

Diana Schofield
The Red House
29 Bolton Street
Lavenham
Suffolk CO10 9RG
Tel: 01787 248074

Turn at The Swan onto Water St then right after 50 yds into private drive to the Priory car park.

Map Ref No: 11

Tim & Gilli Pitt
Lavenham Priory
Water Street
Lavenham, Sudbury
Suffolk CO10 9RW
Tel: 01787 247404
Fax: 01787 248472
e-mail: tim.pitt@btinternet.com

A little pocket of France run by a charming French couple with French staff. They have pulled off a trick rare in the UK, creating a superb hotel that feels like a home. The 18th-century front hides a 15th-century house, full of surprises and utterly lovely. Each of the bedrooms has antique desks and chests of drawers to off-set the superb marble of the perfect bathrooms. You can't escape the beams, the fresh flowers, the sheer generosity and good taste of it all. Catch the late sun in the garden, or the early sun in the courtyard for breakfast.

Rooms: 5 doubles, all en suite, 4 with bath and 1 with shower.

Price: B&B (week only) from £35 p.p. Dinner, B&B, from £52.95 p.p. Single supp. £20.

Breakfast: 7.30-9.30am.

Meals: Dinner from £17.95 p.p. Lunch also available. Meals not available on Mondays.

Closed: First 3 weeks in January.

Lavenham is on A1141. In high street going north, first right after The Swan. In Water St going east, first left after The Swan up Lady St into Market Place.

Map Ref No: 11

Régis & Martine Crépy
The Great House
Market Place
Lavenham
Suffolk CO10 9QZ
Tel: 01787 247431
Fax: 01787 248007
e-mail: greathouse@surflink.co.uk

You may help yourself to the sherry on the oak dresser (17th-century, no less), a hint of the generosity of the house. It is 15th-century, timber-framed and thatched (but good headroom), as pretty as can be, immaculate inside with fine antique furniture and fresh flowers. Guests have their own sitting rooms: soft, grey-green carpet and covers, shelves of books, open log fires. Dine by candlelight and woodburning stove among the beams and mullioned windows; separate tables for breakfast. The impeccable bedrooms have plain walls, good furniture, and thoughtful touches. Delightful people, too.

Rooms: 1 twin/double, en suite (bath & shower). 1 double and 1 single sharing private bathroom.

Price: £25-£28 p.p. Single occ. £30-£35.

Breakfast: 9.30am.

Meals: Dinner £22 p.p. occasionally by prior arrangement. Excellent local pubs & restaurants.

Closed: Occasionally.

From Bury St. Edmunds, A413 towards Haverhill, then B1066 south towards Glemsford for 6 miles to Hartest. After 30 mph signs continue for approx. 0.25 miles, lane is on left (signed Cross Green) on sharp double bend.

Map Ref No: 11

Bridget & Robin Oaten
The Hatch
Pilgrims Lane
Cross Green, Hartest
Suffolk IP29 4ED
Tel: 01284 830226
Fax: 01284 830226

The Cromwellian General Fairfax owned the fireplace; it is splendid, with carved stone pillars and faces, in the dining room with its sumptuous oak panelling and massive moulded beams. The hall has panelling dated 1617 and a fine fireplace. It is a beautiful house, rich in interest, delicate but lived in. Lots of family photos. The bedroom has an ornate Tudor four-poster, sagging beams and good views. The twin room is in the attic, with uneven oak floors, great views and a romantic garret mood. Diana is exceptionally charming - and fresh to B&B, so be nice to her.

Rooms: 1 double and 1 twin, each with private bathroom.

Price: Double £30 p.p., twin £25 p.p.

Breakfast: Until 9.30am.

Meals: Available locally.

Closed: Never!

Janus-like, it looks both ways, Georgian to the front and richly-beamed 1485 Tudor behind. One of the arched Tudor fireplaces in the house was found with the help of Alfred Munnings R.A., a frequent visitor. The house has high ceilings and long windows, so is filled with light. The bedrooms are elegant, formal and very English: flower-patterned wall-paper, padded bedheads, thick curtains, armchairs, standard lamp, lots of books... pretty and full of thoughtful touches. There is a walled garden with a vine-filled greenhouse.

Rooms: 1 twin with bathroom & separate w.c., 1 double, en suite (shower).

Price: £23-£24 p.p. Single occ. £25.

Breakfast: Flexible.

Meals: Available nearby.

Closed: Christmas.

Leave Long Melford on the Clare road, turn right to Stanstead (signed) and right again at the village pub. Follow road for 0.5 miles, the house is set back on the right.

Map Ref No: 11

Diana Banks
Bretteston Hall
Stanstead
Sudbury
Suffolk CO10 9AT
Tel: 01787 280504
Fax: 01787 280504

Take B1115 from Sudbury towards Lavenham for 3.5 miles. Turn right to Lt. Waldingfield. House is on left, 200 yards beyond The Swan.

Map Ref No: 11

Mrs Susan T del C-Nisbett
Wood Hall
Little Waldingfield
Nr. Lavenham
Suffolk CO10 0SY
Tel: 01787 247362
Fax: 01787 248326
e-mail: nisbett@nisbett.enta.net

Keen conservationists and historians, they manage the farm, the wildlife habitats and archaeological sites, and serve their own produce for supper in the main hall. In summer you can eat under the copper beech. Families are welcome and entertained: nature trails, activity sheets, etc... and the Hawkins have a flexibility that will appeal to all. A glorious place, unspoiled 16th-century and lived in by the family for 300 years. Period furniture, walled garden, lovely bedrooms and Juliet, a bundle of energy and enthusiasm.

Rooms: 1 family room with basin, 1 twin and 1 single/twin, all sharing private bathroom.

Price: £20-£25 p.p.

Breakfast: Until 9.30am.

Meals: Dinner £12-£15 p.p. available on request. B.Y.O. wine. Packed lunch up to £6 p.p.

Closed: Never!

From Lavenham take A1141 towards Monks Eleigh. After 2 miles, right to Milden. At crossroads turn right to Sudbury on B1115. The Hall's long drive is 0.25 miles on left.

Map Ref No: 11

Juliet & Christopher Hawkins
The Hall
Sudbury
Nr. Lavenham
Suffolk CO10 9NY
Tel: 01787 247235
Fax: 01787 247235

Rachel Thomas has thought of everything and the result is an idyllic home in an exquisite setting. Guests have the run of this gorgeous 15th-century house: a warm, light drawing room with a grand piano, oak beams, open fireplace; a sun room to catch the evening light; cosy dining room with Suffolk tiles and inglenook fireplace. The guest bedroom area is self-contained, with a king-size bed and many thoughtful touches. Low leaded windows overlook the peaceful gardens which include a grass tennis court. Bicycles are available. Rachel is a delight - and a great cook.

Rooms: 1 kingsize with private bath, shower & w.c.

Price: £24 p.p. Single occ. £30.

Breakfast: Until 9 30am.

Meals: Dinner £15 p.p. by arrangement. Also excellent local pubs.

Closed: Christmas-New Year.

Approx. 4 miles between Hadleigh & A12 on country road, 2 miles from Shelley, 1 mile from Polstead and close to Shelley Priory on O.S. map. Ring for details as many approaches possible!

Map Ref No: 12

Rachel & Richard Thomas
Sparrows
Shelley
Ipswich
Suffolk IP7 5RQ
Tel: 01206 337381

Romantically decorated, oak-beamed bedrooms, one with its own ground-floor entrance. A charming sitting room with inglenook fireplace is available to 'long stayers'. The house itself, dating from the 16th century, is lovely with a walled garden, 400-year-old pond, beautiful lawns and - best of all - the River Box meandering through the grounds. Kiftsgate roses cascade over the huge and very splendid adjacent 17th-century barn. A fairytale house in a fairytale setting. Your hosts are attentive and friendly and your privacy is respected. Hard tennis court available.

Rooms: 1 ground floor twin/double and 1 double, all en suite (bath). 1 single with private bathroom.

Price: £25 p.p.

Breakfast: Until 9.30am.

Meals: Available at excellent local pubs.

Closed: Christmas-New Year.

Were we to award prizes Raewyn would get several; the house is faultless, even voluptuous, and she is a rare mixture of gentleness and fun. The house is tucked away in the valley, away from the road and the garden and lush conservatory face away across long lawns to woods and the Gipping River. There are touches of simplicity amid the sumptuous, cottagey comfort; old beams, white walls and papered walls, floral fabrics and plain ones. The food is sublime, eaten communally in the conservatory. Lovely staff, too, who pamper you in the friendliest Suffolk way. *Children over 5 welcome.*

Rooms: 4 doubles, 3 twins, 2 singles. Some king-size four-posters; 6 have own bath & w.c., 1 has own shower & w.c.

Price: Double/twin £22.50-£35 p.p. Single £18-£42.50. Children (sharing) £5-£16 depending on age.

Breakfast: Until 9.30am.

Meals: Dinner £16-£18.50 p.p. with reductions for children. Not available on Sundays.

Closed: Christmas & New Year.

3 miles from the A12, on the B1068 between Higham and Stoke-by-Nayland. House on south side of road, 300m east of Thorington Street.

Map Ref No: 12

Patrick & Jennie Jackson
Nether Hall
Thorington Street
Stoke-by-Nayland
Suffolk CO6 4ST
Tel: 01206 337373
Fax: 01206 337373

Where A140 joins A14 from Ipswich, take first left at roundabout & follow signs for Pipps Ford.

Map Ref No: 12

Mrs Raewyn Hackett-Jones
Pipps Ford
Needham Market
Ipswich
Suffolk IP6 8LJ
Tel: 01449 760208
Fax: 01449 760561

A fine garden surrounds this lovely Tudor farmhouse - it was owned by Cardinal Wolsey in the 16th century and has Henry VIII's coat of arms over the massive inglenook fireplace where log fires blaze on chilly days. Does Anne Boleyn's ghost still walk here?... well, she hasn't been seen for the last 60 years! It is a big rambling house full of beams, corners and great character. Guestrooms are simply decorated and supplied with fluffy bathrobes. Penny is gentle, well-travelled and, we are told, a very fine cook. You will receive a warm welcome here.

Rooms: 1 double and 1 twin, both with basins and sharing bathroom.

Price: From £18 p.p. Single occ. £21.

Breakfast: Flexible.

Meals: Dinner, 4 courses, £15 p.p. Needs to be ordered in advance.

Closed: Christmas.

5 miles west of Ipswich (off A1071). 200 yards after village P.O. Stores. On left next to farmyard.

Map Ref No: 12

Penny Debenham
Mulberry Hall
Burstall
Nr. Ipswich
Suffolk IP8 3DP
Tel: 01473 652348
Fax: 01473 652110

A rare find, in a town whose attractions are not at first apparent. (Giles the cartoonist drew inspiration from the Ipswich docks!) The Freeths have created a classic Regency-style country-house hotel (2.5 acres of grounds) on the edge of town, warm and elegant with high ceilings, open fires and deep sofas. The wooden panelling in the drawing room is impressive, as are the open fire, the displays of china, and the specially-made Turkish carpet. The bedrooms have French cherry wood furniture and every modern comfort. Nicola cooks fine traditional food.

Rooms: 2 doubles and 1 single, all en suite (bath/shower), 1 double and 3 singles, all en suite (shower).

Price: Doubles from £63 p.p.; single from £47.50.

Breakfast: Until 8.45am

Meals: Lunch & dinner available Monday-Saturday. Packed lunch by arrangement.

Closed: Christmas-New Year & last week in August.

From A14 take A1156 towards town centre. Over two roundabouts, then left at lights into Old Norwich Rd. Hotel 0.25 miles on left, 20 yards beyond Whitton Church Lane.

Map Ref No: 12

William & Nicola Freeth
The Gatehouse
799 Old Norwich Road
Ipswich
Suffolk IP16 6LH
Tel: 01473 741897
Fax: 01473 744 236

Lise is Danish, great fun and a wonderful hostess. The conversion is of a 17th-century barn and stable, beautifully done to a very high standard. The bedrooms have every extra, including plenty of books, and the one in the Carriage Lodge, just steps away from the main house, is ideal for guests with limited mobility. On cool evenings a log fire is lit in the beamed and vaulted drawing room, its terracotta floor scattered colourfully with rugs. Play the baby grand, or use the billiard room; croquet, in the luscious garden, completes the scene.

Rooms: 1 double, en suite (bath/shower), 1 double, en suite (shower). Carriage Lodge: 1 double/twin, en suite.

Price: £25 p.p. Single occ. £36.

Breakfast: Until 9.30am.

Meals: Available locally. You can B.Y.O. wine.

Closed: October-Easter.

Otley is on B1079 and is 6 miles west of Woodbridge and 6 miles north of Ipswich. House is 300 yards north of Otley Post Office on right and up drive.

Map Ref No: 12

Michael & Lise Hilton
Bowerfield House
Helmingham Road
Otley
Suffolk IP6 9NR
Tel: 01473 890742
Fax: 01473 890059
e-mail: lise@bowerfld.demon.co.uk

A beautifully-proportioned house in 7.5 acres of gardens, meadows and woodland. The meadow is a County Wildlife site with orchids and a carpet of wild flowers. Cindy is young and energetic, with enough enthusiasm for her family and her guests. Flagstoned hall, a large oak table in a striking burgundy dining room and a stunning sitting room with French windows. The bedrooms are well furnished and have maps, books, fresh flowers and garden views; one has a wrought-iron four-poster with beautiful embroidered linen. Bathe by candlelight in excellent bathrooms.

Rooms: 1 family room, and 1 single (with basin) sharing adjacent bathroom. 1 double, en suite (bath).

Price: Family/double £22-£25 p.p.; single £18. Fri & Sat £2 p.p. extra.

Breakfast: Flexible.

Meals: Dinner £12.50-£16 p.p., by arrangement. B.Y.O. wine. Lunch & packed lunch available on request.

Closed: Never!

From A12 Woodbridge by pass, exit at roundabout signed Orford and Melton. Follow for 1 mile to lights; there, right and Hall is immediately on right.

Map Ref No: 12

Mrs Lucinda de la Rue
Melton Hall
Woodbridge
Suffolk IP12 1PF
Tel: 01394 388138
Fax: 01394 388982

A remote and ancient farmhouse, an aesthetic treat. It is charmingly scruffy in parts, flagstoned, filled with beautiful and interesting things, surprising, uplifting, fun, exquisitely unmodernised... yet hugely comfortable. The library is crammed with books, the kitchen is a beachcomber's haven. This is an estuarine corner of rare loveliness; the views are wide and clean, you can stroll to the river to be among the gulls, avocets and duck. Solitary, winter-bleak splendour with an engagingly relaxed, interesting, artistic and cultured architect. Come if you are easy and open, and do what you want.

Rooms: 2 doubles sharing guest bathroom.

Price: £25 p.p. Single supp. £15.

Breakfast: Flexible.

Meals: Good selection of local pubs & restaurants.

Closed: Sometimes!

From Orford Market Square take lane towards castle and 1st right past castle marked 'Gedgrave Only, No Through Road'. House is on left after 0.5 miles.

Map Ref No: 12

Mr Hugh Pilkington
Richmond House
Gedgrave
Nr. Orford
Suffolk IP12 2BU
Tel: 01394 450102
Fax: 01394 450102

Old and beamy, brick floors, open fires, comfortable settles, pine tables and chairs, blackboard menu, genuinely good food, good local ales, cosy and attractive... it is all you could wish for. The bedrooms are in the same league: up a narrow staircase, one four-poster, beamy and flawlessly attractive as befits such an ancient and decent pub. Bathrooms are small, but there is no room for bigger ones. Plain carpets are just right, as are the cotton duvets. It is on the road, but quiet at night and only a short walk from the famous Maltings and its music, one of the country's most remarkable combinations.

Rooms: 2 doubles and 1 single, all en suite (bath).

Price: £27.50 p.p. Single occ. £35.

Breakfast: Until 9.30am.

Meals: Lunch & dinner available every day.

Closed: Christmas Day & Boxing Day evening.

From A12 take A1094 towards Aldeburgh. Turn right at Snape Church onto B1069 and follow Snape Maltings' signs. The Crown is on the left hand side at bottom of the hill.

Map Ref No: 12

Diane & Paul Maylott
The Crown Inn
Snape
Suffolk IP17 1SL
Tel: 01728 688324

Off to a flying start, just five minutes from the Snape Maltings and the Aldeburgh Festival, but a house worth including anywhere. It is a beamy old farmhouse, with a good 16th-century slope to the floors and two lovely bedrooms with armchairs, attractive furniture, books and fresh flowers. There are views over the four acres of garden and woodland, with spectacular snowdrops and daffodils in early spring. The entrance is most attractive too, the hall opening into the dining room, with fresh flowers on the large old dining table and a fine open fireplace.

Rooms: 1 double and 1 twin, sharing private bathroom.

Price: £22.50 p.p.

Breakfast: Flexible.

Meals: Available locally.

Closed: Christmas & New Year.

You will be spoilt lavishly, though Jenny's vivacious manner lends a light touch. And Sternfield House graciously plays its part - from the long drive sweeping through 26-acre woodland and parkland gardens, to the plump cushions heaped in luxurious bedrooms, each with its impeccable colour scheme. The Queen Anne mansion's dining room is airily stately, acres of polished table. Everywhere, grandeur is softened by design. There's a temple in the gardens, impressively floodlit at night, plus swimming pool, tennis court and full-size snooker-table. *Children over 12 welcome.*

Rooms: 1 double and 2 twins/doubles, all en suite (bath).

Price: £40 p.p. Single occ. £55.

Breakfast: Flexible.

Meals: Available locally.

Closed: Christmas.

From A12 south of Saxmundham, take B1121 signed to Benhall. First left at crossroads into Grays Lane. House is 45m on left.

Map Ref No: 12

Virginia Reed
Benhall Cottage
Grays Lane
Benhall, Saxmundham
Suffolk IP17 1HZ
Tel: 01728 602359
Fax: 01728 602359

From the A12, take the B1121 to Saxmundham; Sternfield is signed 2nd on the right. House is just over bridge on left before church.

Map Ref No: 12

Jenny Thornton
Sternfield House
Saxmundham
Suffolk IP17 1RS
Tel: 01728 602252
Fax: 01728 604082

You can see the wooden runners for the early window shutters, and the 12th-century moat is listed. It is a gorgeous old house, 13th-century in parts, with sloping floors and unstained beams. The dining room, for the candle-lit dinners at the large table (proper napkins), was once the dairy. The family room has a billiard table and toy cupboard, and the sitting room a baby grand, open fire and lots of books. There's an all-weather tennis court in the large garden. Elizabeth is both delightful and generous: tea and homemade cake on arrival, local honey, homemade bread and marmalade for breakfast.

Rooms: 2 twins and 1 double, sharing bath with w.c. Downstairs basin & w.c. also available.

Price: £20 p.p. No single supp. Children 10-15, £10-£15

Breakfast: Flexible.

Meals: Dinner & supper available on request (24 hrs' notice preferred).

Closed: 13 December-13 January.

A classic of its kind, irreproachably restored and decorated (Michael is an interior designer). It is a Grade II listed 17th-century house with 15th-century timber-framed origins, recreated to make you feel like minor royalty. Beautiful furniture, dramatic window treatments, an elegant panelled drawing room in soft yellows and blues with wild silk curtains, Delft-tiled fireplace, open fire, sofas, plenty of lamps and a door onto the garden. The bedrooms are superb, with shuttered windows. Michael loves house parties, so why not come with friends...?

Rooms: 2 doubles and 1 twin, all en suite (shower).

Price: £35-£65 p.p.

Breakfast: Flexible.

Meals: Dinner, for 6 or more (you can invite friends) and packed lunch, by arrangement.

Closed: Never!

Take A1120 (Yoxford to Stowmarket) to Dennington. B1116 north for approx. 3 miles. Farm on right 0.9 miles north of Bell pub.

Map Ref No: 12

Elizabeth Hickson
Grange Farm
Dennington
Woodbridge
Suffolk IP13 8BT
Tel: 01986 798388

From A12 in Yoxford take the A1120 towards Peasenhall. Hope House is 0.5 miles on the left, set back from road.

Map Ref No: 12

Michael Block
Hope House
High Street
Yoxford
Suffolk IP17 3HP
Tel: 01728 668281
hopehouseyoxforduk@compuserve.com

A summer-soft fishing village central to the 1920s Arts & Craft movement and still a refuge for artists. The ferry across the tiny boat-tangled river to Southwold has been rowed by the same family for five generations. Swim, sail, fish for crabs, paint, walk the beach to Dunwich. The Bell, 600 years old, has ancient beams, flagstone-and-brick floors, settles, nooks and crannies, open fires, fresh flowers and adult-only areas. Sue, welcoming and attractive, has poured energy and good taste into the small bedrooms. A happy place.

Rooms: 4 doubles, 1 twin, all en suite (shower). 1 family room (double & 2 singles) with private bathroom.

Price: £30 p.p. Single occ. £35. Family room £80-£100.

Breakfast: Until 9.30am.

Meals: Lunch & dinner available from Inn menu. Packed lunches available on request.

Closed: Never!

It is the sort of place whose address, if you are in the village for the day, you scrawl hopefully on a scrap of paper. Walberswick is enchanting, and Ferry House is too: built in the 1930s for a playwright, using a butterfly design to catch the light, it has Art Deco touches, hand-painted tiles, simple but pretty rooms, fresh flowers everywhere, lots of books and a sense of fun. Make your own toast at breakfast (a nice touch). There's a warm cloakroom for wet birdwatchers' clothes and a welcoming glass of sherry. Your hostess is as nice as her village. *Children over 10 welcome.*

Rooms: 1 double with private w.c. & basin and 2 singles sharing adjacent w.c. & basin and a guest bathroom.

Price: From £18 p.p.

Breakfast: Until 9.30am.

Meals: Dinner available locally. Packed lunch available on request.

Closed: Christmas week.

From A12 take B1387 to Walberswick. The Bell is on the right, at the far end of the village near the river.

Map Ref No: 12

Sue Ireland-Cutting
The Bell Inn
Ferry Road
Walberswick
Suffolk IP18 6TN
Tel: 01502 723109
Fax: 01502 722728

From A12 take B1387 to Walberswick. Ferry House is on the left at far end of village, near the river.

Map Ref No: 12

Mrs C Simpson
Ferry House
Walberswick
Southwold
Suffolk IP18 6TH
Tel: 01502 723384
Fax: 01502 723384

No historical approximation here; it is carved into the big beam - 1600 - and there's a correspondingly old-fashioned welcome. It's all so natural and relaxed. Sarah cooks excellently in her Aga-warm kitchen; she's intelligent and well-travelled and is easy to talk to. The interior style is simple farmhouse, endearingly hotchpotch and delightfully unfussy. Here's a house lovingly built for comfort. You'll appreciate that in those few seconds between sliding into the linen sheets and falling soundly asleep in this peaceful hamlet. *Children over 10 welcome.*

Rooms: 1 double, 1 single and 1 twin, sharing bathroom.

Price: From £22.50 p.p.

Breakfast: 8-9.30am.

Meals: Dinner from £15 p.p. by arrangement.

Closed: Christmas.

This lovely old farm - 400 acres of mixed arable and dairy - is Suffolk at its rural best. At the end of a half-mile drive, the house is 16th century and as comfortable as it is unpretentious. The rooms are generous, with plenty of books and pictures, armchairs, beams... deliciously cosy. Guests have their own sitting room with an open fire, overlooking the patio and garden (home-grown vegetables and fruits are often served at dinner in the beamed dining room). You can walk to the pub, and Southwold and the sea are eight miles away. Pat is delightful and loves having people to stay.

Rooms: 1 double, en suite (bath), 1 twin, en suite (shower) and 1 twin/double with private bathroom.

Price: £16-£20 p.p. Single supp. £4.

Breakfast: 8.30-9am.

Meals: Dinner & packed lunch available on request.

Closed: Never!

Take A12 towards Wangford. Turn left signed Stoven/Uggeshall. After 1 mile, 1st on left before church.

Map Ref No: 12

Sarah Jupp
Church Farmhouse
Uggeshall
Southwold
Suffolk NR34 8BD
Tel: 01502 578532
Fax: 01953 888306

From A12, take A144 Halesworth road. In Bramfield turn off by Queen's Head on Walpole road. Farm is 0.75 miles on right.

Map Ref No: 12

Patricia Kemsley
Broad Oak Farm
Bramfield
Halesworth
Suffolk IP19 9AB
Tel: 01986 784232

These old Suffolk houses combine bricks and beams in the softest way. This one, 16th-century, is no exception; stay to enjoy it all day if you wish. It is old-fashioned yet friendly, warm and cottagey, with lots of beams and antique furniture, William Morris-type floral sofas and chairs. The dining room is a treat, once a cheese-room. You can wander in and out of the large kitchen for a chat with Rosemary, the kindest of women. But you have your own wing, so can be private. Four miles away is Wingfield Old College and gardens, home of the arts summer festival and, seven miles away, Bressingham gardens.

Rooms: 2 doubles and 1 twin, each with private adjacent bathroom.

Price: From £23.50 p.p. Single occ. from £26.

Breakfast: Flexible.

Meals: Dinner available locally.

Closed: Christmas week.

From Scole/A140 right onto A143 towards Gt Yarmouth. After 7 miles right at Harleston onto B1116 to Fressingfield. Pass church and Fox & Goose on left. At top of hill right then left into Priory Road.

Map Ref No: 12

Stephen & Rosemary Willis
Priory House
Priory Road
Fressingfield, Eye
Suffolk IP21 5PH
Tel: 01379 586254
Fax: 01379 586254

This late-Georgian parsonage, in a pretty village setting, has all the warmth and cosy comfort of a traditional English home plus warm colours, light streaming in through French windows, the wrap-around snugness of plump sofas, and those deft touches that make all the difference - like the dark green bath robes in your room. Only 25 minutes to Waterloo, but you could be a galaxy away. There is sherry by the log fire, home-cooked food using free-range meats and local produce, and chats over dinner with your well-travelled, articulate and relaxed hosts.

Rooms: 1 twin/double and 1 double, both en suite (shower) and 1 double with private bathroom. All available as singles.

Price: £25-£45 p.p.

Breakfast. 7-9am or by arrangement.

Meals: Dinner, 4 courses, from £15.00 p.p. Light supper £10 p.p.

Closed: Never!

At M25 junction 13 take A30 to Egham and Bagshot. At next roundabout take A30 to Basingstoke. Follow A30 uphill to lights. Turn right, take 3rd right, at T-junction turn left. House is immediately on right.

Map Ref No: 5

Sandi & Peter Clark
The Old Parsonage
Parsonage Road
Englefield Green
Surrey TW20 0JW
Tel: 01784 436706
Fax: 01784 436706

Surrey & Berkshire

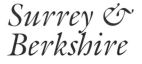

The Italianate garden of this large, handsome 1780s manor is quite divine. You can play tennis and pretend you play croquet; it's the perfect spot to lose track of time and it's all so English you can almost smell the cucumber sandwiches. Quietly rural, you feel a world away from Woking. Guestrooms have good antique furniture and pretty bedspreads and garden views. There are six acres of garden in 100 acres of vineyards, plus home-laid eggs and garden fruit for breakfast. *Children over 8 welcome.*

Rooms: 3 doubles, all en suite (bath).

Price: From £35 p.p. Single supp. £12.50.

Breakfast: Until 9.30am.

Meals: Available locally.

Closed: Christmas & Easter.

So near London and Guildford it is a surprise to bump along Littlefield's farm track and find this lovely old house, isolated in 400 acres of farmland. A very easy-going John clearly enjoys the higgle and piggle of his 1550s house - wooden floors, big open fires, worn carpets and rugs, window seats, beamed ceilings, church panel doors, original wattle and daub, big deep baths, lovely rooms with views, weird and wonderful timbered walls. Outside, a traditional English rose garden is walled in with red brick - and beyond, two acres of super-kempt lawn and tree (his son is a green keeper!).

Rooms: 1 twin with private bath and 2 doubles, both en suite (bath).

Price: £30 p.p. Single supp. £10.

Breakfast: Until 9.30am.

Meals: Suppers, with wine, £20 p.p. by arrangement.

Closed: Never!

Go west on A319 through Chobham (church on left). Continue towards Knaphill and turn left into Carthouse Lane. Manor signed on right.

Map Ref No: 5

Teresa & Kevin Leeper
Knaphill Manor
Carthouse Lane
Woking
Surrey GU21 4XT
Tel: 01276 857962
Fax: 01276 855503

From London, A3 for 20 miles. 3 miles after joining the A323, at a black and white roundabout, house track is 300 yards on left and through woods.

Map Ref No: 5

John & Pooh Tangye
Littlefield Manor
Littlefield Common
Guildford
Surrey GU3 3HJ
Tel: 01483 233068
Fax: 01483 233686

Gillian welcomes guests from all over the world (she's an English language teacher), yet she and David will make you feel like their first ever. Over tea and delicious homemade lime cake, conversation is lively and informed. The house is just as delightful: part 16th, 18th and 19th century, it has exposed timber frames, bold colours - like the dining room red. In the walled garden with its rambling wooden barn, the distant rumble of the A3 reminds you of how well placed you are for Gatwick and Heathrow. This beats even the best airport hotel.

Rooms: 1 twin, en suite (bath/shower), 1 twin/double with private bath; 2 singles (1 with basin) sharing shower room.

Price: £22-£27 p.p.

Breakfast: Until 9.00am.

Meals: Available locally.

Closed: Christmas & New Year.

You will fall under Greenaways' spell the moment you enter. In a vast sitting room, low-slung beams and striking colours jostle for your attention. A sturdy, turning oak staircase leads you to the bedrooms; a peek at them all will only confuse you - they are all gorgeous. There's an ornate bedstead in the Chinese room and in another, an oak bedstead and beams. A further room has a hint of French decadence: golds, magentas and silks. All this and a glorious garden - no wonder so many return time and again.

Rooms: 1 twin and 1 single sharing bathroom; 1 double, en suite (bath).

Price: £30-£37.50 p.p. Single occ. £45.

Breakfast: Until 9am.

Meals: Available locally.

Closed: Never!

A3 South, 5 miles after Guildford, Eashing is signed left before service station. House 150m on left behind white fence.

Map Ref No: 5

David & Gillian Swinburn
Lower Eashing Farmhouse
Eashing
Nr. Godalming
Surrey GU7 2QF
Tel: 01483 421436
Fax: 01483 421436

A3 to Milford. From Milford A283 to Petworth. Pickhurst Road is off the green, third house on the left with a large black dovecote.

Map Ref No: 5

Sheila Marsh
Greenaway
Pickhurst Road
Chiddingfold
Surrey GU8 4TS
Tel: 01428 682920
Fax: 01428 685078
e-mail: jfvmarsh@nildram.co.uk.

High it is, looking across 2.5 acres of smooth lawns to the village and the Surrey hills. The 1532 rambling farmhouse has the sort of family clutter that makes you feel immediately at home. You have the big, log-fired living room, stone-flagged dining room and snug study for yourselves while the three prettily furnished bedrooms share a bathroom upstairs. Unlike many houses with masses of beams, low ceilings and dark furniture, this is light and inviting. Patrick is quiet and gently courteous; Carol is kind and loves children. There are cots and Z-beds aplenty.

Rooms: 2 doubles and 1 twin, sharing bathroom.

Price: £20-£22.50 p.p. Single occ. £22-£25.

Breakfast: 6.30-9.30am.

Meals: Available locally.

Closed: Christmas & Easter.

Originally a 16th-century inn, the farm is now a haven of peace. The pond is part of what used to be a moat; a bridge takes you to a small island. Classical music drifts across the garden from the conservatory while you swim or play tennis. Inside, low beams, wattle-and-daub walls, log fires, rugs and, in the dining room, heavy oak Jacobean-style furniture. One bedroom has a king-size brass bedstead, the attic bathroom has a whirlpool. Ann and David are relaxed, unpretentious, easy hosts.

Rooms: 1 double & 1 twin, both en suite (bath).

Price: £25 p.p. Single occ. £40.

Breakfast: Until 9.30am.

Meals: Available locally.

Closed: Never!

From A3, 1st exit after M25 (signed Ripley/Ockham). Through Ripley & West Clandon, over dual carriageway (A246) onto A25. 3rd right to Shere. There, right to Cranleigh. House is 5 miles on left, 1 mile past Windmill pub.

Map Ref No: 5

Patrick & Carol Franklin Adams
High Edser
Shere Rd
Ewhurst/Cranleigh
Surrey GU6 7PQ
Tel: 01483 278214
Fax: 01483 278200

At crossroads in Leigh, south towards Norwood Hill. After 1 mile, take first right after sign to Mynthurst, then continue up drive for 0.5 miles. House on right.

Map Ref No: 5

Ms Ann Dale
Herons Head Farm
Mynthurst
Leigh
Surrey RH2 8QD
Tel: 01293 862475
Fax: 01293 863350

It's a privilege to share Denise's elegant Regency home. She is entertaining and helpful, does everything for you and has a well-judged respect for privacy; guests have their own entrance. Such a tempting house and gardens, yet so close to London (20 minutes). Choose from the Florentine or Venetian room - both have a private patio garden where you can have breakfast - or, the Sienna room at the top of the house with a silver-leaf four-poster and view of the Thames. Fluffy towels, fresh flowers and lots of attention to detail.

Rooms: Florentine (double) with private bathroom, Venetian (twin/double), en suite bath and Sienna (double/triple), en suite bathroom.

Price: £38-£45 p.p.

Breakfast: 7.30-9am.

Meals: Light supper, prices on request.

Closed: Christmas.

Turn left out of Richmond tube; walk up High Street & up Richmond Hill. Last house at top of Richmond Hill on left, next door to Hotel. Or take a taxi: approx £3.50 from tube.

Map Ref No: 5

Denise O'Neill
Doughty Cottage
142a Richmond Hill
Richmond
Surrey TW10 6RN
Tel: 0181 332 9434
Fax: 0181 332 9434

The first thing that strikes you at Meadow House is the garden and it's no surprise to learn that Harriet is a landscape gardener. She has used her talents to beautiful effect. Banks and beds of flowers wind round and frame two central features - a secluded swimming pool and the 15th-century house itself. Inside, there are timbered walls and small windows, peep holes to that enticing garden. Guests have pretty and immaculate bedrooms with good quality linen and a degree of privacy in their own section of the house. There's a good combination of care, flair and perfectionism.

Rooms: 1 twin and 1 double, sharing private bathroom.

Price: £30 p.p. No single supp.

Breakfast: Until 9am.

Meals: Good food available locally.

Closed: Weekends, Christmas & Easter.

From Newbury, A339 towards Basingstoke. After 4/5 miles, left (B3051). After 2.25 miles, right to Wolverton Common. 300 yds on, take track on right. House 1st on right at end.

Map Ref No: 4

Tony & Harriet Jones
Meadow House
Ashford Hill
Newbury
Berkshire RG19 8BN
Tel: 0118 981 6005
Fax: 0118 981 6005

Parts date back to the 16th century; today it's a working farmhouse and a home to which Mary welcomes her guests in a natural and instantly likeable way. The house is surrounded by a two-acre garden and rolling fields. Her delicious meals are largely home-grown - lamb and veg particularly - and you eat in the beamed kitchen. The bedrooms are simply and attractively decorated, are bright and airy and look out onto the garden, traditional barns and fields. One of the most modern bathrooms has a 16th-century beam. The sitting room has a large open fire and there is a huge selection of books.

Rooms: 3 twins/doubles, two en suite (bath/shower) and 1 with adjacent private bath/shower.

Price: £25 p.p. Single supp. £10.

Breakfast: Until 8.30am.

Meals: Dinner, £18 p.p., by arrangement.

Closed: Never!

From junction 14 of M4 take A338 north towards Wantage. After 0.5 miles take first turning left (B4000). House is on the first farm road on the right after the Pheasant Inn.

Map Ref No: 4

Mary & Henry Wilson
Fishers Farm
Shefford Woodlands
Hungerford
Berkshire RG17 7AB
Tel: 01488 648466
Fax: 01488 648706
e-mail: fishersf@globalnet.co.uk

417

In two acres of beautifully landscaped gardens, Mizzards Farm is a lovely 16th-century farmhouse on a site with a medieval history. It has its own lake, an upstairs conservatory, heated covered pool, outdoor chess, croquet lawn and rare bantams for company. Splendid breakfasts in the spectacular vaulted dining room, and the general atmosphere is of relaxed elegance. The bedrooms are comfortable and attractive, one with a four-poster and correspondingly grand marble bathroom. Harriet and Julian are keen to advise on walks in this designated AONB. *Children over 8 welcome.*

Rooms: 1 twin, 1 double and 1 four-poster, all en suite (bath/shower).

Price: £27-£31 p.p. Single supp. by arrangement.

Breakfast: 8-9am.

Meals: Dinner available locally.

Closed: Christmas.

Sussex

From A272 at Rogate, turn towards Harting/Nyewood. Cross humpback bridge; drive is first turning on the right. Signed.

Map Ref No: 5

Harriet & Julian Francis
Mizzards Farm
Rogate
Petersfield
Sussex GU31 5HS
Tel: 01730 821656
Fax: 01730 821655

John and Lois have spent 28 years raising four children in their rambling Sussex farmhouse, just off the road, farming sheep and creating a well-stocked garden and grass tennis court. Informal and civilised, they invite you into their log-fired drawing-room and into their busy life with friends, family, village and chocolate labrador. Bedrooms are family-style, the smaller one blue with an animal frieze and great views. The house is thoroughly lived-in and easy going; mix in and enjoy it.

Rooms: 1 double, with extra single bed, en suite (bath); 1 twin sharing bathroom with owner's family.

Price: Double £22.50 p.p. Twin from £17.50 p.p.

Breakfast: Flexible.

Meals: Packed lunch £5 p.p. with prior notice.

Closed: Christmas.

A wooded track leads to this beautiful, mellow 17th-century farmhouse, with tall chimneys and a cluster of overgrown outbuildings surrounding a pond. Wood-panelled walls and timber beams, a vast open brick fireplace, an Aga, mullioned leaded windows and welcoming sofas create an atmosphere of relaxed, country-house charm. The large and comfortable, timbered bedrooms (one canopied bed incorporates original oak panelling) overlook fields and rolling lawns, where guests may relax in complete peace, accompanied only by birdsong and the occasional grazing sheep. *Children by arrangement.*

Rooms: 1 double with private bathroom, 1 twin/double/family, en suite (bath). 1 small single for families.

Price: £21-£25 p.p. No single supp. Advance booking only.

Breakfast: Flexible.

Meals: Good pubs nearby.

Closed: Never!

From A3, take Midhurst turning onto A272. Just after Trotton village sign turn right (on dangerous bend). House is 1st on right (B&B sign).

Map Ref No: 5

John & Lois Field
Mill Farm
Trotton
Petersfield
Sussex GU31 5EL
Tel: 01730 813080
Fax: 01730 815080

Directions given on booking.

Map Ref No: 5

Maggie Paterson
Fitzlea Farmhouse
Selham
Nr. Petworth
Sussex GU28 0PS
Tel: 01798 861429

Deer come to your window, miles of unspoiled woodland walks start on your doorstep. Not a B&B but a tranquil, tiny, modern-pine, self-contained annexe hideaway for a cosy pair of independent nature-lovers. Welcoming hosts live in the listed cottage and replenish the refrigerator daily with bread, croissants, hams, cheeses, yoghurts, real coffee... There are kettle and toaster but no cooking equipment. It's spotless and comfortable with all mod cons. You have your own entrance and a garden terrace too. This is 'deep' Sussex.

Rooms: Self-catering studio: 1 double with shower.

Price: From £20 p.p.

Breakfast: Self-service, so any time!

Meals: Local pubs (e.g. Unicorn at Heyshott) within walking distance.

Closed: Never!

From Midhurst, A286 towards Chichester. After Royal Oak pub on left, Greyhound on right, go 0 5 miles, left to Graffham and Heyshott. On for 2 miles, do not turn off, look for white posts and house sign on left.

Map Ref No: 5

Alex & Annabelle Costaras
Amberfold
Heyshott
Midhurst
Sussex GU29 0DA
Tel: 01730 812385

A typically-Sussex brick and flint cottage set in over an acre of its own grounds and surrounded by beautiful downland country. Neil has completely restored the forge and decorated with flair and great care. Red brick flooring, earth-coloured drapes and rugs, terracotta-washed plaster between the beams on the walls. There are two ground floor rooms; one fitted out for those with limited mobility and one with its own garden door. Upstairs rooms are reached via steep, winding staircases and have those lovely downland views.

Rooms: 3 twins/doubles, 1 single, 1 double, all en suite; 1 single with private bathroom.

Price: Double £25-£45 p.p. Single £35-£79.

Breakfast: Cooked: until 9.30am (week), 10am (Sunday). Continental: flexible.

Meals: Supper/dinner available by arrangement. Also, White Horse opposite.

Closed: Last week of October, part of February.

Take A286 north from Chichester, then left onto B2141 to Chilgrove. Cottage is opposite the pub.

Map Ref No: 5

Mr Neil Rusbridger
Forge Cottage
Chilgrove
Nr. Chichester
Sussex PO18 9HX
Tel: 01243 535333
Fax: 01243 535363

Olde Worlde charm at its most authentic. The Lodge was built in pure Neo-Gothic style as the gatehouse to the local manor and has kept its other-world, other-age atmosphere (delicious church windows). It sits in a large rambling garden, is totally secluded and instantly wraps you in peace. There is a wood-burning stove in the garden room for chilly days, a plant-filled conservatory to introduce the garden, two warm, elegant bedrooms and a delightful hostess.

Rooms: 3 doubles, en suite (2 bath and 1 shower).

Price: £25 p.p. Single supp. £20.

Breakfast: Flexible.

Meals: Dinner available locally.

Closed: Never!

Kippers and porridge for breakfast, homemade cakes for tea - Vivien spoils her guests while husband Tim manages a local racehorse stud. The Flint House was built by Napoleonic prisoners of war and was once part of the Goodwood estate. Bedrooms are in the old cattle byres - originally converted for the Reads' growing family - and are good-sized with attractive furniture and decor, fresh flowers and a pretty yellow kitchen for making (real) coffee and tea. Lovely views from the garden and there's a tennis court.

Rooms: 2 twins/doubles, en suite (bath and shower).

Price: £25-£35 p.p. Single occ. £30-£35.

Breakfast: Flexible.

Meals: Available locally.

Closed: Christmas.

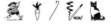

Village is 3 miles W of Chichester on the B2178. The lodge is 170m on the left after Salthill Road. Look for the sign for Oakwood School.

Map Ref No: 5

Jeanette Dridge
Chichester Lodge
Oakwood School Drive
East Ashling, Chichester
Sussex PO18 9AL
Tel: 01243 786560

A272 to Midhurst, then A286 to Singleton. Left turn signed 'The Coast': up over Downs, pass racecourse, take next turning right signed Lavant. House is first on right after 0.5 miles.

Map Ref No: 5

Tim & Vivien Read
The Flint House
East Lavant
Chichester
Sussex PO18 0AS
Tel: 01243 773482

A 'genuine fake', this very beautiful 15th-century mansion was built at vast expense in the 1930s out of innumerable medieval bits - stone mullions, moulded doorways, oak beams, carved doors - recovered from the original courthouse and other ancient ruins. It rambles, has nooks and crannies, tapestries and all things Gothic and big, high-ceilinged, old-furnished, new-bathroomed bedrooms. Only the (much-renovated) chapel is authentic. Superb public rooms and a magnificent garden complete the picture.

Music is one of the most relaxing gifts and Mary amply demonstrates this, as does her peaceful 16th-century home looking out over Chidham harbour to picturesque Bosham. She and her Bechstein, cello and double bass await guests with the appropriate talents - so do bring your violin (or viola). It will be relaxed and very informal; that's how she and her five cats like it. And you will like the quietly cultured atmosphere, antiques and paintings. Tea by the fire when you arrive on chillier days, and a big welcome for non-musicians too.

Rooms: 1 twin with shared bathroom and 1 double with private bath.

Price: £19-£34 p.p. Single £18-£27.

Breakfast: Flexible.

Meals: Available locally.

Closed: Christmas.

Rooms: 31 doubles and 1 single, all en suite.

Price: £67.50-£150 p.p. Single from £125.

Breakfast: 7.30am-9.30am (week); 8-10am (weekend).

Meals: Dinner £32 p.p. Lunch £17.50 p.p.

Closed: Never!

From Chichester head for Portsmouth. Pass Tesco on right. 3rd exit off roundabout, to Bosham/Fishbourne. Follow A259 for 4 miles, pass garage on right. Next left into Chidham Lane. House is last on left, 1 mile down.

From Littlehampton A259 west to Climping. At blue sign for Bailiffscourt turn into Climping St and continue up lane to reach hotel.

Map Ref No: 5

Map Ref No: 5

Mary Hartley
Easton House
Chidham Lane
Chidham, Chichester
Sussex PO18 8TF
Tel: 01243 572514
Fax: 01243 572514

Sandy & Anne Goodman
Manager: Pontus Carminger
Bailiffscourt Hotel
Climping
Sussex BN17 5RW
Tel: 01903 723511
Fax: 01903 723107

A Lutyens manor - "The best of the bunch", he called it himself - of mighty Elizabethan proportions, proudly displaying dressed stone inside and out, a great sitting hall with minstrels' gallery, vaulting stone doorways, high mullioned, leaded windows and a glorious Lutyens garden as well. The wood and leather in library/bar and hall are properly in keeping, the dining tables by Ambrose Heal. Guest suites are exquisite, each seductive and different, all very smart, perhaps even grand, as is the gourmet food.

Rooms: 7 twins/doubles, all en suite; 2 doubles with private bathrooms.

Price: £164.50 per room. Single occ. £105.75.

Breakfast: 8-10am.

Meals: Lunch & dinner available on request.

Closed: Christmas & New Year.

Little Thakeham lies off the A24 north of Storrington.

Map Ref No: 5

Tim & Pauline Ractliff
Little Thakeham
Merrywood Lane
Storrington
Sussex RH20 3HE
Tel: 01903 744416
Fax: 01903 745022

They were building this house 10 years before Columbus... lots of history in one gorgeous spot. It's changed since and the smother of roses, clematis and honeysuckle has come on well. In the 1600s, (straighter) timbers were added to give the great hall an upstairs. Alan and Caroline have spent three years transforming the hall into your B&B dream. They love the house, love sharing it. Comfortable, fresh, country-style bedrooms, log-fired sitting rooms, fine furnishings, natural materials. Cows moo and farmers still work the land (almost) as diligently as they always did.

Rooms: 2 doubles, both en suite (1 with bath and 1 with bath and shower). 1 double can be let as family suite with adjoining single room.

Price: From £24 p.p. Single occ. £38. Single £22.

Breakfast: Flexible.

Meals: Packed lunch available.

Closed: Christmas- New Year.

From A23 take Henfield exit. In Sayers Common right into Reeds Lane. At T-junction left into Twineham Lane and immediately fork right towards Henfield. 2nd left up Blackstone Lane. House is in centre of hamlet.

Map Ref No: 5

Alan & Caroline Kerridge
Yeoman's Hall
Blackstone
Nr. Henfield
Sussex BN5 9TB
Tel: 01273 494224
Fax: 01273 494224

It's not surprising that people love to hold their wedding and anniversary parties here because it is very good looking, has friendly and professional management and the food is ambrosial. Rooms are distributed between the c.1520 house and a c.1990 addition but all have a smart country-house look helped along by lots of antiques and, predominantly, Colefax & Fowler and Zoffany materials. Business people and those wanting a quick dose of spoiling come here in winter and many Americans and Europeans in summer.

Rooms: 4 twins, 5 four-posters, 12 doubles and 1 single, all en suite.

Price: From £57.50-£122.50 p.p.

Breakfast: Until 10am. Full English £5 p.p. extra.

Meals: Dinner from £29.50 p.p. Lunch from £18.50 p.p.

Closed: Never!

First it was a farm, then a pub (the old beer cellar remains). What seems small on the outside opens out into a rambling, higgledy piggledly 16th-century period piece inside, with quirky angles, exposed timbers and a rustic character. It's all down to the dedication and effort of Frances, who did the renovation herself - shower rooms, everything. And she landscaped the delightful gardens where nightingales and owls enjoy the woodland. She is an independent character, and always happy to share a drink and a chat in front of the inglenook fire with her guests.

Rooms: 1 double and 1 twin, both en suite (shower); 1 single, en suite (bath).

Price: Double £25 p.p. Twin £22.50 p.p. Single £25.

Breakfast: Flexible.

Meals: Dinner, 2 courses, £12 p.p.

Closed: Never!

4.5 miles after end of M23 (south), left onto B2115 towards Haywards Heath. Cuckfield 3 miles on & hotel at end of Ockenden Lane, just off High Street opposite Talbot Inn.

Map Ref No: 5

Sandy & Anne Goodman Manager:
Mr K. Turner
Ockenden Manor
Ockenden Lane
Cuckfield
Sussex RH17 5LD
Tel: 01444 416111
Fax: 01444 415549

From Gatwick, take M23 South and follow signs to Cuckfield. There, right at 1st mini-roundabout, left at 2nd and right at 3rd. Left at T-junction. Copyhold Lane is 1st on right, after entrance to Borde Hill Gardens.

Map Ref No: 5

Frances Druce
Copyhold Hollow
Copyhold Lane
Borde Hill, Haywards Heath
Sussex RH16 1XU
Tel: 01444 413265

Rarely have we met such dedicated hosts, Jennifer organising behind the scenes, Graham proving that nothing is too much trouble. He makes the preserves, too, and will book a table at the village pub for you. Visitors from 53 nations have enjoyed the comforts of this unspoilt, wisteria-clad 1930s bastion of old-Englishness set to the gentle music of fantails. It is surrounded by peaceful views over lovely gardens, has a huge fruit and veg plot that could feed an army, and log fires in winter. *Children over 10 welcome.*

Rooms: 1 double with private bath & w.c.; 2 twins sharing 1 bathroom and 2 w.c.s.

Price: £29 p.p. Single supp. £10.

Breakfast: Flexible.

Meals: Village inn serves evening meals.

Closed: Never!

Simply arriving here is special - the view takes the breath away, the blue lake shimmers, the weathered bricks and tiles of the 18th-century farmhouse promise warmth and welcome, a promise kept by charming Pauline. They run a Shetland pony stud, their garden runs down to the lake (trout fishing possible) and Pauline serves tea on the terrace (guests may also use her Aga). The bedrooms have glorious views and fluffy towels. The epicentre for famous gardens and historic houses. *Children over 12 welcome.*

Rooms: 1 twin and 1 double (with basins) and 1 single, all sharing 1 bathroom. 1 w.c. downstairs. 2 self-catering cottages available.

Price: £23-£26 p.p. No single supp. Cottages £185-£495 per week.

Breakfast: Flexible.

Meals: Restaurants & pubs nearby.

Closed: Christmas.

From M25 take A22 to Maresfield. Once in the village go under the grey stone arch opposite the church and the pub and over 5 speed bumps. South Paddock is first house on left.

Map Ref No: 5

Graham & Jennifer Allt
South Paddock
Maresfield Park
Nr. Uckfield
Sussex TN22 2HA
Tel: 01825 762335

From Wadhurst take B2099 south for approx 1.5 miles, left into Wards Lane, follow road for 1.5 miles to Newbarn. Last part of road is unsurfaced.

Map Ref No: 6

Chris & Pauline Willis
Newbarn
Wards Lane
Wadhurst
Sussex TN5 6HP
Tel: 01892 782042
Fax: 01892 782042

This listed 17th-century house is beside the church in the heart of a tiny village, just ten minutes from Glyndebourne. Yes, there are scrummy picnic hampers; Alison was chef to the Beatles. More unexpected, your host gives tennis coaching - he's a former world racquets champion - so, clearly, there is a tennis court, also swimming pool and croquet lawn in the large, pretty gardens. Toast your toes after a South Downs walk in the drawing room's inglenook. Bedrooms are comfortably and attractively furnished. Easy-going and informal Sussex at its bucolic best.

Rooms: 1 double and 2 singles, sharing bathroom.

Price: Double £20 p.p. Single £25.

Breakfast: Flexible.

Meals: Dinner £15 p.p.

Closed: Christmas & Easter.

The Stone House has belonged to the Dunn family for 500 years and Peter and Jane have managed to keep the feel of 'home'. The decorations are fabulous - nothing 'hotelly' here, except luxury and service you won't find in many grander establishments, plus croquet and billiards. Jane cooks (Master Chef Award!): fresh fish every day, game from the estate, fruit and veg from the beautifully laid out gardens. Sumptuous picnic hampers for Glyndebourne (chairs and tables provided) are an added treat.

Rooms: 1 double/single, 3 twins/doubles and 2 four-posters, all en suite; 1 suite with 2 rooms & bathroom.

Price: £50-£90 p.p. Single occ. £55-£75.

Breakfast: 8.30-9.45am.

Meals: Dinner £24.95 p.p. Lunch, by arrangement, £18.50 p.p.

Closed: Christmas & New Year.

From Boship roundabout on A22, take A267 and then first right to Horsebridge and then immediately left to Hellingly. Globe Place is next to church, in Mill Lane.

Map Ref No: 6

Alison & Willie Boone
Globe Place
Hellingly
Sussex BN27 4EY
Tel: 01323 844276
Fax: 01323 844276

Take B2096 from Heathfield, 4th turning on right marked Rushlake Green. Follow to R. Green, 1st left by the green, keeping it to your right. Small crossroads, house signed to left.

Map Ref No: 6

Peter & Jane Dunn
Stone House
Rushlake Green
Heathfield
Sussex TN21 9QJ
Tel: 01435 830553
Fax: 01435 830726

The Collins moved from a smart hotel in Brighton to this rural haven secluded in 40 acres of rolling grounds surrounded, in turn, by 1,000 acres of Forestry Commission woods - just the birds, foxes and deer to create a bit of traffic. Ask for a pathway map at the farmhouse and spend your days watching wildlife. Or visit nearby historic Battle where William beat Harold so long ago. Paul and Pauline are delighted with their pretty home and happy to welcome guests into the beamed, inglenooked dining room and excellent bedrooms.

Rooms: 3 doubles, all en suite (bath).

Price: £24.50 p.p. Single occ. £39.

Breakfast: Usually 8-10am.

Meals: Supper available by arrangement.

Closed: January.

Alison and Paul Slater's 40-acre farm is deliciously laid-back and peaceful, at the end of a bumpy old track, with a two-acre trout lake, lawn tennis court, croquet lawn and wisteria-clad pergola. You may fish or boat on the lake, or swim in it, and the farm is surrounded by woodland walks. Mouth-watering home-cooked food, using home-grown produce, is served in the candlelit dining room, preceded by drinks in the cosy, beamed bar. Bedrooms are simple but comfortable, one with a four-poster, and four even have small wood-burners. It is informal and generous.

Rooms: 10 twins/doubles, all en suite (bath); 2 family rooms with private bathroom.

Price: £38-£44 p.p. Single supp. up to £25. Dinner, B&B, £50-£62 p.p.

Breakfast: 8.30-9.30am.

Meals: Dinner, 4 courses, £22.50 p.p.

Closed: 3 January-11 February.

From Battle on A271 take first right to Heathfield. After 0.75 miles right into drive.

Map Ref No: 6

Paul & Pauline Collins
Fox Hole Farm
Kane Hythe Road
Battle
Sussex TN33 9QU
Tel: 01424 772053
Fax: 01424 773771

From Battle take A2100 towards Hastings. Approx. 1.5 miles past Battle, by sharp right road sign, turn left to Hemingfold. Farm track is 0.5 miles.

Map Ref No: 6

Alison & Paul Slater
Little Hemingfold Hotel
Telham
Battle
Sussex TN33 0TT
Tel: 01424 774338
Fax: 01424 775351

People swoop back like swallows for the garden. The trimmed lawn hugs a huge ornamental pond and there is a heated pool kept at 88° in the walled garden. By another tiny pond you can breakfast in summer if you are not in the sun-drenched dining room, with its long wooden table and starched napkins. The house is full of beautiful things and, though there is no sitting room for guests, one is made to feel totally at home... so much so that you may stay here all day in the garden. Bathrooms are superb, and one of the bedrooms overlooks both garden and sea.

Rooms: 1 twin, en suite (shower); 1 double with private bathroom.

Price: £30 p.p. Single supp. £10.

Breakfast: 8-9.30am. Earlier by arrangement.

Meals: Pub nearby.

Closed: Christmas & New Year

"Teddy bears inside, hedgehogs outside and a really excellent cat". This most welcoming, rule-free townhouse in lovely history-laden Rye also has fine antiques, masses of books and paintings, occasional groups of amateur dramatists in the big and otherwise quiet garden, a Smugglers' Watchtower and a small library for rainy days. Sara is lively, attentive and fun and will give you big organic/free-range breakfasts as well as information about what to do and see. *Children over 12 welcome.*

Rooms: 2 doubles and 1 twin, en suite (2 with bath and 1 with shower).

Price: £30-£42 p.p. Single occ. £45-£65.

Breakfast: 8-9.30am (week); 8-10am (Sunday).

Meals: Dinner available nearby.

Closed: Never!

From Rye take A259 to Winchelsea; after Bridge Inn, sharp left up steep hill signed Winchelsea. After medieval arch, 1st left, house 200 yards, 1st on left.

Map Ref No: 6

Mrs Sarah Jempson
Cleveland House
Winchelsea
Sussex TN36 4EE
Tel: 01797 226256
Fax: 01797 226256

In Rye follow signs to town centre and enter Old Town through Landgate Arch into High Street. West Street is third on left. House is half-way up on left.

Map Ref No: 6

Sara Brinkhurst
Little Orchard House
West Street
Rye
Sussex TN31 7ES
Tel: 01797 223831
Fax: 01797 223831

Perfect: there is a small library for rainy days. There is a lovely atmosphere too, an easy trust, ample character and some fine furniture. The house is on one of the most beautiful, ancient, cobbled streets of Rye and has a colourful past as, variously, wool-store, school and home of the American poet Conrad Potter Aitken. The galleried chapel is now the dining room, there is a winter fire in the hearth and immense attention to details. A super little hotel run by delightful people.

Rooms: 10 doubles, all en suite; 1 double & 1 single sharing bathroom. 1 honeymoon suite.

Price: £22.50-£54 p.p.

Breakfast: 8-9.30am (week); 8.30-10am (weekend).

Meals: Available locally.

Closed: Never!

From London, into centre of Rye on A268, left off High Street onto West Street, then 1st right into Mermaid Street. House on left. Private car park, £3 a day for guests.

Map Ref No: 6

Jenny & Francis Hadfield
Jeake's House
Mermaid Street
Rye
Sussex
Tel: 01797 222828
Fax: 01797 222623

Don't forget to telephone if you're running late

The house (mainly 1857) is dominated by a 20-foot-high conservatory, designed by Judy and Jeremy. Breakfasts are here beneath a Roxanne balcony, inundated with morning light. It connects with a sitting room, with deep sofas, bookshelves, a real fire. It's a very sociable house too - that's down to Judy - with an honesty bar and a large, round dinner table. The first floor bedrooms are off a large landing from which a staircase leads through a rabbit warren of passages to the third guest bedroom. There's a tennis court and a pool.

Rooms: 1 double and 1 twin, both en suite (shower) and sharing further bathroom; 1 twin with private bathroom.

Price: £30 p.p. Single supp. £5.

Breakfast: 8-10am.

Meals: Dinner, £20 p.p., by arrangement. B.Y.O. wine.

Closed: Christmas & New Year.

Warwickshire

From Shipston take Banbury Road to first crossroads (about 300 yards). Turn right and wind on for 3 miles, ignoring any right turns. House is last on right before T-junction.

Map Ref No: 10

Judy & Jeremy Arnold
The Butts
Cherington
Nr. Shipston-on-Stour
Warwickshire CV36 5HZ
Tel: 01608 686226
Fax: 01608 686524

An air of calm pervades this lovely 17th-century farmhouse - superb thatched barn, too - and envelopes you as you pass through the heavy iron and oak door to a friendly welcome and a real rest. The interior has a timeless feel with its cool, stone-flagged hall and simple country antiques. Fresh, light bedrooms have mullioned windows. Flowers spill out between the courtyard paving stones by the pretty garden. Visit Kiftsgate garden and don't miss Hidcote - surely one of the most imaginative and idiosyncratic gardens ever created? *Children over 10 welcome.*

Rooms: 1 double and 1 twin, en suite (bath); 1 single, en suite (shower).

Price: From £28 p.p. Single supp. £3.

Breakfast: Flexible.

Meals: Dinner, 3 courses, from £17 p.p. Supper, 2 courses, £13 p.p. Packed lunch £5 p.p. All by arrangement.

Closed: January & February.

From Stratford-upon-Avon take A3400 towards Oxford. After 5 miles, right by church in Newbold-on-Stour & follow signs to Blackwell. Fork right on entering Blackwell. Entrance to house is just beyond thatched barn.

Map Ref No: 10

Mr & Mrs L Vernon Miller
Blackwell Grange
Blackwell
Shipston-on-Stour
Warwickshire CV36 4PF
Tel: 01608 682357
Fax: 01608 682357

'Less is more' may be enigmatic in its original context, but to the easy-going Howards it means a more personal, friendly service for guests. They ran a bigger B&B for 17 years, before moving to this place, a totally secluded, converted 18th-century barn, with exposed timbers and sloping upstairs ceilings. It is beautifully, brightly decorated throughout in a fresh cottage style; walls positively glow in the sunlight. The four-poster suite has its own front door. They keep sheep, horses and poultry so there are plenty of fresh free-range eggs for breakfast. *Children over 8 welcome.*

Rooms: 1 double/twin/family, en suite (bath/shower) and 2 doubles, en suite (1 shower and 1 bath/shower).

Price: £19-£22 p.p. Single occ. £25.

Breakfast: Flexible.

Meals: Available locally.

Closed: Christmas.

From Stratford-upon-Avon take A422 to Pillerton Priors, then follow sign to Pillerton Hersey. There, turn down Oxhill Bridle Rd, opposite War Memorial. House is at the end.

Map Ref No: 10

Carolyn & John Howard
Dockers Barn Farm
Oxhill Bridle Road
Pillerton Hersey, Warwick
Warwickshire CV35 0QB
Tel: 01926 640475
Fax: 01926 641747

The garden reaches out to the Stour river with its waterside willows. If you can't stir yourself to make a close inspection, sit on the terrace and watch the sun set over the North Cotswolds. Angie and Chris have an easy-going manner that is infectious. Angie decorates with strong colours; Chris, an interiors' photographer, has an eye for arranging things. He also bakes bread most mornings. Flagstones and wooden floors downstairs; upstairs, one Art Deco-ish bedroom and the other cosily pink with patchwork quilt, cream sofa and canopied bed.

Rooms: 1 double, en suite (bath); 1 family (double and single) and private bathroom.

Price: £25 p.p. Single supp. £15.

Breakfast: At 8.30am

Meals: Available locally.

Closed: Christmas.

Here's a big, old house in the country, minus the expected creaks and draughts and with every mod con. Carpets are thick, beds four-poster and sumptuous. This feels like a small hotel (there's a helipad for those wanting to make a big entrance!), yet it's very much the McGoverns' home. Plush green sofas sit by the stone inglenook and you can have drinks here before eating in the candlelit conservatory. (Mark is a Master of Cheese and once ran a restaurant.) The garden is lush and landscaped and there are fields all around - look out for the fat Hebridean sheep; they look like small buffalo!

Rooms: 2 doubles, both en suite (shower).

Price: £42.50 p.p. Single supp. £27.

Breakfast: Flexible.

Meals: Dinner, 3 courses, £19.50 p.p.

Closed: Never!

From Stratford, go south on A3400 towards Shipston. After 3 miles, signed on right.

Map Ref No: 10

From Stratford take A4200, over Clopton bridge, immediately left onto Tiddington Road then 1st right onto Loxley Rd. Last house on left with white electric gates.

Map Ref No: 10

Angela & Chris Wright
Alderminster Farm
Alderminster
Nr. Stratford-upon-Avon
Warwickshire CV37 8BP
Tel: 01789 450774
Fax: 01789 450774
christopher_denley.wright@virgin.net

Ms Kate McGovern
Glebe Farm House
Loxley
Stratford-upon-Avon
Warwickshire CV35 9JW
Tel: 01789 842501
Fax: 01789 842501
e-mail: scorpiolimited@msn.com

Originally part of the Ragley estate owned by the Marquis of Hertford, this delightful barn conversion has a large comfortable sitting/dining area. Gravelside is on a hill and the light airy bedrooms have magnificent views over farmland to the Cotswold Hills beyond. Gourmet *à la carte* breakfasts and a hard tennis court complete the picture... with a labrador called Mattie to retrieve the stray tennis balls or take you for a walk. Service indeed in a real country hideaway.

Rooms: 1 twin and 2 doubles, all en suite (shower).

Price: £25-£30 p.p. Single occ. £35-£40.

Breakfast: 7.30-9am.

Meals: Excellent local pub/restaurants nearby.

Closed: Never!

Drink in the views. The greenness of the surrounding countryside will revive flagging spirits, the peace will soothe the frazzled. David and Julia are a well-travelled and unassuming couple devoted to their ancient house and garden. Mallards glide over the pond and a stream runs by the 400-year-old yew. Inside, Cotswold stone walls, comfortable sofas, beamed dining and drawing room and huge inglenooks complete the peaceful scene while uneven floors enhance the character of this 300-year-old house.

Rooms: 2 doubles, sharing bathroom.

Price: £25 p.p. No single supp.

Breakfast: Flexible.

Meals: Supper, £12-£18 p.p., by arrangement.

Closed: Christmas & New Year.

From Stratford A46 towards Evesham. After 4 miles left to Binton. Fork left at Blue Boar. House 350m down hill on right. Turn into drive, house on left.

Map Ref No: 10

Denise & Guy Belchambers
Gravelside Barn
Binton
Stratford-Upon-Avon
Warwickshire CV37 9TU
Tel: 01789 750502
Fax: 01789 298056

From A423 turn off to Wormleighton and Priors Hardwick. After 1.8 miles, left for Priors Hardwick. First hard left on S-bend (No exit sign). House on right on concrete road behind farm buildings.

Map Ref No: 10

Mr David Gaunt
Hollow Meadow House
Priors Hardwick
Nr. Rugby
Warwickshire CV22 8SP
Tel: 01327 261540
Fax: 01327 261540

Kim has the sort of kitchen city dwellers dream of: big, old and welcoming. It's the hub of the house. She fizzes with good humour and energy and takes pride in those times when family and guests feel easy together. You will be offered tea on arrival, or even a walk round the village with the dogs. Hers is a large 1900s country house with tennis court, terrace, fine garden, croquet lawn and homemade jams. The rooms are large, soft and supremely comfortable. A special place.

Rooms: 1 twin and 1 double, each with private bathroom.

Price: £22-£25 p.p. Single supp. £8.

Breakfast: Flexible.

Meals: Dinner, £18.50 p.p., by arrangement

Closed: Never!

Cathy's great sense of humour carries her through each gloriously eventful day. This is a paradise for families - there's so much room to play and so much to see: suckler cows, pet turkeys, Christmas geese and free-range Saddleback pigs. The farmhouse, built in 1640, was extended 25 years ago using old bricks and beams. Tiny timbered corridors lead to large bedrooms with wooden floors and leaded windows (the family room has everything needed for a baby). Neighbouring the farm is the magnificent lake, Shrewley Pools.

Rooms: 1 large family with kingsize, single and cot, 1 twin, both en suite (bath).

Price: £22.50 p.p. Single supp. £2.50.

Breakfast: Flexible.

Meals: Dinner with home-reared meat, packed lunch & children's high tea all by arrangement.

Closed: Christmas & New Year.

From Banbury A361 north. At Byfield village sign left into Twistle Lane, straight on into Priors Marston. House is white, 5th on left with cattle grid, after S-bend.

Map Ref No: 10

Kim & John Mahon
Marston House
Priors Marston
Rugby
Warwickshire CV23 8RP
Tel: 01327 260297
Fax: 01327 262846

From Warwick take A4177 towards Solihull. At Five Ways roundabout, 1st left, follow for 0.75 miles; signed down track on left.

Map Ref No: 10

Cathy Dodd
Shrewley Pools Farm
Haseley
Warwick
Warwickshire CV35 7HB
Tel: 01926 484315

We challenge you to find anything else of such good value so close to Birmingham. Built in 1737, well-and-truly done-up in 1988, everything about this place is HUGE! The kitchen, with Aga and stone floors, gives onto a stunning patio and conservatory where you can eat breakfast. Drawing room, bedrooms and bathrooms are plush, big and comfortable. Denise, quiet at first, has an infectious laugh and runs her B&B with careful attention to detail. *Prior booking essential. Children over 12 welcome.*

Rooms: 2 doubles and 1 twin, all en suite (baths).

Price: £22.50 p.p. Single supp. £12.50.

Breakfast: Flexible.

Meals: Supper, £17.50 p.p., by arrangement.

Closed: Never!

At M6 junction 4, take A446 for Lichfield. At sign to Coleshill South get in right lane and turn off. From High St, turn into Maxstoke Lane. After 4 miles take 4th right. House 1st on left.

Map Ref No: 10

Mrs Denise Owen
Hardingwood House
Hardingwood Lane
Fillongley, Nr. Coventry
Warwickshire CV7 8EL
Tel: 01676 542579

Valerie is a talented interior designer and fashion historian - both passions are apparent as soon as you see the Threlfall's half of the 16th-century manor house. Dotted around the house you find fashion prints, photographs, a collection of hat boxes and dressmakers' dummies. Valerie is huge fun. In the ballroom, with its wooden floor, grand piano and window seats you can imagine the elegant ribaldry of the days when it hosted 'coming-out' balls. The dining room is red and hung with William Morris fabrics and paper.

Rooms: 1 double, en suite (bath) and 1 twin with private shower.

Price: £24-£30 p.p. Single supp. £5.

Breakfast: Until 9.50am.

Meals: Available locally.

Closed: Christmas & New Year

Wiltshire

In the centre of the village is the White Hart pub. 100m due east is a tall Cotswold stone wall with stone pillars. Turn in and the house is on the right.

Map Ref No: 4

Valerie & Roger Threlfall
1 Cove House
Ashton Keynes
Wiltshire SN6 6NS
Tel: 01285 861226
Fax: 01793 814990

The original granary for Malmesbury Abbey was here; now there is this lovely honey-coloured country farmhouse, with Cotswold stone roof with moss and lichen, traditional walled garden (veg, fruit and flowers), flagstoned floors and views through old doors and windows. And it is right next to a fine church in a classically pretty village. The views from the surprisingly modern bathroom are inspiring - cattle peacefully grazing in the paddock; the church from another, and little window seats to sit on. It is all delightful, and comfortable, too. Helen is lovely.

Rooms: 2 doubles, one en suite and one with private bathroom.

Price: £20-£22.50 p.p. Single occ. £25.

Breakfast: Until 10am.

Meals: Dinner, 3 courses, £12.50 p.p. Packed lunch also available, both with notice.

Closed: Christmas & New Year.

A429 Malmesbury to Cirencester. In Crudwell, at Plough right signed Minety/Oaksey. Straight on, then left between church and tithe barn pillars.

Map Ref No: 4

Helen & Philip Carter
Manor Farmhouse
Crudwell
Malmesbury
Wiltshire SN16 9ER
Tel: 01666 577375
Fax: 01666 823523

The quiet seclusion of Liz and Colin's home is delightful whatever the season; in winter large comfy sofas envelop you and fires warm you; in summer, eat on the lawn in the cool shade of the arbour. The bright conservatory with its huge oak table is the sort most of us can only dream of. The cottage garden supplies the fresh vegetables and herbs (mostly organic) which Liz uses to magnificent effect. Liz and Colin are marvellously easy and flexible; Colin will gladly show you the sights then bring you home for dinner. Perfect.

Rooms: 1 twin, en suite (bath) and 1 twin with private bathroom.

Price: £25-£27.50 p.p. Single supp. by arrangement.

Breakfast: Flexible.

Meals: Dinner, 3 courses, £18 p.p. by arrangement.

Closed: Christmas & Easter.

From A429 take B4040 through Charlton, past Horse & Groom pub. 0.5 miles on, left signed 'Bullocks Horn - No Through Road'. Continue to end of lane. Turn right. House is first on left.

Map Ref No: 4

Colin & Liz Legge
Bullocks Horn Cottage
Charlton
Malmesbury
Wiltshire SN16 9DZ
Tel: 01666 577600
Fax: 01666 577905

From the front it is a characteristic townhouse in sight of the Benedictine Abbey; from the back it is a country house with views over the Avon River and Wiltshire. Inside, there is a sense of sunlit space, the foyer/dining room has a gallery, there are old, rare, well-loved possessions, books (they used to run a book shop here) and a fine conservatory. There is also a meditation room. Your hostess is great fun; both she and Dick enjoy having guests in this, the oldest borough in England.

Rooms: 1 twin, en suite (bath), with single attic room for overflow. Separate shower also available.

Price: Twin £22.50 p.p. Attic overflow £20.

Breakfast: Flexible.

Meals: Dinner available locally.

Closed: Never!

Doi is relaxed and friendly: she does B&B because she loves it. Breakfast is cooked just as you want it, when you want it. In summer you can while away warm evenings in the vine-hung, thyme-carpeted arbour in the garden. Cotswold stone is star here: house, yard, flower beds, delicious walled garden are all softly golden. Gently-decorated bedrooms have space, views, flowers and old photographs; one has a half-tester bed. The dining room has dark blue walls, wooden floors and a solid oak table with tapestry chairs.

Rooms: 2 doubles: 1 en suite (bath) and 1 with private bath & shower.

Price: £20-£22 p.p. Single supp. £5.

Breakfast: Flexible.

Meals: Dinner £12.50 p.p. by arrangement, B.Y.O. wine. Also local pubs.

Closed: Christmas.

From top of High Street left at Market Cross. House is 100m on left next to the large traffic mirror.

Map Ref No: 4

Dick & M.E. Batstone
St. Aldhelms
14 Gloucester Street
Malmesbury
Wiltshire SN16 0AA
Tel: 01666 822145

Take B4042 from Malmesbury towards Wootton Bassett. Left to Lea & Charlton. In Lea, right opposite school. House is along drive through fields.

Map Ref No: 4

Tony & Doi Newman
Winkworth Farm
Lea
Nr. Malmesbury
Wiltshire SN16 9NH
Tel: 01666 823267

Big, generous beds, and it is within eight acres of parkland and garden, in an ancient hamlet. This is the sort of impeccably managed house that appeals particularly to American visitors and to those who love their comforts: huge main rooms with big windows looking over the perfectly manicured garden, lots of big flower arrangements, chintz-covered chairs and everything neat and tidy. Bedrooms are smaller, with skylights and sloping beamed ceilings. Helga can tempt you with croquet, tennis and meals on the lawn in summer.

Rooms: 1 twin, 1 double and 1 single. Private or shared bathroom available.

Price: £25-£30 p.p.

Breakfast: Flexible.

Meals: Dinner £12.50-£15 p.p. Available on request.

Closed: Never!

From M4 junction 17, west along A420. Turn right to Upper Wraxall. Take first left in village opposite pond. Coach House at end of this private drive.

Map Ref No: 4

Helga & David Venables
The Coach House
Upper Wraxall
Nr. Bath
Wiltshire SN14 7AG
Tel: 01225 891026
Fax: 01225 892355
e-mail: venables@compuserve.com

Breakfast on the terrace and gaze over the honey-coloured collage of Regency Bath below, a stunning spectacle from this lofty vantage point. Much-travelled Anne's Cotswold stone house is an oriental excursion, enriched by batiks, silk paintings and other Malaysian memorabilia. Exotic plants and hand-painted pots fringe the garden pond full of carp and smaller, shimmering fish. Anne's high-powered working background as a Far-East head-hunter (sic!) may seem at odds with her relaxed, friendly manner; now she channels her considerable vitality and energy into caring for guests.

Rooms: 1 twin/family, en suite (shower) and 1 double, en suite (bath and shower); 1 double/single with private bathroom.

Price: From £22-£28 p.p. Single occ. £27-£33.

Breakfast: Flexible.

Meals: Excellent pub, within walking distance.

Closed: Never!

M4 exit 18, A46. A46 joins A4, then left for Chippenham. At r'bout, A363 (Bradford on Avon). Bear left under bridge, into Bathford. After 1.5 miles left after pub (Lower Kingsdown Rd). Bear right at bottom, house 300 yds on left.

Map Ref No: 4

Anne Venus
Owl House
Kingsdown
Nr. Box
Wiltshire SN13 8BB
Tel: 01225 743883
Fax: 01225 744450
e-mail: venus@zetnet.co.uk

A medieval manor house and all that goes with it, plus the necessary modern touches where they matter. It looks imposing outside - arched, mullioned windows, jutting gables, tall chimneys - while the interior is, quite breathtakingly, manorial, with all the cultured trappings you would expect. Henry VIII housed Archbishop Cranmer here, so it seems appropriate that he is commemorated by a huge engraved Elizabethan stone fireplace. Bedrooms are sunny, luxurious and charming with big beds and views over the grounds. Bradford is delightful, and Bath is close by.

Rooms: 3 twins/doubles, all en suite (bath/shower).

Price: £35-£40 p.p. Single occ. £60.

Breakfast: 8.15-9.20am.

Meals: Only for parties.

Closed: Christmas & New Year.

A36 Warminster road out of Bath for 5 miles, left onto B3108, under railway bridge and up hill. First right, turn off Winsley by-pass into old village and then 1st left after 30 mph signs, into lane marked 'except for access'.

Map Ref No: 4

John & Elizabeth Denning
Burghope Manor
Winsley
Bradford-on-Avon
Wiltshire BA15 2LA
Tel: 01225 723557
Fax: 01225 723113

It was built by a local baker in 1807, on a steep hillside with spectacular southern views over the lovely old Cotswold-stone town. The oak sail gallery has been meticulously restored, as well as the Victorian spiral staircase and pointed Gothic windows. The curves of the main part of the mill have created womb-like rooms, decorated in pale pinks and greens with vibrant Tahitian fabrics and hand-woven South American rugs. The beds - king-size circular, water, and Gothic iron - add a touch of fun. Dinners, too, are exotic, with recipes collected during their travels.

Rooms: 2 doubles, 1 en suite (bath) and 1 en suite (shower); 1 suite, en suite (bath).

Price: £34.50-£49.50 p.p. Single occ. £69-£89.

Breakfast: 8-9am.

Meals: Dinner, vegetarian only, £20 p.p. avail. Mon, Thurs, Sat by prior arrangement. B.Y.O. wine.

Closed: January & February.

Coming from the N on A363, mini-roundabout at Castle pub, take road downhill towards town centre. After 50m turn left into private drive, immediately before first house on pavement.

Map Ref No: 4

Peter & Priscilla Roberts
Bradford Old Windmill
Masons Lane
Bradford-on-Avon
Wiltshire BA15 1QN
Tel: 01225 866842
Fax: 01225 866648

Sue and Allan bought this Victorian manor house two years ago and have transformed it with imagination and style into a comfortable and elegant country house. The large bedrooms are well furnished and overlook the colourful gardens and orchards with distant views of Salisbury Plain. The elegant drawing room leads out through French windows to the terrace and lawns. The village is dominated by the magnificent 14th-century Priory Church - home every August to a music festival. Many lovely walks surround the house. *Children over 8 welcome.*

Rooms: 1 twin, en suite (bath/shower) and 1 twin/double with private shower & w.c.

Price: First-night rate £28 p.p., £25 for subsequent nights. Single supp. by arrangement.

Breakfast: Flexible.

Meals: Dinner & packed lunch by prior arrangement.

Closed: 20 December-2 January.

From Westbury, B3098 to Bratton, then to Edington and left to Priory Church. First left into Lower Road, house on left opposite last thatched cottage.

Map Ref No: 4

Susan & Allan Edwards
The Manor House
Edington
Nr. Westbury
Wiltshire BA13 4QW
Tel: 01380 831210
Fax: 01380 831455

Codford nestles under the southern fold of Salisbury Plain in the renowned Wylye Valley in deepest Wiltshire. Bluff Richardson-Aitken runs a tight ship but shows a heart of gold to visitors who enjoy the cheerful routine in his 18th-century cottage which was once the home of the parish sexton. Interested in wine and a keen cook, he makes a point of preparing local sausages for breakfast. The spacious, bright double bedroom with its floral curtains, fitted wardrobes and traditional furniture overlooks the gardens. The drawing room with exposed beams is elegant and comfortable.

Rooms: 1 twin with private bathroom with possible use of single for member of same party.

Price: £20 p.p.

Breakfast: Flexible.

Meals: Lots of good places nearby.

Closed: Christmas.

Codford is on the A36, 7 miles south of Warminster. Church Lane leads to St Mary's church and is signed for the ANZAC War Cemetery nearby.

Map Ref No: 4

Mr & Mrs Richardson-Aitken
Glebe Cottage
Church Lane
Codford St. Mary
Wiltshire BA12 0PJ
Tel: 01985 850565
Fax: 01985 850565

The cockerels that fought in the garden pit here were reputedly the last in the South to do so. It is a treat to stay in the Woodford Valley and from the hill behind the garden you can see Stonehenge. The garden is enclosed by a thatched cob wall and contains, among other unusual plants, a Judas tree and a Tulip tree. The house is full of intriguing bits and pieces. There is an ethnic twist to the bedroom furnishings but it is very much 'country house': large sofas, pastel walls, pale carpets, spaniel and labrador, and a large and attractive dining room. *Children over 7 welcome.*

Rooms: 1 twin with adjacent single, en suite (bath/shower).

Price: £28-£30 p.p. Single supp. £14.

Breakfast: Flexible.

Meals: Dinner, 3 courses, £18 p.p. by arrangement.

Closed: Christmas & New Year.

Festooned with rambling roses, this mellow brick farmhouse stands in superb gardens, in bloom from January to September, with over 50 varieties of clematis, architectural shrubs and specimen trees to interest the discerning gardener. There are two themed guest rooms: the Hat Room, displaying hats from around the world, and the Raffles-style Singapore room, furnished in bamboo. Penny O'Brien is a keen walker, and a tennis court is available for those with energy to spare. Try candle-lit dinner (plan ahead) in the intimate, wooden-floored dining room.

Rooms: 1 twin, en suite (shower) and 1 double with private bathroom.

Price: £25-£28 p.p. Single occ. £35-£38.

Breakfast: Flexible.

Meals: By arrangement £18-£20 p.p.

Closed: Never!

From A303, take road to Amesbury. Over lights, right at mini-roundabout. Left fork, after 1 mile left at Heale Gardens. House 0.5 miles on right just before phone box. Door is in the cob wall immediately on the right.

Map Ref No: 4

Philip & Ann Danby
Fighting Cocks
West Amesbury
Salisbury
Wiltshire SP4 7BH
Tel: 01980 622381
Fax: 01980 626362

A36 from Salisbury-Southampton. After 6 miles, through traffic lights, then 3 miles later, take left (signed Landford Wood). Go down narrow lane through lodge gatehouses, pass chapel on left, then left, house signed.

Map Ref No: 4

Mrs Penelope O'Brien
Landsbrook Farm
Landford Wood
Nr. Salisbury
Wiltshire SP5 2ES
Tel: 01794 390220
Fax: 01794 390220

What could be more seductive than the smell of home-baked bread wafting out of the kitchen? It sets the scene for this fine George I farmhouse in a quiet spot off the main road, on the edge of the New Forest. The rooms are full of character, ample and charming, with patchwork quilts, brass beds, stencils. Sue Barry is equally characterful and, as a Blue Badge Guide, is well qualified to tell you about the area. Homemade jams, honey and elderflower cordial, and several black labradors snuffling about.

Rooms: 1 twin/family; 2 doubles, each en suite (shower) and 1 single with private bathroom.

Price: Twin/doubles £21-£25 p.p. Single supp. £10.

Breakfast: Until 9am.

Meals: Available locally.

Closed: Christmas & New Year.

It is a rare treat to have your milk fresh from the cow. This rather grand Victorian Gothic farmhouse is a working, tenanted, arable and dairy farm owned by the Earl of Pembroke. There are very large bedrooms furnished in the period of the house with impressive garden views and a billiard room. In the summer, the terrace doors are thrown open for an *al fresco* breakfast. Everything is grand but cosy. The whole estate is 1,400 acres and a Site of Special Scientific Interest, treasured for its wild flowers and butterflies.

Rooms: 2 twins: 1 en suite (shower) and 1 with private shower room; 1 double/family with private bathroom.

Price: £22-£25 p.p. Single occ. £30.

Breakfast: Flexible.

Meals: Dinner available locally.

Closed: Christmas & 31 December.

From Salisbury A36 towards Southampton. After about 5 miles look for sign on left before lights at junction A36/A27. Follow the signs.

Map Ref No: 4

Sue Barry
Brickworth Farmhouse
Brickworth Lane
Whiteparish, Salisbury
Wiltshire SP5 2QE
Tel: 01794 884663
Fax: 01794 884186

From Salisbury A36 towards Warminster/Bath. Left at Stoford into Great Wishford. Pass church and turn right at Royal Oak pub. House signed on right after 2 miles.

Map Ref No: 4

Patricia Helyer
Little Langford Farmhouse
Little Langford
Salisbury
Wiltshire SP3 4NR
Tel: 01722 790205
Fax: 01722 790086

No townies, Christopher and Emma will plunge you into their particular enthusiasms: hunting, shooting and fishing. A deer's head lords it over the dining room and the couple will even organise tank spotting! The garden slopes down towards Enford, with views of the water meadows. The interior has been done with flair: seagrass flooring, tartans, creams and greens. Emma's an accomplished cook and uses organic ingredients; Christopher knows about wine. *Children over 8 welcome* and there's a donkey trap!

Rooms: 1 double, with private bathroom and also single bed. In the barn: 1 double, en suite with twin attic room for children.

Price: £20-£25 p.p.

Breakfast: Flexible.

Meals: Dinner £17 p.p. Lunch & picnics also available on request.

Closed: Never!

Few Victorian houses exude such an air of repose as you saunter up the drive past kempt lawns. Inside, a bright, galleried hallway sets the mood which the Cravens carry with them. The perfect peace of the setting helps: you can walk through the gate onto Salisbury Plain. Guestrooms have sweeping views; the double has an 'Empire' feel, a beautifully decorated (4'6") bed with an oval Japanese picture set in the headboard; the twin has space and a pretty fireplace. The elegant drawing room sums up Cleeve House - glorious, unpretentious comfort.

Rooms: 1 twin and 1 (small) double, with basin, sharing bathroom and w.c.

Price: £23 p.p. Single occ. £25.

Breakfast: Until 9.45am.

Meals: Dinner £16.50-£18 p.p. by arrangement. Also excellent local pub.

Closed: Christmas.

From Salisbury A345 towards Marlborough. Right into Enford village, cross Avon. At T-junction right and then immediately left. House is signed.

Map Ref No: 4

Christopher & Emma Younghusband
Hill House
Long Street
Enford Pewsey
Wiltshire SN9 6DD
Tel: 01980 671202
Fax: 01980 671212

From Marlborough, take A345 through Pewsey into Upavon. Left at garage, over bridge. Immediately left at pottery shop. House is at end of Vicarage Lane.

Map Ref No: 4

Richard & Tuppie Craven
Cleeve House
Upavon
Pewsey
Wiltshire SN9 6AA
Tel: 01980 630812
Fax: 01980 630892

They knew how to build houses in the very old days, for the manor house, set in 20 acres of field and paddock is 16th century. Mrs Firth loves traditional pursuits, such as horse-riding (dressage and hunting) and cooking. She grows loads of fruit and veg and knows where to track down the best local produce. So, farmhouse-honest, or *Cordon Bleu*, the food oozes country freshness and nutritional values that are satisfyingly 'old-world' - as is the 400-year-old dining table where you eat.

Rooms: 1 kingsize, en suite (shower); 1 twin, en suite (bath) and 2 singles with either private bath or shower.

Price: £19-£21 p.p.

Breakfast: 7.30-9am.

Meals: Dinner, 4 courses inc. wine, £15 p.p. by arrangement. Reduction for 2 courses.

Closed: 23-31 December.

Serena is friendly, gutsy and open with a lovely sense of humour and an artistic streak; she paints in oils. She and her two spaniels welcome guests with equal enthusiasm to their thatched 18th-century cottage. The pretty, pastel bedrooms with fabric headboards, co-ordinated bed linen and lovely botanic paintings overlook the garden. From the bathroom you can see the dovecot and the distant canal. The setting is lovely and the peace restorative. *Children over 5 welcome.*

Rooms: 1 double and 1 twin, both sharing private bathroom.

Price: £22.50 p.p. Single supp. up to £10.

Breakfast: Flexible.

Meals: With prior notice.

Closed: Christmas.

From Devizes either take A360 to Salisbury or A342 to Andover. After 4 miles either from A342 or from A360 at West Lavington along B3098. Manor is 0.25 miles east of Easterton, 1 mile west of Urchfont.

Map Ref No: 4

Janet Firth
Eastcott Manor
Easterton
Devizes
Wiltshire SN10 4PL
Tel: 01380 813313

From Marlborough on A345 into Pewsey. After station, right to Woodborough. Follow road through village. The Manor House is on the right, St. Cross is next door up a lane on the left.

Map Ref No: 4

Serena Gore
St. Cross
Woodborough
Pewsey
Wiltshire SN9 5PL
Tel: 01672 851346

Flagstone floors lead you into book-lined, red bricked rooms scattered with family photographs and fresh flowers. Stylishly cluttered, cosy and with an adoring family retriever and pug, it's a seductively easy place to settle into. Clarissa is a professional cook and looks after you with bundles of energy and enthusiasm. Bedrooms are bright and simply decorated: walls and throws are cream, beds are wooden. Outside, there are five acres of gardens, a tennis court, a swimming pool and chickens that provide fresh eggs for breakfast.

Rooms: 1 twin, en suite (shower), 1 twin/double, en suite (bath) and 1 double with private bathroom.

Price: £23-£26 p.p. Single occ. from £30.

Breakfast: Flexible.

Meals: Dinner, 4 courses, £20 p.p.

Closed: Never!

A more beautiful setting would be hard to find. In the valley of the Kennet River - which flows briskly past the foot of an immaculate lawn - is a house that deserves to be in a glossy magazine. It looks every inch a dolls' house, but Jeremy and Heather add a deft human touch. The elegance of breakfast taken in the conservatory is balanced by the comforting hubbub emanating from the family kitchen. Upstairs, the cleverly converted bedrooms are ingeniously clustered around the chimney breast. Time here slips by effortlessly; many people come to visit the mysterious crop circles.

Rooms: 1 double, en suite (bath) and 3 singles with shared bathroom.

Price: Double £25 p.p. Single £30.

Breakfast: Flexible.

Meals: Available locally. Lunch/packed lunch available on request.

Closed: Christmas.

From Marlborough take A346 for 3 miles. Right to Wootton Rivers. In village, turn right (opp. Royal Oak pub) and drive for 0.7 miles. Drive on right after sign for Clench Common.

Map Ref No: 4

Clarissa Roe
Clench Farmhouse
Clench
Nr. Marlborough
Wiltshire SN8 4NT
Tel: 01672 810264
Fax: 01672 811458

From Hungerford A4 towards Marlborough. After 7 miles right towards Stitchcombe, down hill (bear left at barn) and left at T-junc. On entering village house is on left.

Map Ref No: 4

Jeremy & Heather Coulter
Fisherman's House
Mildenhall
Nr. Marlborough
Wiltshire SN8 2LZ
Tel: 01672 515390

On the Down behind the house was fought the Battle of Roundway in 1643. Today you are left in peace to take in the horizon-sweeping views, cosseted by two charming, easy-going hosts; Richard is a wine enthusiast and Pippa a skilled cook who works wonders with fresh ingredients to produce imaginative food. You have the run of the house and its gardens. Chickens range free in the stable yard and there's a grass tennis court. The bedrooms are large and luxurious, the whole house is elegantly furnished and decorated. *Children over 13 welcome.*

Rooms: 2 large twins/doubles, both en suite (bath); 2 smaller doubles sharing a bathroom.

Price: £29-£35 p.p. Single supp. £18 in small double.

Breakfast: Flexible.

Meals: Dinner, £22 p.p., by arrangement.

Closed: Christmas & Easter.

West along A4. Left just before Calne signed Heddington. 2 miles to Ivy Inn and T-junct. Left. House on left opposite church 50 yards on.

Map Ref No: 4

Richard & Pippa Novis
Heddington Manor
Heddington
Nr. Calne
Wiltshire SN11 0PN
Tel: 01380 850240
Fax: 01380 859176

Elegant, embracing and unpretentious, this Georgian rectory is perched high on a hillside with views to Worcestershire and Herefordshire. The three acres of garden with mature trees display a colour and fragrance with year-round interest. This is a much-loved family home with antiques, big sofas, open fires, family photos and Rockingham china. Bedrooms have books, quilted counterpanes and high, old-fashioned beds with good sheets and blankets. The long, polished dining table is set with silver. Dinners are delicious, so bring your own wine and eat in. *Children over 14 welcome.*

Rooms: 1 double with private bathroom; 1 twin, en suite (shower).

Price: £26 p.p. Single supp. £5.

Breakfast: Until 9am (week), 9.30am (weekend).

Meals: Dinner £20 p.p. B.Y.O. wine.

Closed: Occasionally.

Worcestershire

Going east on the A456 between Ludlow and Tenbury, take lane in front of the Rose & Crown, on bend before Tenbury turn. Rectory is 1.5 miles on left.

Map Ref No: 9

John & Rosemary Matthews
The Old Rectory
Boraston
Tenbury Wells
Worcestershire WR15 8LH
Tel: 01584 811088

Good food, good wines and a warm welcome await you at this lovely old house. You'll be singing the praises of Ann, who does the cooking, and Tony, a wine importer, when their combined knowledge and palpable enjoyment are on show at meal times. When they held occasional 'Wine Weekends' they discovered that they loved entertaining so much that they threw open the doors of their 18th-century home full-time. Take a post-prandial stroll into their long, calming garden with the Malverns as your backdrop.

Rooms: 1 twin/double and 1 double, each en suite (bath); 1 double with private bathroom.

Price: £22-£26 p.p. Single occ. £29.50. Winter breaks available.

Breakfast: Between 8-9am.

Meals: Dinner, 4 courses, £15.90 p.p.

Closed: Christmas & New Year.

At the foot of the majestic Malvern Hills, so there are stunning views all around. A fine 15th-century house that was subsequently Georgianised, Welland Court is surrounded by 23 acres and a two-acre trout-stocked lake (guests may fish here). Inside, you are bound to enjoy the dazzling black-and-white floored hall, antique-filled dining and drawing rooms and large bedrooms (where the house Scotch awaits you). *Cordon Bleu* dinners at the beautifully-set mahogany dining table.

Rooms: 1 twin, en suite (shower), 1 twin and 1 twin/double, en suite (bath/shower).

Price: £35 p.p. Single supp. £10.

Breakfast: Until 9.30am.

Meals: Dinner, inc. aperitif & wine, £35 p.p. available on request.

Closed: Never!

Turn off M50 at junct.1 onto A38 toward Worcester. After 1.5 miles left towards Upton-on-Severn, cross River Severn. At T-junction, right onto B4211. Left onto (B4209) towards Malvern Wells. Farm 3rd on right.

Map Ref No: 9

Ann & Tony Addison
Old Parsonage Farm
Hanley Castle
Worcester
Worcestershire WR8 0BU
Tel: 01684 310124
Fax: 01684 310124
e-mail: oldparsonagewines@msn.co

West on A4104 to Upton-upon-Severn. Once there, cross river, turn left up main street, continue for 3 miles until phone box on left. Turn left at sign and take left fork.

Map Ref No: 9

Philip & Elizabeth Archer
Welland Court
Upton-upon-Severn
Worcestershire WR8 0ST
Tel: 01684 594426
Fax: 01684 594426

Flamborough Head juts out into the North Sea, battered by weather and history. The Manor House is a splendid refuge: maple flooring and rugs on the ground floor, dark green walls and old oak table in the dining room, cosy book-filled sitting room with brocade sofas, oak furniture, shuttered windows. Perhaps a coal fire in your room or you may have the vast carved 17th-century four-poster. The bathrooms have marble and Victorian fittings (cast-iron baths). Geoffrey is an author, Lesley runs a shop that has kept the art of Gansey knitting alive. A smashing place. *Children over 8 welcome.*

Rooms: 1 double with private bathroom; 1 twin/double, en suite (bath).

Price: £30-£35 p.p. Single supp. £8.

Breakfast: Flexible.

Meals: Dinner £21 p.p.

Closed: Christmas.

Yorkshire

From Bridlington take B1255 to Flamborough. Follow signs to the lighthouse, past church on right. House is on the next corner (Lighthouse Road and Tower Street).

Map Ref No: 16

Lesley Berry & Geoffrey Miller
The Manor House
Flamborough
Yorkshire YO15 1PD
Tel: 01262 850943
Fax: 01262 850943

Some 'guests' had to sleep outside when it was a children's hospital. Dulce and Ian took seven winters to restore the Hall to its former beauty. The house now feels very much like a family home; big, comfortable bedrooms with armchairs, fresh flowers and excellent bathrooms. Another labour of love is the two-acre walled garden which includes a nursery and 'potager'. The flowerbeds are a gardener's dream, the lawns are sweeping and there is a grass tennis court. Dulce is a liveryman of the Worshipful Company of Gardeners.

Rooms: 2 twins/doubles, en suite (bath and shower). 1 twin with private shower.

Price: £25 p.p. Single supp. £5.

Breakfast: Until 9.30am.

Meals: Dinner, 3 courses, £17.50 p.p. Supper £12.50 p.p.

Closed: Never!

From Bawtry, east on A631. Approaching Gringley on the Hill, 1st left after school sign. Continue 150m. House on left with iron gates.

Map Ref No: 15

Ian & Dulce Threlfall
Gringley Hall
Gringley on the Hill
Yorkshire DN10 4QT
Tel: 01777 817262
Fax: 01777 816824

If you don't know what a Clun or Lonk is, use it as an excuse to make a trip to this unusual restaurant with rooms. The answer is somewhere on the walls. There's a rambling eccentricity downstairs; the lighting is atmospheric, the front bar is distinctly French with heavy wood, marble and comfy chairs. Some bedrooms have antique French beds and two of them look out onto the parsonage where the Brontës lived - now a museum. At night, the restaurant fills with chatter.

Rooms: 1 twin, 1 double and 1 single: all with private bathrooms.

Price: Twin/double £34.74 p.p. Single, £49.50.

Breakfast: Until 9am.

Meals: Set menus up to £13.50 p.p. À la carte up to £25 p.p.

Closed: Two weeks after Christmas & two weeks in June.

From A629 take B6142 to Haworth. Follow Brontë Parsonage Museum signs. Use their car park as Weaver's backs onto it! Ignore signs for Brontë Village.

Map Ref No: 15

Colin & Jane Rushworth
Weaver's
15 West Lane
Haworth
Yorkshire BD22 8DU
Tel: 01535 643822
Fax: 01535 644832

Ann, cultured, interesting and attentive, is a one-off. So, too, is her house. The combination of host and home will fill you with *joie de vivre*. Sit at the large bay window and look down on York's only residential square or sweep down the central stone staircase and venture forth to tease every secret out of the historic city. The house, completed in 1852, is graciously proportioned and unconsciously stylish. Rooms are enormous, colours are bold and Anne has created a lovely secluded garden at the back.

Rooms: 1 twin with private shower; 2 doubles, en suite (1 with shower and 1 with bath).

Price: £35 p.p. Single supp. £10.

Breakfast: Until 10.30am.

Meals: Available locally.

Closed: Occasionally.

A stream runs through the garden and there's wildlife all around: very peaceful indeed. Only a mile from the spa town of Harrogate, this old mill cottage is a good base for sight-seeing. Over 200 years old, it has oak beams and an old stone arch that used to be the dairy and is now the breakfast corner. Peter and Marion are quiet hosts, their only concern being your rest and well-being. Peter was a professional golfer for 20 years and can arrange for you to play. There's a small library, and a guest sitting room. *Children over 12 welcome.*

Rooms: 2 twins: 1 en suite shower and 1 private bath/shower; 1 double, en suite (shower).

Price: £21 p.p. Single supp. £9.

Breakfast: Until 9am.

Meals: Available locally.

Closed: Christmas & New Year.

In the south-west side of the city just off the Holgate road, which is part of the A59 from York to Harrogate.

Map Ref No: 15

Mike & Anne Beaufoy
18 St. Paul's Square
York
Yorkshire YO2 4BD
Tel: 01904 629884
Fax: 01904 643428

Off the A61 north of Harrogate, signed on the road.

Map Ref No: 15

Peter & Marion Thomson
Knox Mill House
Knox Mill Lane
Harrogate
Yorkshire HG3 2AE
Tel: 01423 560650
Fax: 01423 560650

The light pouring through all those beautiful stone-mullioned windows bathes the whole, glorious house. The sun drenches the conservatory, filled with plants and views over the garden and beyond. Take your pre-dinner drinks in the oak-panelled, log-fired drawing room and sleep in bedrooms of style and simplicity. If time allows do stroll down past the pedigree Aberdeen Anguses to the banks of the Nidd, or you can play tennis. Pamela is ever-cheerful and kind, serving home-grown food and home-baked bread. *Children over 12 welcome.*

Rooms: 2 twins, both en suite (bath); 1 double with private shower & bath.

Price: £35 p.p. No single supp.

Breakfast: Until 9.30am, or by arrangement.

Meals: Dinner £18.50 p.p.

Closed: Christmas.

Although an old-fashioned inn with lots of old-world charm, the place is fun too; even the ghost in the 12th-century cellars has a sense of humour, turning the beer taps off! The family is fully involved and the food is seriously good. The bedrooms are fine - most have beamed ceilings - and one has a Victorian brass bed and, in the bathroom, a free-standing bath. The sitting room is strewn with local guide-books and maps, cosy with old armchairs and sofas. The river runs wide and shallow under the bridge, through a very English landscape; and the village is deeply sleepy.

Rooms: 2 family rooms, 1 single, 2 twins, 6 doubles, all en suite (bath or shower).

Price: £45-£52.50 p.p. Dinner, B&B from £65 p.p.

Breakfast: Until 9.30am.

Meals: Dinner in restaurant £22.95 p.p. Bar food from £7.50 p.p.

Closed: Never!

Off B6451 4 miles south of Pateley Bridge. Stone entrance is between Dacre Banks & hilltop hamlet. Look out for Dacre Aberdeen Angus sign.

Map Ref No: 15

Pamela Holliday
Low Hall
Dacre
Nr. Harrogate
Yorkshire HG3 4AA
Tel: 01423 780230

A59 west from Harrogate, then B6160 north at Bolton Bridge. Continue to Burnsall. Hotel next to bridge.

Map Ref No: 15

Elizabeth & Andrew Grayshon
The Red Lion
By the Bridge at Burnsall
Nr. Skipton
Yorkshire BD23 6BU
Tel: 01756 720204
Fax: 01756 720292
e-mail: redlion@daelnet.co.uk

Ray was the first Englishman since the war to work at the *Georges Cinq* in Paris - bravely. He has created a slice of English Heaven: snug sitting rooms, creaking staircases, log fires, close to the River Nidd; and Wath is a conservation village. The restaurant is elegantly attractive - creamy colours and a vast selection of liquids, not least malt whiskies. Dine on fish and local game in convivial surroundings; Ray is a gentle and articulate Yorkshireman with a gift for cooking. We wish there were more such superb restaurants-with-rooms.

Rooms: 2 twins & 3 doubles, all en suite. 2 doubles with private facilities. 6 en suite rooms in 'Stable Courtyard' annexe.

Price: £35 p.p. Single occ. £45.

Breakfast: Until 10am.

Meals: Dinner (all p.p.), 2 courses, £13.75; 3 courses £17.50, 4 courses £19.10. À la carte, 3 courses £25.

Closed: Christmas Day.

It's hard to believe that High Fold was once a barn, given its present-day elegance. Our inspector's form is littered with "wonderfuls". "The house is a jewel," he says. The house, deceptively small from the outside, regales you with space and style once inside. The eye is caught constantly: tapestries, paintings, plants rising up from corners, regal blue and gold curtains, and all set off perfectly by lighting. The upstairs bedroom has an arched window above the bed, a sloping ceiling and views of Wharfedale. Downstairs rooms are good for those with impaired mobility. *Pets by arrangement.*

Rooms: 3 twins/doubles: 2 en suite (bath), 1 en suite (shower).

Price: £28 p.p. Single supp. £7.

Breakfast: From 8.30-9am.

Meals: Dinner, 4 courses, £16 p.p.

Closed: January.

From Ripon, B6265 to Pateley Bridge. Over bridge, then right, signed Wath. After 1.5 miles, right over humpback bridge, signed.

Map Ref No: 15

Ray & Jane Carter
The Sportsman's Arms
Wath-in-Nidderdale
Pateley Bridge
Yorkshire HG3 5PP
Tel: 01423 711306
Fax: 01423 712524

B6160 into Kettlewell. After 1st bridge, 1st right, then 1st left. Road bears left after 400 yds but house is straight on, 400 yds on right.

Map Ref No: 15

Robin Martin & Tim Earnshaw
High Fold
Kettlewell
Skipton
Yorkshire BD23 5RJ
Tel: 01756 760390

A perfectly proper house run with faultless precision by John and Harriet - wine buff and interior decorator respectively. Right next door to Fountains Abbey and Studley Royal (here are the most complete remains of a Cistercian abbey in Britain), you are spoiled for things to do and see; consider your options in the manicured garden. As you drink your tea deer may wander up to the fence. Just two beautifully decorated bedrooms and bathrooms that are enough to make you want to put down roots. *Golf, riding and clay pigeon shooting can be arranged.*

Rooms: 2 twins, both en suite (bath).

Price: £40 p.p. Single supp. £10.

Breakfast: Flexible, by arrangement.

Meals: Dinner £20 p.p. by prior arrangement.

Closed: Christmas & New Year.

A superbly solid Georgian house with sweeping views across the Vale of York, yet only three minutes walk from the heart of the village. Set in 28 acres that run down to the River Swale (fishing available), it has black sheep, ducks, horses and ponies, a croquet lawn and a tennis court. The house - largely renovated by the amusing Sam and Annie - is a treat: the large, stylish rooms are all extremely cosy with quirky touches, and the big beamed bedrooms have lots of books, antiques, window seats. One even has a four-poster.

Rooms: 1 twin/double, en suite (shower); 2 doubles, 1 en suite (bath) and 1 with private bathroom.

Price: £25 p.p.

Breakfast: Until 9.30am.

Meals: Dinner £20 p.p. by arrangement, or good food available at four pubs a walk away.

Closed: Occasionally in winter.

Off A1 to Ripon. Take B6265/Pateley Bridge road for 2 miles. Left into Studley Roger. House last on right.

Map Ref No: 15

John & Harriet Highley
Lawrence House
Studley Roger
Ripon
Yorkshire HG4 3AY
Tel: 01765 600947
Fax: 01765 609297

From A1(M) take Boroughbridge exit. North side of Boroughbridge follow Easingwold/Helperby sign. In Helperby, right at T-junction, right up Hall Lane. Left in front of school.

Map Ref No: 15

Sam & Annie Key
Laurel Manor Farm
Brafferton-Helperby
York
Yorkshire YO6 2NZ
Tel: 01423 360436
Fax: 01423 360437

Mid-way between London and Edinburgh, on the banks of the River Swale lie the twin villages of Brafferton and Helperby - of Saxon and Viking origins respectively. In a quiet corner you will find Brafferton Hall, a c.1720 Dower House. All here is delightfully English: there are cricket bats in the umbrella stand, old chests, thick rugs, hot water bottles and antique floral eiderdowns. The drawing room is pale grey with a large bay window; Sue and John will have tea with you here. They are so easy-going that you'll soon feel you belong.

Rooms: 3 doubles: 2 en suite (shower) and 1 with private bathroom; 1 single, en suite (shower).

Price: £35-£38 p.p.

Breakfast: Until 10am.

Meals: Dinner £19 p.p., & lunch available on request.

Closed: Never!

From A1 take Boroughbridge exit. North of Boroughbridge follow Easingwold & Helperby signs for 4 miles. In village right at T-junc. & right again up Hall Lane. Hall on left opp. school.

Map Ref No: 15

John & Sue White
Brafferton Hall
Brafferton-Helperby
York
Yorkshire YO6 2NZ
Tel: 01423 360352
Fax: 01423 360352

Just head for the castle; its ruins are still superb and Richard III lived here in better days. This is a wonderful spot whence you may even glimpse York Minster and where walks start at the front door. The elegant drawing room has a fine high-backed sofa and log fire, fine rugs, good paintings and antiques. The bedrooms are pretty and comfortable, full of thoughtful touches. Jenny, a Scot, is fun, down-to-earth and a prodigious cook; Richard is a retired academic agricultural economist. A relaxed and special place. Your dog is welcome to sleep in the kennels.

Rooms: 1 four-poster and 1 double, both en suite (bath).

Price: £33-£35 p.p. No single supp.

Breakfast: Until 9.30am.

Meals: Dinner, 4 courses, £17.50 p.p. by arrangement.

Closed: Occasionally.

North from York on A64. After about 5 miles, left signed Flaxton and Sheriff Hutton. In S. Hutton, 1st right and house 150m on right, signed.

Map Ref No: 15

Jenny & Richard Howarth
Castle Farm
Sheriff Hutton
Yorkshire YO6 1PT
Tel: 01347 878341

The hotel was built in the early years of Victoria's reign to accommodate visitors who came to the spa seeking relief from insomnia, skin rashes and so on. It still offers relief: plump cushions, a snug cocktail bar, baby-sitting, bedboards for lower-back sufferers and all the joys of a good village hotel. The straight-forward, excellent rooms (all similar) are split between the main house and the cottage across the village green. There is a garden, a bistro and a restaurant, delicious traditional food, lots of Yorkshire prints and helpful staff.

Rooms: In hotel: 5 doubles, 3 twins, 2 singles, all en suite (bath). In cottages: 3 doubles, 5 twins/doubles, all en suite (bath).

Price: From £40 p.p. Single occ. £60.

Breakfast: Until 9.30am.

Meals: Dinner, 3 courses, from around £20 p.p.

Closed: Never!

From York, A64 North. After 7.5 miles, left signed Hovingham. After 6 miles, at crossroads, left onto B1257, signed Hovingham. Hotel 2 miles on in centre of village.

Map Ref No: 15

Debbi & Euan Rodger
The Worsley Arms Hotel
Hovingham
Yorkshire YO6 4LA
Tel: 01653 628234
Fax: 01653 628130

This spot, on the edge of the North York Moors National Park, was chosen for its views and the house arranged to soak up as much of the scenery as possible, from the Pennines to the Wolds. Although built in the 60s, the house, which has 2.5 acres of mature hillside garden, is stylish, elegant and spacious. One of the rooms has lemon and blue matching quilts and curtains, large dressing room and big, dove-grey modern, uncluttered bathroom; all are comfortable. Phillip and Anton love what they are doing, so you will be treated like angels, with those sublime views thrown in for good measure. *Children over 12 welcome.*

Rooms: 2 kings/twins, both with en suite bathroom and 1 double with private bathroom.

Price: Kingsize £40 p.p.; double £32.50 p.p. Single supp. £10.

Breakfast: 8-9.30am.

Meals: Dinner, 4 courses, £20 p.p. Packed lunch by arrangement.

Closed: Christmas & New Year.

From Thirsk take A19 south, then 'caravan route' via Coxwold and Byland Abbey. First house on left, just before entering Ampleforth.

Map Ref No: 15

Anton van der Horst & Phillip Gill
Shallowdale House
West End
Ampleforth
Yorkshire YO62 4DY
Tel: 01439 788325
Fax: 01439 788885

Only the Moors lie behind this solid, stone farmhouse, five yards from the National Park, in farmland and woodland with fine views... marvellous walking country. The house is full of light and flowers. The pretty sitting room has deeply comfortable old sofas, armchairs and fine furniture. Rich colours and hunting prints give the dining room a warm and cosy feel. The Orrs have poured affection into this house, and the result is a home that's happy and remarkably easy to relax in... wonderful.

Rooms: 2 twins/doubles, 1 en suite (shower), 1 with private bathroom.

Price: £25 p.p. Single supp. £10.

Breakfast: Until 9am.

Meals; Dinner, 3 courses, including wine, £22.50 p.p.

Closed: Never!

A stone cottage perched on top of a ridge with glorious views across Rosedale Moor. Eighty-five acres of fields, 80,000 Christmas trees, woods and a stream with footpath access to the moor and forest, abundant wildlife including nightjars, badgers and deer. The spotless bedrooms, all on the ground floor, are furnished in pine and all have garden views. The large guest sitting room takes in those great views of the North York Moors and Cropton Forest Park. Plenty of simple farmhouse cooking. *Children over 12 welcome.*

Rooms: 1 twin and 1 double, en suite (bath /shower) and 1 double, en suite (bath).

Price: £24 p.p. No single supp.

Breakfast: Until 9am.

Meals; Dinner, 4 courses, £14 p.p. Special diets catered for, with notice.

Closed: Never!

From A170 between Kirkbymoorside & Pickering turn into Sinnington. On village green keep river on your left, fork right between cottages. Turn up lane bearing right uphill, past church, signed.

Map Ref No: 15

From Thirsk towards Pickering on A170 take left signed Cropton. At New Inn, right into village and out other side. After 0.25 miles, you'll see 3 farm gates on left. House drive through middle one.

Map Ref No: 15

John & Jane Orr
Hunters Hill
Sinnington
York
Yorkshire YO62 6SF
Tel: 01751 431196
Fax: 01751 432976

Julie Richardson
Burr Bank Cottage
Cropton
Pickering
Yorkshire YO18 8HL
Tel: 01751 417777
Fax: 01751 417789
e-mail: jrbb@dial.pipex.com

YORKSHIRE

Gerry rode the winner of the Grand National in 1960! He is now a race starter, still surrounded by horses. Bring your own and it can muck in with the others - plenty of paddock and good riding. In the house: chairs, tables and sofas afloat on a sea of light twisted carpet; an open fire, stripped pine doors; bedrooms with views to the moors. Outside: a formal lawn, rough grass tennis court and croquet lawn, a pond with a fountain, a paved patio. Even dogs are welcome; the whole place is easy-going and great for children, with Avril unflappable.

Rooms: 2 doubles and 1 twin with basins, all sharing bathroom & w.c.

Price: £16 p.p. No single supp.

Breakfast: Flexible.

Meals: Dinner £9 p.p. B.Y.O. wine.

Closed: Christmas Day.

From A6108 (Ripon to Richmond road) turn off 0.35 miles north of Masham, towards Healey. Continue through Healey to junction signed Colsterdale. Take right fork. House is 1st on left.

Map Ref No.15

Avril & Gerry Scott
Pasture House
Healey
Masham
Yorkshire HG4 4LJ
Tel: 01765 689149
Fax: 01765 689990

"Sod it," we thought, "why not include this extraordinary house?" Man has met Nature in rare harmony, taken it to his bosom and put it to work. Where turf, tree and tangled bush serve our purposes so elegantly there is hope, yet, for mankind. Hidden from prying eyes you may take root in the knowledge that nobody will find you, yet the many other small residents will keep you company day and night. There's a 'green' approach to catering and you head into the hills for closer communion with nature when it calls.

Rooms: 1, richly carpeted, in mossy green. On-hill facilities (w.c. and running water).

Price: 20p p.p. Single occupancy never an option; price includes bug sprays and mouse traps.

Breakfast: Breakfast: Berries, in season.

Meals: Meals: Pick your own.

Closed: Always.

Deep in the forest, right at top of track, turn left up the grassy bank, through small gap in hedge. House straight in front of you.

Mr & Mrs S. Hack
Dun Mowin'
Dun Sinane
Yorkshire SOD IT

The Madells work hard so that "people should not go away unhappy". This is not going to happen! The restaurant has an excellent reputation - you are generously fed and any of the 6,000 bottles in the cellar is served by the glass! The sitting rooms are country-house elegant and relaxing. The bedrooms, from large to cosy, each have sherry and a radio; you can hear race horses ambling past in the morning on their way to the Moor. The house even has a marriage license. But all of this would be blossom in the wind without Everyl's unflagging dedication and kindness.

Rooms: 2 four-posters, both en suite (shower); 1 twin/double and 2 doubles, all en suite (bath/shower).

Price: £35-£45 p.p. Single supp. £10.

Breakfast: Until 10am.

Meals: Dinner from £19.50 p.p. Lunch from £15.50 p.p. Booking essential for both.

Closed: Never!

The hills of Bishopdale rise up on both sides of the house, the countryside is awesome and the great air of the Dales will drive any city stuffiness from your lungs. High Green is a small Georgian house beside the village green of a quiet little Yorkshire village. On warm summer afternoons, tea and scones are served in the manicured walled garden. The rooms are ordered and unfussy (residents' lounge and separate tables); more of a guest house than a B&B, and in a marvellous position. One room is fully equipped for handicapped guests.

Rooms: 1 twin, en suite (bath/shower); 2 doubles, 1 en suite (shower) and 1 with private bath/shower.

Price: £25-£28.50 p.p. Single supp. £10. Small children free, up to age 12, £5-£10. Over 12, adult rate.

Breakfast: At 8.30am.

Meals: Dinner £16.50 p.p.

Closed: 31 October-late March.

Southbound from A1 at Scotch Corner via Richmond and Leyburn. House at top of hill on right on entering village square.

Map Ref No: 15

Everyl & Brian Madell
Waterford House
19 Kirkgate
Middleham
Yorkshire DL8 4PG
Tel: 01969 622090
Fax: 01969 624020

From Leyburn take A684 to Aysgarth. Turn left into Thoralby. House is on the right next door to post office.

Map Ref No: 15

Pat & Ted Hesketh
High Green House
Thoralby
Nr. Leyburn
Yorkshire DL8 3SU
Tel: 01969 663420
Fax: 01969 663420

Gone are the shepherds, but the house lives up to its name ('Helm' is Norse for shelter). Teeming with Wensleydale history, it has an underground dairy with stone cheese shelves, a seeping well, once used for cooling milk, and a stone cheese press. There are fine views from the Bainbridge room and from the cotton-sheeted walnut bed in the Askrigg room. The bold, yellow back room has a small window with occasional views of cows' legs! The dinner menu will taunt those who can't stay. *Children over 10 welcome.*

Rooms: 2 doubles, both en suite (1 with bath and 1 with shower); 1 twin, en suite (shower).

Price: £28-£34 p.p. Single supp. £12.

Breakfast: Until 9am.

Meals: Dinner, 3 courses, £16 p.p. Cheese £2 p.p.

Closed: Mid-November-early January.

A perfect place from which to explore the Dales. Built in 1760 to house the racing stables of John Pratt, the hotel bears its heritage proudly. The Parlour bar drips with riding and country paraphernalia, original saddle hooks are embedded in the ceiling, the Silks Room is decorated with framed jockey's shirts while the Clubroom restaurant features John Pratt. Bedrooms are excellent, some with a French mood, one with a stately four-poster. They all have fine linen, excellent duvets and pretty quilts.

Rooms: 1 twin and 2 doubles, all en suite (shower); 1 family, 1 suite and 6 doubles, all en suite (bath).

Price: £39.50-£62 p.p. Single supp. £10.50-£13.

Breakfast: Until 9.30am.

Meals: Available in restaurants & bars.

Closed: Never!

From Askrigg towards Bainbridge, after 2/3 miles, you'll see lay-by on left. Turn right at no-through road sign. Up hill for 0.5 miles, last house on right.

Map Ref No: 15

Barbara & John Drew
Helm
Askrigg
Leyburn
Yorkshire DL8 3JF
Tel: 01969 650443
Fax: 01969 650443
e-mail: drewhelm@compuserve.com

In the centre of Askrigg.

Map Ref No: 15

Liz & Ray Hopwood
The King's Arms Hotel & Restaurants
Market Place
Askrigg in Wensleydale
Yorkshire DL8 3HQ
Tel: 01969 650258
Fax: 01969 650635
e-mail: rayliz@kahaskrigg.prestel.co.uk

In the heart of the Yorkshire Dales National Park, this is a superb base for walkers. If you're arriving by car, take the 'over the top' road from Buckden to Hawes for stunning views. Gail and Ann bake their own bread, make jams and marmalade and cook very good sausages. Their dinners are prepared with fresh, local produce and are utterly delicious. One (very pink) room has a four-poster and all rooms have marvellous views of Wensleydale. (The local cheese factory has been bought by the locals.) *Pets by arrangement.*

Rooms: 2 four-posters, 1 twin and 1 double, all sharing bathroom or shower room.

Price: £18-£19 p.p. Single supp. £5-£8.

Breakfast: At 8.30am.

Meals: Dinner, 4 courses, £12 p.p. (not Thursdays).

Closed: 31 October-31 January.

Standing at the top of the village green with sweeping views of Swaledale, the Burgoyne has a dignified and august air. Peter and Derek have created a crisp yet comfortable interior: cool mints, bold greens, delicate lighting and cushions as plump as Christmas geese. The bedrooms are all big and some - one with deep pink walls and another with long, red, silk curtains - are dramatic. For those with limited mobility there's a ground-floor bedroom. Peter's superb cooking - with fresh, local ingredients - coupled with Derek's careful choice of wine guarantees an excellent evening.

Rooms: 4 doubles, all en suite (bath); 3 twins, 1 en suite (shower) and 2 with private bathroom.

Price: £35-£62.60 p.p. Single occ. from £60.

Breakfast: Until 9.30am.

Meals: Dinner £23 p.p.

Closed: 2 January for six weeks.

The house is approx. 320m off the A684 on the road north out of Hawes, signposted Muker and Hardraw.

Map Ref No: 15

Ann Macdonald
Brandymires
Muker Road
Hawes
Yorkshire DL8 3PR
Tel: 01969 667482

From Richmond, A6108, then B6270 to Reeth. House on village green.

Map Ref No: 15

Peter Carwardine & Derek Hickson
The Burgoyne Hotel
On The Green
Reeth, Richmond
Yorkshire DL11 6SN
Tel: 01748 884292
Fax: 01748 884292

Geraldine is a *Cordon Bleu* cook who will bake cakes for tea and make you feel totally at home. A grand piano will tempt the musically gifted and the three dogs will lead the way as you explore the large garden. Bedrooms are light, airy and elegant and the cast-iron bath in one is custom-built for wallowing, and surrounded by fresh greenery. The yellow, beamed dining room is gloriously sunny and breakfast is a feast. You'll find it easy to relax.

Rooms: 1 twin leading to small single and 1 four-poster, all sharing a bathroom and let only to members of the same party.

Price: £30 p.p. Children £15.

Breakfast: Until 9am.

Meals: Dinner, £15 p.p., on request.

Closed: Never!

Oriella goes the extra mile for you and her flamboyancy and style make light of the practicalities of having guests. She is arty, fun-loving and kind: she'll leave out fruit cake if you're peckish, provide a driver, sit and chat or leave you to choose some music. There are tapestries, mirrors, thick oak tables and oriental pieces, something to catch the eye at every turn. The bedrooms are big, chintzy/paisley and one has a seven-foot square bed! A Georgian jewel. *Children over 13 welcome.*

Rooms: 2 doubles and 1 twin, all en suite (2 with bath/shower and 1 with bath).

Price: £40-£45 p.p.

Breakfast: Until 10.30am.

Meals: Dinner, 4 courses, £25 p.p.

Closed: Never!

From A1 north take Catterick turn-off, then left on to the Hackforth road. After 1 mile, bear right on s-bend onto single-track road. Follow through farm. Left at white boulders.

Map Ref No: 15

Geraldine Burton
The Manor House
East Appleton
Richmond
Yorkshire DL10 7QE
Tel: 01748 818495

Leave A1 at Leeming Bar, take A684 to Bedale. 0.5 miles out of town, turn off A684 to Newton-Le-Willows. Right at T-junction, left at Wheatsheaf pub, then immediate right through gates.

Map Ref No: 15

Oriella Featherstone
The Hall
Newton-Le-Willows
Bedale
Yorkshire DL8 1SW
Tel: 01677 450210
Fax: 01677 450014

Prepare to be amazed. In every room and in every corner of the *breathtaking* garden, the marriage of natural beauty and sophistication exist in a state of bliss. The four Doric columns at the entrance draw you through the hall into the dining room and to views of the Swale Valley. Beds from Heals, oak furniture, cast-iron baths, myriad prints and paintings and one double bed so high you wonder how to get onto it. Tim and Austin, both ex-English teachers, have created something unique and very special.

Half a skip from the centre of this pretty old market town with its castle ramparts, theatre, pubs and Saturday market, step off the cobbled street and you find yourself in a country garden on the edge of stunning views of the Swale Valley. The owners of this elegant listed Georgian house are full of flair and humorous enthusiasm... there is *trompe l'œil* everywhere. Guests have excellent rooms on the ground floor and the view-filled conservatory for breakfast. Turner painted Easby Abbey; you could do the same from the garden here.

Rooms: 1 twin with private bathroom; 1 double, en suite (shower).

Price: £22 p.p. Single supp. £6.

Breakfast: Flexible.

Meals: Available locally.

Closed: 24-26 December.

Rooms: 1 double and 1 twin, each en suite (bath and shower).

Price: £28 p.p. Single supp. £10.

Breakfast: Until 10am.

Meals: Available in Richmond.

Closed: Never!

From Scotch Corner (A1 30 miles north of Wetherby) follow signs to Richmond. In Richmond turn left at library and left into Frenchgate. House is at top on right with black railings.

From Richmond Market Place, house is at bottom of the hill opposite Barclays Bank. Look for a green door with 'MGH'.

Map Ref No: 15

Map Ref No: 15

Maggie & Brian Fifoot
58 Frenchgate
Richmond
Yorkshire DL10 7AG
Tel: 01748 823227
Fax: 01748 823227

Austin Lynch & Tim Culkin
Millgate House
Richmond
Yorkshire DL10 4JN
Tel: 01748 823571
Fax: 01748 850701
oztim@millgatehouse.demon.co.uk

A massive virginia creeper covers this amazing house. Richard's ancestors look down from the stone stairs onto the oak hall. There are fireplaces, paintings, high plasterworked ceilings and acres of space. Bedrooms have a light, airy feel, pale-painted walls and gracefully worn furniture. After croquet or tennis you can soak in a cast-iron bath or choose a leather-bound tome from the big-windowed library. The tiered lawn descends to the mighty Tees and your hosts spread an atmosphere of *joie de vivre*: they love having guests. Incredible value.

Rooms: 2 twins, both with private bathrooms.

Price: £30 p.p. No single supp.

Breakfast: Flexible, with notice.

Meals: Dinner, 3 courses, from £15 p.p. By arrangement.

Closed: 10 December-1 February.

David and Ann will pour you an early-evening drink and even give you a choice of sitting rooms; in one of these, two facing sofas give an even share of the log fire. Ann asks which newspaper you'd like in the morning and when you pull back the curtains you will see her cycling over the village green to get it. Such unassuming generosity. There's much fine furniture and the beds have linen sheets, blankets and quilted eiderdowns. The room at the front has a colossal bathroom and the one at the back looks over the enchanting garden.

Rooms: 1 twin, en suite (bath); 1 double with private bathroom.

Price: £30 p.p. No single supp.

Breakfast: Until 10am.

Meals: Available locally.

Closed: Christmas & Easter.

From A1, exit onto B6275. North for 4.2 miles. Turn into drive (on left before Piercebridge) and take 1st right fork.

Map Ref No: 15

Caroline Wilson
Cliffe Hall
Piercebridge
Darlington
Yorkshire DL2 3SR
Tel: 01325 374322
Fax: 01325 374947

From A1 at Scotch Corner roundabout right to Middleton Tyas. Continue 1 mile. Pass the Shoulder of Mutton. House is on village green on right with white gate.

Map Ref No: 15

David & Ann Murray
Foresters Hall
Middleton Tyas
Richmond
Yorkshire DL10 6QY
Tel: 01325 377722

These are the nicest and most genuine farming folk imaginable. Even in the mayhem of the lambing season they will greet you with a smile, tea and homemade biscuits. Their farmhouse is as unpretentious as they are: there's one bedroom here and three in converted outbuildings, pine-furnished with country textiles, garden views and modern shower rooms. Some have old oak beams. And always the Pearsons' delightful, straightforward manner.

Rooms: 1 family, 1 twin, 1 double and 1 single, all en suite (shower). Gate Cottage: 1 double, en suite.

Price: £19.50-£30 p.p.

Breakfast: Until 10am.

Meals: Dinner £12 p.p.

Closed: 1 December-28 February.

For 250 years this has been a farm, always in the same family; so deep are the farming traditions that some of the oil paintings are of old family cows. It is a splendid country house of the most traditional kind, at the end of a long, tree-lined drive and in very English parkland. A stone-flagged hall leads to an exquisite dining room that breathes family history. The bedrooms have oak chests, deep basins and magnificent wardrobes that sigh with age. Everywhere there is the nobility of wood and fine furniture. Croquet and tennis available.

Rooms: 2 doubles, en suite (bath). 1 twin with private bathroom and separate shower.

Price: £25 p.p. Single supp. £5.

Breakfast: Until 9am.

Meals: Dinner £15 p.p.

Closed: 1 December-1 April.

From Northallerton, take A167 north towards Darlington for 4 miles. House is on right, and signed.

Map Ref No: 15

John & Mary Pearson
Lovesome Hill Farm
Lovesome Hill
Northallerton
Yorkshire DL6 2PB
Tel: 01609 772311

From A19 take A172 towards Stokesley for 3 miles. Turn left, go straight over crossroads. Drive to house is 0.25 miles ahead on right.

Map Ref No: 15

Major & Mrs Julian Kynge
Potto Grange
Nr. Northallerton
Yorkshire DL6 3HH
Tel: 01642 700212
Fax: 01642 700212

A peaceful, informal spirit pervades this elegant, bay-windowed farmhouse - it exudes warmth and friendliness. Anne goes to great lengths to make you comfortable and her cooking is delicious. The house, which harmoniously incorporates the former cottage and dairy buildings, has pale, fresh colour schemes, an interesting collection of books and superb views. The big guestrooms face south and you will be drawn to explore the gentle rolling dales, the bleak, wild moors, the coastline and York and Durham. *Children over 12 welcome.*

Rooms: 1 twin and 1 twin/double, both with private bathrooms.

Price: £31 p.p. Single supp. £10.

Breakfast: Flexible.

Meals: Dinner £20 p.p. by arrangement.

Closed: December & January.

The views go on forever, the wildlife comes to you. Lose yourself in 164 acres of parkland and woodland: bridle paths lead you from the farm to the moors and take you past wild geese on the flight pond, cantering Soay sheep and even comical rheas and wallabies. Martin and Margaret are interested, involved people: you feel your presence counts. Inside, china knick-knacks and florals contrast with the bright whiteness of the rooms. Guests must take dinner. You won't mind in the slightest. *Children over 12 welcome.*

Rooms: 2 doubles and 1 twin, 1 en suite (bath) and 2 with private bath/shower.

Price: Dinner, B&B £42.50-£47.50 p.p. Single supp. £10.

Breakfast: Until 9.30am.

Meals: Dinner, 5 courses, included.

Closed: Christmas.

Going north on A19 take A172 towards Stokesley. Pass sign on right to Carlton and Busby. House is 0.5 miles further on the left, with tree-lined drive.

Map Ref No: 15

Anne Gloag
Busby House
Stokesley
Yorkshire TS9 5LB
Tel: 01642 710425
Fax: 01642 713838

Take B1257 south from Stokesley to Great Broughton. Left at village hall onto Ingleby Road to Church at Ingleby Greenhow. Entrance opposite church. House is 0.5 miles away.

Map Ref No: 15

Margaret & Martin Bloom
Manor House Farm
Ingleby Greenhow
Great Ayton
Yorkshire TS9 6RB
Tel: 01642 722384
e-mail: mbloom@globalnet.co.uk

SCOTLAND

"The birthplace of valour, the county of worth!
Wherever I wander, wherever I rove,
The hills of the Highlands forever I love."

Robert Burns

The Taylors moved to this creeper-clad old manse after retiring from farming. The rooms are large and bright, there is a fine cantilever staircase up from the hall, and the dining room's long windows frame good rural views. The big comfortable bedrooms, with shutters and long curtains, have more character than luxury. The colourful walled garden full of clematis, honeysuckle and roses, hides a small vegetable garden and orchard and an ornamental pond. Beyond, fields rise and there is deep rural seclusion. Genuinely nice people and good, easy conversation. *Children over 12 welcome.*

Rooms: 1 twin and 1 double, sharing bathroom.

Price: £21.50 p.p. No single supp.

Breakfast: Until 9.30am.

Meals: Dinner, £12.50 p.p., by arrangement.

Closed: Christmas & New Year.

Borders & Lowlands

From A1 towards Duns on B6438 for 5.5 miles. Left at church noticeboard. On for 0.25 miles. After Bonkyl church second right through black gate.

Map Ref No: 19

Libby & Martin Taylor
Kirkside House
Bonkyl
Nr. Duns
Berwickshire TD11 3RJ
Tel: 01361 884340
Fax: 01361 884340

However elegant and lovely the house may be, David and Sue bring it down to earth; Sue is a delightful character and you will enjoy good conversation with them both. The best room is the drawing room, formal but seductively so, with open fires, antiques, a great old atlas lying open, lots of magazines. From the handsome hall rises the cantilevered stone staircase to the bedrooms, two of them elegant with writing desks and high ceilings, one of them more country-comfy, with lots of books and old pine furniture. Sue is a trained cook and uses home-grown organic veg; her porridge is delicious. *Children over 12 welcome.*

Rooms: 1 twin, en suite (bath), 1 twin with private bathroom and 1 double, en suite (shower).

Price: £33 p.p, Single supp. £10.

Breakfast: Until 9.00am.

Meals: Dinner, 4 courses, £22 p.p. by arrangement. Packed lunches from £10 p.p.

Closed: Christmas & New Year.

2.5 miles north of Earlston A68, turn east for Birkenside. 150m after narrow bridge, at right-hand bend, keep straight on and then immediately left through stone archway.

Map Ref No: 19

Sue & David Sillar
Birkhill
Earlston
Borders TD4 6AR
Tel: 01896 849307
Fax: 01896 848206
e-mail: birkhill@aol.com

A hands-on farm made for children to wander or work: pitch in - milk a cow, watch the lambing and collect eggs. Winter log fires for chilly farmhands of all ages; warmth, too, in the welcome and care lavished on visitors by Sheila and Martyn in the family farmhouse. Simple comfortable rooms, bright from big windows and, everywhere, an eccentric 1700s nooks-and-crannies mood prevails. There are heart-stopping views, old Border keeps and a spider-web of stone walls sweeping up to the Eildon Hills where Robert the Bruce's heart lies buried.

Rooms: 1 family with private bath and 1 double, en suite (shower).

Price: £20 p.p. Single supp. £5.

Breakfast: 8.30am, or as agreed.

Meals: Dinner from £12 p.p.

Closed: Never!

From Galashiels take A7 past Torwoodlea golf course and right to Langshaw. After 2 miles right at T-junction, then left at Earlston sign in Langshaw. House is white, in trees, signposted at farm road.

Map Ref No: 19

Sheila & Martyn Bergius
Over Langshaw Farm
Galashiels
Selkirkshire TD1 2PE
Tel: 01896 860244

Jill and Johan, relaxed and kind, willingly collect and deliver walkers. They traded Dutch polders for a bumpier horizon - the stupendous view of rolling Border country says why. A tranquil old house, it is big all over: views, rooms, windows, beds, log fire in the huge bay-windowed drawing room. Even bathrooms are lofty, and the wood-burning stove heats the whole house for 20 tons a year. There are modern creature comforts but the oak-filled tick-tocking atmosphere is pleasingly nostalgic. You're in Scotland... go on, try haggis for breakfast .

Rooms: 2 doubles and 1 twin, all en suite (1 bath and 2 showers).

Price: £19-£24 p.p. Single supp. £10.

Breakfast: Flexible.

Meals: Walker's supper, £8-£9.50 p.p., by prior arrangement.

Closed: 23-27 December.

"Leave it better than you found it" - your hosts' philosophy of land ownership (they have planted an amazing vegetable garden) applies equally to improvements wrought for their guests' well-being. As soon as you round the bend and see their secluded Georgian farmhouse, wrapped in the bubbling Bowmont's river valley, the magic begins its work. Peace, informality, an immaculate interior of gentle taste and genial hosts who enjoy company. Cheery bedrooms with good beds, crisp linen, flowers and books, overlook gardens, the river and the Cheviots. And Ann cooks most ably with fine fresh ingredients.

Rooms: 1 twin and 1 double, both with private bathrooms.

Price: £25 p.p. Single occ. £30.

Breakfast: Flexible.

Meals: Dinner £18 p.p. 24 hours notice needed.

Closed: 23 December-4 January.

From Jedburgh, A68 for Edinburgh. Left after 3.5 miles to Ancrum. Fork left to Denholm before village. After 1.75 miles, right signed Lilliesleaf. Bear left, then left to Ancrum Craig.

Map Ref No: 19

From Kelso take B6352 to Yetholm. Bear right down High Street (B6401). 1 mile; left to Belford-on-Bowmont. After 3.5 miles drive on right by phone box.

Map Ref No: 19

Jill & Johan Hensens
Ancrum Craig
Jedburgh
Borders TD8 6UN
Tel: 01835 830280
Fax: 01835 830259

Ann & Peter Mather
Belford-on-Bowmont
Yetholm
By Kelso
Roxburghshire TD5 8PY
Tel: 01573 420362

In a peaceful village, this former manse is a happy and much-loved house; energy and affection have been poured, too, into the lovely and once-derelict garden. You will warm to the naturalness of it all. You have the drawing room - with old pictures and a log fire - to yourselves, and if you stay for dinner you'll eat, maybe, fish or game, good country food. Your hosts are keen on country life and its sporting activities, although no longer take part. Some amazing floral wallpapers and comfortable bedrooms. The rooms are let to the same party, so you can make up your own rules.

Rooms: 2 twins and 1 single let only to members of the same party, sharing bathroom.

Price: £20 £25 p.p.

Breakfast: Until 9.30am.

Meals: Dinner £15 p.p. by prior arrangement.

Closed: Occasionally.

Astonishingly, the remains of a medieval 'motte' (fortified mound) are now inside the big walled garden at Applegarth. The Pearsons keep hunting dogs yet the wetlands bird sanctuary is just down the lane. The house is ideally placed on the road half way between deep south and far north but in utterly quiet surroundings. The worn old sandstone building beside the crowded graveyard contains big pristine bedrooms and bathrooms. There is a warm family air to it all, with furniture a mix of old comfort and old elegance. *Children over 10 welcome.*

Rooms: 1 double with private bath; 2 twins, both en suite (bath).

Price: £30.00 p.p. Single supp. £5.

Breakfast: Flexible.

Meals: Dinner £20 p.p.

Closed: Never!

From A74M take junction 20 onto B722 to Eaglesfield. Take 2nd left after 350m signed Middlebie. In Middlebie, house and gate are next to church.

Map Ref No: 19

J Milne-Home
Kirkside of Middlebie
Lockerbie
Dumfries & Galloway DG11 3JW
Tel: 01576 300204

M74 junction 17 to Lockerbie then B7076 to Johnstonebridge. First right after approx 1.5 miles and in 100 yards left back over m-way bridge. After 1 mile, right at T-junction then 2nd left to 'The Church'. House is next to Chuch.

Map Ref No: 19

Frank & Jane Pearson
Applegarth House
Lockerbie
Dumfries & Galloway DG11 1SX
Tel: 01387 810270
Fax: 01387 811701

Knockhill is superbly authentic: a 17th-century motto - 'too small for envy, for contempt too great', stone stairs, carved oak furniture, grandfather clocks, old horse-driven gin mill, impeccable tennis and croquet courts. The warm, chuckly Morgans glow with country health as they farm their land and harness their horses. The atmosphere is informal and unfussy: people are friends within hours. Stoop to enter the beamed and eaved attic room and discover the unusual shower and loo arrangement. Rooms are simple but have fine views and bathe in the same warm welcoming air.

Rooms: 2 twins: 1 with private bath and 1 with private shower.

Price: £25-£30 p.p. No single supp.

Breakfast: Flexible.

Meals: Dinner £18 p.p.

Closed: Christmas & New Year.

The Victorian billiard table is full-size, there are 20 acres of rhododendrons and woods, a turf-and-gravel maze, a croquet lawn, lots of books, some fine paintings and sculpture, and the log fires are lit for breakfast. Christopher is a vintage car enthusiast and keen gardener; Mary is an excellent cook, using food from their own garden. They are warm hosts and the house feels relaxed, even with an elegant and formal sitting room. The bedrooms are large, bright, and well-furnished, with good rugs, old long dressing mirrors and the odd *chaise longue. Children over 12 welcome.*

Rooms: 3 twins/doubles, all en suite (bath/shower).

Price: £29-£32 p.p. Single occ. £38.

Breakfast: Until 9.15am.

Meals: Dinner £16 p.p. available on request. Packed lunch from £3.50 p.p.

Closed: 1 November-Easter.

At M74 junction 19 follow signs to Dalton (B725) for 1.5 miles. Right at crossroads, to Lockerbie, 1 mile on and right at small stone lodge. House is at top of long unsurfaced drive.

Map Ref No: 19

Yda & Rupert Morgan
Knockhill
Lockerbie
Dumfries & Galloway DG11 1AW
Tel: 01576 300232
Fax: 01576 300818

From Dalbeattie south-east on B793. Auchenskeoch is 7 miles down this road on right. Turn right, and after 30 yards, left through gate posts.

Map Ref No: 18

Christopher & Mary Broom-Smith
Auchenskeoch Lodge
By Dalbeattie
Dumfries & Galloway DG5 4PG
Tel: 01387 780277
Fax: 01387 780277

You can sink into the sofas without worrying about creasing them; it is a beautiful 18th-century Scottish Georgian house, yet there's not a hint of formality. The Dicksons, engaging and sociable, are at ease here and you will be, too. The sitting and dining rooms connect through a large arch; family pictures, rugs on wooden floors, a feng shui cabinet. In the bedrooms: a cast-iron bed, elegant linen, excellent furniture and masses of light and good books. There are 200 acres of grazing land, a dog, cat, donkey, and free-ranging hens. The place and the people are among the best.

Rooms: 2 twins/doubles, both with private bath and shower.

Price: £30 p.p. Single supp. £6.

Breakfast: Until 10am.

Meals: Dinner £20 p.p. may be available on request.

Closed: 15-28 December.

A gem of near-luxurious comfort, a genuine greeting and great style - that is Killern. Here, you dine elegantly off a mahogany table, bathe extravagantly in a pink or blue 'temple of delight', sleep in a bedroom with views, enjoy cosmopolitan conversation and very good food with much-travelled Alison. Galloway, 'a microcosm of Scotland', with its heathery hills, ancient oak woods and stunning coastline is at your door; there are archaeological and architectural treasures and lots of history to discover. Superb value.

Rooms: 1 twin and 1 double, both with private bathrooms.

Price: £19 p.p. No single supp.

Breakfast: Flexible.

Meals: Dinner £12 p.p.; supper £10 p.p., both by arrangement. Good local hotels & pubs.

Closed: Occasionally.

A75 ring road round Dumfries towards Stranraer. Through Crocketford to Springholm & right to Kirkpatrick Durham. Left at village crossroads, after 0.8 miles go up drive on right by white lodge to Chipperkyle.

Map Ref No: 18

From Dumfries take A75 signed Stranraer to Gatehouse of Fleet. There, turn right at Anwoth Hotel. After 1.4 miles turn left signed Ornochenoch. After 0.4 miles left up steep farm road. Killern is on left.

Map Ref No: 18

Willie & Catriona Dickson
Chipperkyle
Kirkpatrick Durham
Castle Douglas
Dumfries & Galloway DG7 3EY
Tel: 01556 650223
Fax: 01556 650223

Mrs Alison Foster
Killern
Gatehouse of Fleet
Castle Douglas
Kirkcudbrightshire DG7 2BS
Tel: 01557 814398

"One of the loveliest houses I've seen," said our inspector. The owners have real warmth and interest to match the vibrant, multi-hued brightness of their generous William Adam house. They also have ancestors to oversee the dining table, a club fender before the drawing-room fireplace, a garden room with masses of books and one bedroom described as a green-combed retreat with a Rajahstani bedhead. All the bedrooms feel private (around corners, in other wings), beautiful and different with superb decor. And adjective-defying Galloway is all around.

Rooms: 1 double, en suite (bath), 2 twins/doubles, en suite (1 bath and 1 bath and shower).

Price: £25 p.p. Single supp. £5.

Breakfast: Flexible.

Meals: Dinner £16 p.p. by arrangement.

Closed: Occasionally.

Sir David Hunter Blair, in 1821, razed the old castle to create this magnificent Regency one, cared for with affection by James and much of it unchanged. It is too rich a treat to fit this brief passage; bring your friends and have the whole place to yourselves - it is worth the considerable cost. The rooms are huge, the furniture is original, the library has walls of leather-bound tomes, there is a billiards room on the expected scale, a family museum, an art gallery full of Scottish colourists, 2000 acres. A castle, yet still, exquisitely, a home.

Rooms: 4 four-posters, 2 doubles, 5 twins, 6 singles, all en suite bathrooms or sharing bathroom with 1 single.

Price: £100 p.p. Bookings made only for one party at a time. Minimum 4 people.

Breakfast: Flexible.

Meals: Dinner £65 p.p. includes all drinks. Lunch from £17.50 p.p.

Closed: Christmas.

From Stranraer take A77 towards Portpatrick for 1.5 miles. Go straight on at A716 towards Drummore. Drive is on left after approx. 1 mile at junction with B7077 signed Newton Stewart.

Map Ref No: 17

Peter & Liz Whitworth
Kildrochet House
By Stranraer
Wigtownshire DG9 9BB
Tel: 01776 820216
Fax: 01776 820216

South from Maybole on B7023 through Crosshill, then left onto B741 towards Straiton. After 2 miles, estate wall. Lodge and gates on left and signed.

Map Ref No: 18

James Hunter Blair
Blairquhan Castle
Straiton
Maybole
Ayrshire KA19 7LZ
Tel: 01655 770239
Fax: 01655 770278

Culzean Castle, by Robert Adam, is awe-inspiring by any castle standards. The top floor, including six double bedrooms, is probably the most interesting hotel address in Scotland, especially loved by Americans because it was presented to General Eisenhower for his lifetime use. The rooms are exquisitely decorated in elegant country house rather than castle style with inimitable views of the wild coast to the Isle of Arran and Ailsa Craig. Fresh flowers everywhere and *Cordon Bleu* cooking from Susan Cardale. A show piece of the National Trust for Scotland.

Rooms: 5 twins: 3 en suite, 2 with shared bathroom. 1 double, en suite (bath & shower).

Price: £75-£150 p.p. Single occ. £100-£210.

Breakfast: Until 9.30am.

Meals: Dinner, £40 p.p., inc. house wine, by arrangement.

Closed: 1 November-31 March.

They are young, kind, relaxed and interesting. Our inspector hugely enjoyed them. It is a fine house, too, with views to the River Doon flowing past the garden. The atmospheric drawing room is stately and half-panelled. There is a lot of oak, plus cream colours, bay windows, oils on the walls, and large sliding doors to the dining room. The bedrooms are done in fresh colours, blues and whites, with good linen and towels, fine furniture, decorative wash bowls, shutters rather than curtains. Easy elegance and wonderful people and the sea is only a mile away.

Rooms: 1 double and 1 twin sharing private bath and 1 twin, en suite (shower).

Price: £35 p.p. Single supp. £10.

Breakfast: Until 9.30am.

Meals: Dinner £21.50 p.p. Supper £13 p.p.

Closed: Never!

A719 into Alloway on south side of Ayr. Follow Tam O'Shanter signs. Doonbrae opposite Burns Monument by Alloway church.

Map Ref No: 18

From A77 in Maybole take A719 for 4 miles following signs for Culzean Castle.

Map Ref No: 18

Jonathan Cardale
The National Trust for Scotland
Culzean Castle
Maybole
Ayrshire KA19 8LE
Tel: 01655 760274
Fax: 01655 760615

John & Moira Pollock-Morris
Doonbrae
40 Alloway
Ayr
Ayrshire KA7 4PQ
Tel: 01292 442511
Fax: 01292 442511

A very special house: a summation of 1900s Arts and Crafts thought and deed, it has innate grace of space and form in its one-room-thick layout, and gathers its beautiful gardens in a peaceful embrace. The harmony goes on inside, where soft colours and superb design are enhanced by Bob and Isobel, whose eye for complementary ancient and modern is acute. Contemporary oils, decorative wrought-ironwork and myriad other crafted details, including a spectacular 16th-century Florentine ceiling in the log-fired drawing room. Fine food matches your surroundings in the more informal dining room.

Rooms: 1 twin, 1 double and 1 twin/double, all en suite (1 bath and 2 bath and showers).

Price: £29 p.p. Single supp £10.

Breakfast: 8-10am (week); 8.30-10.30am (Sunday).

Meals: Dinner £17.50 p.p.

Closed: 3 January-28 February.

From Biggar take A702 for Edinburgh. Just outside Biggar take right on A72 for Peebles and Skirling. Big wooden house on right facing village green.

Map Ref No: 19

Bob & Isobel Hunter
Skirling House
Skirling
By Biggar
Lanarkshire ML12 6HD
Tel: 01899 860274
Fax: 01899 860255
e-mail: skirlinghouse@dial.pipex.com

This Georgian manse is a real family home where Gwen welcomes guests who want to combine proximity to Edinburgh (30 minutes by train to the castle) with the peace and pace of a charming country town. Rooms are nicely proportioned with big beds, one's a four-poster, and different views; one looks onto the surrounding garden, one into town and the highest over the rooftops and out to sea - which is a two-minute walk from the house. Behind the town there is a steep and imposing hill for a great walk. Potato scones for breakfast, lots of attention to detail: a friendly haven.

Rooms: 1 double, en suite (shower), 1 four-poster, en suite (bath) and 1 twin with private bathroom.

Price: £25-£30 p.p. Single supp. £5-£10.

Breakfast: Flexible.

Meals: Restaurants in town.

Closed: Christmas & New Year.

From Edinburgh, A1 signed Berwick. Left onto A198, follow signs into North Berwick. Right into Station Rd signed 'The Law', to 1st crossroads, left into town centre - house on left behind wall.

Map Ref No: 24

Gwen & Jake Scott
The Glebe House
Law Road
North Berwick
East Lothian EH39 4PL
Tel: 01620 892608

Take to heart the Latin inscription 'No one shall enter here except in truth and peace' (trans.) on the door's arch. There are secrets sealed at Inveresk - from the heavy long-locked safe to the still hidden Roman tunnel. Two enormous bow-fronted pine-floored rooms are in the tower. The dining room has brick-red walls and a black carved fireplace; there is a pale lemon, and ornately vaulted, plasterwork ceiling in the drawing room above. Alice's flower paintings, as bold and brilliant as her native America, are, colourfully, everywhere.

Rooms: 1 family and 1 double, en suite (bath); 1 twin with private bathroom.

Price: £25-£40 p.p. Single supp. £5.

Breakfast: Usually 7.30-8.30am.

Meals: None, but available within walking distance.

Closed: Never!

From Edinburgh, A199 (A1) to Musselburgh. There follow signs to Inveresk Lodge. At top of Brae Hill right into cul-de-sac (signed St. Michael's). 2nd drive on right, bear right past cottages to house at right end of drive.

Map Ref No: 19

Alice & John Chute
Inveresk House
3 Inveresk Village
Musselburgh
East Lothian EH21 7UA
Tel: 0131 665 5855
Fax: 0131 665 0578
e-mail: chute.inveresk@btinternet.com

A lot of thought has gone in to Murrayfield Gardens, safe in a leafy suburb 10 minutes from the city centre... and the result is great comfort in elegant surroundings. It's a fine first floor flat with big bay windows, thick carpets, deep sofas, made exotic with dashes of Asiana, such as lacquer-work demi-lunes from Hong Kong, an old stamping ground of Tim's. Rooms are grandly comfortable, with wonderful beds and views across the road to the rugby ground and on to the Pentland Hills. Bathrooms are a delight, too; clean, fresh and unobtrusive - one is hidden in a 'cupboard'. *Children over 7 welcome.*

Rooms: 2 twins/doubles, both en suite (1 bath/shower and 1 shower); 1 double with private bathroom.

Price: £35-40 p.p. Single supp. £5.

Breakfast: Until 9am.

Meals: Dinner, £22.50 p.p., by arrangement.

Closed: Christmas week.

From city centre (direction of Glasgow), follow for 1 mile and Murrayfield Gardens is on right. To access, take next right, then right again, to end and right into road.

Map Ref No: 19

Tim & Christine MacDowel
22 Murrayfield Gardens
Edinburgh EH12 6DF
Tel: 0131 337 3569
Fax: 0131 337 3469
e-mail: macnetic@dial.pipex.com

A rare thing in Edinburgh, an entire undivided Georgian house, in a lovely terrace (1821) very close to the city centre. The house is blessed with fine features: a cantilever staircase and cupola, a bow-walled dining room, spiral stairs that lead down to the basement where the guest rooms are. Susie and Andrew have done everything well and bright coloured rooms will be better kitted out than most poly-starred hotel rooms. But the comfort here comes with a personal touch, very nice hosts who can give you inside knowledge of this most beautiful of Scottish cities.

Rooms: 1 twin and 1 double, both en suite (shower) and 1 single, en suite (bath).

Price: £35-£40 p.p. No single supp.

Breakfast: Flexible.

Meals: Huge variety close by.

Closed: Christmas.

Take Queensferry Road out of Edinburgh towards Forth Road Bridge. 250 yards off west end of Princes Street, before bridge, bear left.

Map Ref No: 19

Andrew & Susie Hamilton
16 Lynedoch Place
Edinburgh EH3 7PY
Tel: 0131 225 5507
Fax: 0131 226 4185
e-mail: susie.lynedoch@btinternet.com

Sarah is one of the nicest people we met - she is genuine, enthusiastic and humorous and treats you like a friend. The house, 1830s Georgian, buzzes with life; it's homely, yet stylish. Lots of the decoration is extraordinary, some of it inherited from the previous Italian owner - light chocolate meets muddy pink, gold cornicing, murals - unusual but stunning. A cupola lights the stairwell and, in the bedrooms, striking colours; one room has an enormous bathroom, one a sitting area (pictured). Guests have no sitting room, but the kitchen is huge and welcoming, so it doesn't matter a jot. This, after all, is Edinburgh.

Rooms: 1 twin and 1 double sharing bathroom; 1 double with private bathroom.

Price: £23-£37 p.p. Single occ. £28-£35.

Breakfast: Flexible.

Meals: Not available, but masses of restaurants nearby.

Closed: Never!

In Edinburgh, 500m north of Botanic Gardens.

Map Ref No: 19

Sarah Nicholson
44 Inverleith Row
Edinburgh EH3 5PY
Tel: 0131 552 8595
Fax: 0131 551 6675

An attractive Victorian town-house in a quiet, cobbled lane close to the centre of Edinburgh. Enjoy what Scotland's capital has to offer or relax in the privacy of the pretty, walled back garden. Rise from your four-poster bed, fling open the shutters (this is not city air) and breakfast in the family kitchen or *al fresco* on the terrace. Clarissa is involved in the arts and can advise on what to do, and where to eat; or you may just wish to relax by the log fire in the private sitting room.

Rooms: 1 double, en suite (bath).

Price: £30-£40 p.p.

Breakfast: Flexible.

Meals: Available locally.

Closed: 23-29 December.

Three Georgian houses in one, nine guest rooms, a dining room to seat a house party of twenty and a friendly private-home feel. From some top rooms you can see over to the Forth, Fife and the sea, amazing from a city centre. Despite the numbers the scale remains human, the antiques breathe family history, the private garden over the road is yours to wander in. You are the guest of a bright, easy-going, chatty hostess. This sophisticated base once belonged to William Playfair, Edinburgh's famous Georgian architect.

Rooms: 2 triples, 2 twins, 4 doubles and 1 single, all en suite.

Price: £40-£50 p.p. Variable single supp.

Breakfast: 8-9am (week); 8.30-9.30am (weekend).

Meals: Lots of places to eat nearby.

Closed: Never!

From centre of Edinburgh take A702 south, to Peebles. Go past the Churchhill Theatre (on left), to lights. Albert Terrace is first right after theatre.

Map Ref No: 19

Clarissa Notley
1 Albert Terrace
Churchhill
Edinburgh EH10 5EA
Tel: 0131 447 4491

Abercromby Place lies parallel to Queen Street just north of the city centre in what is known as 'New Town'. Private parking.

Map Ref No: 19

Eirlys Lloyd
17 Abercromby Place
Edinburgh EH3 6LB
Tel: 0131 557 8036
Fax: 0131 558 3453
e-mail: eirlys.lloyd@virgin.net

Annie's terraced fisherman's cottage faces a salmon and trout river. It is full of light, flowers, books, original watercolours and lithographs complemented by floral fabrics and European pottery. Previously a professional cook, she produces an imaginative breakfast to tempt any palate - omelettes with herbs from her garden, fishcakes with dill, homemade jams and real coffee. Bedrooms are fresh, airy and very comfortable. Annie has guests from all over the world and really does take care of them.

Rooms: 1 double, en suite (shower) and 1 twin with large private bathroom (down narrow stairs).

Price: £16-£18 p.p. Single supp. by arrangement.

Breakfast: Flexible.

Meals: Good restaurants nearby.

Closed: Never!

From Edinburgh take A199 (A1) to Musselburgh bridge (about 7 miles). Eskside West is on right, just before bridge. Number 53 is by old Roman footbridge.

Map Ref No: 19

Annie Deacon
53 Eskside West
Musselburgh
Edinburgh EH21 6RB
Tel: 0131 665 2875

On a quiet leafy road not far from the centre, a Victorian terrace house with original mosaic hall floor and big bay windows. A downstairs guestroom gives onto the garden and the upstairs room has a lovely, large bed and garden views, too; both rooms are freshly decorated and quiet. You are fully independent but Iola is a willing guide to fascinating Edinburgh if you wish. Breakfasts are something special - Iola roasts her own muesli, makes her own bread and jam and offers the full Scottish feast.

Rooms: 1 twin and 1 double, both with private bathrooms.

Price: £26 p.p. Ask about single supp.

Breakfast: Flexible.

Meals: Available locally.

Closed: 23-26 December.

Enter Edinburgh on A702. 0.5 miles from by-pass fork right down Braid Road, after pedestrian crossing. No. 60 is 0.5 miles on left after mini-roundabout. Free on-street parking.

Map Ref No: 19

Iola Fass
60 Braid Road
Morningside
Edinburgh EH10 6AL
Tel: 0131 446 9356
Fax: 0131 447 7367
e-mail: fass@dial.pipex.com

See No. 559 for another special place N.W. of Edinburgh.

A long tree-lined drive, an elegant farmhouse, good furniture, space, fun and a huge welcome await you here. The farm runs down past tennis and croquet lawns almost to the Rock and Spindle beach, the views are spectacular, the coastline walks exhilarating, the cooking (by both hosts) excellent; they have their own lobster pots and love to use local produce. Come join the family.

Rooms: 2 twins: 1 en suite and 1 with private bath; 1 double, en suite (shower).

Price: £28-£32 p.p. Single occ. £38-£42.

Breakfast: Flexible.

Meals: Dinner £22 p.p.

Closed: Never!

East Scotland

From St. Andrews take A917 for 2 miles towards Crail. Kinkell's drive is in the first line of trees on left after St. Andrews.

Map Ref No: 24

Sandy & Frippy Fyfe
Kinkell
St. Andrews
Fife KY16 8PN
Tel: 01334 472003
Fax: 01334 475248
e-mail: gt38@dial.pipex.com

The Goodsmans love entertaining at their Victorian Gothic village school and schoolmaster's house, now converted and furnished in an easy, comfortable, country-house style. Furniture is mostly 'old family' with open fires and woodburning stoves. James knows a lot about Scottish history, especially of the local area, and likes to share his enthusiasm; Victoria cooks well and her giant Scottish and English breakfasts are served in the conservatory/breakfast room or, in the coldest months, in the dining room. *Children over 12 welcome.*

Rooms: 1 double, en suite (bath) and 1 twin, en suite (shower).

Price: £26-£28 p.p. No single supp.

Breakfast: Flexible.

Meals: Dinner, £20 p.p., by arrangement.

Closed: Christmas & New Year.

Take B937 north from A91, 6 miles west of Cupar; immediate right turn into Collessie village. House is second on right through black iron gates.

Map Ref No: 24

James & Victoria Goodsman
The Old Schoolhouse
Collessie
Fife KY15 7UU
Tel: 01337 810744
Fax: 01337 810746

Whistlebare was once a shepherd's cottage built between two bubbling burns. The house has been expanded but the idea remains the same: a haven among sheep farms on the green-swarded Ochills. The Claverings once travelled a lot - the lamb (home-grown) was expertly curried and fruited - but they've settled here now. "Simple farmhouse accommodation for people who love the country," proclaims Jenny. Relax in the original cottage, deep-walled and cosy with wing-back armchairs, bright sofa and fireplace.

Rooms: 2 twins: 1 en suite (bath) and 1 with private bath.

Price: £22 p.p. No single supp.

Breakfast: Flexible.

Meals: Dinner £15 p.p.

Closed: 20 December-end January.

From A91 just over M90 from Milnathart, right for Stronachie, following road, going over crossroads and up hill to Little Craigow on left. House is next on right with stone-pillared driveway.

Map Ref No: 23

Jenny Clavering
Whistlebare
Milnathort
Kinross KY13 7RP
Tel: 01577 864417
Fax: 01577 864417

Under five miles from the motorway is this lovely manse, tragically burnt down but rebuilt with great taste, elegance and style. A light-coloured wood predominates and rooms are warm with cornicing, thick carpets, combed ceilings, lots of space... very comfortable in every way. Joanna is new to the world of B&B, but clearly enjoys the company of others, and will greet you without pretension and with her two dogs. Guests eat in the wonderful country kitchen, the true heart of the house, which is always informal and fun, or in the conservatory in finer weather. A genuine welcome here.

Rooms: 1 double, en suite (bath/shower), 1 large single with private bathroom.

Price: £28 p.p. No single supp.

Breakfast: Flexible.

Meals: Dinner, £15 p.p., by arrangement.

Closed: Christmas & New Year.

From Edinburgh, cross Forth Road Bridge. Follow M90 to junct 8 (Glenfarg) - 3 miles to village, through village and first right signed Arngask. 1st large house on right.

Map Ref No: 23

Joanna Cameron
The Old Manse
Arngask
Glenfarg
Perthshire PH2 9QA
Tel: 01577 830394

This is a maverick house, an extraordinary hunting lodge-cum-folly with its ornamental gates and Tuscan-style tower. And far below the fast-flowing River Devon with its kingfishers, herons and dippers. The property goes up the other bank and long walks on high ground await those who dare cross the suspended bridge! You couldn't wish for a more gracious welcome. Klas (Swedish) and Nayana and family (Sri Lankan) put emphasis on basics: guests should feel well cared for; beds should be top quality (duvets and pillows of goosedown); showers should be powerful; and Nayana's food should continue being exceptional.

Rooms: 4 doubles, sharing 2 shower rooms.

Price: £25 p.p. Single supp. £5.

Breakfast: Flexible.

Meals: Dinner, £15 p.p., by arrangement, or country pub next door.

Closed: Never!

From M90 going North, exit 6 at Kinross. Stay on A97 for 6 miles signed Kincardine Bridge, then right onto A823 signed Crieff. 4 miles to Glendevon and house is first on left.

Map Ref No: 23

Klas Buring & Nayana Silva
Glentower House
Glendevon
Dollar
Perth FK14 7JY
Tel: 01259 781587
Fax: 01259 781501

You will love Kippenross; it might be the fruit and flora of the plasterwork in the duck-egg blue morning room. It could be the polished and creaking mahogany staircase that springs from the oak-parqueted hall past ancestral portraits to the Colefax and Fowler bedrooms. Or the stunning grounds, which are almost an arboretum, landscaped nearly 200 years ago; there are miles of river to splash and fish in. Most likely, though, it will be the gentle and unstuffy hospitality which you most enjoy. A runaway Highland bull and orphaned red squirrel are recent friends; you will quickly join them.

Rooms: 1 twin with private shower; 1 twin and 1 twin/double, both en suite (bath/shower).

Price: £30-£35 p.p. Single supp. £10.

Breakfast: Flexible.

Meals: Dinner £22 p.p.

Closed: Never!

They started here as farmers, went on to do B&B and have ended up with a hotel, a warm, friendly and eclectic sort of place, full of music (jazz to opera) and interest. It is run by a very spirited family: son Tom cooks (superbly), a fabric designer daughter accounts for the dramatic and innovative bedrooms, Rob and Jean chat, serve and greet. Rob and another son still run the farm, too. The place seems to evolve at its own pace; a large vegetable garden is now growing. It is virtually at the end of the road, close to Loch Voil where you can go boating. Dynamic, lovely... and fascinating.

Rooms: 2 twins, 5 doubles, 3 suites, all en suite (bath or shower).

Price: £32.50-£45 p.p. Single supp. £12.50.

Breakfast: Until 9.30am.

Meals: Dinner £22.50-£27.50 p.p. Sunday lunch £18.50 p.p.

Closed: Never!

From junction 11 of M9 take B8033 towards Dunblane. Get in right hand lane and take 1st right across reservation to lodge. Keep on drive over bridge up hill to Kippenross.

Map Ref No: 23

Sue & Patrick Stirling-Aird
Kippenross
Dunblane
Perth FK15 0LQ
Tel: 01786 824048
Fax: 01786 823124

Turn off A84 at Kings House Hotel following signs to Balquhidder. Continue beyond Balquhidder to end of Loch Voil. Monachyle (pink) is up drive on the right.

Map Ref No: 23

Rob, Jean & Tom Lewis
Monachyle Mhor
Balquhidder
Lochearnhead
Perthshire FK19 8PQ
Tel: 01877 384622
Fax: 01877 384305

Arrive along a mile of wood and rhododendron to this imposing (if not very beautiful), third house on this historic and fortifiable site. The remains of ramparts from earlier castles rear over the Victorian dell with its ferny burn and waterfall. The gardens are 'fantastic' (our inspector) with huge, exotic 200-year-old trees, beautifully laid-out walks, wallaby graves - the usual! The house is magnificent on the inside too, with beautiful rooms in elegant style. Your hosts are great fun and add delicious food and wonderful bedrooms to the many reasons to stay at Dupplin. *Children over 12 welcome.*

Rooms: 6 twins/doubles, all en suite.

Price: From £55 p.p. Single supp. £15-£55.

Breakfast: Until 9am.

Meals: Dinner, 3 courses, £28 p.p. with 24 hours notice.

Closed: Christmas & New Year.

From M90 roundabout, A93 towards Perth for 1 mile, then sharp right onto B9112 for Dunning. After 2.7 miles, wrought-iron gates on right.

Map Ref No: 23

Derek & Angela Straker
Dupplin Castle
By Aberdalgie
Perth
Perthshire PH2 0PY
Tel: 01738 623224
Fax: 01738 444140
e-mail: dupplin@netcomuk.co.uk

Penny and Roddy are naturals at hospitality and it's not long before you feel fully ensconced in your own wing of their lovely 18th-century farmhouse. There's only one guest room, up its own staircase with its own bathroom and views of the Vale of Strathmore. Penny is a marvellous cook, and breakfast eggs are laid by her rare-breed hens; fruit and veg are home-grown too. Everything possible is done to make your stay more comfortable. All in all this is a really friendly home where you are well looked after. You are also within easy reach of Scone and Glamis Castle.

Rooms: 1 twin, en suite (bath).

Price: £30 p.p. Children £15. Under 3s free if sharing parents' room. No single supp.

Breakfast: Flexible.

Meals: Dinner £18 p.p. Must be booked in advance.

Closed: Christmas & New Year.

From Perth A94 north towards Coupar Angus. After Perth airport 2nd right signed Rait/Kilspindie. House drive on left after 1 mile, over cattlegrid & 200m up farm drive.

Map Ref No: 23

Roddy & Penny I'Anson
Montague House
Balbeggie
Perth
Perthshire PH2 7PR
Tel: 01821 640656
Fax: 01821 640788

In 1914, whisky potentate A.K. Bell perched his Edwardian summer house in deer woods and rabbit meadows high above the fertile Tay valley. Now it is Garry and Jenny who entertain here, taking real pleasure in your company, as you will in her scrumptious cooking. The rooms are elegant and restrained. The panoplied four-poster is almost worth getting married for. Beautiful big bathrooms with all the original clunky chrome and iron, and enamel-gleaming hot towel rails that might grace a '57 Chevy. Downstairs is lined with light oak, and with Persian rugs on the floor. *Children over 12 welcome.*

Rooms: 2 twins with private bathrooms; 1 double (four-poster), en suite (bath/shower).

Price: £36 p.p. Single supp £10.

Breakfast: Flexible.

Meals: Dinner £22 p.p.

Closed: Christmas & New Year.

'I would love to stay here myself,' wrote our inspector. Deep in the countryside you have complete peace and old-fashioned Scottish hospitality. The gardens, somewhat wild, ramble over 20 acres and there are fine lawns with some magnificent trees. Inside, there are big comfortable bedrooms with very good beds, a wonderfully ornate and high-ceilinged drawing room and a similarly fine dining room where you eat *en famille*. Silla does traditional country cooking (lots of game).

Rooms: 2 twins, en suite (bath).

Price: £33 p.p. Single supp. £36.

Breakfast: Flexible.

Meals: Dinner £20 p.p. Packed lunch available.

Closed: Never!

From Perth take A93 towards Braemar through Guildtown. The Lodge is on the right after 1 mile, with green railings. Pass Lodge and continue up drive, keeping left to reach Campsie Hill.

Map Ref No: 23

Garry & Jenny Barnett
Campsie Hill
Guildtown
Perth
Perth PH2 6DP
Tel: 01821 640325
Fax: 01821 640785

From Perth A94 to Coupar Angus. In town right to Dundee, 100m right signed Enverdale Hotel; continue past hotel for 0.25 miles, round sharp bend. House 100m on right.

Map Ref No: 23

Peter & Silla Keyser
Balgersho House
Coupar Angus
Perthshire PH13 9JE
Tel: 01828 627397

A 170-acre private loch where birds can be watched and pike fished; a great organ halfway up the main stairs with air pumped from a separate building in the grounds; a 16th-century central building with wings added in 1780 to a design filched from Adam. "One of the prettiest houses in Scotland"? It is a very historic, very traditional country house run by delightful people. The bedrooms are big and utterly charming - our inspector said his was the most comfortable he'd had in Britain! *Children over 12 welcome.*

Rooms: 1 twin and 1 double, both en suite (1 bath and 1 shower and bath). Adjoining twin available only for children sharing parents' bathroom.

Price: £30-£40 p.p. Single supp. £5-£10.

Breakfast: Flexible.

Meals: Bistro nearby.

Closed: Christmas & New Year.

Rattrays have lived here for five centuries. One forebear escaped death in 1747 because the judges were reluctant to hang the world's best golfer. The gorge view from a circular balcony that rings the drawing room is not just dramatic... it's unbelievable! The 300 acres of "Sublime-Style designed natural" woodland provide fabulous walks. A house full of character and antiques awaits you. The French room is pink and has a four-poster. Meals may be exotic-eastern - Lachie is enthusiastic, Nicky practical, about cooking. A fun and easy-going young couple.

Rooms: 1 four-poster, en suite (bath) and 1 twin with private adjacent bathroom.

Price: £30 p.p. Single supp. £10.

Breakfast: 8-9am.

Meals: Dinner £15 p.p. Sometimes available on request.

Closed: 22 December-5 January.

From Blairgowrie turn onto A923 signed to Dunkeld. Look for sign saying 'Kinloch. Drive safely' and then take first opening to left after sign.

Map Ref No: 23

Kenneth & Nicolette Lumsden
Marlee House
Kinloch
Blairgowrie
Perthshire PH10 6SD
Tel: 01250 884216

From Blairgowrie take A93 towards Braemar for 2 miles. Just before end of 30mph limit there is a sharp right-hand bend and drive (also on right). Follow drive for 1 mile.

Map Ref No: 23

Nicky & Lachie Rattray
Craighall-Rattray
Blairgowrie
Perth PH10 7JB
Tel: 01250 875080
Fax: 01250 875931
e-mail: oh54@dial.pipex.com

The house was begun as a tower in 1585 and added to until Victorian times (with turrets, etc) and into the present century. Inside it is delightfully old-fashioned. The rooms are large and comfortable with open fires which are lit in cooler weather. Paul is a conservationist and writer and both he and Louise love having guests whom they welcome with grace and humour. This is a lovely family home and visitors can roam freely on the estate with its parkland, woods and heather moorland.

Rooms: 1 four-poster with private bathroom; 1 double and 1 single with shared bathroom.

Price: Double £30 p.p. Single £35.

Breakfast: Flexible.

Meals: Dinner, £15-£20 p.p., by arrangement.

Closed: Christmas & New Year.

Peacocks strut their stuff and the chickens range free. The garden is full of fine vegetables, fruit and honey, too. It is all delightful, elegant but rural and even nicer than the photo. The conservatory - almost Mediterranean - has vines and creepers, an orange tree, a garden umbrella, wicker chairs and doors to the garden. In the snug sitting room is an open fire, with oriental tapestry and fresh flowers. The dining room has fine etchings and swords on the walls. The bedrooms are in a clean unfussy style - crisp colours - and hugely comfortable. *Children over 12 welcome.*

Rooms: 2 twins & 1 twin/double, each en suite (bath).

Price: £32-£36 p.p. No single supp.

Breakfast: Until 9.00am.

Meals: Dinner £21 p.p.

Closed: Christmas & New Year.

From Blairgowrie, A926 to Kirriemuir. After 5 miles left to Alyth. Straight through town on Airlie St. After 2.5 miles round sharp left bend. Bamff drive on right.

Map Ref No: 23

In Pitlochry turn into E Moulin Road. Take 4th turning on the right into Tomcroy Terrace to the end. Turn right up the drive.

Map Ref No: 23

Paul & Louise Ramsay
Bamff House
Alyth
Blairgowrie
Perth PH11 8LF
Tel: 01828 632992
Fax: 01828 632347

Alastair & Penny Howman
Auchnahyle
Pitlochry
Perthshire PH16 5JA
Tel: 01796 472318
Fax: 01796 473657

This 1865 shooting lodge has the most wonderful position right by Loch Tummel and the country-house feeling survives. Owned and run by Norma and Richard, it's a very personal place. Rooms have bags of character, too. The drawing room has an amazing centrepiece fireplace with Bacchanalian scenes in relief; bedrooms have window seats, combed ceilings, large bathrooms... and all of them have varying degrees of loch view. The turret contains two bathrooms so you can stare out, immersed and transfixed, at the lake. The hotel also has a boat and bikes and walking is superb. Great value.

Rooms: 1 family suite, 10 double or twin, 8 en suite (shower) and 3 en suite (bath).

Price: £37-£50 p.p.

Breakfast: Until 9.30am.

Meals: Dinner around £20 p.p.

Closed: Mid-January-end February.

Elizabeth grew up on an Angus farm and Jim was 'factor' of the woods and tumbling rivers at Glen Tanar Estate. They seem to know everything about the area: walking, fishing, eating, history or local scandal and eccentricities. Their Victorian villa is a real Scottish family B&B, with a mix of reproduction and antique furniture, gilt-framed pictures and fresh flowers carefully arranged throughout, and all 'facilities' you need in the big bedrooms. They are glad to pick you up from Aberdeen airport so you could soon be sitting in the lush garden.

Rooms: 2 twins, en suite (shower) and 1 double with private bath.

Price: £24 p.p. Single supp. £8.

Breakfast: Flexible.

Meals: Dinner £19 p.p.

Closed: Hardly ever!

From A9 going North, past Pitlochry, turn right towards Killiecrankie (B8079), then left over river Garry (signed Strathtummel/Queen's View). House 3.5 miles on left between road and loch.

Map Ref No: 23

Richard & Norma Tomlinson
The Queen's View Hotel
Strathtummel
Pitlochry
Perthshire PH16 5NR
Tel: 01796 473291
Fax: 01796 473515
queensviewhotel@compuserve.com

From A93 Aboyne is 30 miles west of Aberdeen. Gordon Crescent is the lane on the left just after the village green.

Map Ref No: 24

Elizabeth & Jim Thorburn
Birkwood Lodge
Gordon Crescent
Aboyne
Aberdeenshire AB34 5HJ
Tel: 013398 86347
Fax: 013398 86347

An impressive Edwardian house in an idyllic setting on the banks of the river Dee in Royal Deeside. The big, luxurious bedrooms all have excellent views over the river or garden to the hills beyond. There's a snooker table if guests feel up to a challenge and a sauna, too. David is a keen naturalist and fisherman while Meg likes to share her enthusiasm for the historic castles and gardens that surround them. They enjoy welcoming visitors from all over the world and will make you feel completely at home.

Rooms: 1 twin, en suite (bath and shower); 1 twin and 1 double, both with private bathroom. Separate shower room available.

Price: £30 p.p. No single supp.

Breakfast: 8-9.30am.

Meals: Dinner £20 p.p. by arrangement, or available locally.

Closed: Rarely.

This 'Castle Country' breathes history and at the Duncans' own well-restored castle, once home of the Gordons of Park, you may suspect that the odd Jacobite ghost still lurks; you may even sleep in the room where Robert the Bruce slept. Two of the guest suites have four-posters. James is an artist and has an art gallery in the house. Meryl, warmly welcoming, cooks superb Scottish fare which is served by candlelight. The atmosphere, both romantic and mysterious, makes it ideal for house parties.

Rooms: 4 private suites, all en suite.

Price: £28-£40 p.p.

Breakfast: Flexible.

Meals: Restaurant attached. Supper £12 p.p. À la carte dinner around £20 p.p.

Closed: Never!

From Aboyne take A93 towards Braemar. By 50 mph sign turn left down Rhu-na-Haven road. The house is approx 400 yds on the right.

Map Ref No: 24

David & Meg White
Lys-na-Greyne
Rhu-na-Haven Road
Aboyne
Aberdeenshire AB34 5JD
Tel: 013398 87397
Fax: 013398 86441

Castle of Park is on the B9023, a quarter of a mile out of Cornhill village.

Map Ref No: 28

James & Meryl Duncan
Castle of Park
Cornhill
Aberdeenshire AB45 2AX
Tel: 01466 751667
Fax: 01466 751667

Grange means 'granary' and this area used to supply the 12th-century monks of Kinloss with oats and barley. Grange House is surrounded by fields and woods well beyond its own eight acres of grounds. A late Georgian manse with Victorian additions it has been sensitively re-done, with light and airy bedrooms and a comfortable drawing room with a baby grand piano and plenty of reading material. It is only an hour from Aberdeen airport and close enough for you to enjoy the little fishing villages of the Moray coast.

Rooms: 1 double, en suite (shower) and 1 twin, en suite (bath).

Price: £25 p.p. No single supp.

Breakfast: Flexible.

Meals: Dinner, 3 courses, £18 p p

Closed: Occasionally.

With listed buildings a sense of history is usually assured; at this 1776 country mansion, history extends into the orchard where King Malcolm was murdered among the windfalls about 1,000 years ago. Blervie makes B&B history for, among many things, "the best porridge in Scotland" and the use of stones and a fine stone staircase from ruined Blervie Castle. Fiona and Paddy are still restoring; there are antiques, lots of decorative antlers, guns and violins, one full four-poster. Paddy grows and cures his own tobacco. *Children over 10 welcome.*

Rooms: 1 twin/double with private bath and 1 double (four-poster), en suite (bath).

Price: £30 p.p. No single supp.

Breakfast: Flexible.

Meals: Dinner £20 p.p.

Closed: Christmas & New Year.

From Keith, take A95 towards Banff. After 3.5 miles left (signed Grange Church). Left again opposite the church.

Map Ref No: 28

Doreen & Bill Blanche
Grange House
Grange
Keith
Banffshire AB55 6RY
Tel: 01542 870206
Fax: 01542 870206
e-mail: wd.blanche@zetnet.co.uk.

From A96 follow signs to Forres; turn south at the clocktower, straight across at the next roundabout and leave the town on B9010. Pass the hospital and after 1 mile follow Mains of Blervie sign. Turn right at farm.

Map Ref No: 27

Paddy & Fiona Meiklejohn
Blervie
By Forres
Moray IV36 0RH
Tel: 01309 672358
Fax: 01309 672358
e-mail: meiklejohn@btinternet.com

For another superb house in the Highlands please see entry 621.

Caroline grew up in this Gulf stream micro-climate and has an easy intimacy with the area, so she can show you bike rides, walks and beaches, summer ceilidhs, Highland games and village dances. Robert had 'Les Ambassadeurs', the renowned Park Lane club. He now farms with a few sheep, horses and fowl. You can stoke your own fires in the cosy cottages or pine-vaulted studio, but you may prefer the Manse's warm dark woods, rugs and finer furniture. You'll eat well: butcher's sausages and drop-scones or even, at dinner, venison off the hill. *Dogs by prior arrangement.*

Rooms: Main House: 2 doubles with private baths and 1 single, en suite (bath). Stable studio: 1 double, en suite (shower).

Price: £30 p.p. Single supp. £8.50.

Breakfast: Flexible.

Meals: Dinner, 5 courses, £20 p.p. Supper, 2 courses, £10 p.p. B.Y.O. wine.

Closed: Never!

Highlands & Islands

From Inverness, A9 north. Cross Dornoch bridge. 14 miles later take A839 to Lairg. Cross bridge in Rogart and take sharp right turn uphill. House is 1.5 miles on, on right, next to church.

Map Ref No: 27

Robert & Caroline Mills
St Callan's Manse
Rogart
Sutherland IV28 3XE
Tel: 01408 641363
Fax: 01408 641313

The Road to the Isles was built to take Highland cattle to Lowland markets. Along it you find Telford's famous eight-gate lock on the Caledonian Canal, Fort William fort, many dramatic Scottish memories... and Garramore. This imposing 19th-century house, built as a Highland sporting lodge, sits in six acres of woodland garden (hundreds of species of trees and shrubs) just a few minutes from the sea. The superb conversion provides big, interesting rooms. The Moores pride themselves on their warm hospitality and meals of good local produce.

Rooms: 1 family (double & single bed) and 1 double, both en suite (bath); 1 twin with private shower room; 3 family rooms (double & single bed) sharing 2 bathrooms.

Price: From £18 p.p.

Breakfast: 8-9.30am, or by arrangement.

Meals: À la carte dinner, May-September. Rest of year, homemade supper by arrangement.

Closed: Never!

From Fort William take A830 to Mallaig. Garramore is approx. 3 miles past Arisaig and 1 mile before Morar.

Map Ref No: 22

Julia & Sophie Moore
Garramore House
South Morar
Nr. Mallaig
Inverness-shire PH40 4PD
Tel: 01687 450268
Fax: 01687 450268

The Campbells' quietly luxurious B&B is 10 minutes' walk from Fort William. They renovated it from rubble; all is now spick, span and freshly flowered. Ponder over breakfast as the boats sail by on Loch Linnhe. From your room (our favourite is the pale green, angled front double with wooden bed and *chaise longue*) you may, if very lucky, see whales. Ride the cable car to what seems to be the top of the world, or climb Ben Nevis, then return to candlelight for a 'wee dram' before the coal fire.

Rooms: 2 doubles, en suite (shower) and 1 double, en suite (bath).

Price: £33 p.p. Single occ. £66.

Breakfast: Flexible.

Meals: Available locally.

Closed: Mid November Easter

From Glasgow take A82 to Fort William. 200 yards after Fort William sign take right turn up Ashburn Lane, next to Ashburn guest house. The Grange is on left at top of lane.

Map Ref No: 22

Joan & John Campbell
The Grange
Grange Road
Fort William
Inverness-shire PH33 6JF
Tel: 01397 705516

On 50 acres of wild, ferny lochside grounds is Invergloy, a converted coach house and stables in the beautiful Great Glen, north of Fort William. There are lovely views of Loch Lochy and surrounding mountains from the guest drawing room. This is a peaceful, no-smoking home run by Margaret, a professional musician and James, a retired chemical engineer. Two of the bedrooms have low ceilings and one room has twin beds foot-to-foot. There are excellent walks from the house and guests can use a rowing boat from the private shingle beach. There's a tennis court, too. *Children over 8 welcome.*

Rooms: 3 twins, en suite (2 with shower and 1 with bath and shower).

Price: £21 p.p. Single supp. £10.

Breakfast: At 8.30am.

Meals: Good restaurants in area.

Closed: Never!

In the perfect peace of rural Scotland, Colin, a polyglot tour guide, and Fiona, wine buff and keen cook (shortbread, ice-cream, jam and bread are all hers), are passionately Scottish. The fine organic garden gives the fruit, the river yields its salmon, the moors provide game in winter. Two big luxurious rooms with gigantic beds are in the lovely, traditionally-furnished farmhouse; two others are in sunny, rose-clad, self-contained and fully-equipped Gled Cottage a few minutes away. The Grahams are likeable and energetic and have two delightful young boys.

Rooms: 1 twin with private bath & shower. 1 double and 2 double/twins en suite (bath/shower)..

Price: From £30-£35 p.p. Single supp. £15.

Breakfast: 8.30-9am.

Meals: Dinner £20 p.p.

Closed: Never!.

From Spean Bridge, head north on A82. After 5 miles, house is signed on left.

Map Ref No: 22

Margaret & James Cairns
Invergloy House
Spean Bridge
Inverness-shire PH34 4DY
Tel: 01397 712681

On M9 going north, junc 10 onto A84 towards Doune. After 5 miles, left on B826 towards Thornhill. Mackeanston Ho. on left after 2.2 miles.

Map Ref No: 23

Fiona & Colin Graham
Mackeanston House
Doune
Highlands
EH3 6ES
Tel: 01786 850213
Fax: 01786 850414

This former ferryman's house is small, welcoming, homely, informal... simply charming. Just 50 yards from the River Spey where ospreys and otters fish and dippers dip. Explore the wonderful countryside or sit in the garden with a pot of tea. The sitting room is cosy with a wood-burning stove and lots of books (no television). Elizabeth, free spirit, lived in the Sudan and still enjoys travelling. You will eat very well here. Heathery honeycomb, homemade wholemeal soda bread and preserves, herbs from the garden and fresh veg. A superb base for nature lovers and very good value.

Rooms: 1 double, 1 twin, 2 singles, all sharing 1 bathroom & 2 w.c.s.

Price: £18.50-£19 p.p.

Breakfast: Flexible.

Meals: Dinner £13.50 p.p. Packed lunches £4.50 p.p.

Closed: Occasionally, please check.

Dip one of their rods, or an oar, in the loch, or walk the land that has been in the family for three generations. This was once their holiday home and they are delighted to live here properly; there are still holiday touches, like the hot water bottles and electric blankets in the old bedrooms. The house is comfortable without being imposing, an 1850 original with later add-ons, mostly clad in gleaming white wood. Christina is lively, down to earth and a great hostess. You will be given home-bee honey, fruit and veg from the garden; and the two llamas add an exotic touch.

Rooms: 1 double, en suite (bath) and 1 twin with private bath or shower.

Price: £25 p.p. Ask about single supp.

Breakfast: Until 9.30am.

Meals: Dinner £15 p.p.

Closed: Christmas & New Year.

From B970 take the road to Boat of Garten. House on left just before river Spey. From A9 follow main road markings through village. Pass golf club and cross river.

Map Ref No: 23

Elizabeth Matthews
The Old Ferryman's House
Boat of Garten
Inverness-shire PH24 3BY
Tel: 01479 831370
Fax: 01479 831370

North of Aviemore for 16 miles, left onto B851 signed Fort Augustus. Continue over bridge, through Inverarnie to Farr and past children's playground. House 2nd gate on left, signed.

Map Ref No: 23

James & Christina Murray
Farr Mains
Farr
Inverness
Inverness-shire IV1 2XB
Tel: 01808 521205
Fax: 01808 521466

You can only reach Skiary by boat or on foot. Enveloped in the wilds of Loch Hourn it is lost to the outside world. No electricity, no roads, no neighbours: just mountains, waterfalls (there is a burn and pool yards up the hill for swimming), otters in the loch, deer feeding along the shoreline. The tiny, pine-lined cottage is the last inhabited dwelling of a once busy fishing village. You will be pampered, with 'hotties', early morning tea and log fires. Wonderful meals are served in the lochside greenhouse dining room. John's ferry service for guests down and across the loch makes spectacular walking accessible from Skiary.

Rooms: 3 twins with shared bathroom.

Price: Dinner, B&B £60 p.p. Full board £385 p.p. per week.

Breakfast: Flexible.

Meals: Light/packed lunch & dinner included in price.

Closed: Mid-October-mid-March.

From Invergarry A87 N; left after 5 miles towards Kinloch Hourn. Stop at phone box near Tomdoun Hotel to tell Everetts of your arrival. Continue about 15 miles to Kinloch Hourn, at end of road, where hosts will meet you.

Map Ref No: 22

John & Christina Everett
Skiary
Loch Hourn
By Invergarry
Highlands PH35 4HD
Tel: 01809 511214

Rural simplicity and elegance in rare harmony... Di and Inge are delightful and deeply committed to the place. They stripped the sitting-room to its original stone and pine-clad walls, put in a wood-burning stove, brought in sheep, goats and chickens and resolved to serve the finest of local and home-grown food. People now come from far away to eat here, and they have won accolades galore. Dine (part of the package) with white cotton, silver and china; sleep in small but pretty bedrooms. A caring, warm and cheerful haven and hauntingly beautiful views.

Rooms: 1 twin and 2 doubles, each en suite (shower).

Price: Dinner, B&B £45-£50 p.p. Minimum 2-night stay. Singles only taken in April and October, supplement £20.

Breakfast: 8.30am.

Meals: Dinner included.

Closed: November-March.

Little Lodge is just off B8021 Gairloch to Melvaig road, shortly after turning to North Erradale.

Map Ref No: 26

Di Johnson & Inge Ford
Little Lodge
North Erradale
Gairloch
Highlands IV21 2DS
Tel: 01445 771237

The ocean laps on every side; the curlew's cry echoes across the bay. Utterly solitary, this house could not be more exposed, nor more romantic. Warm and enjoyably quirky with a crackling log fire, Art Deco lamps and snaking S-shaped bookshelves. Pop art hangs above the beds; huge bath and magnificent showers in big bathrooms. Mairi and Roger use high quality local ingredients for their delicious meals and share their extensive local knowledge with guests. There is no TV... it's not that sort of place.

Rooms: 2 doubles, en suite (bath/shower) & 1 twin, en suite (shower); 1 twin, en suite, in adjacent croft.

Price: Dinner, B&B £55 p.p. Single supp. £10.

Breakfast: Flexible.

Meals: Dinner included. Packed lunches £6 p.p.

Closed: 1 November-28 February & 1-15 July.

Turn off A832 at Laide Post Office. Follow the road to Mellon Udrigle. Turn left at bottom of hill as entering village and continue until track reaches house, at the very end of the road.

Map Ref No: 26

Roger & Mairi Beeson
Obinan Croft
Opinan
Laide
Highlands IV22 2NU
Tel: 01445 731548
Fax: 01455 731635
e-mail: rj&mc.beeson@obinan.co.uk

The most idyllic dwelling. The sea loch ripples beyond the garden gate; herbs flourish by the front porch; fruit ripens in the unruly walled garden. Clambering from the road down a steep, muddy field prepares you well for this slightly shambolic, utterly charming crofthouse. Honeymooners have an exclusive suite in the old boathouse. Help yourself to any boats lying around but beware of the 'dodgy dinghy'. Tony is very informal, funny and imaginative, cooking purely vegan food that leaves even meat-eaters in raptures.

Rooms: 1 double, en suite and 2 doubles sharing bathroom.

Price: Dinner, B&B £35-£40 p.p. Single supp. £7.

Breakfast: Flexible.

Meals: Included. "Bring your own wine (& cow's milk if addicted)".

Closed: Never!

Turn off A835, 9 miles south of Ullapool. Follow road to Ardindrean. Park car by phone box & walk down steep muddy path to right through field to cottage on shore.

Map Ref No: 26

Tony Weston
Taigh-na-mara Vegetarian Guesthouse
The Shore
Ardindrean, Lochbroom, Nr. Ullapool
Highlands IV23 2SE
Tel: 01854 655282
Fax: 01854 655292
e-mail: tony@scotlandthegreen.co.uk

Gordon is gently passionate about opera, art and life. The place is powerful, moving, magnetic... an artistic cauldron; in winter there are plays, concerts and recitals. The sublime food is a symphony orchestrated by Gordon and Charles. The furniture is a combination of traditional, antique and modern with superb fabrics, a 'deafening' Pugin wallpaper and red silk on the walls of the long corridor. There are open fires, comfortable sofas, books, fresh flowers and pictures everywhere.

Rooms: 4 singles, 4 doubles and 4 twins, all en suite (bath).

Price: £54-£60 p.p.

Breakfast: Until 11.30am.

Meals: Dinner, à la carte, average price £25 p.p.

Closed: Christmas & New Year.

The shells are ground to the finest of white sands, white to set off the coast's gold and azure to creamy perfection. Scarista sits among flowers. Ian (merchant banker turned perfectionist cook) and Jane (artist and mildly eccentric hostess) took on a lot moving from their Islington roots to this remote Outer Hebridean manse. Now there is a fire in the library, rich colour glowing from drawing room pictures and rugs, and always the impossibly lovely view. Ask for the white cotton-quilted front bedroom. *Children over 8 and babies welcome.*

Rooms: 2 doubles, 1 twin, 1 double suite and 1 twin suite, all en suite. Most rooms in annexe.

Price: £55-£62.50 p.p. Single supp. £15.

Breakfast: 8.30-9.30am.

Meals: Dinner £30 p.p.

Closed: Early October-mid-April.

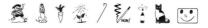

A939 north to Nairn, left onto A96 and into town. At roundabout, straight over (not left). Hotel signed half a mile on left.

Map Ref No: 27

J. Gordon Macintyre
Clifton House
Nairn
Highlands IV12 4HW
Tel: 01667 453119
Fax: 01667 452836
e-mail: macintyre@easynet.co.uk

From Tarbert take A859 signed to Rodel. Scarista is 15 miles on the left after the golf course.

Map Ref No: 25

Ian & Jane Callaghan
Scarista House
Isle of Harris
Western Isles HS3 3HX
Tel: 01859 550238
Fax: 01859 550277
e-mail: scarista@compuserve.com

An older, long-serving, Gaelic-speaking islander is likely to answer your summons when the service bells ring in the pantry. They keep their staff by staying busy in the low season and, as the hived off old billiard room is the only pub, community ties are strong, especially on Saturday's packed Ceilidhs. Elsewhere the atmosphere is quiet - Victorian ease without stuffiness. The pale old lavender-and-moss green, couched drawing room gives way to polished wood in the dark oaken hall. A much-loved place, and the craggy coast views are always stupendous.

Rooms: 9 doubles, 9 twins and 1 single, all en suite.

Price: Double £49-£79 p.p. Single £49.

Breakfast: 8-10am.

Meals: Dinner £28.50 p.p. Sunday lunch £17 p.p. Bar & conservatory meals also available.

Closed: Never!

White cottages bob by the quay in the remote, tiny fishing village, sparkling in the salty breeze. If a thirsty appetite nags after your day's Hebridean adventures there is always The Stein. At the beer-seasoned bar Angus stocks real ale and 62 single malts under the blackened joists of his rough hewn, fire-warmed hostelry. The food is delicious too, and if cosiness comes from contrast and setting then the clean, closely eaved, blue-carpeted and pine-panelled rooms above are perfect. Watch from your window the catch landed, hauled from the sea to your plate, impossibly fresh.

Rooms: 3 doubles and 1 single, sharing shower room & bathroom.

Price: £19.50 p.p.

Breakfast: Flexible.

Meals: Dinner, 3 courses, approx. £10 p.p.

Closed: 25 December-1 January.

From Bridge of Skye take A850 to Broadford. There take A855 towards Portree. Travel through Portree to Staffin and then follow road through to Flodigarry. The hotel is on the right.

Map Ref No: 25

Andrew Butler
Flodigarry Country House Hotel
Flodigarry
Isle of Skye IV51 9HZ
Tel: 01470 552203
Fax: 01470 552301

From Isle of Skye bridge take A850 to Portree. There follow sign to UIG for 4 miles. Then left on A850 towards Dunvegan for 14 miles. Hard right turn to Waternish on B886. Stein is 3.5 miles along on loch side.

Map Ref No: 25

Angus & Teresa McGhie
Stein Inn
Stein
Waternish
Isle of Skye IV55 8GA
Tel: 01470 592362
Fax: 01470 592362

After a lifetime in the diplomatic service Donald and Rosemary enjoy putting people at ease. Their home is an oasis of comfort and charm encircled by mountains and sea. The house is light and bright with superbly comfortable beds; through the windows, complete with wooden shutters, you have dramatic views across the loch to Dunvegan village, famous for its castle. The local minister would once row to work; you may prefer to walk among the Iron Age duns (forts) in the hills and cliffs. Return to the house party atmosphere and dinner in the loch-side conservatory. *Pets by prior arrangement.*

Rooms: 1 twin & 1 double, en suite (baths and showers).

Price: From £30 p.p. Prior booking essential.

Breakfast: Flexible.

Meals: Dinner £18 p.p.

Closed: Christmas & New Year.

Lady Claire MacDonald of MacDonald radiates such an ebullient elegance and charm that resistance is useless. Her interest and willingness to take up your cause are completely sincere. Downstairs hang a supporting cast of ancestors who coolly attest to the maturity and grace of hospitality in this much-loved and luxurious 17th-century home. Upstairs many of the snug and pretty pastel-papered rooms expand to spaciousness with sea loch views. Dining off silver and crystal you may expand a little yourself - Claire's cookery is properly famous (and much published).

Rooms: 5 doubles and 5 twins, all en suite.

Price: £40-£90 p.p. Single supp. by arrangement.

Breakfast: Flexible.

Meals: Dinner £35 p.p.

Closed: 30 December-7 February.

From Skye Bridge follow signs to UIG until Sligachan Hotel. Take left fork to Dunvegan (22 miles). There, left (just before bakery) signed Glendale. White house in trees after 0.75 miles.

Map Ref No: 25

Donald & Rosemary MacLeod
Kinlochfollart
By Dunvegan
Isle of Skye IV55 8WQ
Tel: 01470 521470
Fax: 01470 521470

From the Bridge of Skye follow signs south on A851 to Armadale-Mallaig ferry. Lodge is signed on the left down a forestry road, approx 20 minutes from the bridge.

Map Ref No: 22

Lady Claire MacDonald
Kinloch Lodge
Sleat
Isle of Skye IV43 8QY
Tel: 01471 833214
Fax: 01471 833277

The views over the harbour are life-affirming and the superb rooms at the front drink them in. The old oak door revolves you through to the vast hall, great oak staircase, antlers and trophies. It feels old and rather grand, slightly Edwardian. The dining room has great ruched floral curtains, pink table-cloths and patterned carpet; it all fits. The sitting room has heavy-patterned furniture, a grand piano and more of those ineffable views. Wicker, cushioned chairs in the very glassy conservatory (more views). Great value, especially facing inland. Sue puts the place at ease.

Rooms: 1 suite, 11 twin, 11 doubles and 2 singles, all en suite (bath or shower).

Price: From £38-£88 p.p.

Breakfast: Until 9.30am.

Meals: Dinner from £12.50-£23 p.p. Bar lunches from £5 p.p.

Closed: 18 December-18 January.

In Tobermory follow signs for Main Street. Go to harbour, take first left up steep hill, then 1st very sharp right. Hotel 200m on right.

Map Ref No: 22

Sue & Michael Fink
Western Isles Hotel
Tobermory
Isle of Mull
Tel: 01688 302012
Fax: 01688 302297

The Burn tumbles through the garden down to Loch Scridain, not far from Ben More, Mull's highest mountain; glorious country. If you go to Iona you will pass close by. Six bedrooms, an elegant dining room and a beautiful tile-floored sun-room with vines over the ceiling. This is comfort at its most attractive; remote and romantic, yet accessible - in every way. Colin and Jane are among the most helpful, experienced people in this book and enthusiastic and knowledgeable about Mull. The peace and quiet are perfect, and the woodland walk down to the sea is dreamy.

Rooms: 3 twins and 3 doubles, all en suite (bath).

Price: £35-£45 p.p. Ask about single supp.

Breakfast: Until 9am.

Meals: Dinner from £25 p.p. Packed lunch by request.

Closed: Rarely! Please check.

From car ferry at Craignure or Fishnish take A849 towards Bunessan & Iona ferry; turn right on B8035 towards Gruline. After 4 miles turn left at converted church. Tiroran is 1 mile along minor road.

Map Ref No: 21

Colin & Jane Tindal
Tiroran House
Isle of Mull PA69 6ES
Tel: 01681 705232
Fax: 01681 705240

The house, warm and simple, is perfect for the setting - the real star of this place. The water is crystal clear, seals - even dolphins or a whale - swim by. Climb up from the rugged coastline of fell and rocky outcrop and watch the sun set over Iona, Coll and Tiree; then turn round and see the almost heavenly red glow. Sailors sail in just for John's cooking. Eleanor works by day at her silversmithing; you can drop in to see her. They are both free spirits inhabiting a cheerful, cosy and eccentric enclave with cabin-like bedrooms and white walls that reflect the glorious light. Special indeed.

Rooms: 2 twins and 1 double sharing 2 bathrooms.

Price: From £16 p.p.

Breakfast: Until 9am.

Meals: À la carte dinner always available.

Closed: Rarely! Please check.

4 miles beyond Bunessan on road to Iona ferry, take right to Kintra. After 1.5 miles turn left down track and through iron gate. Cottage is on shore.

Map Ref No: 21

John & Eleanor Wagstaff
Red Bay Cottage
Deargphort
Fionnphort
Isle of Mull PA66 6BP
Tel: 01681 700396

Fiona, delightful and very low key, did her Ph.D. on Iona's geology. It is a mystical and beautiful isle, whence came Christianity to Scotland. The Argyll's rooms are cottagey-simple, but comfortable and homely; go for the ones with a sea view. Well-thumbed books, games, and cosy fires in the sitting room. The dining room has antiques and family portraits. The last ferry from Mull is at 6.15pm so plan your journey; there is a sense of fun in being marooned on Iona for the night. The hotel has its own organic garden. Gordon paints and pots in an old croft house near the Abbey.

Rooms: 3 doubles, 4 twins, 2 family and 6 singles, all en suite (bath or shower), plus 2 singles with shared bath.

Price: Dinner, B&B £57-£62 p.p.

Breakfast: 8.15-9am.

Meals: Dinner, 5 courses, included.

Closed: Early October-Easter.

Oban ferry to Craignure on Mull, then west to Fionnphort for Iona ferry. Hotel on seashore. Cars not allowed on Iona but can safely be left at Fionnphort.

Map Ref No: 21

Mrs Fiona Menzies
Argyll Hotel
Iona PA76 6SJ
Tel: 01681 700334
Fax: 01681 700510

Perched on the edge of a cliff above Crinan Harbour, Fernfield has simply breathtaking views towards the Western Isles. The light, elegant upstairs drawing/dining room is a perfect vantage point - the sunset has been known to stop dinner in its tracks. Paintings, charts, artefacts and maps reflect Michael's lifelong affair with the sea. You'll enjoy Monica's home-cooking, from her bread, marmalade and cakes to her imaginative dinners. Bedrooms are small, pretty and comfortable and, like the rest of the house, recently, lovingly renovated. *Children over 12 welcome.*

Rooms: 1 double, en suite (bath); 1 double and 1 single sharing a bathroom.

Price: En suite £28 p.p. Double and single £26 p.p.

Breakfast: Flexible.

Meals: Dinner £19 p.p. & packed lunches by arrangement.

Closed: Christmas & New Year.

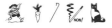

From Lochgilphead take A813 towards Oban. After 3 miles take B841. After 5 miles when you see harbour, fork right & then left. Pass row of cottages. Take 1st driveway on left & then fork left between wooden gates.

Map Ref No: 22

Michael & Monica Stewart
Fernfield
Crinan
Argyll PA31 8SW
Tel: 01546 830248
Fax: 01546 830282

Farm or manor? On land or on water? The views are stupendous; wander as you wish and admire them. The house is elegantly white, the farm definitely working; yet the eye always comes to rest on the waters and boats of Loch Craignish. The drawing room is the original 16th-century bothy with coved ceiling, four-foot-thick walls and log fire. The Services have a 400-acre hill farm but find time for real hospitality and delicious food, including shellfish from the Ardfern landings. The downstairs loo doubles as the library.

Rooms: 1 double, en suite (bath), plus 2 singles and 1 double, sharing bathroom and sitting room.

Price: £30 p.p. No single supp.

Breakfast: Until 9.00am.

Meals: Dinner £20-£35 p.p. Lunch (packed also available) on request.

Closed: 22 December-3 January & fourth week of August.

From A816 take B8002 to Ardfern. Go through village. 0.75 miles beyond church right by Heron's Cottage, and up drive to Corranmor.

Map Ref No: 22

Hew & Barbara Service
Corranmor House
Ardfern
By Lochgilphead
Argyll PA31 8QN
Tel: 01852 500609
Fax: 01852 500609

You can borrow the boat on the loch for rowing or fishing (brown trout); that is a treat in itself. This is very much a simple family home, run with undue modesty by the gentle and lovely Gill and her ex-rugby pro husband. He is an oyster farmer, big and full of life. They have the gift of making one feel at home. There are lots of family photos, deep red sofas in the sitting room, rugs, plenty of books and games. There's a big old pine double bed in one colourful and large room, with bright linen and good views across the loch.

Rooms: 1 twin/double, en suite (bath/shower).

Price: £22.50 p.p. Single supp. by arrangement.

Breakfast: Until 9am.

Meals: Available locally.

Closed: November-end of February.

Under the youthful eye of the Millers, this huge, solid Scottish house sings. Their enthusiasm and passion have blown away any hint of intimidation. This is an easy-going place; you have the run of the house and the biggest compliment is that you settle in easily and forget that you're a guest. Breakfast can be a social affair; plates make way for maps, fresh coffee is brewed and new friends are made. Post-dinner - Bella is an excellent chef - Charlie may join you for a cigar in the billiard room. Bedrooms are comfortable, the peace remarkable and the scenery is mountains, loch, coast and forest.

Rooms: 4 doubles and 3 twins, all en suite.

Price: £35 p.p. Single supp. £15.

Breakfast: Until 9am.

Meals: Dinner £20 p.p. by arrangement.

Closed: Never!

A816 north from Lochgilphead to Kilninver, then left on B844 towards Easedale. Farm on right opposite Loch Seil, after 2 miles(signed).

Map Ref No: 22

Ms Gill Cadzow
Duachy Farm
Kilninver
By Oban
Argyll PA34 4QU
Tel: 01852 316244
Fax: 01852 316244

From Connel village head north over the bridge on A828 and through Benderloch. 5 miles on, just past right to Bonawe, are black gates (on right). Drive down, over bridge to house.

Map Ref No: 22

Charlie & Bella Miller
Barcaldine House
Barcaldine
Nr. Oban
Argyll PA37 1SG
Tel: 01631 720219
Fax: 01631 720219
e-mail: barcaldine@breathe.co.uk

Loch Linnhe is 200 metres away, so views are stunning. Light floods in, there are windows everywhere and the walls are white to reflect the sun. The daughter's modern art hangs above a classical marble fireplace in the sitting room, whose ceiling is the roof. The dining room connects open-plan, with good simple long oak table. The bedrooms are nicely minimalist, with cool fresh apple greens, light yellows, white, fresh flowers, candles, books and views. The two-acre garden is 100% organic, fertilised by seaweed, the pony and free-range chickens. Relaxed and interesting people.

Rooms: 1 double, en suite (shower) and 2 twins sharing bath and shower.

Price: £18.50-£25 p.p. Single supp. by arrangement.

Breakfast: Until 9.15am.

Meals: Available locally.

Closed: Christmas & New Year.

After a bumpy, private, two-mile drive you are in peace, just a stroll from Loch Linnhe and in 11 acres of lawns, gardens and impressively ancient woodlands. Neil grew up here and still wears a kilt; Philippa, fun and bubbly, does a lot of cooking. The stage is now set for a dramatic entrance: an oak-panelled hall with roaring fire, leather sofas, a barrel window with long views, billiard room in grand style. The bedrooms are in grand old country-house style, floral curtains and chairs, good period furniture. Entertaining, beautiful, traditional.

Rooms: 1 four-poster, 2 twins, 3 doubles, all en suite (bath).

Price: £39 p.p. No single supp.

Breakfast: Until 9.30am.

Meals: Dinner £24 p.p.

Closed: Never!

North from Oban on A85, then A828. Continue up to the village of Duror, then left, signed Cuil. House on left after 0.5 miles.

Map Ref No: 22

Bridget Allen
Druimgrianach
Cuil Bay
Duror
Argyll PA38 4DA
Tel: 01631 740286

North from Oban on A85, then A828. Continue for about 30 miles to Kentallen and house drive signed left just after the town sign.

Map Ref No: 22

Philippa & Neil Sutherland
Ardsheal House
Kentallen of Appin
Argyll PA38 4BX
Tel: 01631 740227
Fax: 01631 740342
e-mail: ardsheal97@aol.com

Robert wears his old-school, fishing-mad, gentleman's heart engagingly on his tweed sleeve. This 1960s lodge conceals a rich rococo interior of 18th-century style and comfort. He has dragged and ragged the walls to a warming vibrancy and is the perfect host - turning his gatherings into country house parties. The pretty garden is terraced down to the River Awe with its stone road bridge. He'll gladly brave the evening's midges and take you to the barrage where the salmon leap. The rooms are just what you need - fresh flowers, simply furnished, light and airy.

Rooms: 2 twins/doubles and 1 twin, all en suite (bath).

Price: £30 p.p. Single supp. £7.

Breakfast: 8.15-9.15am.

Meals: Dinner £20 p.p.

Closed: 1 November-1 March, but will open by special arrangement.

Earle and Stella retired here from their Hampshire prep school and have a gentle schoolmasterly concern and reserve, although Stella will flash a conspiratorial wink if you are in danger of taking them too seriously! "Stella is a fantastic cook and does everything," Earle says, "except buttle". The bedrooms are big and comfortably angled under the eaves. This is a peaceful house which is practically paddling (you certainly can) in Loch Baile Mhic Chailen... a Highland diamond sparkling at the feet of the towering Bens Sguilard and Fhionnlaidh.

Rooms: 1 twin and 1 double, en suite (bath); 1 twin with private shower.

Price: £20-£27 p.p. No single supp.

Breakfast: Flexible.

Meals: Dinner £17 p.p.

Closed: Never!

From A85 (Oban road) travel 23 miles west from Crianlarich. Take right signed 'Inverawe Fisheries' just before bridge over river. House is first on left after high hedge. If you reach Taynuilt you have travelled 3 miles too far!

Map Ref No: 22

Robert Knight
Bridge of Awe Lodge
Taynuilt
Argyll PA35 1HT
Tel: 01866 822642
Fax: 01866 822510

20 miles south of Ballachulish on the A828. On reaching the inner end of Loch Creran turn off main road, following signs to Invercreran House Hotel. After Hotel on left, house is 1 mile further on.

Map Ref No: 22

Earle & Stella Broadbent
Lochside Cottage
Fasnacloich
Appin
Argyll PA38 4BJ
Tel: 01631 730216
Fax: 01631 730216

History broods over this fine house at the foot of Glencoe; the massacre was ordered here and it was burnt down by Hanoverian troops in 1746. Rebuilt in 1764, it has fine rooms and antiques but nothing overly grand. The drawing room has a warm, historical feel to it, deep red walls, deep sofas, fine furniture and an open fire. It is a good place for an after-dinner whisky; Liz's food is very, very good - local produce and fish straight from the water. The Duke of Argyll in 1760 wrote: "..the best hospitality I ever had on my travels was at Ballachulish House". *Children over 3 welcome.*

Rooms: 4 twins and 3 king-size, all en suite (bath).

Price: Dinner, B&B £67 p.p.

Breakfast: Until 9.30am.

Meals: Dinner included. Children £3.50.

Closed: Christmas & New Year.

Only wildlife breaks the silence around this elegant former manse on a beautiful loch with dazzling views of the mountains of Kintail. You can wander the large garden (complete with burn), or follow the forest or loch walks, see pine martens and deer, perhaps seals and otters, and even eagles. Dinner is equally interesting, with Scottish seafood - or even sushi - a speciality; afterwards, settle in front of a log fire and listen to some of the huge collection of classical music. Anne and Uilleam love their work and all things Gaelic.

Rooms: 2 doubles with private bathrooms.

Price: £35 p.p. Single supp. £10.

Breakfast: Flexible.

Meals: Dinner, 4 course table d'hote, £?? p.p. by arrangement. B.Y.O. wine.

Closed: November-April (although can open by arrangement).

House is just south of Ballachulish Bridge, 250m off A828 Oban to Fort William road. If approaching from north, 40m beyond Ballachulish Hotel on left.

Map Ref No: 22

John & Liz Grey
Ballachulish House
Ballachulish
Argyll PA39 4JX
Tel: 01855 811266
Fax: 01855 811498

Down Glenshiel on the A87 and left at Shiel Bridge to Ratagan and Letterfearn. Over stone bridge and on for 1 mile. Right at next sign for Ratagan and Letterfearn. Duich House is 3 miles on left.

Map Ref No: 22

Anne Kempthorne
Duich House
Letterfearn
Glenshiel
Ross-shire IV40 8HS
Tel: 01599 555259
Fax: 01599 555259
e-mail: duich@mcmail.com

WALES

Built in 1821, and Grade II listed, this lighthouse is of unique design, with an internal collecting well, a stone spiral staircase, slate-bedded entrance hall and a Lamp Room with a full 360-degree view of hills and sea. All rooms are wedge shaped ("like portions of Camembert") and you'll sleep in either a kingsize waterbed or a pine four-poster. This is, we think, our only house that has a flotation tank and after you've bobbed around imagining yourself in the Dead Sea, you shower in an old BT phone box! Aromatherapy and reflexology are also on offer. Oh, there's a life-sized Dalek at the foot of the stairs, too.

Rooms: 2 twins/doubles, both en suite.

Price: £37.50 p.p. Single occ. £55.

Breakfast: Flexible.

Meals: Available locally. You can B.Y.O. wine.

Closed: Never!

From M4, A48 to Newport, then B4239 to St. Brides. Drive for 2 miles and turn left at B&B sign, into long, winding private road.

Map Ref No: 3

Frank & Danielle Sheahan
West Usk Lighthouse
St. Brides Wentloog
Newport NP1 9SF
Tel: 01633 810126/815860
Fax: 01633 815582

South Wales

One of very few Grade I listed buildings in the country - this Tudor manor possesses staggeringly ancient beauty. Under-floor heating warms the flagstones (once Julia found a lamb settling in), the dining room is lit by candles in Tudor candlesticks (even at breakfast) and some of the stone window frames retain the original 1600 finger moulding. Bedrooms have dramatic mountain views and there is a fascinating herb and knot garden plus a newly-planted yew maze. A grand, historic house, yet conservation and commitment to the environment are evident everywhere. Sumptuous dinners include Welsh wines and cheeses.

Rooms: 3 doubles, all en suite (bath).

Price: From £35 p.p. Single supp. £10.

Breakfast: 8.30-9am (week); 9.30-10am (weekend).

Meals: Dinner, 4 courses £25 p.p. by prior booking

Closed: Never!

The Welsh bard Elis Aethwy wrote of this area: "So pleasant with the world at bay. Glanrannel in my soul will stay." It doesn't take long to get his drift when you escape into the grounds of this Victorian gentleman's residence. The wedding-cake white house overlooks a lake stocked with Chinese carp and trout, a stream and lush parkland... and perhaps even a red kite. The local staff are cheerfully hospitable and the rooms have good views. Menus include fish from their own river and produce from local farms.

Rooms: 2 twins, 3 doubles and 2 triples, all en suite except one with basin and private bathroom.

Price: £36 p.p. Single supp. £5.

Breakfast: Flexible.

Meals: Dinner, £16 p.p. for residents. Lunch & bar snacks available.

Closed: 1 November-31 March.

North from Abergavenny on A465. 5 miles later left to Pantygelli. After 0.25 miles right up stone track between house and bungalow.

Map Ref No: 9

Julia Horton Evans & Ken Peacock
Penyclawdd Court
Llanfihangel Crucorney
Nr. Abergavenny
Monmouthshire NP7 7LB
Tel: 01873 890719
Fax: 01873 890848

North up the A482 for 6 miles; hotel signed on left. Follow hotel signs for 1 mile.

Map Ref No: 8

David & Bronwen Davies
Glanrannell Park Country House Hotel
Crugybar
Llanwrda
Carmarthenshire SA19 8SA
Tel: 01558 685230
Fax: 01558 685784
e-mail: glanparkhotel@btinternet.com

Bring a notebook for Sue's recipes: her vegetarian dishes, with much organic fruit and vegetables, are exceptional. In the attractive dining room, revel in her good food and sparkling conversation and discuss fishing and country life with Nick (he loves sailing, too, and will captain his 22-foot boat for you). You may lie in a deep bed with embroidered sheets and contemplate the heart-healing view or wallow in the big bath under the timbers, with one of the books from the bathroom library. The bedrooms in this 200-year-old farmhouse are big and beautifully furnished and Sue will greet you like a dear friend.

Rooms: 2 twins/doubles, both en suite (bath).

Price: £24 p.p. Single occ. £28.

Breakfast: Flexible.

Meals: Dinner, 3 courses with wine, £15 p.p. Packed lunch £5 p.p.

Closed: Christmas Day & Boxing Day.

From Llandovery take A40 towards Llandeilo. At Llanwrda right for Lampeter (A482). After 1 mile, first right past M H Evans. Over bridge and up hill; first left. House is 1st on right.

Map Ref No: 8

Sue & Nick Thompson
Mount Pleasant Farm
Llanwrda
Carmarthenshire SA19 8AN
Tel: 01550 777537
Fax: 01550 777537

Events have not invaded the serenity here. Enter via the courtyard with its clock tower and mellow stonework; you are drawn into the embrace. The river, with a spectacular 30-foot waterfall, runs through the estate. On both banks are unspoiled woods hiding unharried wildlife. The farmyard seethes with pot-bellied pigs, poultry, peacocks and pigeons. Bring a party of friends, recite poetry, paint... "Absolutely magical," wrote our inspector. *Six self-catering cottages and flats.*

Rooms: 1 double and 1 twin/double, both en suite (shower); 1 double with shared bathroom.

Price: From £18 p.p.

Breakfast: Flexible.

Meals: Dinner, 4 courses, from £10 p.p.

Closed: November-February (except for large groups).

From M4 to Pont Abraham Services take 2nd exit marked Llandeilo & Ammanford. There, left at 2nd set of lights. After 2 miles, right opp. bus shelter and Golf Club on left. House is 1 mile up on right.

Map Ref No: 8

Carole, Katy & Julian Jenkins
Glynhir Mansion
Llandybie
Ammanford
Carmarthenshire SA18 2TD
Tel: 01269 850438
Fax: 01269 851275

How comforting to find an old 14th-century house saved from years of neglect and brought back to life! 'Freddie' has done a tremendous job and restored her 'Church of David Higher' in traditional country style - brass beds, chintz and patchwork, terracotta and beams.The house is surrounded by tall trees and lush acres within a stone's throw of the babbling River Towy (with private fishing), a designated SSSI. On fine days guests can ride out in a horse and carriage for picnics.

Rooms: 1 family suite (2 rooms), 2 doubles (1 bath, 1 shower) and 1 twin (bath), all en suite.

Price: £25 p.p. Single occ. £37.

Breakfast: 8-9am or by arrangement.

Meals: Dinner £25 p.p.

Closed: Christmas.

The Quinns' house is somewhat deceptive. It looks like a neat two-up, two-down from the front, but once inside the front door you need a map! The original early 19th-century cottage has been constantly enlarged and is now delightfully higgledy piggledy. Guests usually forget about lunch after one of Jennifer's breakfasts, sometimes served in the little garden: Welsh Rarebit, fried laverbread, bacon and eggs any way you like; the Quinns give such a touching level of care. Only 100 yards from the harbour and near the beach. *Careful dogs are welcome to bring well-trained owners.*

Rooms: 1 twin/triple with shared bathroom and 1 double, en suite (shower).

Price: Twin/triple £16 p.p; double £17.50 p.p. No single supp. Under 3s free, 3-12s half price.

Breakfast: Fairly flexible.

Meals: Dinner available locally.

Closed: Occasionally. Please check.

Take B4300 from Carmarthen for about 5 miles to Capel Dewi. Leaving village follow sign on left and go down the drive off the main road.

Map Ref No: 8

Fredena Burns
Capel Dewi Uchaf Farm
Capel Dewi Road
Capel Dewi, Nr. Carmarthen
Carmarthenshire SA32 8AY
Tel: 01267 290799
Fax: 01267 290003
e-mail: frmretreat@aol.com

From Carmarthen A477. At Kilgetty r'bout left onto A478. 1.5 miles after railway bridge left into Sandyhill Rd (becomes Stammers Rd). House on left.

Map Ref No: 7

Malcolm & Jennifer Quinn
Primrose Cottage
Stammers Road
Saundersfoot
Pembrokeshire SA69 9HH
Tel: 01834 811080

Cresswell House - the old Quaymaster's house - sits on the bank of the River Cleddau which literally laps against the garden wall. Boldly decorated in sympathy with its Georgian interior, the house has excellent river views. Philip and Rhian relish producing imaginative and memorable food for dinner and breakfast; homemade sausages, fishcakes and home-smoked salmon are often on the menu. Then go and walk off the excesses along the miles of river footpaths to watch kingfishers, herons and cormorants. There's a fine old-fashioned inn just a minute's walk away.

Rooms: 1 twin with private bathroom; 1 double, en suite (shower) and 1 four-poster, en suite (bath).

Price: £20-£22.50 p.p. Single occ. £25.

Breakfast: Flexible.

Meals: Dinner £18.50 p.p. Packed lunches available on request.

Closed: Christmas.

From A477 take A4075. Turn left at the garage selling 4x4s. House is on the left after 1.4 miles, just before bridge.

Map Ref No: 2

Philip Wight
Cresswell House
Cresswell Quay
Nr. Pembroke
Pembrokeshire SA68 0TE
Tel: 01646 651435

Imagine an almost perfect, green hillside setting with mountain views in nearly every direction and then set a garden designer loose. This is what this gentle, charming and endearing couple are keen to share with you - together with their enormous capacity for fun, their family heirlooms (each with attached story), formal drinks before superb dinners, immaculate airy rooms, fluent Norwegian, piles of books, and a talent for conversation and reflection. The house is closed from noon to 4.30pm, but that is for the cleaning that makes it sparkle. There is a profound sense of peace and quiet here. *Children over 12 welcome.*

Rooms: 1 twin, en suite (shower) and 2 doubles, en suite (bath).

Price: £26 p.p. + £4 surcharge for 1-night bookings.

Breakfast: 8.15-10.15am.

Meals: Dinner, 3 courses, including aperitif & wine, £25 p.p.

Closed: November-Easter.

From A487 to Nevern, past pub, over bridge. First left before church, up hill, bear right at fork. 100 yards on left after Trefach Farm, driveway is marked.

Map Ref No: 7

Wendy & Sydney Beresford-Davies
Glasdir Bach
Nevern
Nr. Newport
Pembrokeshire SA42 0NQ
Tel: 01239 820623

The dramatic course of the River Cych is a wonderful prelude. With trout fishing at the bottom of the garden and the Pembrokeshire coastal path only seven miles away, this is a beautiful, easy-going haven for lovers of the outdoors. Very much a family home with comfortable, traditionally decorated bedrooms, a cosy book-lined library and a more formal drawing room with grand piano. Breakfast is served at a sunlit table in the window of the great dining room that houses many reminders of the long family history and overlooks the stunning grounds. Tony and Sarah are friendly, easy and unstuffy.

Rooms: 1 twin and 1 double, en suite (bath/shower). 1 double with shared bathroom.

Price: £35 p.p. Single occ. £45.

Breakfast: Flexible.

Meals: Dinner available locally.

Closed: 1 November-1 March.

M4 to Carmarthen, A484 Cardigan road, until Cenarth, left onto B4332. Continue for 1.5 miles to yellow Nags Head pub. Turn left. Llancych is 1 mile on left.

Map Ref No: 7

Antony & Sarah Jones-Lloyd
Llancych
Boncath
Pembrokeshire SA37 0LJ
Tel: 01239 698378
Fax: 01239 698686

These lucky people live in Britain's only coastal National Park. No traffic jams or crowded beaches, but an acre of lawned gardens, big bedrooms and great sea views to enjoy. The coast path is a mile away at Ceibwr Bay, a dramatic spot. (The neighbours' dog, Heidi, can guide you on a walk to the bay... really.) Patricia and David welcome you to their beautiful home which has lots of books and many original paintings. Lifts are arranged to Poppit Sands or Newport for guests wishing to walk the majestic coast path.

Rooms: 2 doubles and 1 twin, all en suite (shower).

Price: £20-£25 p.p. Single supp. £10.

Breakfast: Usually 8.30-9am.

Meals: Dinner, 3 courses, £14 p.p. Packed lunch £3.75 p.p.

Closed: 1 December-1 February.

From Cardigan by-pass towards Cardigan at southern r'bout. Left by Eagle Inn to St Dogmaels. Sharp right at end of High St, head for Moylegrove. Bear left (signed Glanrhyd) when there, uphill. House on right, past church.

Map Ref No: 7

Patricia & David Phillips
The Old Vicarage
Moylegrove
Nr. Cardigan
Pembrokeshire SA43 3BN
Tel: 01239 881231
Fax: 01239 881341
e-mail: davidhphillips@compuserve.com

Plentiful birdlife adds an audible welcome to Broniwan: tree-creepers, wrens and redstarts all nest in ivy-covered walls or mature beech trees. This is a small and peaceful farm just five miles from the sandy coast of Cardigan where Carole and Allen unfussily draw you into their home, serving tea and Welsh cakes on your arrival. They are organic farmers so you will eat well. This traditional farmhouse has wonderful views of the Preselli hills from its large panelled windows. The rooms are cosy with warm, natural colours in paintings and woollen tapestries. There is a pretty garden for relaxing.

Rooms: 1 twin, en suite (shower) and 1 double with private bath.

Price: £20.00 p.p. No single supp. Reduced weekly rate.

Breakfast: 8-9.30am generally, or can be flexible.

Meals: Dinner £10.00 p.p. Light supper £5.00 p.p. Packed lunch on request.

Closed: Never!

Mid Wales

From Aberaeron A487 for 6 miles towards Brynhoffnant. Left at B4334 to Rhydlewis; left at Post Office & shop, 1st lane on right, then 1st track on right.

Map Ref No: 8

Carole & Allen Jacobs
Broniwan
Rhydlewis
Llandysul
Ceredigion SA44 5PF
Tel: 01239 851261
Fax: 01239 851261
e-mail: 101535.2310@compuserve.com

A Regency gem reached via a winding parkland drive, with magical glimpses of the mansion on the way. No disappointment close up. Encounter peace and tranquillity and a house dripping with elegant style and spoiling comfort everywhere you go. Magnificent ancient mirrors, airy conservatory, four-posters and claw-foot baths. Dinner, truly sumptuous, can be taken in the lovely dining room. This is a sporting estate with riding, shooting and fishing arranged in season. Or, even better, woodland walks in totally unspoilt countryside.

Rooms: 1 double, 1 twin and 1 single, each with private bathroom.

Price: £35 p.p.

Breakfast: Flexible.

Meals: Dinner £25-£30 p.p. available on request.

Closed: 1 December-1 March.

It is grand and magnificent, yet Graham and Sue somehow manage the difficult trick of making you feel at ease and at home. The house has known many incarnations (parts of the cellar are 11th-century!); its sympathetically restored 18th-century façade shields a fine entrance hall with a ball-gown wide staircase and high-ceilinged, seductively decorated rooms. The music room has echoes of Jane Eyre and the halls are dotted with old family portraits. There are 70 acres of sumptuous parkland, woodland and gardens. Fine dining in the restaurant or brasserie.

Rooms: 3 twins/doubles, all en suite (bath).

Price: £40 p.p. Single supp. £15. Dinner, B&B, £55 p.p. Reduced prices for longer stays.

Breakfast: Until 10am.

Meals: Dinner, 3 courses, for non-residents, from £19.50 p.p.

Closed: January.

From Lampeter west towards Aberaeron on A482. After 9 miles, in village of Ciliau Aeron, right to Pennant. Another 2 miles, over stone bridge, left through gates, past lodge and up drive.

Map Ref No: 8

Nigel & Wendy Symons Jones
Monachty Mansion
Pennant, Llannon
Aberaeron
Ceredigion SY23 5JP
Tel: 01545 570215
Fax: 01545 571707

Entering Aberystwyth, turn left into Devil's Bridge Road and immediately left again onto B4340. Follow road to signposted drive and follow for approx 0.5 miles.

Map Ref No: 8

Sue & Graham Hodgeson-Jones
Nanteos Mansion
Rhydyfelin
Aberystwyth
Ceredigion SY23 4LU
Tel: 01970 624363
Fax: 01970 626332
e-mail: nanteos@btinternet.com

Where the Snowdonian mountains come down to the crystal sea, you will hear only the waves on the shore and the sheep on the hill. Pentre Bach promises some of the best sunsets you'll ever see. The Smyths grow their own organic veg and Margaret was mid-Wales Cook of the Year 1994; their dinner menu is worthy of the best restaurants. The old stone farmhouse has good-sized, warmly-carpeted, pastel-quilted rooms with great views. The Smyths are committed to conservation and 'green' living: you'll enjoy them.

Rooms: 1 twin and 2 doubles, all en suite (shower) plus extra bath available. 3 self-catering cottages for 4, 6 and 7 people.

Price: £22-£27 p.p. Single supp. £6 or full-room rate when busy.

Breakfast: Flexible.

Meals: Dinner £14.95 p.p. Packed lunch available on request.

Closed: Christmas & New Year. Cottages open all year.

People return again and again to this 17th-century inn with its crooked passages, low ceilings and friendly atmosphere. The bedrooms are cosy rather than grand, although one has a four-poster bed, and there's a family room in the roof space with stone walls and sloping ceilings. Personal bits and pieces scattered around add to the warmth and homeliness. The bar/bistro is dark and atmospheric (lots of little pockets to explore) or you can eat in the restaurant or outside on the paved forecourt overlooking the unspoilt village.

Rooms: 1 twin and 6 doubles, all en suite.

Price: £40-£45 p.p. Single occ. £55.

Breakfast: 7.30-9.30am.

Meals: Dinner, 3 courses, £18.95 p.p.

Closed: Never!

Off A493 Dolgellau-Tywyn coast road, 12 miles from Dolgellau. Entrance 40m south of old stone bridge in Llwyngwril.

Map Ref No: 8

Nick & Margaret Smyth
Pentre Bach
Llwyngwril
Nr. Dolgellau
Caernarfon & Merioneth LL37 2JU
Tel: 01341 250294
Fax: 01341 250885

Turn off A483 between Welshpool and Newtown following signs to Berriew. The hotel is next to the church.

Map Ref No: 8

Mr & Mrs Thomas
The Lion Hotel and Restaurant
Berriew
Nr. Welshpool
Powys SY21 8PQ
Tel: 01686 640452
Fax: 01686 640604

An elegant 1920s fishing lodge, set in 27 acres of garden and woodland. If you're an angler (like your host), there are 800 yards of double-bank salmon and trout fishing to cast your line in; or simply sit back and enjoy the sound of water flowing past your window. Inside, there's a cosmopolitan feel, with a mixture of English antiques and oriental overtones from the many rugs and paintings collected on their Middle and Far Eastern travels. Yolande, your enthusiastic hostess, attends to all those little extras that make your stay memorable. A great place for house parties, too. *Fishing available by advance booking.*

Rooms: 3 doubles, all en suite (bath/shower).

Price: From £30 p.p. Single supp. £10.

Breakfast: Flexible.

Meals: Dinner £16 p.p.

Closed: 1 November-28 February.

Years of restoration and conversion work on the Legges' Grade II* listed watermill have produced spectacular results. The origins of the building have been honoured, even the dining room has been created amid the corn-milling machinery. Lots of wood, flagstone and terracotta with wood-burning stoves, comfortable chairs and a riverside garden. The bunkhouse and camping facilities in the old cider orchard give the mill an informal ambiance with a planet-friendly bias. Food is vegetarian and truly delicious! A brilliant base for exploring on foot, horseback, bicycle or canoe.

Rooms: 1 twin and 1 double (Continental bath/shower) and 1 double, en suite (shower).

Price: £19.50 p.p. Single supp. £10.

Breakfast: Flexible.

Meals: Vegetarian dinner, 3 courses, £10.50 p.p; simple vegetarian supper £4.50 p.p. Available on request.

Closed: Christmas.

From Abergavenny head for Crickhowell, then right, through Talgarth, towards Builth Wells. After Erwood look for lay-by & discreet sign on right which is entrance to drive.

Map Ref No: 8

Jeremy & Yolande Jaquet
Pwll-y-Faedda
Erwood
Builth Wells
Powys LD2 3YS
Tel: 01982 560202
Fax: 01982 560732
e-mail: yolande@btinternet.com

12 miles north of Brecon on A470. The mill is set slightly back from the road on the left between the villages of Llyswen and Erwood.

Map Ref No: 8

Alistair & Nicky Legge
Trericket Mill Vegetarian Guesthouse
Erwood
Builth Wells
Powys LD2 3TQ
Tel: 01982 560312
Fax: 01982 560768

Penpont is magnificent in its grounds on the River Usk and folded into the gentle Brecon hills. It has not a whiff of pretension yet a relaxed stateliness of its own: great one-table dining room, grand oak staircase with balustrades turned on an angle and the original candle holders to light your way to bed, vast bedrooms (one with tapestried walls) and vast atmosphere. You may fish with flies, overflow into tents (£2.50), show off on the tennis court, borrow wellies and just walk - wonderful! Come not to be cosseted but to be welcomed into an easy-going family home of unexpected beauty.

Rooms: 1 twin, en suite; 1 double with own shower and basin; 1 double with 3 singles and another double with 2 singles, sharing 2 bathrooms. Self-contained flat sleeps 12.

Price: £25-£28 p.p. Children half price. Babies cot free if you bring bedding.

Breakfast: Flexible, within reason!

Meals: Evening meals for groups - but book ahead.

Closed: Christmas (for B&B). Self-catering, never!

From Brecon west on A40 through Llanspyddid. Pass second telephone kiosk on left. Entrance to house is on right. (Approx 4.5 miles from Brecon).

Map Ref No: 8

Davina & Gavin Hogg
Penpont
Brecon
Powys LD3 8EU
Tel: 01874 636202
Fax: 01874 636202

You can hear the auctioneer rattling through the bids on market day if you sit at the bottom of the long and expansive walled garden. Behind the Georgian façade is a fine 1620s house with tall-ceilinged, dark-beamed hall and dining room. You creak up the oak stairs to bedrooms past shelves gratifyingly full of books. Big windows, original pargeted ceilings, views over the garden from two of them. The food is good, too; a delightful place with a most welcoming family.

Rooms: 2 doubles, 1 twin, all en suite (shower).

Price: £22-£25 p.p. Single occ. £30.

Breakfast: Until 9.30am.

Meals: Dinner £15 p.p. Packed lunch £5 p.p.

Closed: December & January.

Follow one-way system to High St. Left at Midland bank, then right into Lion St. House is big and yellow, on left. Parking at rear through green gates.

Map Ref No: 8

Helen & Nigel Roberts
Cantre Selyf
5 Lion Street
Brecon
Powys LD3 7AU
Tel: 01874 622904
Fax: 01874 622315
e-mail: cantreselyf@imaginet.co.uk

As if the Brecon Beacons didn't have enough to offer with their gentle grandeur, here's a real family holiday that gives you canal cruising too, in beautifully painted barges on its doorstep. The guest wing has its own entrance - come and go as you choose - and a wicker-chaired conservatory. Most guest rooms have a sitting area; the attic rooms have timber beams and sloping ceilings. Prices are so reasonable, stay a while - but book early for high seasons and holidays, for it gets busy.

Rooms: 1 double and 1 twin, both en suite (bath); 2 doubles, both en suite (shower).

Price: £20 p.p. Single occ. £25.

Breakfast: 8.30-9am.

Meals: Available locally.

Closed: End of October-mid-March.

The Parks love their house and readily share their passion for it. Grade I listed and 16th-century, it has elaborate plasterwork, dark oak panelling and mullioned windows that frame, beautifully, the Llynfi valley and the distant Brecon Beacons. Exponents of the Arts & Craft movement created the huge garden terraces in 1910, using old stone roof tiles; it's a perfect place to drink in the scenery. Bedrooms are luxurious and light, all have views and are decorated with Farrow & Ball colours. Delicious food with garden produce emanates from the huge kitchen. *Children over 12 welcome.*

Rooms: 1 four-poster, 1 double and 1 twin, all en suite (bath/shower).

Price: From £35 p.p. Single supp. £10.

Breakfast: Flexible.

Meals: Dinner, £22 p.p., by arrangement.

Closed: December, January & February.

From Abergavenny take A40 to Brecon. After 15 miles turn left to Talybont-on-Usk. There, turn right on to B4558 to Pencelli. Drive through Pencelli for 1 mile, over canal, then immediately right. Signed Cambrian Cruisers.

Map Ref No: 8

Nicola & Bob Atkins
Ty Newydd, Cambrian Cruisers
Pencelli
Brecon
Powys LD3 7LJ
Tel: 01874 665315
Fax: 01874 665315

From M4, junction 24 and A449 to Raglan, then follow A40 through Abergavenny and Crickhowell to Bwlch. Right onto B4560 and 3.5 miles after Llangors, right to house.

Map Ref No: 8

Miles & Patricia Park
Trefecca Fawr
Brecon
Powys LD3 0PW
Tel: 01874 712195
Fax: 01874 712196

Between them the Winstones have five generations connected with the hotel business. Mrs Winstone greets you, puts flowers everywhere and carries luggage. Mr Winstone cooks with a Belgian bias (French without the portion control). The rooms are cottagey, with limed oak panelling in the drawing room. Sociability is encouraged by the absence of bedroom TV so guests stay up late, comparing notes and gossiping after an excellent dinner. To help things along, Mrs Winstone, Belgian herself, will serve Belgian beer of all sorts.

Rooms: 3 twins and 4 doubles, all en suite.

Price: £34 p.p. Single occ. £40-£65.

Breakfast: 8-9am (week); 8-9.30am (Sunday).

Meals: Dinner £27 p.p. Lunch available on request.

Closed: December, January & 1-14 February.

A place steeped in history (Charles I slept here) and stonework (the lions deserve close scrutiny), this Elizabethan manor stands on a Druid sanctuary, has some (purloined?) Norman bits, a minstrels' gallery in a panelled banqueting hall and possibly the only Renaissance gardens left intact, but underground, in Britain. It is splendid but not grand, a home not a hotel; there are no modern gadgets and the Beetham's enthusiasm for their estate and their country is contagious. Come and be enchanted.

Rooms: 3 twins, 2 four-posters, 4 doubles, 2 singles - 9 en suite, 2 with shared bathroom.

Price: Twins/doubles £37-£50 p.p. Singles £41-£46.

Breakfast: 8.15-9.15am.

Meals: Dinner £19.50 p.p.

Closed: Christmas & New Year.

On A438 Brecon-Hereford road, 27 miles from Hereford, 11 miles from Brecon, 4 miles from Hay-on-Wye, signed.

Map Ref No: 8

Mr & Mrs M Winstone
Three Cocks Hotel
Three Cocks
Nr. Brecon
Powys LD3 0SL
Tel: 01497 847215
Fax: 01497 847339

Three Cocks is 12 miles NE of Brecon on A438 in Hereford direction. At Three Cocks Hotel turn right, then first right again to Felindre. Right at junction, past Three Horseshoes. Manor is on right.

Map Ref No: 9

Roger & Dawn Beetham
Old Gwernyfed Country Manor
Felindre
Three Cocks, Brecon
Powys LD3 0SU
Tel: 01497 847376

This handsome Georgian house with its fine gardens and pillared portico could frame your wedding photographs. The Morrows have brought new life to the old hall, with great decorative flair. The drawing room has Italianate gilded ceilings in contrast to the library which is truly snug. Bedrooms are decked out in a mix of period and contemporary and every piece of furniture is special. Duck-down duvets, oak floors, high ceilings, stone staircases, fruit in the rooms and good fresh food. Ancient trees in the grounds and a walled vegetable garden. Pretty Berriew is nearby.

Rooms: 3 twins/doubles, 6 doubles and 1 single, all en suite.

Price: £25-£45 p.p. Single occ. £37.50-£67.50.

Breakfast: Flexible.

Meals: Dinner £18.50 p.p. Hampers also available.

Closed: Never!

6 miles south of Welshpool on A483. Driveway is on the right 50m after The Nags Head Hotel.

Map Ref No: 9

Tim & Nancy Morrow
Garthmyl Hall
Garthmyl
Montgomery
Powys SY15 6RS
Tel: 01686 640550
Fax: 01686 640550

Please remember to 'phone ahead if you are going to arrive late!

In this superbly-preserved example of Neo-Gothic architecture (1861), the hall is dominated by the oak staircase winding to the galleried landing full of pictures, the decor painstakingly restored. Beautiful shower rooms are totally up to date and Karon and Ken seem to know what you need. The bright sunny bedrooms, Sunflower, Orchid and Bluebell, give lovely views over the bracken-gilt Berwyn Mountains. The weeping ash in the garden is 138 years old and Pistyll Rhaeadr, Wales' highest waterfall, is just up the lane.

Rooms: 1 twin, 1 double and 1 family, all en suite (shower). Self catering cottage sleeps 2.

Price: £20-£23 p.p. Single supp. £5.

Breakfast: From 8.45am.

Meals: Dinner £15 p.p. by prior arrangement; also available locally. Packed lunch available on request.

Closed: Never!

North Wales

12 miles west of Oswestry on the B4396. In village, right after Midland bank into Waterfall Street.

Map Ref No: 8

Karon & Ken Raines
Bron Heulog
Waterfall Street
Llanrhaeadr Y M Mochnant
Powys SY10 0JX
Tel: 01691 780521
Fax: 01691 780630
e-mail: kraines@enta.net

Centuries of use have polished the oak floors and doors of this imposing, Elizabethan hall run by delightfully unimposing people. Uneven floors scattered with rugs and matting, big, open fire recesses, low, heavy doors and deep window sills all induce a tender historical nostalgia. Add the comfy leather sofas, huge vases of flowers and high soft beds and you begin to get the feel of this warm, hospitable working farmhouse. Outside, there are attractive farm buildings, a formal orchard and lush lawns leading to 400 acres of open fields. *Children over 8 welcome.*

Rooms: 1 double, en suite (bath); 1 twin with private bathroom.

Price: £32 p.p. Single supp. £10.

Breakfast: Until 9am.

Meals: Dinner, 4 courses, £19.50 p.p.

Closed: November-March (except for parties of four).

The only sound is the baa-ing of the sheep and the occasional whistle of the light railway - take it to historic Bala and travel back in time. The house stands high above Bala Lake (Llyn Tegid), the largest natural lake in Wales, where non-motorised water sports beckon. The views across to Snowdonia are breathtaking. Inside the old stone house, the decor is peaceful too - waxed pine, light colours, simple, unfussy furnishings (real patchwork quilts). Olwen is a lovely, bubbly lady who likes people and poetry. A super place.

Rooms: 1 double with en suite bath and 1 twin with private bathroom.

Price: £19.50 p.p. No single supp.

Breakfast: Flexible.

Meals: Packed lunch available.

Closed: Never!

From Oswestry follow signs to Llansillin on B4580. Through Llansillin and take left at 1st crossroads. Glascoed is 0.5 miles along on left at stone gateway.

Map Ref No: 8

Ben & Louise Howard-Baker
Glascoed Hall
Llansillin
Nr. Oswestry
Powys SY10 9BP
Tel: 01691 791334

On entering Bala on A494 turn left, drive across head of lake. Right on B4403 to Llangower & cross bridge. Go straight ahead. Take 2nd gate on right.

Map Ref No: 8

Olwen Foreman
Plas Gower
Llangower
Bala
Gwynedd LL23 7BY
Tel: 01678 520431
Fax: 01678 520431

Set upon a gentle hillside with views to sea and mountains, the house is a Welsh delight in old stone, its walls showing the bumps of four centuries. The Thompsons have delved deep into the rich history of the building and its past owners - fascinating. They are relaxed and welcoming (they especially appreciate walkers) and their dinners are worth a journey. Guestrooms in the main house have original doors and beams and maybe a four-poster; in the converted barn you will find new country pine. Excellent bathrooms, rich colours, lovely old feel.

Rooms: 4 doubles (2 four-posters), 2 family and 1 twin, all en suite.

Price: £29-£35 p.p.

Breakfast: Flexible.

Meals: Dinner, 3 courses, from £15 p.p. Packed lunch £4-£5 p.p.

Closed: Never!

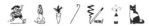

Cotton-wool puffs of smoke may emerge from the forest across the lake as trains from the steam age chug through. All very suitable, for the house itself is a heady cocktail of restoration, history and architectural miscellany. Monks built it as a retreat in the 16th century; the Georgians left their mark, as did the 1950s. It is comfortable, dark-wooded, oak-carved, and immensely friendly; fine bone china in the bedrooms, too. The lake is a magnet for bird-life and there are four acres of wood, lawns and uncomplicated formal gardens... and a grass tennis-court. Glorious.

Rooms: 1 double, en suite (shower), 1 double and 1 twin, each with private bathroom.

Price: £36 p.p. No single supp.

Breakfast: Until 10.30am.

Meals: Dinner, 4 courses, B.Y.O. wine, £16 p.p. by arrangement.

Closed: November-Easter.

Follow A496 north from Barmouth. Pass through Llanaber. After last house on left Llwyndû farmhouse is signposted on the right.

Map Ref No: 8

Peter & Paula Thompson
Llwyndû Farmhouse and Restaurant
Llanaber
Barmouth
Gwynedd LL42 1RR
Tel: 01341 280144
Fax: 01341 281236
e-mail: petethompson@btinternet.com

Leave Bala on A494, travel 1 mile, then, just before the 'approaching bend' road sign, turn sharply right into the first part of a triple entrance.

Map Ref No: 8

Mair & Jack Reeves
Fron Feuno Hall
Bala
Gwynedd LL23 7YF
Tel: 01678 521115
Fax: 01678 521151

In the heart of Snowdonia, encircled by mountains, the house has stunning views... fields, crags, lots of sky. The exterior is stone, walls are wobbly, doorways low and the lovely cottagey bedroom has cane and country furniture with an adjoining sitting room just for you. Calm, tranquil surroundings; warm, friendly, generous people; wonderful walks.

Rooms: 1 double, en suite (bath/shower) and own sitting room.

Price: £20 p.p. No single. supp.

Breakfast: 8-9am.

Meals: Sometimes available on request, but good eating places nearby.

Closed: Christmas.

Haven't you always dreamed of sleeping in a hayloft? The typical honey-coloured former cow byre opposite the 15th-century wattle-and-daub house has been sensitively converted for guests, keeping its low sloping ceilings, beams and small windows; you can still see the outlines of the original thick stone walls. The easy furniture adds to the relaxed atmosphere, the staircase creaks, the sitting room looks over the Vale of Clwyd and your jolly hosts will drop and collect you from Offa's Dyke walks. *Children over 10 welcome.*

Rooms: 1 double and 1 triple, both en suite (shower).

Price: £17.50 p.p. Single occ. £20.

Breakfast: Flexible.

Meals: Dinner £9 p.p. Packed lunches £3 p.p. Also nearby inn.

Closed: Never!

From Beddgelert head south on A4087 for 2.5 miles. In Aberglaslyn Pass, left over stone bridge. After 0.25 miles left into Nantmor. At top of village, left in front of a large chapel. House is 300 yards along a tarmac road.

Map Ref No: 8

Tim & Gay Harvey
Cwm Caeth
Nantmor
Caernarfon
Gwynedd LL55 4YH
Tel: 01766 890408

Take A494 east from Ruthin. Left opposite Griffin Hotel onto B5429. After 0.5 miles turn right to Llangynhafal. After 2 miles, Esgairlygain is signed on right about 100m past Plas Draw.

Map Ref No: 8

Irene Henderson
The Old Barn
Esgairlygain
Llangynhafal, Ruthin
Denbighshire LL15 1RT
Tel: 01824 704047
Fax: 01824 704047

Guarded by a tiny cannon brought back long ago from the Hong Kong Yacht Club, this is the only remaining fortified house on the Welsh/English border and it was built over 500 years ago by the family who occupy it now. The medieval dining hall, in the tower, has a barrel-vaulted ceiling (from which the Mayor of Chester was hanged in 1465), mullioned windows, portraits, coat of arms and family motto: "*Heb Dduw - Heb ddim:* (without God there is nothing)". The Tower bedrooms have mullioned windows, portraits, antique furniture and big beds. There are four acres of formal gardens in which to dream.

Rooms: Tower: 1 double, en suite (bath); 1 double with private bathroom. Main house: 1 twin with private bathroom.

Price. £30 p.p. Single supp. £10.

Breakfast: Until 9.00am.

Meals: Not available. Eating places within 2 miles.

Closed: 22 December-3 January.

From Wrexham, on A541 towards Mold, left onto B544. After roundabout, turn left. Travel 0.4 miles until reaching the large black gates on right, past Nercwys sign.

Map Ref No: 14

Charles & Wendy Wynne-Eyton
Tower
Nercwys
Mold
Flintshire CH7 4ED
Tel: 01352 700220

A magical and intriguing house, Golden Grove is pure Elizabethan, built by Sir Edward Morgan in 1580. Oak panelling and heavy rustic furniture, myriad maze-like passages, rich jewel colour schemes (the breakfast room is red, the dining room a subtle aquamarine). The dog-leg staircase is Queen Anne and the hall is hung with family pictures, paintings and prints. The family foursome tend the formal garden and run a farm as well as their excellent B&B. Friendly, fascinating, worth the trip. *Children over 12 welcome.*

Rooms: 1 twin and 1 double, each with private bath & w.c.; 1 double with en suite bath.

Price: £35 p.p. Single occ. £45.

Breakfast: 8-9.30am.

Meals: Dinner £21 p.p. Good food also available locally.

Closed: 1 December-mid January.

Turn off A55 onto A5151 for Prestatyn. At Spar shop before Trelawnydd, turn right. Branch left immediately. Over first crossroads and right at T-junction. Gates are 170m on left.

Map Ref No: 14

Ann & Mervyn &
Ann & Nigel Steele-Mortimer
Golden Grove
Llanasa, Nr. Holywell
Flintshire CH8 9NA
Tel: 01745 854452
Fax: 01745 854547
e-mail: golden.grove@lineone.net

STOP PRESS! Two more lovely houses

High on Edinburgh's exalted Georgian escarpment, this eyrie mixes 19th-century elegance with Danish and Middle Eastern style. Brass beds, burnished pine floors and a vast hall with a stairway that floats regally above a magnificent sitting room; the Castle can be glimpsed through the trees. Erlend swapped the rigours of daily deadlines (he was a Scottish Correspondent) for freelancing and advanced egg scrambling. Breakfasts are a full 'Franco-Scottish affair' with oak-smoked salmon. The Cloustons will meet you from the train or take you on a tour. It's relaxed and fun.

Rooms: 1 twin with basin and private bathroom (Victorian bath and shower) and 1 double with basin and private adjacent shower.

Price: From £35 p.p. Single occ. £50.

Breakfast: Flexible.

Meals: Available locally.

Closed: Hardly ever.

Heriot Row is parallel to Princes Street, three major blocks north.

Map Ref No: 19

Erlend & Hélène Clouston
41 Heriot Row
Edinburgh EH3 6ES
Tel: 0131 225 3113
Fax: 0131 225 3113
email: erlendc@lineone.net

A rare combination of relaxed informality and seriously good food – Sukie has a fast-growing reputation as one of Scotland's top chefs. She takes daily delivery of superbly fresh ingredients, has her own smokehouse, picks wild fungi. Bill readily shares his enthusiasm for local scenery, wildlife, history and culture; nothing is too much trouble. Pretty, comfortable sofas, log fires, loads of books and family pics. Plants and flowers frame Ben Nevis in the conservatory. Guests' children can eat and play with the Barbers'. They are a wonderful family. Wheelchair access throughout.

Rooms: 2 family, 2 twin, 2 double and 1 single, all en suite; 1 single with private bathroom.

Price: £50-£75 p.p. with dinner. Children £5 plus food when sharing with parents.

Breakfast: Flexible.

Meals: Dinner included, but open to non-residents (£27.50 for 5 courses). BYO wine. Lunch always available.

Closed: Never!

On A82, 1 mile north of Spean Bridge turn left just after Commando Memorial on to B8004 to Gairlochy. Old Pines is 300 yards down road on right.

Map Ref No: 22

Bill & Sukie Barber
Old Pines Restaurant with Rooms
Spean Bridge
By Fort William
Highlands PH34 4EG
Tel: 01397 712324
Fax: 01397 712433
e-mail: goodfood.at.oldpines@lineone.net

Alastair Sawday's Special Places to Stay in Ireland

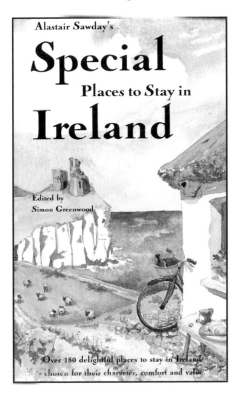

Alastair Sawday's

Special

Places to Stay in

Ireland

Edited by
Simon Greenwood

Over 180 delightful places to stay in Ireland
- chosen for their character, comfort and value.

All the magic of Ireland in our choice of lovely places to stay.

Ireland - one of the last havens in Western Europe still unspoilt by mass tourism - is the perfect setting for the fifth Sawday guide. Our inspectors have collected a series of gems that nestle in this wide and wild land where taking in weary travellers is part of the Celtic tradition. The Irish of today are definitely worthy descendents of their ancestors on this score.

Each of the 200-odd B&Bs, farmhouses, mansions and family-run hotels boasts something that makes it truly special - usually a welcome stemming not from the contents of your wallet but from your hosts' genuine enjoyment in meeting people.

We have weeded out any hint of over-commercialism, pretension or half-heartedness in the owners' approach and brought you the loveliest, gentlest, most seductive places to stay in this green and misty country.
Full colour photography, masses of detail, reliable practical information. Available for £10.95.

Alastair Sawday's
French Bed & Breakfast

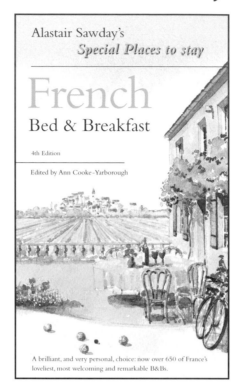

Alastair Sawday's
Special Places to stay

French
Bed & Breakfast

4th Edition

Edited by Ann Cooke-Yarborough

A brilliant, and very personal, choice: now over 650 of France's loveliest, most welcoming and remarkable B&Bs.

Put this in your glove compartment; no visitor to France should be without it!

It has become a much-loved travelling companion for many thousands of visitors to France. What a treat it is to travel knowing that someone else whom you can trust has done the researching, agonising and diplomatic work for you already. Wherever you are there will be, not too far away, a warm welcome from a French (or even English) family keen to draw you into their home and give you a slice of real French hospitality.

The selection has been honed over 4 editions, and is delectable. We can **almost** guarantee you a good time! And you will, too, save a small fortune on hotel prices.

One reader wrote to tell us that we had changed her life! Well, we don't claim to do that, but it does seem that we have changed the way thousands of people travel.

Over 660 places. Price: £12.95.

Alastair Sawday's Special Places to Stay in Spain and Portugal

The guide that takes you to the places that your friends would (privately) recommend.

No other guide gives you this wonderful selection of remarkable places to stay in both Spain and Portugal. To the magic that we worked for Spain in our first edition, with its 200 Special Places, we now add the magic of Portugal. Its houses and hotels are quite delightful, with an atmosphere all of their own. We have found about 80 of them, great country houses and little beach-side hotels, old religious buildings etc... all of them selected because they, and their owners, are special in some way. So, you can now find authenticity, character and charm in every corner of Spain and Portugal, and wonderful value for all budgets.

Order your copies from us, or harry your local book-shop. Price £10.95.

Alastair Sawday's Paris Hotels

Alastair Sawday's
Special Places to stay

Hotels

2nd Edition

Edited by Ann Cooke-Yarborough

Things change so quickly... how on earth are you to know which hotels are still attractive and good value? Which *quartiers* are still livable and quiet? Where has the long arm of the corporate hotel world NOT reached?

Well, you are lucky to hear of this book... it will rescue your week-end! This second edition follows a successful first edition, still with just a small, select number of our very favourite hotels.

Ann Cooke-Yarborough has lived in Paris for years and has tramped the streets to research and upgrade this second edition. She has chosen with an eagle eye for humbug. Unerrringly, she has selected the most interesting, welcoming, good-value hotels in Paris, leaving out the pompous, the puffed-up, the charmless and the ugly.

Trust our taste and judgement, and enjoy some good descriptive writing with the colour photos, the symbols, the light touch and you have a gem of a book. Price: £8.95.

ORDER FORM for the UK, See over for USA.

All these books are available in the major bookshops but we can send them to you quickly and without effort on your part. Post and packaging is FREE if you order 3 or more books.

	No. of copies	Price each	Total value
French Bed & Breakfast – 4th Edition		£12.95	
Paris Hotels		£8.95	
Special Places to Stay in Spain & Portugal		£10.95	
Special Places to Stay in Britain – 3rd Edition		£12.95	
Special Places to Stay in Ireland		£10.95	
Add Post & Packaging: £1 for Paris book, £2 for any other, **FREE** if ordering 3 or more books.			
TOTAL ORDER VALUE *Please make cheques payable to Alastair Sawday Publishing*			

All orders to: Alastair Sawday Publishing, 44 Ambra Vale East, Bristol BS8 4RE Tel: 0117 9299921. (Sorry, no credit card payments).

Name

Address

Postcode

Tel   Fax

If you do not wish to receive mail from other companies, please tick the box ☐   GB3

ORDER FORM for USA.

These books are available at your local bookstore, or you may order direct. Allow two to three weeks for delivery.

	No. of copies	Price each	Total value
French Bed & Breakfast – 4th Edition		$19.95	
Paris Hotels		$14.95	
Special Places to Stay in Spain & Portugal		$19.95	
Special Places to Stay in Britain		$19.95	
Special Places to Stay in Ireland		$19.95	
Add Post & Packaging: $4 for Paris book, $4.50 for any other.			
TOTAL ORDER VALUE *Please make cheques payable to Publishers Book & Audio*			

All orders to: Publishers Book & Audio, P.O. Box 070059, 5446 Arthur Kill Road, Staten Island, NY 10307, phone (800) 288-2131. For information on bulk orders, address Special Markets, St. Martin's Press, 175 Fifth Avenue, Suite 500, New York, NY 10010, phone (212) 674-5151, ext. 724, 693, or 628.

Name

Address

Zip code

Tel   Fax

REPORT FORM

Comments on existing entries and new discoveries.

If you have any comments on existing entries, please let us have them.

If you have a favourite house or a new discovery, please let us know.

Please send reports to: Alastair Sawday Publishing, 44 Ambra Vale East, Bristol BS8 4RE, UK.

Report on:

Entry no. _____   New Recommendation ☐ Date _____

Names of owners _____

Name of house _____

Address _____

_____

_____ Tel. No: _____

My reasons are _____

_____

_____

_____

_____

_____

_____

_____

_____

_____

_____

_____

_____

_____

_____

_____

_____

_____

_____

_____

_____

_____

_____

_____

My name and address:

Name _____

Address _____

_____

Tel. No.: (only if you don't mind) _____

I am not connected in any way with the owners of this property

Signed _____

Please send the completed form to:
Alastair Sawday Publishing, 44 Ambra Vale East,
Bristol BS8 4RE, UK.

THANK YOU SO MUCH FOR YOUR HELP!

INDEX OF NAMES

INDEX OF PLACES

Alastair Sawday's
Special Walking Holidays

Do you enjoy walking, and drool over the kind of properties we feature in our books? Do you enjoy real farmhouses more than modern hotels, breathtaking countryside more than frenetic cityscapes, regional cooking more than fast food?

If so why not experience things feet first and join our travel company's Special Walks?

We have run tours since 1984 and this new programme includes our favourite European areas and two special holidays in South India and Sri Lanka. The tours are for 6-9 nights and cost about £800 (not including flights). All holidays will combine:

* Wonderful properties run by friendly and interesting hosts

* Charming and knowledgeable local guides who generally live in the areas and know it's best-kept secrets

* Walks of varying lengths so you may walk as much or as little as you like (6-12 miles a day)

* Fantastic fresh food; mouth-watering picnics

* Small groups of like-minded people (minimum 6, maximum 14)

And of course your luggage will be transported for you.

For more details please complete the following coupon and send it to us.
Alastair Sawday Tours, 44 Ambra Vale East, Bristol BS8 4RE

....

Name: ,... Age: ....

Address: ....

....

Tel no: .... Fax No: .... E-mail: ....

Which areas are you interested in? (please circle): Andalucia, Spanish Pyrenees, The Lot, Provence, Burgundy, Dordogne, Tuscany, Umbria, Italian Lakes, Romania, Austria, Norway, South India, Sri Lanka

Others:...

Dates I prefer: ....

Friends who may also be interested: ....

GARDENS

OF ENGLAND AND WALES

OPEN FOR CHARITY

1999

This book is sponsored by

CARR SHEPPARDS

MEMBERS OF THE LONDON STOCK EXCHANGE

WITH MAPS

THE NATIONAL GARDENS SCHEME

GARDENS OF ENGLAND AND WALES
OPEN FOR CHARITY
1999 EDITION PUBLISHED FEB/MARCH

Price: £5.75 including UK postage; Airmail to Europe £6.75; Australia A$20.00; New Zealand NZ$24.00; USA US$20.75; Canada CDN$22.50.

To The National Gardens Scheme; Hatchlands Park, East Clandon, Guildford, Surrey, GU4 7RT. Tel 01483 211535 (Fax 01483 211537)

Please send.......copy/copies of *Gardens of England and Wales* for which I enclose PO/cheque for...

Postal orders and cheques should be made payable to The National Gardens Scheme and crossed. If sending money from abroad, please use an international money order or sterling, dollar or eurocheques; other cheques are not acceptable. Add $2 for clearance.

Name Mr/Mrs/Miss (Block letters)...

Address...

....

The books will be posted on publication. If you wish to receive acknowledgement of your order, please enclose an s.a.e.

Trade terms Supplies of this book on sale or return should be ordered direct from our trade distributors: Seymour, 1270 London Road, Norbury, London, SW16 4DH (Tel 0181 679 1899)

Portfolio, Unit 3c, West Ealing Business Centre, Alexandra Road, London, W13 0NJ (Tel: 0181 579 7748)

The National Gardens Scheme is a registered charity, number 279284.   **A.S.P.**

CHARITY ROSE ORDER FORM   A.S.P.

Please complete and send to David Austen Roses Ltd, Bowling Green Lane, Albrighton, Wolverhampton WV7 3HB. Tel 01902 373 931 (quoting AS99).

1 'Charity' shrub rose   £7.50 incl. VAT, plus £4.25 p&p
3 'Charity' shrub roses   £19.25 incl. VAT, plus £4.25 p&p

PLEASE PRINT IN BLOCK CAPITALS

Please send me................................. 'Charity' roses

Date.......................... (Mr/Mrs/Miss/Title)............................

Name...

Address..

Postcode.................................Tel. No...

I enclose a cheque/PO value £................................. payable to David Austin Roses Ltd or debit my Access/Visa account to the above amount.

Card No...

Expiry date.............................Signature..

The National Cycle Network